The Cambridge Companion to
Late Medieval English Kingship

For more than 100 years, scholars have written about late medieval kingship, and a vast body of published work now exists on the subject. However, in all this rich coverage, no accessible introduction to the subject exists. *The Cambridge Companion to Late Medieval English Kingship* addresses this need by bringing together, within a single volume, a series of themed chapters which consider key aspects of the workings of the English monarchy between 1200 and 1500. Featuring leading experts in the field, each chapter provides a concise and accessible guide, offering insights, synthesis and explanation to help readers understand not only how kings ruled but also what made their rule more – or less – effective. By adopting a holistic approach to kingship, the contributors also consider how kingship impacted on the king's subjects, thereby illuminating the complex interplay of cooperation and conflict that shaped both the monarchy and the wider polity in late medieval England.

GWILYM DODD is Associate Professor of Medieval History at the University of Nottingham. He is the author of *Justice and Grace: Private Petitioning and the English Parliament in the Late Middle Ages* (2007) and more than sixty scholarly articles and chapters, and is also editor and co-editor of numerous essay collections.

Cambridge Companions to History

Cambridge Companions to History provide accessible and thought-provoking introductions to key topics, eras, places and figures, invaluable to both the student and scholar. Edited by leading academics, each volume contains specially-commissioned essays by a team of expert contributors from around the world, presenting cutting-edge research and suggesting new paths of inquiry for the reader. Companions are designed not only to offer a comprehensive overview of their chosen topic, but also to provoke debate and discussion. Like the highly successful Cambridge Companions to Literature and Cambridge Companions to Philosophy series, these volumes are ideal for use by students, and will be of interest also to the curious general reader.

A full list of recent titles in the series can be found at the following address: www.cambridge.org/history-companions

The Cambridge Companion to
Late Medieval English Kingship

Edited by
GWILYM DODD
University of Nottingham

CAMBRIDGE
UNIVERSITY PRESS

Shaftesbury Road, Cambridge CB2 8EA, United Kingdom

One Liberty Plaza, 20th Floor, New York, NY 10006, USA

477 Williamstown Road, Port Melbourne, VIC 3207, Australia

314–321, 3rd Floor, Plot 3, Splendor Forum, Jasola District Centre, New Delhi – 110025, India

103 Penang Road, #05–06/07, Visioncrest Commercial, Singapore 238467

Cambridge University Press is part of Cambridge University Press & Assessment, a department of the University of Cambridge.

We share the University's mission to contribute to society through the pursuit of education, learning and research at the highest international levels of excellence.

www.cambridge.org
Information on this title: www.cambridge.org/9781009382021
DOI: 10.1017/9781009382045

© Cambridge University Press & Assessment 2026

This publication is in copyright. Subject to statutory exception and to the provisions of relevant collective licensing agreements, no reproduction of any part may take place without the written permission of Cambridge University Press & Assessment.

When citing this work, please include a reference to the DOI 10.1017/9781009382045

First published 2026

A catalogue record for this publication is available from the British Library

A Cataloging-in-Publication data record for this book is available from the Library of Congress

ISBN 978-1-009-38202-1 Hardback
ISBN 978-1-009-38207-6 Paperback

Cambridge University Press & Assessment has no responsibility for the persistence or accuracy of URLs for external or third-party internet websites referred to in this publication and does not guarantee that any content on such websites is, or will remain, accurate or appropriate.

For EU product safety concerns, contact us at Calle de José Abascal, 56, 1°, 28003 Madrid, Spain, or email eugpsr@cambridge.org

Contents

List of Figures page viii
List of Maps xi
List of Contributors xii
List of Abbreviations xiv
Preface xv

Part I Chronology and Context

1 Events, Personalities and Reputations: The Thirteenth Century from 1216   3
ANDREW M. SPENCER

2 Events, Personalities and Reputations: The Fourteenth Century   24
DAVID GREEN

3 Events, Personalities and Reputations: The Fifteenth Century to 1485   44
A. J. POLLARD

Part II Kingship in Practice

4 Governance and Politics   67
GWILYM DODD

5 Finance   89
   CHRIS GIVEN-WILSON

6 Justice   109
   ANTHONY MUSSON

7 Warfare and Chivalry   131
   ANDY KING

8 The Royal Court and Household   151
   MATTHEW HEFFERAN

9 Queens and the Royal Family   171
   J. L. LAYNESMITH

Part III   The King and His Subjects

10 The Clergy   195
   ALISON K. MCHARDY

11 The Nobility   217
   JAMES BOTHWELL

12 The Gentry   237
   PETER COSS

13 Citizens   257
   ELIZA HARTRICH

14 The 'Public'   278
   HELEN LACEY

15 The King's Subjects beyond the Realm   298
   PETER CROOKS

Part IV Representations

16 Art and Architecture 323
   LAURA SLATER

17 Kingship and Historical Writing 359
   SARAH L. PEVERLEY

18 Conceptualisations of Kingship 379
   CHRISTOPHER FLETCHER

Part V Reflection

19 English Kingship in a European Context 401
   JOHN WATTS

   Index 423

Figures

P.1 Genealogy 1: The English royal family in the thirteenth and fourteenth centuries. *page* xxi
P.2 Genealogy 2: The English royal family in the fifteenth century. xxii
4.1 Edward I presiding over parliament (Wriothesley Garter Book, c. 1530 (RCIN 1047414).) (Photo by DeAgostini/Getty Images.) 78
8.1 The great hall built at Eltham Palace, c. 1470s. (Photo by Print Collector/Getty Images.) 158
9.1 Tomb effigy of Queen Eleanor of Castile, Westminster Abbey, c. 1291–3. (Photo by Angelo Hornak/Corbis via Getty Images.) 188
16.1 Choir screen at York Minster, c. 1452–61. (Photo by Angelo Hornak/Corbis via Getty Images.) 324
16.2 View of Westminster, with Parliament House (the former St Stephen's Chapel), Westminster Hall and Westminster Abbey, 1647. (Photo by Henry Guttmann Collection/Hulton Archive/Getty Images.) 326
16.3 Jewel Tower, Westminster Palace, c. 1365. (Photo by English Heritage/Heritage Images/Getty Images.) 327
16.4 Antiquarian copies of decoration in the Painted Chamber, Westminster Palace, c. 1819–20. (Photo by Sepia Times/Universal Images Group via Getty Images.) 329
16.5 Depiction of St Stephen's Chapel, Westminster Palace in 1830. (Photo by The Print Collector/Getty Images.) 330

16.6 Interior of Westminster Hall, Westminster Palace, c. 1395. (Photo by Pawel Libera/Getty Images.) 332
16.7 Interior of crossing and east end of Westminster Abbey, c. 1245–53. (Photo by John Harper/Getty Images.) 334
16.8 Sanctuary pavement before the high altar, Westminster Abbey, 1268. (Photo by Dan Kitwood/Pool/AFP via Getty Images.) 336
16.9 Coronation Chair, Westminster Abbey, c. 1300–1. (Photo by Werner Forman/Universal Images Group/Getty Images.) 338
16.10 Interior of St George's Chapel, Windsor Castle, c. 1475–1528, restored 1863–73. (Photo by Tim Graham Photo Library via Getty Images.) 341
16.11 Interior of Great Hall, Winchester Castle, 1222–35. (Photo by Franz Marc Frei/Getty Images.) 342
16.12 Caernarfon Castle, Gwynedd, Wales, 1283–1330. (Photo by Gallo Images/Getty Images.) 342
16.13 King's College Chapel, Cambridge, 1446–1536. (Photo by Ian Cumming/Design Pics Editorial/Universal Images Group via Getty Images.) 344
16.14 Eton College Chapel, Berkshire, 1441–83. (Photo by DeAgostini/Getty Images.) 346
16.15 Obverse of the Great Seal of Edward I, 1272–1307. (Photo by Bettmann/Getty Images.) 348
16.16 Detail of the double tomb of Henry IV and Joan of Navarre in Canterbury Cathedral, 1420s. (Photo by RDImages/Epics/Getty Images.) 350
16.17 Eleanor Cross at Hardingstone, Northamptonshire, 1291–3. (Photo by Dave Porter/Getty Images.) 351
16.18 Westminster Abbey portrait of Richard II, c. 1395. (Photo by Fine Art Images/Heritage Images/Getty Images.) 353
16.19 Interior left wing of the Wilton Diptych, c. 1395 (London, National Gallery NG44451). (Photo by Imagno/Getty Images.) 354
16.20 Interior right wing of the Wilton Diptych, c. 1395 (London, National Gallery NG4451). (Photo by Fine Art Images/Heritage Images/Getty Images.) 355

17.1 A depiction of Richard III with his wife, Anne Neville, and son, Edward in the armorial roll-chronicle by John Rous, The Rous Roll, c. 1483–5 (London, British Library Additional MS 48976). (Photo by Universal History Archive/Universal Images Group via Getty Images.) 373

Maps

4.1 Locations visited by Edward I, 1291–1307 (reproduced with permission from D. Boucoyannis, *Kings as Judges: Power, Justice, and the Origins of Parliaments* (Cambridge, 2021), frontispiece   page 72
10.1 Dioceses of late medieval England and Wales   196
13.1 Royal and seigneurial boroughs by population size, c. 1290 (source: B. M. S. Campbell, 'Benchmarking Medieval Economic Development: England, Wales, Scotland, and Ireland, c. 1290', *Economic History Review* 61 (2008), 896–945 (Table 4, pp. 908–9)   260
15.1 England and the Plantagenet dominions in the later Middle Ages (reproduced from P. Crooks, 'Before Humpty Dumpty: The First English Empire and the Brittleness of Bureaucracy, 1259–1453', in *Empires and Bureaucracy in World History: From Late Antiquity to the Twentieth Century*, ed. P. Crooks and T. H. Parsons (Cambridge, 2016), p. 260)   300
19.1 Western Europe, c. 1300 (reproduced from J. Watts, *The Making of Polities: Europe, 1300–1500* (Cambridge, 2009), p. 160)   408

Contributors

JAMES BOTHWELL is Lecturer in Later Medieval English History at the University of Leicester

PETER COSS is Professor Emeritus of Cardiff University

PETER CROOKS is Associate Professor in Medieval History at Trinity College Dublin, University of Dublin

GWILYM DODD is Associate Professor of History at the University of Nottingham

CHRISTOPHER FLETCHER is Associate Research Professor at the French National Centre for Scientific Research (CNRS) at the University of Lille

CHRIS GIVEN-WILSON is Emeritus Professor of Medieval History at the University of St Andrews

DAVID GREEN is Professor of History at Harlaxton College, the British Campus of the University of Evansville

ELIZA HARTRICH is Senior Lecturer in Late Medieval History at the University of York

MATTHEW HEFFERAN is Assistant Professor of Medieval and Early Modern History at the University of Nottingham

ANDY KING is Lecturer in History at the University of Southampton

HELEN LACEY is Associate Professor of Medieval History at Mansfield College, University of Oxford

J. L. LAYNESMITH is Visiting Research Fellow at the University of Reading

ALISON K. MCHARDY is Reader Emerita of History, University of Nottingham

ANTHONY MUSSON is Head of Research at Historic Royal Palaces

SARAH L. PEVERLEY is Professor of Medieval Literature and Culture at the University of Liverpool

A. J. POLLARD is Emeritus Professor at Teesside University

LAURA SLATER is Associate Professor in the History of Medieval Art and Architecture at the University of Cambridge and Fellow of Peterhouse, Cambridge

ANDREW M. SPENCER is Senior Tutor and Fellow in History of Gonville & Caius College, University of Cambridge

JOHN WATTS is Professor of Later Medieval History at the University of Oxford and Fellow and Tutor in History at Corpus Christi College, Oxford

Abbreviations

BIHR	*Bulletin of the Institute of Historical Research*
BJRL	*Bulletin of the John Rylands Library*
CCR	*Calendar of Close Rolls*
CPR	*Calendar of Patent Rolls*
EETS	Early English Text Society
EHD, 1189–1327	*English Historical Documents, 1189–1327*, ed. H. Rothwell (London, 1975)
EHD, 1327–1485	*English Historical Documents, 1327–1485*, ed. A. R. Myers (London, 1969)
EHR	*The English Historical Review*
Foedera	*Foedera, conventions, literae etc.*, ed. T. Rymer, 3 vols. in 6 parts (London 1816–30)
HR	*Historical Research*
JBS	*Journal of British Studies*
JEH	*Journal of Ecclesiastical History*
JMH	*Journal of Medieval History*
ODNB	*Oxford Dictionary of National Biography*
PROME	*Parliament Rolls of Medieval England*, ed. C. Given-Wilson, P. Brand, A. Curry *et al.* (Leicester, 2005) – online edition
RS	Rolls Series
SR	*Statutes of the Realm*, 11 vols. (London, 1810–28)
TNA	The National Archives
TRHS	*Transactions of the Royal Historical Society*

Preface

There were only two things which had a near continuous presence in ordering the lives of almost everyone living in late medieval England. One was religion, as mediated through the rules, customs and clerical offices of the church. The other was kingship. Kingship refers, in the first instance, to the position, office or dignity of a king. By definition, a king was undisputed ruler of the realm, an individual whose powers were theoretically unrivalled and who – in the late medieval period – was considered to possess a semi-sacral status as God's chosen representative on Earth. But the king was also just a man, an individual who, as much as anyone else, was constrained by the human condition and whose actions were shaped by the full panoply of the personal attributes he possessed – frailties as well as strengths. The study of kingship is therefore, above all else, a study of the man sitting on the throne; but as a concept or idea, kingship also implies a system of governance operating within a polity (i.e. a society organised politically) with the king at its head. Exercising direct political power – that is, having the king as the ultimate focus of real political authority and legitimacy – made late medieval England's system of governance a monarchy in the truest sense of this term.

The king was the focal point of the nation's public life: there was very little in which he was not involved, either directly or by association. In his name laws were enacted, taxes imposed and wars fought, but very often he imposed justice, negotiated taxation and led armies (and did much else besides) in person. He was looked to, to set the highest standards in personal piety, military prowess and cultural sophistication. He had at his disposal a vast pool of patronage, primarily in the form of land, money and local office, which he needed to distribute wisely and proportionately, in a way that allowed him to pursue his projects for the whole kingdom without upsetting the delicate balance of power in the localities. All this reminds us that the late medieval period was still very much an age of *personal*, or personality-driven, kingship. All important decisions affecting the life of the nation, and countless decisions affecting the lives of individuals, emanated from, and through, him. It was a system which worked well and effectively when the king had the requisite skills and temperament to do his job properly; but a system which relied so heavily on one individual contained within it the potential to come off the rails, if he persistently failed to do his job and his actions directly threatened the security of his subjects and the stability of the realm.

For obvious reasons, then, contemporaries were heavily invested in kingship: it mattered to everyone that the king ruled wisely and in the interests of the kingdom. Thus, late medieval kingship was not just about the art of ruling; it was also about how the king's actions impacted his subjects. It was also a system that relied on the consent, cooperation and service of the people, as seen most clearly in the way the king depended on hundreds of unpaid individuals to implement royal policy on his behalf. This broader participation in, and reaction to, royal governance meant that kingship was as much moulded and shaped by the king's subjects as it was by the king himself, and concomitantly, it also meant that the king was as much bound by the norms and expectations of kingship as his people were bound by their obligations to him as his subjects. Studying late medieval kingship is thus a complex and multifaceted task. It requires investigation into the personalities, abilities and achievements of individual kings, the events that shaped their rule, relations with their subjects, the nature and workings of royal government and the representation of kingly rule in the writings, theoretical works and material cultures of the day.

Scholarship on late medieval English kingship enjoys an extremely long and illustrious pedigree, but it is a point of some surprise to note that *The Cambridge Companion to Late Medieval English Kingship* is the first publication of its type. More than a century of research has produced countless articles, chapters, monographs and editions on different aspects of the subject. Dozens of scholars have devoted their careers to uncovering the lives of particular kings, as well as the achievements, contexts and challenges of kingly rule across the thirteenth, fourteenth and fifteenth centuries. Traditionally, the royal biography has dominated the field. With the publication in 2023 of David Carpenter's second volume on Henry III, we have a complete set of late medieval royal biographies published in the Yale English Monarchs series, extending from the reign of King John to Richard III. Numerous essay collections published over the years also offer detailed consideration of specific elements of different reigns.[1] In the past few decades, scholars have increasingly turned their attention to more theme-based approaches. There have been important conceptual reappraisals of royal power by Christopher Fletcher on Richard II, and John Watts and Katherine Lewis on Henry VI.[2] Other works have considered the king's relations with his nobilities,[3] while others have considered the connections between the king and the wider body of his subjects.[4] There have been important interdisciplinary contributions;[5] and generations of students have benefited from a large assortment of syntheses on particular themes or periods.[6] All these works – and many more besides – add depth, as well as breadth, to our understanding of what late medieval English kingship entailed, how it was conceived, how it was received and how it performed – or was performed. This Cambridge Companion volume addresses the need for a synthesis of this vast body of scholarship. It takes as its chronological focus the period from the start of the reign of Henry III in 1216 to the death of Richard III in 1485. Altogether eleven kings ruled England in this time, ranging from the fifty-six-year rule of Henry III to the seventy-eight days of Edward V's reign (see Figures P.1 and P.2 for lines of succession and genealogies).

There is no better time to focus on this era of English kingship. The increasing interdisciplinarity of late medieval political studies and emphasis on political history as a cultural phenomenon have generated a rich intellectual environment in which new approaches and methodologies have flourished alongside a strong and enduring commitment to empiricism. Students of late medieval English kingship now also have access to a sizeable body of translated sources, including most of the main chronicles of the period, the parliament rolls and a number of important source collections.[7] In recent years, moreover, a growing body of work has considered the interconnectivity of the English monarchy with the wider world.[8] From this scholarship we have a much better understanding of how English kingship compared to other European models, how these monarchical systems often developed in step with each other and how the rulers of the period frequently faced the same challenges and conditions. Thanks to this work, however, we can also see what made English kingship distinctive: the unusually intensive nature of royal authority; the elaborate administrative, political, fiscal and legal structures of the state; and the highly organised and integrated polity, including, as time passed, an increasingly politicised peasantry. In a period of great change, the English monarchy provided a clear locus of institutional continuity; but within this overall organisational framework the nature of kingship developed significantly, in response to far-reaching political, economic, social and cultural developments. It makes the subject, and the period, immensely rewarding to study.

This companion offers accessible chapters written by leading specialists on all the different aspects of late medieval English kingship. Each chapter covers a broad field and assumes no prior knowledge. Chapters in Part I outline key events and the personalities and personal attributes of the kings who ruled in the three centuries under consideration. Some key historiographical trends are also considered. Chapters in Part II consider how late medieval English kings ruled. Here, the focus is as much on what was expected of a king as on what they did (and how successful they were in doing it). These chapters also explore the relationship between the personal rule of the king, on the one hand, and the exercise of royal authority through the wider apparatus of royal government, on the other hand. Part III considers kingship from the perspective of the king's subjects. The focus here is on the integrated nature of the English polity. These chapters demonstrate ways in which the king's subjects interacted with the king and with royal authority, whether they were members of his family, his servants, courtiers and friends, or his supporters, critics and opponents. Part IV explores representations of English kingship in narrative and theoretical writings, as well as in art, architecture and other forms of visual culture. The final chapter in Part V offers broader reflections on the nature of English kingship in comparison to other contemporary models of

European monarchy. Beyond general outlines, authors have been allowed to develop their topics in directions that reflect their own approach to the subject. In this way, each chapter is self-standing and individual. A short 'Further Reading' list at the end of each chapter provides the starting point for readers wishing to explore topics in more detail.

It remains for me to thank Liz Hanlon and Victoria Phillips at Cambridge University Press for providing unstinting support and encouragement for this project from its very inception, and to Linsey Hague for her assistance and expertise during the copy-editing stage. I should also like to thank the contributors to this volume for their authoritative and finely crafted chapters, for meeting in timely fashion the deadlines I set and for their patience in the editing and copy-editing process. I wish to thank Deborah Boucoyannis, John Watts and Peter Crooks for generously allowing me to use maps that have appeared in previous publications and Oliver Dodd for producing Maps 10.1 and 13.1. It has been a great privilege and pleasure working with the contributors to this volume. I have learned much from them. My hope is that the fruits of their labours will guide and assist readers through this most fascinating of topics and that the publication will act as a stimulus for future research into this incredibly rich and diverse field.

Notes

1. E.g. G. L. Harriss, ed., *Henry V: The Practice of Kingship* (Oxford, 1985); A. Goodman and J. L. Gillespie, eds., *Richard II: The Art of Kingship* (Oxford, 1999); J. Bothwell, ed., *The Age of Edward III* (Woodbridge, 2001); G. Dodd and A. Musson, eds., *The Reign of Edward II: New Perspectives* (York, 2006); G. Dodd and D. Biggs, eds., *The Reign of Henry IV: Rebellion and Survival, 1403–1413* (Woodbridge, 2008); A. King and A. Spencer, eds., *Edward I: New Interpretations* (York, 2020).
2. E.g. J. Watts, *Henry VI and the Politics of Kingship* (Cambridge, 1996); C. Fletcher, *Richard II: Manhood, Youth, and Politics, 1377–99* (Oxford, 2008); and K. Lewis, *Kingship and Masculinity in Late Medieval England* (Abingdon, 2013).
3. E.g. A. K. Gundy, *Richard II and the Rebel Earl* (Cambridge, 2013); and A. M. Spencer, *Nobility and Kingship in Medieval England: The Earls and Edward I, 1272–1307* (Cambridge, 2014).

4. E.g. G. Dodd, *Justice and Grace: Private Petitioning and the English Parliament in the Late Middle Ages* (Oxford, 2007); H. Lacey, *The Royal Pardon: Access to Mercy in Fourteenth-Century England* (York, 2009); and M. Hefferan, *The Household Knights of Edward III: Warfare, Politics and Kingship in Fourteenth-Century England* (Woodbridge, 2021).
5. E.g. R. Firth-Green, *A Crisis of Truth: Literature and Law in Ricardian England* (Philadelphia, 1999); J. Nuttall, *The Creation of Lancastrian Kingship: Literature, Language and Politics in Late Medieval England* (Cambridge, 2007); W. M. Ormrod, *Winner and Waster and Its Contexts: Chivalry, Law and Economics in Fourteenth-Century England* (Cambridge, 2021).
6. E.g. M. Prestwich, *English Politics in the Thirteenth Century* (Basingstoke, 1990); W. M. Ormrod, *Political life in Medieval England, 1300–1450* (Basingstoke, 1995); M. Hicks, *Political Culture in the Fifteenth Century* (London, 2003); C. Carpenter, *The Wars of the Roses, 1437–1509* (Cambridge, 2008); or they take a reign-by-reign or narrative-based approach, e.g. A. J. Pollard, *Late Medieval England 1399–1509* (Harlow, 2000); J. Hamilton, *The Plantagenets: History of a Dynasty* (London, 2005); M. Jones, ed., *New Cambridge Medieval History VI, c. 1300–c. 1415* (Cambridge, 2015).
7. E.g. *Chronicles of the Revolution: 1397–1400*, ed. and trans. C. Given-Wilson (Manchester, 1993); *The Reign of Richard II: From Minority to Tyranny, 1377–97*, ed. and trans. A. K. McHardy (Manchester, 2012); *The Reign of Edward II, 1307–27*, ed. and trans. W. R. Childs and P. R. Schofield (Manchester, 2022).
8. E.g. J. Watts, *The Making of Polities: Europe, 1300–1500* (Cambridge, 2009); C. Fletcher, J.-P. Genet and J. Watts, eds., *Government and Political Life in England and France, c. 1300–c. 1500* (Cambridge, 2015); P. Crooks, D. Green and W. M. Ormrod, eds., *The Plantagenet Empire, 1259–1453* (Donington, 2019).

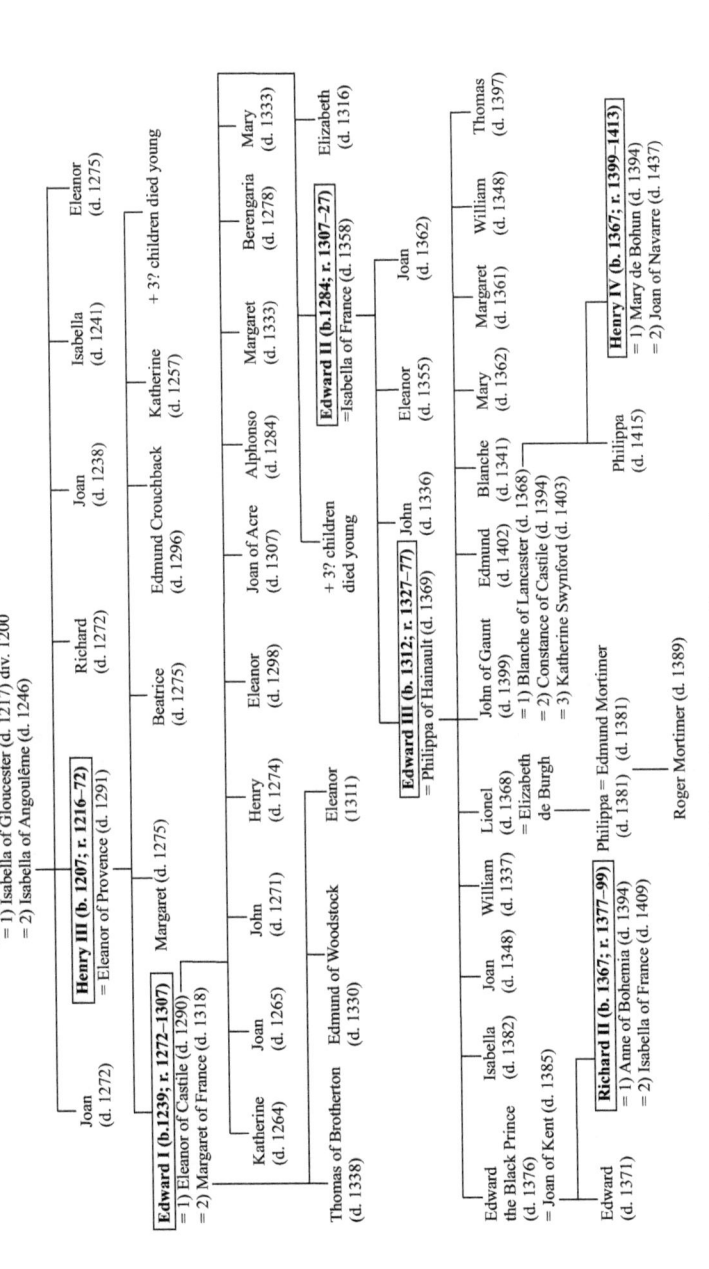

P.1 Genealogy 1: The English royal family in the thirteenth and fourteenth centuries.

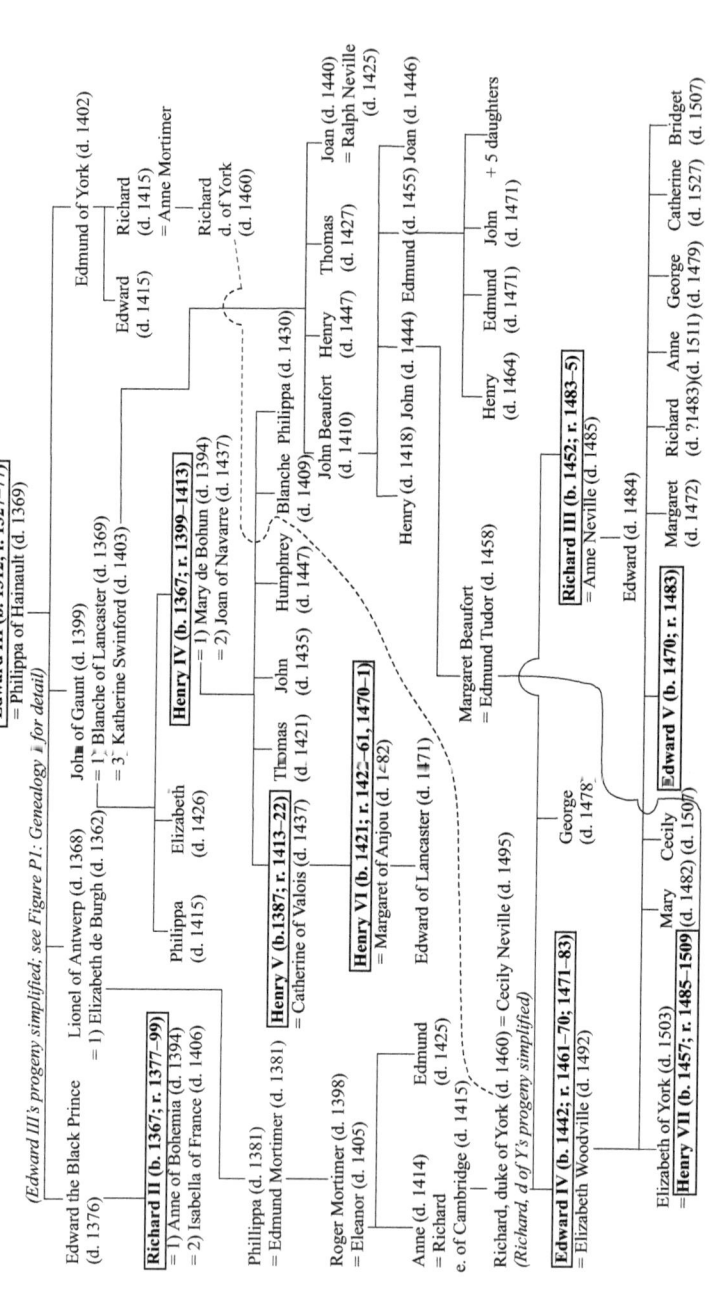

P.2 Genealogy 2: The English royal family in the fifteenth century.

Part I

Chronology and Context

ANDREW M. SPENCER

1

Events, Personalities and Reputations
The Thirteenth Century from 1216

The Statute of York in 1322 recognised that 'in time past ... troubles and wars have happened in the realm', blaming this on the various attempts to restrict royal power in the thirteenth century[1] Reform, sometimes led by the crown and sometimes imposed upon it, was a key theme in the reigns of Henry III (1216-72) and Edward I (1272-1307). Two other themes, focused on the king's interests beyond the borders of England, had significant effects on relations between the king and his English subjects, as the king sought to access their manpower, money and materiel. These interests were the king's claims to sovereignty over all Britain and protecting his remaining lands in France. When these factors all came together, as they did in the pivotal periods of 1258-67 and from 1294, it led to upheavals and strife in the realm which punctuated long periods of peace in England under both kings.

The Minority of Henry III: 1216-1234

Henry III had probably the hardest inheritance of any king of England. Only nine, he was the first minor to accede since 978 and did so in the midst of civil war and foreign invasion. When King John died at Newark (Notts.) on 19 October 1216, Henry was at Corfe Castle (Dorset). London was in enemy hands and so he was crowned just nine days later at Gloucester Abbey. In addition to Prince Louis of France, John's English opponents were aided by Llywelyn ap Iorwerth, prince of Gwynedd, and by Alexander II, king of Scots, both of whom were seeking to undo concessions made to John. The rebels' greatest asset, however, had been John himself who had alienated so many of his subjects.

On the other hand, young Henry had five key factors in his favour. First, although many had deserted John, some key magnates had remained loyal. These included the two greatest marcher lords, Ranulf, earl of Chester, and William Marshal, earl of Pembroke, as well as the warlike foreigner cleric Peter des Roches, bishop of Winchester, England's richest see. Secondly, papal support for John's dynasty remained firm and it was the papal legate, Guala, who had crowned Henry. Thirdly, Dover Castle remained in the hands of John's justiciar, Hubert de Burgh, and while it did Louis's maritime supply lines remained insecure. Fourth, the advisors around the young king had, in Magna Carta, a ready-made offer for the realm. John's repudiation of the charter had precipitated the war in the autumn of 1215, but Louis had not adopted it. Suitably altered to make it more amenable to royal taste, it could be offered as a new deal between crown and people. The charter was reissued on 12 November 1216. Finally, and perhaps most significantly, the young king was not his father. This 'fine little knight' was innocent of his father's sins.[2] For many, the reason for the war died with John.

Notwithstanding this, it still had to be fought and won. William Marshal, around seventy years of age, was chosen as *rector* of the king and kingdom and for a time the result hung in the balance. In 1217, however, the royalists won two crucial victories. Louis's forces were beaten at Lincoln in May, while in August Hubert de Burgh defeated a French fleet off Dover, thereby finally relieving the siege of the 'key to England'. The treaty of Kingston in September recognised Henry as king. Shortly afterwards Magna Carta was again confirmed.

In some ways, the remainder of Henry's minority was a success. He grew slowly to manhood and maturity under the guidance of de Burgh, and the latter's ascendancy was a generally peaceful period. Magna Carta was confirmed once more in 1225 and the fact of Henry's minority meant that Hubert relied on regular councils of magnates to ensure broad support for his regime and the decisions he was taking, as well as providing consent for taxation. By the late 1230s, these assemblies had acquired a new name: parliament. On the other hand, political tensions continued to simmer. A bloody siege at Bedford in 1223 precipitated the exile of the bishop of Winchester and Falkes de Breauté, one of John's cadre of foreign knights. In 1227, Richard of Cornwall quarrelled with his brother the king and with de Burgh. Not for the last time, the quarrel ended with Richard being bought off and abandoning his baronial allies.

Through all this, de Burgh retained Henry's confidence until failure in France in 1230. Louis VIII of France had overrun Poitou in 1224 and its recovery was Henry's priority. Louis's early death in 1227, and the accession of his young son, Louis IX, seemed to offer Henry an opportunity. Henry finally landed in Brittany in 1230 in alliance with its duke. The campaign came to nothing, however, and Henry returned to England disappointed. Peter des Roches returned in August 1231 and the bishop began to play on Henry's frustrations. Peter painted a tempting vision of a different type of kingship, encompassing the plenitude of royal power. Henry took the proffered apple, dismissing Hubert from his office of justiciar. A series of charters granted by Henry in the past few years were overturned by royal fiat. Most significant of these was the confiscation of the manor of Upavon (Wilts.) from Gilbert Basset, a close associate of Richard Marshal, earl of Pembroke, the greatest domestic magnate of all, who promptly rebelled. Although Marshal died during the rebellion, his cause triumphed and the bishop's party was removed by a chastened and penitent Henry in the spring of 1234. This marks the definitive end of Henry's minority and the start of his personal rule. Henry was twenty-seven and that we can date his personal rule as late as this says much about the king Henry had become.

The Personal Rule of Henry III: 1234–1258

All three themes mentioned at the beginning of the chapter, those of domestic reform, the expansion of English royal authority over Britain and the defence of his French territories, were key elements of Henry's personal rule and also came together to bring it to a close with the revolution of 1258. At the heart of the narrative lies Magna Carta and the type of king Henry tried to be. The definitive 1225 version of Magna Carta was much shorter than its 1215 predecessor, thirty-seven chapters down from sixty-three, and was much less prejudicial to royal authority but it promised a version of kingship very different from the one proposed to Henry by Peter des Roches in 1232. A Magna Carta king would abide by his own laws, take counsel from the leading men of the kingdom and, above all, would behave regularly towards his subjects. Magna Carta was not a plea for *less* royal government and justice but an attempt to depersonalise and regularise it. Under Magna Carta, the king's subjects would know what to expect when they came into contact with the crown. Thus, the estates and dependants (widows and heirs) of tenants-in-chief were protected from arbitrary exactions from the crown, while those who came before royal courts would know that the king's justice would not be bought, sold or delayed.

There was much, however, that Magna Carta had left unsaid. There was nothing, for instance, on how the king's ministers should be appointed or on how the king might distribute patronage. Moreover, the security clause of twenty-five barons charged with the enforcement of the charter in 1215 had been removed. The cry of 'Magna Carta in danger' was a leitmotif of the years of Henry's personal rule. One final problem of ruling within the confines of Magna Carta was money. Henry was poor. The loss of most of the French lands, combined with a period of high inflation, had hit Plantagenet finances hard. Two key methods by which John had kept his coffers full were the manipulation of both royal justice and the feudal rights of the crown. With these now constrained, Henry urgently needed to find alternative sources of revenue to fund his ambitions. The most obvious source was taxation on the movable goods of his subjects, which could bring in easily twice the annual revenue of the crown. The problem was that during the course of Henry's minority, the idea had crystalised that such taxes could only come from an assembly of magnates. If parliament were to be persuaded, they first needed to trust the king to spend the money wisely and secondly they might demand concessions in return. Both were problematic in Henry's personal rule and repeated refusals of his demands followed.

Henry fell back instead on other methods of raising money which antagonised the layer of landholders below the barons, the gentry. Henry increased the amount of money that sheriffs had to produce each year; the judicial and forest eyres became more a vehicle for raising revenue than one designed to bring justice to the localities; and a series of heavy taxes on England's Jews forced them to pressure their own creditors, who were frequently local gentry. This, coupled with Henry's lax attitude towards the abuses committed by magnates, led to consistent calls for reform at parliaments in the 1230s and 1240s, most notably in 1244 when a plan for reform, the so-called Paper Constitution, was drawn up which bore striking similarities to that eventually imposed in 1258.[3] Unwilling or unable to reform voluntarily, Henry left himself vulnerable to having reform forced upon him. Henry's one significant attempt at reform came in the late 1230s, starting with the Statute of Merton and then temporary reforms to local government.[4] Two men were central to these efforts: William Ralegh, the author of the legal tract known as *Bracton*, and William of Savoy, uncle of Henry's queen, Eleanor of Provence, who arrived with her in 1236 and immediately gained Henry's trust. Unfortunately, reform stalled following Henry's falling out with Ralegh and William of Savoy's death in 1239.

Savoyard influence, however, did not end here. Henry cultivated the relationship with this powerful and influential family, making Peter of Savoy one of the great magnates in England, securing Boniface's election as archbishop of Canterbury and giving lavish fees to Thomas and Queen Eleanor's mother, Beatrice. Henry hoped to increase his influence on the continent in this way, also through his marriage alliance with the Holy Roman Emperor, Frederick II, and by cultivating the lords of Poitou, all with the hope of regaining his lost lands in France. Such a strategy, however, came to nought when in 1242, after years of planning, Henry's key potential ally in Poitou, his stepfather Hugh de Lusignan, rebelled before Henry was ready. By the time Henry arrived, Lusignan had been defeated and Henry was chased humiliatingly back to Gascony. Frederick II was too engulfed in his own wars to aid him, while the Savoyards kept their powder dry, conscious of their marriage links with the Capetians. Henry's mother, Isabella of Angoulême, died in 1246 and the following year several of her children arrived in England seeking the patronage of their half-brother, Henry III. Henry responded with characteristic generosity and the Lusignans quickly established themselves as a rival foreign faction to the queen's Savoyard relatives.

With his ambitions in France frustrated, Henry began to look further afield, his gaze eventually alighting upon Sicily. Henry's pursuit of the

Sicilian throne for his younger son, Edmund, was simultaneously utterly impractical and ruinously expensive. Henry's trust in the Savoyards, who were pushing the idea, and his devotion to the papacy led him into disastrous deals with successive popes that left him facing excommunication if he defaulted, the sulphurous displeasure of the English church, who were left to foot his bill, and the incredulous non-cooperation of the English baronage.

Henry's problems were compounded by a major rebellion in Wales. Up to 1256, Wales and Scotland had been two of Henry's more striking successes. The northern border remained relatively quiet, secured by royal marriages with both Alexander II and III. The seizure of Alexander III, still a minor, by Scottish lords in 1257, though, threatened temporarily to disturb the peace once again. More serious, however, was the rebellion of Llywelyn ap Gruffydd in Gwynedd. While Henry had largely accepted the hegemony of Llywelyn ap Iorwerth, he took advantage of the latter's death in 1240 and his astute purchase for the crown of the earldom of Chester to seize the four cantrefs west of the Dee from Llywelyn's heir, Dafydd, in 1241. As so often, however, Henry failed to follow through on a promising position. In 1241, Dafydd had promised that were he to die without heirs Gwynedd would escheat to the crown. When Dafydd died in 1246, however, Henry made no effort to make good on this promise at a time when the principality was divided between the rival sons of Dafydd's half-brother, Gruffydd. Instead, he allowed the brothers to fight things out and Llywelyn ap Gruffydd thus emerged as the undisputed ruler of Gwynedd by 1255. In November 1256, Llywelyn crossed the Clwyd into the four cantrefs held by the king's son and heir, Lord Edward, overrunning them easily. In June 1257, Edward's attempted counterattack was spectacularly defeated. Desperate for money, and with no help coming from his parents or the Savoyards, Edward turned instead to the Lusignans and moved in the winter of 1257–8 from the Savoyard to the Lusignan camp.

Henry's position was collapsing in the spring of 1258 when he summoned a parliament to ask once again for the realm's support for the Sicilian project. The king had alienated the church, the gentry and the Savoyard party. He was running out of allies. Henry's personal rule ended as it started, with a denial of justice in breach of Magna Carta.

Then he had been repenting for the disseisin of Gilbert Basset and others; now he refused to give justice to John Fitz Geoffrey, a well-connected curial baron, who was appealing against Aymer de Lusignan, bishop-elect of Winchester. On 12 April, Fitz Geoffrey joined six other barons in a sworn pact of mutual support and on 30 April they marched in full armour into Westminster Hall, with Roger Bigod, earl of Norfolk, at their head, and demanded that the king accept reform.[5] Henry, naked of all meaningful support beyond the Lusignans, had no choice but to agree.

Henry III – Reform, Rebellion and Peace-Making: 1258–1272

While Magna Carta sought to regularise royal authority, the reformers of 1258 intended to exercise that authority themselves.[6] It was corporatised into the hands of a council of fifteen magnates. A justiciar, Hugh Bigod, was appointed to hold a general eyre (in essence a super royal judicial commission that stood above all other jurisdictions) to investigate abuses. Henry was effectively shoved aside while the council undertook virtually all business. The reform movement began as a palace coup against the Lusignans, who were forced into exile, but it was not confined to the court. From almost the very start, however, there were splits about just how far-reaching reform should be. Some, like the queen and Peter of Savoy, were content with the expulsion of the Lusignans; others, such as Richard de Clare, earl of Gloucester, wished to reform the conduct of the king's ministers but not to investigate abuses by the barons' own men.

The man who emerged as the leader of the most radical reformers was Simon de Montfort, earl of Leicester. Montfort arrived in England in 1230 with nothing more than a famous name, a silver tongue and a claim to the earldom of Leicester. By 1239, the time of his first quarrel with Henry III, he was earl of Leicester, had married the king's sister and had become one of Henry's closest counsellors. Following that initial quarrel, the two remained bitterly co-dependent upon each other: Henry requiring Montfort's military and diplomatic capabilities and Montfort needing Henry's goodwill to sustain and develop his landed position.

Montfort never laid aside his material ambitions, but he was unwavering in his commitment to wholesale reform of the realm and clashed repeatedly with anyone showing less commitment to reform than he did. The path of reform in these years is complex to trace but falls essentially into three broad phases: first up to the finalising of the treaty of Paris in December 1259; secondly, the king's slow and uncertain recovery of power until the spring of 1263; followed by civil war until the summer of 1267.

Following the conclusion of the Oxford parliament in the summer of 1258, the three major achievements of the reform programme were Hugh Bigod's general eyre, the so-called Provisions of Westminster in 1259 which accomplished much legal and administrative reform locally and the treaty of Paris which sought to achieve a permanent settlement with the Capetians over the residue of the Angevin Empire.[7] Negotiations over a settlement had begun with Henry meeting Louis in 1254 and continued intermittently for several years afterwards. Under its eventual terms, Henry agreed to do homage to Louis for Gascony as duke of Aquitaine, obtaining residual rights in the strategically vital Agenais and the dioceses of Périgueux, Cahors and Limoges. In return, he gave up his other claims. The treaty was to have both major short- and long-term consequences, but it cemented the ties of friendship and kinship between the two kings.

Henry travelled to France in November to conclude the treaty and, safe in Paris and away from many of the council, he began to regain some freedom of action. Henry remained there until April 1260 and, on his return, conducted a cold war against his opponents as he sought to regain power. The two leading reformers were now Montfort and Lord Edward, the king's own son and heir, who, having first opposed reform, was now filled with youthful reforming zeal. Gradually, over the course of the next eighteen months, Henry gained the ascendancy and by November 1261 he had overthrown the council. He was aided by the pope's quashing of the reformers' oath and by Lord Edward's defection from reform. Most of all, however, he was aided by a general sense that being in the king's goodwill was a better place to be than outside it. Only Montfort refused to yield, going into exile bitterly complaining of the faithlessness of the English.

Sadly for England, Henry had learned little from earlier mistakes. Errors abounded over the next two years. Most important of these were his failure to reconcile effectively with Montfort, leaving him as a dangerous outsider brooding on his wrongs; his factional persecution, led by the queen, of the former associates of Lord Edward who had been cast aside; his decision not to allow the eighteen-year-old Gilbert de Clare to inherit his father's lands early following Gloucester's death in July 1262; and renewed military defeat at the hands of Llywelyn ap Gruffydd, who resumed hostilities in late 1262.

In April 1263, Montfort, invited by Edward's former friends, returned and Henry's position collapsed. Foreigners now became a particular focus for the rebels and a 'Statute against Aliens' was imposed in July 1263, alongside a general resumption of reform under the umbrella title of the Provisions of Oxford. It was not to last, however, and, following the return of Edward's former friends to the prince's fold, a strong royalist party emerged. Civil war was only averted in December 1263 by seeking intervention from Louis IX. The reformers' case was intricate and elaborate but it was Henry's much more simple case, that the king should have the freedom to appoint and dismiss his own ministers, that won Louis's approbation. In the mise of Amiens, issued in January 1264, he quashed the provisions utterly.[8]

Such a one-sided judgement, however, only precipitated civil war. Despite early success at Northampton in April, the king's forces were lured south and, at Lewes (Sussex) on 14 May 1264, defeated by Montfort's much smaller baronial army. King Henry, Lord Edward, Richard of Cornwall and his son all now fell into Montfort's hands and England came under the effective rule of 'King Simon'. Montfort attracted passionate support from many in the church and the younger members of the baronage and from many towns, especially London. He sought to secure broader support for his regime at the two famous parliaments of June 1264 and January–March 1265. Knights of the shire, two from each county, were summoned to both meetings and, at the latter, borough representatives too. Never had the authority of the crown been brought so low as at the Hilary Parliament of 1265 when Lord Edward was denuded of his estates in favour of Montfort and Henry agreed to sustain the current governmental arrangements, acknowledging the right, even the duty, of his subjects to ignore his commands and take up arms against him if he sought to resile from reform.

Regarded by the papacy and the French as a rogue state, Montfort's regime was vulnerable to invasion and to threats from within. As he and his family plundered royalist estates, Montfort was open to the charge of greed and tyranny. He had allied himself with Llywelyn, England's enemy, to aid him against the recalcitrant royalist marcher lords; royalist sympathy remained strong in the north; while his sudden imprisonment of the earl of Derby aroused the suspicion and fear of Gilbert de Clare, earl of Gloucester, the one man powerful enough to challenge Montfort for supremacy. In collusion with Gloucester, Edward escaped custody and joined up with the marcher lords and other royalists. Montfort came west but eventually found himself trapped at Evesham on 4 August 1265. Rather than retreat, Montfort decided upon a martyr's crown and was killed, along with many of his closest supporters. Such was the targeted slaughter, not seen on an English battlefield for two centuries, that one chronicler described it as 'the murder of Evesham, for battle it was none'.[9]

The royalists were victorious, but a permanent peace remained beyond their grasp for nearly two years, largely because of an ill-advised decision to disinherit all the rebels. This was reversed by the Dictum of Kenilworth in October 1266, which allowed the rebels to buy back their lands at agreed rates of compensation, but it was not until June 1267, after the earl of Gloucester occupied London, that a final peace was reached. Shortly afterwards, negotiations began with Llywelyn and in September a treaty was agreed at Montgomery that recognised him as prince of Wales, giving him the homage of all the other native Welsh rulers and conceding the four cantrefs.[10] It cost Llywelyn 25,000 marks but achieved the highwater mark of native Welsh power. It was not to last. In the final years of Henry's reign, the crusade returned to centre stage but this time with Lord Edward as the lead actor, joining Louis IX's crusade in 1270, going first to Tunis then the Holy Land where he won honour, if little else, before leaving Acre in September 1272. His father died on 16 November and Edward was proclaimed king in his absence. His long apprenticeship was over.

Edward I – Command and Conquer: 1272–1290

Edward did not return to England until August 1274. In the meantime, he had spent time in Gascony, strengthening his administrative and diplomatic position there. Edward remained much interested in the duchy and returned for almost three years between 1286 and 1289. In 1279, at Amiens, Edward gained the Agenais and Saintonge from Philip III of France, fulfilling the terms of the treaty of Paris and securing Gascony's frontiers.

Domestically, Edward sought to restore the rights and prestige of the crown which had been laid low and to adopt those principles of reform he regarded as compatible with the crown's dignity. Parliament was the key vehicle through which these objectives were achieved. Edward's kingship in these years of success was parliamentary kingship. In most years, parliament met twice a year, sometimes with the 'commons' element of knights and burgesses and sometimes without. In parliament, the king could take counsel from his subjects, listen to their petitions and dispense justice. He could also, if he demonstrated necessity, obtain their consent for taxation, as in 1275, 1283 and 1290. Finally, what parliament offered the king was a platform for legislation. Between 1275 and 1290, Edward's parliaments passed at least ten major statutes which transformed the operation of English law and formed the bedrock of its functioning for centuries afterwards.[11] In local government, Edward generally appointed substantial local landholders as sheriff, long demanded by the localities, while through his *quo warranto* inquiries into the exercise of local franchises, he established the important principle that all franchises were held from the crown. Through investigation, through listening to and acting upon his subjects' concerns and in the interests of the crown, Edward was demonstrating that reform could enhance the power of the crown rather than diminish it.

A final plank of restoring the crown's position was in Wales. Llywelyn overestimated his strength and underestimated his opponent. Edward, with the full weight of the English state behind him, was much more formidable than he had been earlier. Llywelyn refused to do homage until his grievances were addressed and so Edward, having consulted parliament, declared war in 1276. All Llywelyn's gains at Montgomery were reversed in the short war that followed. A further rebellion in 1282–3 led to the death of Llywelyn in battle and his brother Dafydd on the scaffold. Independent native Wales disappeared and the future of Wales's relationship with England was established in the Statute of Rhuddlan in 1284.[12] The first English prince of Wales, the future Edward II, was born at Caernarfon that same year as the new castle, one of a ring of castles around Snowdonia that Edward constructed, was being built around him.

Edward I – War on All Fronts: 1290–1307

Edward took the cross once more in 1288 and determined to head east again, a desire made more urgent by the fall of Acre in 1291. This influenced his conciliatory approach to provocations from the new French king, Philip IV. Philip was listening to the strong anti-English faction at the French court who wished to unpick the concessions of the treaty of Paris and expel the king of England from France once and for all. A complaint by Norman sailors against the English and Gascon piracy gave Philip the excuse to summon Edward to appear before the Paris *parlement* to answer for the Gascons' actions. Edward was keen to avoid war and was prepared to accept the temporary surrender of Gascony as part of a secret negotiated settlement. Philip reneged on the deal, however, refused to withdraw the summons to the *parlement* and declared the duchy forfeit when Edward failed to appear.

Winning Gascony back would take a huge effort given that Philip's resources were so much greater than Edward's own. He would need military service not only from his English subjects but also, he believed, from Wales and Scotland and he summoned support from both. He also sought allies in the Low Countries to threaten Philip with a war on two fronts. It was Edward, however, who found himself at war with multiple opponents. His expedition to Gascony had to be curtailed to deal with a rebellion in Wales in 1294–5 and then he had to deal with the Scots after they concluded an alliance with the French.

Edward had maintained good relations with Alexander III of Scotland, building on Scottish support for the royalist cause during the Barons' War. The question of English sovereignty over Scotland, long claimed but rarely achieved previously, was left unresolved while Alexander lived. Alexander's death in 1286, followed four years later by that of his sole granddaughter Margaret of Norway, left Scotland vulnerable to civil war between the many possible candidates for the throne. The Scots turned to Edward to adjudicate. This was natural, any new king of Scots would need the approval of his powerful southern neighbour and, besides, many of the claimants, and their allies, were Edward's vassals anyway. At the close of the 'Great Cause' in 1292, Edward pronounced in favour of John Balliol, the man with the strongest claim.[13] All the candidates had been forced to accept Edward's overlordship of Scotland. Like Edward in France, Balliol quickly discovered how difficult it was to have a superior lord to whom your own subjects could appeal over your head. Despite his own experiences in France, Edward showed no empathy for Balliol's position in his handling of Scotland. It is not surprising, then, that the Scots sought French assistance to resist Edward's demands for service. Edward marched north in 1296 and within just a few weeks Balliol's kingship was overthrown. Rather than pass the Scottish crown to the Bruces, Edward relegated the status of the kingdom of Scots to merely a land under his direct rule, establishing an English administration under Earl Warenne.

It seemed by 1297 as if Edward could finally turn his attention to France and in the nick of time, as in January an Anglo-Gascon force was defeated at Bellegarde leaving Edward's position in Gascony precarious. His plans to reinforce Gascony and to launch a second front in Flanders, however, were disrupted by protests domestically. The crisis of 1297 began over the king's demands for military service and metamorphosed into a crisis over taxation. Edward's demands for unpaid service overseas from all those with an income as little as £20 per annum met with mass non-compliance at the muster in July. Edward was forced to offer pay but with his expensively procured allies in the Low Countries getting desperate for Edward's arrival, the king was unable to wait for a parliament to grant him the necessary tax to pay for his army. Instead, he claimed consent for a tax from those around him in his chamber. The earls of Norfolk and Hereford, who had emerged as spokesmen for the discontented, described the tax as a tallage (an arbitrary tax imposed upon serfs) and attempted to prevent the exchequer from collecting it.[14]

Despite the widespread discontent, Edward nonetheless departed for the continent in August with a sizeable force. While his army spent more time fighting its allies than the French, its very presence forced Philip to agree a truce in October. Edward married Philip's sister, Margaret, in 1299 and a final peace was agreed in 1303. It had cost around £500,000 but Gascony had been saved. That still left Scotland to settle. While the seriousness of the domestic crisis in 1297 has been debated, what brought it to a conclusion was news of the defeat of Earl Warenne's English army at Stirling Bridge on 11 September by William Wallace. Though Edward beat Wallace at Falkirk the following August, a combination of persistent Scottish resistance, continuing political discontent at home and the difficulties of campaigning in Scotland meant that it was not until 1304 that Edward was finally able to pacify Scotland again.

With the war seemingly over, Edward was able to turn his mind back to domestic matters. In 1305, he got papal consent to overturn the political concessions he had made between 1297 and 1301 and began to deal with the criminal disorder that had emerged over the past decade through the so-called trailbaston commissions. After a decade of distraction, Edward hoped to return to his previous cooperative and responsive kingship. Such hopes were dashed, however, by the renewal of hostilities in Scotland. Robert Bruce, whose allegiances up to this point had been flexible, made a bid for kingship following his murder of his rival John Comyn at Dumfries in February 1306. The war remained in the balance when Edward I died at Burgh-on-Sands (Cumberland) on 7 July 1307.

If we return to the themes with which we began this chapter, Edward had demonstrated that through parliament he could reform the realm successfully as a Magna Carta king but the crown's demands on its subjects after 1294 led to administrative and judicial developments and tensions that persisted through the following reigns. Most significantly, while Wales had been pacified, England ended the reign of Edward I at war with Scotland and with the status of Gascony and the position of the English kings in France an open question once more. The fourteenth century was dominated by attempts to force an answer to that question.

Personalities

Henry III

One word dominates contemporary and modern discussion of Henry's character: *simplex*. 'Simplex' is not a 'simple' word to translate. It could mean honest and straightforward, but it could also mean unworldly and foolish and was used extensively in both senses by numerous chroniclers to describe Henry.[15] *Simplex* often came with religious overtones, and few would have disagreed with the Westminster chronicler that Henry was a 'devout worshipper of God'.[16] He had other positive qualities: a quirky sense of humour, uxoriousness, a warm heart, loyalty and generosity to his family and an eye for beauty in art and architecture.

Henry's essential decency may have saved his crown in 1264–5 but it did not, unfortunately, make him a good king. Henry was not stupid, but he was less wily than he thought he was and his elaborate plans on the continent came to nothing. Henry occasionally demonstrated flashes of royal anger, but these would often pass without any definite result which enhanced royal dignity or authority. He lacked fixity of purpose and confidence in his own judgements (perhaps a consequence of the reliance on the advice of others developed during his long minority), frequently changing his mind, and even having to guard against this sometimes in official documents, such as his order to the exchequer in 1241 that nothing be taken from his 'hidden' treasure at the Tower 'for any order that the king might make'.[17]

This order also plays to one of Henry's most conspicuous faults, his reckless capacity for overspending in the wrong direction. While the £40,000 spent on the new Westminster Abbey may have been justified, the huge amounts of money he gave to the Lusignans, Savoyards and their supporters produced less tangible results and, in fact, only served to create faction and tension at his court. Henry's open purse to foreigners who arrived at his court contrasts with his cautious patronage of his native nobility. Matthew Paris, the chronicler of St Albans Abbey, despairingly described England under Henry as like 'a vineyard without a wall, in which all who pass along the road gather grapes'.[18]

Part of the frustration the native nobility must have felt was that Henry did not share many of their interests. He loved falconry but showed limited interest in hunting and was hostile to tournaments. Unlike in the reign of Edward I, the great native magnates were not often in attendance at court, while military campaigns were relatively rare in Henry's reign and usually unsuccessful when they did occur. Henry, for all his grand designs, was at heart a peaceful man and, as he declared to the sheriffs in 1261, 'with our utmost desire and all our strength we have not ceased to study and labour ... for the peace and tranquillity of one and all'.[19] Henry only ever wanted peace domestically: with his magnates, between his family and for his subjects. Unfortunately, too often his own actions almost guaranteed that conflict would emerge and, when it did, he was rarely skilled enough to control it.

What did Henry look like? As a boy, Matthew Paris describes him as having a 'pleasant face and golden hair'.[20] The only surviving physical description of him as an adult, however, comes from Nicholas Trevet, writing in the 1320s. Trevet describes him as being of middle height but strong in build with a distinguishing feature of a drooping eyelid.[21]

Edward I

That drooping eyelid was inherited by his eldest son but, while Henry was of middle height, Edward 'towered head and shoulders above the average' according to Trevet, and when he was exhumed in 1774 he was confirmed at six feet two inches: he well deserved his nickname 'Longshanks'.[22] Clearly he was intimidating, so much so that in 1294 the dean of St Paul's apparently dropped dead with fear at having to gainsay the king. Edward's anger was fiercer and much more dangerous than his father's, especially when aimed against those he felt had betrayed him, as the Montforts, Dafydd ap Gruffydd and the Bruces discovered to their cost.

The most famous early description of Edward's character comes from the anonymous author of the *Song of Lewes*, a Montfortian tract composed in 1264:

> A lion by pride and fierceness, he is by inconstancy and changeableness a pard, changing his word and promise, cloaking himself by pleasant speech. When he is in a strait he promises whatever you wish, but as soon as he has escaped he renounces his promise.[23]

Later chroniclers, however, found Edward hard to characterise and it was common to fall back on historic exemplars rather than offer novel individual insights. There was no Matthew Paris or Jean de Joinville to shed light on Edward in the way these chroniclers did for Henry III and Louis IX respectively. We must seek to infer Edward's character, then, from his actions more than from descriptions. Edward was aided by his long apprenticeship and by the fact that he not only looked like a king but acted like one. He could be masterful certainly, but his interests – hunting, hawking, tourneying, Arthurian legends – were those of his greatest subjects as well. It is notable that Edward's relations with his earls were generally very good including, unusually, with those from the generation below him.

Edward's slipperiness, criticised in the *Song of Lewes*, was evident throughout his career, from his conduct in the Barons' War to his renunciation in 1305 of his earlier political and constitutional concessions. While he may have been untrustworthy at times, however, he was also single-minded, and it was a determination to restore the authority of the crown that ran through his career like a golden thread. Never again the humiliations of the period between Lewes and Evesham. If that meant making temporary tactical concessions which could be discarded later, then so be it. This single-mindedness was often beneficial but it could also become a hindrance. Edward rarely saw things from other people's point of view, which often led to resistance when he pushed his own interests too hard. Edward's achievements, nonetheless, were summed up well by the Westminster Chronicle in his obituary, writing that 'while you flourished in your power and might, Fraud lay concealed and honour came to light; Peace gladdened all the earth. The Scots were crushed, Afflicted, beaten, humbled to the dust.'[24]

Reputations The historiography of the thirteenth century and its kings was framed by William Stubbs as the 'struggle for the charters', and this focus has characterised much subsequent writing on the period.[25] In general, historians' judgements of Henry have been negative. Stubbs wrote of the 'series of his follies and falsehoods' which 'accumulated an irresistible weight of national indignation'.[26] R. F. Treharne's judgement in 1932 was much like that of many contemporary chroniclers: 'Though not wholly unattractive as a man, Henry III was devoid of all the qualities which enable a ruler to command success.'[27] The first great age of Henrician studies culminated with Maurice Powicke's two-volume study of *Henry III and the Lord Edward* in 1947. In Powicke's view, Henry was 'capable of energy and passion, watchful, critical and intelligent, quickly responsive to the grandiose, he lacked the dignity of true self-possession. Too often he appears in history as a petulant child or a magnificent potterer.'[28]

A new generation began to reassess Henry's reign in the 1970s, this time with much more attention to the voluminous public sources than previously. A huge amount of new material was produced by John Maddicott, Robert Stacey, Peter Coss, Nicholas Vincent and Margaret Howell and more recently by Adrian Jobson, Louise Wilkinson and Sophie Ambler, shedding new light on aspects of Henry's reign and especially those around the king, from Queen Eleanor to Montfort and his wife, des Roches, and the English church.[29] The big gap in the recent historiography, however, was a comprehensive biography of Henry himself, but David Carpenter has recently corrected this. His two volumes, over forty years in the making, offer the most complete and balanced judgement on Henry so far. He recognises the difficulties Henry faced and the achievements that can be ascribed to him, but, returning to the *simplex* trope, sums him up as 'a king *simplex* in the sense of being pious and innocent but *simplex* too in being naïve and foolish'.[30]

Edward I's reputation has fluctuated rather more than his father's, while remaining generally high. 'With a new reign', Stubbs commented, 'the old antipathies vanish, and the nation rises to its full growth, in accord, for the most part, with the genius of its ruler.'[31] Frederick Tout was less forgiving than Stubbs of Edward's autocratic tendencies, but Powicke ensured that Edward's stock remained high by the 1950s: 'a very great king' was his considered verdict.[32]

This image was clouded, however, from the 1960s, first by Bruce McFarlane's criticisms of Edward's 'masterfulness' in his management of the earls and then the development of this picture by Celtic historians such as Geoffrey Barrow, Rees Davies and others who demonstrated the effects of this masterfulness on Scotland and Wales.[33] Michael Prestwich's Yale biography was published at this 'cyclic low' as he described it.[34] While still critical of the king, Prestwich did much to restore the reputation of a 'formidable king' whose reign was 'a great one'.[35] Since Prestwich's biography, a series of new work on Edward's rule by English historians such as Marc Morris, Caroline Burt, Andrew Spencer, Andy King and Kathleen Neal has further enhanced Edward's reputation. As a recent judgement puts it, Edward's reign 'shows how the powers available to a king of England might be utilised by an intelligent and determined man, with an ability to recognise and employ other intelligent men. Few, if any, wielded them to greater effect.'[36] This flurry of new research on both Henry and Edward shows little sign of slowing down and demonstrates how this period remains one of intrigue and debate for historians. This should come as no surprise as it was a momentous century and many of its political and constitutional questions remain relevant to English and British geopolitics.

Notes

1. *EHD, 1189–1327*, no. 103.
2. *The History of William Marshal*, trans. N. Bryant (Woodbridge, 2016), 187.
3. *EHD, 1189–1327*, no. 34.
4. Ibid., no. 30.
5. Ibid., no. 36.
6. Ibid., no. 37.
7. Ibid., nos. 40–1.
8. *Documents of the Baronial Movement of Reform and Rebellion, 1258–1267*, ed. and trans. R. E. Treharne and I. J. Sanders (Oxford, 1973), no. 38.
9. *Metrical Chronicle of Robert of Gloucester*, ed. W. A. Wright, 2 vols., RS (1887), II, line 11,376.
10. *The Acts of the Welsh Rulers, 1120–1283*, ed. H. Pryce with the assistance of C. Insley (Cardiff, 2005), no. 363.
11. *EHD, 1189–1327*, nos. 47, 49, 51–4, 57–9, 62–4.
12. Ibid., no. 55.
13. The key documents of the Great Cause are in *Anglo-Scottish Relations, 1174–1328: Some Selected Documents*, ed. and trans. E. L. G. Stones (Oxford, 1965), nos. 14–20.
14. *EHD, 1189–1327*, no. 73.
15. Matthew Paris, *Chronica Majora*, ed. H. R. Luard, 7 vols., RS (1872–3), III, 164–5; 'Annales Monasterii de Osneia, AD 1016–1347', in *Annales Monastici*, ed. H. R. Luard, RS, 36 (1864–9), IV, 77; *The Chronicle of Walter of Guisborough*, ed. H. Rothwell, Camden Society, Third Series, 89 (1957), 201.
16. *Flores Historiarum*, ed. H. R. Luard, 3 vols., RS (1890), III, 28.
17. *CCR, 1237–1242*, p. 376.
18. Paris, *Chronica Majora*, V, 514.
19. *Foedera*, I, i, 408–9.
20. Matthew Paris, *Historia Anglorum*, ed. H. T. Riley, 3 vols., RS (1867–9), II, 196.
21. Nicholas Trevet, *Annales Sex Regum Angliae*, ed. T. Hog (London, 1845), 280.

22. Ibid., 281–2.
23. *EHD, 1189–1327*, no. 232.
24. *Flores Historiarum*, III, 330.
25. W. Stubbs, *The Constitutional History of England, in Its Origin and Development*, 3 vols. (Cambridge, 2012, reprint), II, ch. 14.
26. Ibid., II, 4.
27. R. F. Treharne, *The Baronial Plan of Reform, 1258–1263* (Manchester, 1971, reprint), 47.
28. F. M. Powicke, *Henry III and the Lord Edward*, 2 vols. (Oxford, 1947), I, 156–7.
29. N. Vincent, *Peter des Roches: An Alien in English Politics, 1205–1238* (Cambridge, 1996). For the others see Further Reading in this chapter.
30. D. A. Carpenter, *Henry III, 1258–1272: Reform, Rebellion, Civil War, Settlement* (New Haven, CT, 2023), 639.
31. Stubbs, *Constitutional History*, II, 4–5.
32. Powicke, *Henry III*, II, 725.
33. K. B. McFarlane, 'Had Edward I a "Policy" towards the Earls?', *History* 50 (1965), 145–59; G. W. S. Barrow, *Robert Bruce and the Community of the Realm of Scotland* (Edinburgh, 1965); R. R. Davies, *The First English Empire: Power and Identities in the British Isles, 1093–1343* (Oxford, 2000).
34. M. C. Prestwich, *Edward I* (New Haven, CT, 1997), xi.
35. Ibid., 567.
36. *Edward I: New Interpretations*, ed. A. King and A. M. Spencer (Woodbridge, 2020), 8.

Further Reading

Ambler, S., *Bishops in the Political Community of England, 1213–1272* (Oxford, 2017).
Burt, C., *Edward I and the Governance of England* (Cambridge, 2013).
Burt, C. and Partington, R., *Arise England: Six Kings and the Making of the English State* (London, 2024).
Carpenter, D., *The Struggle for Mastery: Britain, 1066–1284* (London, 2003).
  Henry III, 2 vols. (New Haven, CT, 2020–23).
Howell, M., *Eleanor of Provence: Queenship in Thirteenth-Century England* (Oxford, 1998).
Jobson, A., *The First English Revolution: Simon de Montfort, Henry III and the Barons' War* (London, 2012).
King, A. and Spencer, A., eds., *Edward I: New Interpretations* (Woodbridge, 2020).
Maddicott, J. R., *Simon de Montfort* (Cambridge, 1994).
  The Origins of the English Parliament, 924–1327 (Oxford, 2010).

Morris, M., *A Great and Terrible King: Edward I and the Forging of Britain* (London, 2008).
Prestwich, M., *Edward I* (New Haven, CT, 1997).
   Plantagenet England, 1225-1360 (Oxford, 2005).
Spencer, A., *Nobility and Kingship in Medieval England: Edward I and the Earls, 1272-1307* (Cambridge, 2014).
Stacey, R., *Politics, Policy and Finance under Henry III, 1216-1245* (Oxford, 1987).
Wilkinson, L., *Eleanor de Montfort: A Rebel Countess in Medieval England* (London, 2012).

DAVID GREEN

2

Events, Personalities and Reputations
The Fourteenth Century

The fourteenth century saw the arrival of what is often described as the late medieval crisis. A period of famine, war, plague and death on an unparalleled scale – it is hardly surprising that many believed the apocalypse was upon them. Given these vicissitudes it is equally unsurprising that the challenges of kingship became especially acute in this period. The fourteenth century saw the first deposition of an English king by his own people, but it was not the last. Edward II's fate would be shared by his great-grandson, Richard II, who was well aware that a dangerous precedent had been set. Indeed, Richard's cognisance of the events of 1327 and his attempts to prevent them from being repeated proved utterly counterproductive. Because of these contexts, while many of the priorities of kingship remained much as they had been for centuries, there was a new environment in which royal governance had to operate in the fourteenth century. Shaped by a sequence of natural and man-made disasters as well as by a new political milieu, the spectre of deposition loomed large. And yet the 'calamitous fourteenth century' also witnessed a period of spectacular royal success. For much, although not all of his long reign, Edward III, buoyed up by triumphs against the traditional enemies of Scotland and France, enjoyed security on the English throne and could, indeed, contemplate extending his authority to create what might be considered a 'Plantagenet Empire'.

Edward II, 1307–1314

Such extraordinary contrasts – triumph and calamity – seemed unlikely when Edward II succeeded his father, Edward I, in 1307. Certainly, the expense of the Welsh campaigns, the failure to subdue Scotland and ongoing difficulties regarding the duchy of Gascony meant that when Edward received the crown he was confronted with circumstances which would inevitably prove to be challenging. But, by comparison with many of his predecessors, the hand he was dealt at his accession was if not splendid then certainly not disastrous. Many of the (considerable) problems Edward faced in the early years of his reign were, in fact, of his own making. He did, nonetheless, have to operate in a political environment which differed in some significant ways from that which had preceded it. From the very beginning of his administration, he should have been aware that there were particular expectations which he would do well to fulfil. Some of these involved generic priorities that concerned all kings before him such as the defence (and ideally the expansion) of the realm, as well as ensuring patronage was used and distributed appropriately to members of the secular elite and maintaining a good working relationship with representatives of the church. The latter was by no means straightforward given the strife his father had experienced with Pope Boniface VIII (d. 1303) over questions of clerical taxation and, later, the frictions caused by the relocation of the papacy to Avignon (between 1305 and 1309).

However, in addition to these traditional requirements that he encountered in his capacity as head of the body politic Edward was also confronted with some significant new challenges. Laid out in his coronation oath (1308), these suggested that he would be expected to deal more closely with members of the so-called community of the realm than his predecessors. This was a somewhat amorphous body. It comprised not only those who sat in parliament but also those beyond the ranks of the elite. The foundations for a more representative form of government that had been laid in the thirteenth century, and which were seen in legislation such as Magna Carta (1215) and the Provisions of Oxford (1258) and Westminster (1259), were built upon in the years of the late medieval crisis. In many respects, the success or otherwise of royal government in this period rested on how well monarchs maintained a positive working relationship with this 'community'.

When one considers the catastrophic nature of the relationships Edward had with this group the great surprise is that he was not deposed much sooner than proved to be the case. Difficulties began, in no small part, because of the favouritism shown to Piers Gaveston (d. 1312). A Gascon knight who had been part of Edward's household when he had been prince of Wales, Edward's patronage saw him catapulted into the ranks of the peerage. Gaveston married Margaret de Clare (d. 1342) and became earl of Cornwall in 1307 at the outset of the new reign. His new status was shown by the central role he played in the coronation. It would be Gaveston's proximity to the crown and what was seen as his undue influence over the king, alongside deteriorating circumstances in Scotland and spiralling household expenses, that led certain magnates to come together and demand reform. Known as the Ordainers, on account of the Ordinances, the document which laid out the changes they demanded the king implement, the group was led by Thomas, earl of Lancaster (d. 1322). One of the central requirements was that 'as the evident enemy of the king and of his people', Gaveston should 'be completely exiled . . . forever without ever returning'.[1] Under intense pressure, the king acceded to the demands in the late summer of 1311 but immediately began negotiations with the papacy seeking to annul the Ordinances. Additionally, early in 1312, in a move guaranteed to provoke the Ordainers even further, Gaveston returned. Tensions reached such a pitch that the country appeared to be on the brink of civil war. Gaveston was eventually besieged in Scarborough Castle and captured. Perhaps initially seen as a potentially valuable bargaining chip in negotiations with the king, the decision was soon taken by senior members of the opposition to execute him.

Edward II, 1314–1327

This undermined what little trust remained between the king and many of the key figures in the English elite. The monarch's own position then suffered another blow when he was defeated by Robert I of Scotland (Robert Bruce, r. 1306–29) in battle. After a difficult start to his own reign, Robert had slowly established his power before he found himself in a position to look south. A number of raids across the Border made a statement that Edward II could not ignore, and so in 1314 an English army with the king at its head marched to confront the Scots. He met Bruce at Bannockburn. What followed was a calamity for Edward personally and a stain on the reputation of the English monarchy for generations. Bruce's victory severely compromised Edward's authority in England and led to the king being essentially sidelined from major governmental decisions as the earl of Lancaster seized power.

Thomas, however, was not able to maintain his position and, in time, Edward re-established himself. This meant that two major power blocs now existed in the realm and in 1321–2 they came to blows. This civil war between the royal house and the Lancastrians would prove to be only the first in a series of conflicts which would shape and reshape the English political landscape throughout the remainder of the medieval period. Lancaster himself was killed at the battle of Boroughbridge (1322) and Edward alongside his new favourites, Hugh Despenser the Elder and Hugh the Younger, sought to expunge the Ordainers from the realm. Another of those deemed a threat by the new regime was the queen, Isabella (d. 1358). It appears that up until the rise of the Despensers to prominence, Edward and Isabella, known today as the 'She-Wolf of France', had enjoyed a reasonably cordial relationship. That collapsed in the early 1320s. Isabella found her own position severely compromised: her access to funds and even to the king himself became very limited. She, however, could not be completely set aside given her rank and the fact that she was sister to the king of France. When the vexed question of the status of the duchy of Gascony flared up once more in the form of the war of Saint Sardos (1323–5), Isabella found herself despatched across the Channel as part of an embassy to seek a resolution to this dispute. The decision that the heir to the throne (the future Edward III) should pay homage to the French monarch for the duchy was a short-term 'fix' which, in reality, resolved very little. However, once out of the direct influence of the king and his advisors and now having control of the heir, Isabella's position was much enhanced. She refused to return to England with her son unless the Despensers were removed from power. When her demands were rebuffed, she took steps that proved decisive. She sought allies among the English exiles aboard. With their assistance and with the military support that came with the marriage of Prince Edward to Philippa, the daughter of the count of Hainault, she launched an attack on her husband in 1326. Support for the king swiftly dissolved and he fled only to be captured near Neath in Wales.

As the new regime took charge, both of the Despensers were executed, with Hugh the Younger hanged, drawn and quartered, while Edward would become the first English monarch to be deposed by his own people. This was a fait accompli although the decision to replace the king with his son was justified in parliament. A checklist of the king's many failures was read to these representatives of the community of the realm; they outlined his military failures, his mismanagement of his household, his 'unkingly' behaviour and his unwillingness to listen to the wise counsel of the great men of the kingdom. The deposition process was momentous but also relatively straightforward as it did not interfere with the line of succession. Although, for the time being, Isabella and her new paramour Roger Mortimer would take charge, the crown would be worn by Edward III.

The fate, thereafter, of Edward II has been a cause of speculation for many years. Although very many historians argue that the king met his death while imprisoned in Berkeley Castle, a vociferous minority suggest he escaped captivity.[2] Such a notion was first proposed by a papal notary, Manuele Fieschi, in a letter of 1337. Unless the tomb in Gloucester in which Edward is said to lie is opened, such speculation is unlikely to end. But while it is probable that the king did perish in the aftermath of his deposition, the manner of his death has been the subject of lurid conjecture. The tale of his murder by means of a red-hot poker thrust into his anus is only one among many.

Edward III: 1327–1360

The new reign did not mark an immediate change in the fortunes of the monarchy. The regime of Isabella and Mortimer was loathed almost as intensely as that of Edward II and the Despensers, and circumstances deteriorated further when Robert of Scotland enforced a peace treaty considered so iniquitous to England that it became dubbed the 'Shameful Peace' of Northampton (1328). Not long after, perhaps prompted by fears about the extent of Mortimer's avarice, the young king resolved to take matters into his own hands. In 1330, with a group of loyal companions, Edward stole into his mother's chambers while the court was staying at Nottingham Castle. There, he seized Mortimer, who would soon be executed, placed Isabella under house arrest and with this coup began to rule in more than name only.

Taking inspiration from his grandfather, Edward III sought to unite the English aristocracy beneath the royal banner and restore the authority of the monarchy through military means. He first turned his attention to Scotland where the recent death of Robert I and the minority of his son, David II (r. 1329–71), provided an opportunity to support the Balliol family in its own ambitions for the Scottish throne. English armies, some sponsored by the king and some which he led in person, secured several significant victories. The encounters at Dupplin Moor (1332) and Halidon Hill (1333) offered something of a counterpoint to the humiliation of Bannockburn. More significantly, the campaigns led to the creation of a cadre of experienced soldiers trained in particular tactics which would secure even more important victories once the Hundred Years War began.

This conflict with France would become the focus of royal attention for much of the remainder of the reign. At the heart of dispute was Gascony. The status of the duchy had been a cause of friction ever since Eleanor of Aquitaine brought the territory into the English dominions (with her marriage to Henry II in 1152). As king of England Edward III was, in theory at least, sovereign within his realm, but as duke of Gascony he remained subject to his overlord, the king of France. The fact that Edward's own claim to that title had been refuted when the Capetian dynasty failed in 1328 only poured more fuel on this political fire. However, the Hundred Years War would last so long because it also came to involve Scotland, Flanders, Castile and the papacy itself. It was shaped by economic concerns, reshaped notions of national identity and developed governmental structures to enable the state to wage war for longer periods and over wider areas than ever before.

The war erupted in 1337 when Edward refused to comply with the demands of Philip VI, the first king of the Valois dynasty, to turn over Robert of Artois (d. 1342), a French nobleman who had fled French justice and sought sanctuary at the English court. As a vassal of the French crown, Edward, Philip believed, had failed in his responsibilities and his lands in France were forfeit as a result. Edward III's reputation as one of England's most successful medieval monarchs rests, chiefly, on a phase of the war which began in 1346. As this suggests, the first nine years of the conflict were far from glorious. The king sought to establish a series of vastly expensive alliances with foreign princes and disgruntled members of the French elite. There was some success in the form of a naval battle at Sluys in 1340 but the costs involved in this early policy were colossal. They brought about a financial crisis followed by major opposition in parliament. Forced to accept major, albeit short-lived concessions the crisis of 1340–1 marked a turning point in the reign and it also resulted in a change of military strategy which produced spectacular results. The year 1346 was the king's *annus mirabilis*. After landing in Normandy, he launched a *chevauchée* – a widespread raid calculated to cause major devastation to the French countryside and hence to the economic and personal standing of the Valois monarchy. This drew a response from the French crown and Philip and Edward met in battle at Crécy. There, using the tactics which had proved so effective in Scotland, namely the deployment of mixed retinues of longbowmen, infantry and dismounted men-at-arms, Edward secured a shattering victory over his French counterpart. The year's triumph was then made even greater when Philip's Scottish ally, David II, was also defeated and the king himself was captured at Neville's Cross.

Unfortunately for Edward, he was prevented from making even greater political capital from these successes by the ghastly intervention of the Black Death, which arrived on the southern shores of England in 1348. The impact of bubonic plague was both immediate and long-lasting. The contagion returned, albeit with lessening ferocity, throughout the remainder of the Middle Ages. It is likely that on account of endemic plague as well as famine and war the population of England in 1400 fell to 50 per cent of what it had been 100 years previously. The consequences were profound, for labour, agriculture, social structures, attitudes to the church and much besides. As early as 1349, Edward introduced legislation to seek to counter the effects of the plague on a peasantry who suddenly found that their labour was now much more valuable than before. This Ordinance of Labourers was followed by a statute in 1351 and legislation of this sort would be reiterated, amended and discussed in approximately 30 per cent of all parliamentary meetings for the next century.

The peasantry was the group most affected by the plague – numerically and proportionately its members suffered most and yet, ironically, those who survived the plague benefited a great deal from the conditions the Black Death created. But no one was entirely immune. The king's daughter, Joan (of England, 1333–48), died at Bordeaux, en route to cement an alliance by marriage to the son of King Peter of Castile. The letter despatched to the Castilian court after Edward had heard the news is a diplomatic missive but one in which we (seem to) hear the deep sadness of a father who has lost his child and who is seeking to understand this loss.[3] This, perhaps, was all the more difficult for the king because so many of his contemporaries believed the plague to be a manifestation of God's wrath with a sinful people.

Because of the enormous disruption caused by the Black Death, it was some time before English expeditions set out for France in force once more. The most significant among the next campaigns was led by the king's eldest son, Edward of Woodstock, known to posterity as the Black Prince (1330-76). In 1355, he led what became known as the *grande chevauchée* – a devastating raid that cut a swathe through southern France, from the borders of English Gascony to the shores of the Mediterranean and back. It was an act of calculated and extreme devastation. In the following year, a second raid was launched into the Valois heartlands. This challenge had to be met and King John II of France (1350-64) himself drew up his army against the prince not far from Poitiers. The battle proved to be a closer-run affair than Crécy, but the result was the same and in many respects it seemed more significant given that the French king was captured alongside a host of French nobles.

Edward III then sought to make political capital out of military success. In domestic terms this was simple, and he had strong foundations on which to build. Success in warfare and a certain chivalric glamour did much to unite the aristocracy in support of royal ambitions. But Edward also fashioned a good deal of support in parliament, which was developing as an institution in its own right, and among the population at large. He was also moulding a new conception of English identity, one in which the church served as a mouthpiece and the English language was starting to play an important role. In 1362, the king would issue the Statute of Pleading ensuring that many legal cases were to be heard in the vernacular. In short, the king was moulding a political community that extended beyond the ranks of the elite and ensuring that it marched in step with his own objectives.[4]

It proved, however, more difficult to take advantage of circumstances in France, despite the turmoil caused by the king's capture and the humiliation of Poitiers. When negotiations failed in 1359, he launched a further expedition. On this occasion, it appears that Edward had very particular ambitions. He marched on Reims, the coronation city of French kings, and he brought a crown with him. It seems that while sovereignty over Gascony had been the predominant English aim in the Hundred Years War up until this point, briefly it appeared that much more might be gained, nothing less than the French throne itself. However, the siege of Reims failed, as did a subsequent assault on Paris. As a result, Edward agreed to terms and sealed the treaty of Brétigny-Calais in 1360. This involved a vast ransom for the return of John II as well as major territorial concessions. The Plantagenets reacquired many of their ancestral 'Angevin' territories. In return, Edward was to give up his claim to the French throne. However, some key aspects of the treaty were never formally concluded, which, in time, provided an opportunity to reopen the Anglo-French war.

Edward III: 1360–1377

In retrospect, the treaty of Brétigny-Calais marked the end of the most successful phase of Edward III's reign. Indeed, one might argue that the Reims campaign indicated the beginning of a period of (uneven) decline that would continue until the king's death in 1377. This, however, was by no means obvious at the time. At home, the people enjoyed a period of peace and stability. Taxation was relatively low and, despite significant outbreaks of plague, there were few significant disruptions to law and order. Meanwhile, with the pressures of the Hundred Years War relieved for the time being, Edward could turn his attentions elsewhere and to the needs of his family. The king would have been a poor student of history, indeed, not to recognise the dangers that ambitious adult sons could pose to a regime. Hence, Edward of Woodstock was appointed prince of Aquitaine (controlling a lordship which greatly extended the duchy of Gascony), and Lionel of Antwerp became duke of Clarence and the king's lieutenant in Ireland. Discussions began for Edmund of Langley to marry Margaret of Burgundy, which, if they had succeeded, would have created a hugely influential lordship in France and Flanders, and John of Gaunt enjoyed the wealth of the duchy of Lancaster. There are clear imperial ambitions underpinning the various plans Edward III engineered in the early 1360s. However, the family's fortunes would soon decline. Lionel left Ireland, preferring instead a marriage to Violante Visconti of Milan, but he died in 1368, only four months after the match was contracted. The Black Prince misman-aged affairs in Aquitaine, which rose in revolt reigniting the Hundred Years War in 1369. This coincided with a collapse in Edward's health that would see him return to England and, indeed, to predecease his father. The negotiation for the marriage between Langley and Margaret foundered on the need for a papal dispensation. And soon, Edward III's own health began to deteriorate. Consequently, the final decade of the reign saw a retrenchment of the English position in France and growing uncertainty about the future and the succession.

This deterioration led to worries in parliament, especially among the Commons, a group which had been growing in authority over the course of the century. For the first time, in 1376, the knights of the shire and representatives of the boroughs took direct action against some of the servants of the crown and chief figures in the royal household. The so-called Good Parliament was a significant moment in the evolution of the institution, and although many of its actions were repealed in subsequent meetings, it is an indication that a new political force was at work in the realm. With the death of the Black Prince in 1376, the heir to the throne became his remaining son, Richard of Bordeaux, who became Richard II after his grandfather suffered a stroke in 1377 that would prove to be fatal.

Richard II: 1377–1381

Richard's accession returned England to the uncertainties of a minority kingship. However, unlike the situation in 1327 or when Henry III came to the throne in 1216, that minority was not acknowledged explicitly. There was no regency. Instead, a series of continual councils took charge for the opening years of the young king's reign. This indicates that succession planning was not all that it might have been. The death of the Black Prince and the decline of Edward III had certainly made this process difficult. So too did the general unpopularity of John of Gaunt and the unconventional marital history and personal reputation of Richard's mother, Joan, 'the Fair Maid' of Kent. In actuality, Joan was a highly capable figure and Gaunt probably offered a stability to his nephew's regime, although there is no doubt that he had considerable ambitions for himself and the Lancastrian dynasty.

The new administration immediately faced a series of challenges. The situation in France continued to deteriorate and funds were needed urgently to bolster the frontiers of Gascony. Tax collection had become commonplace throughout Edward III's reign, although there had been considerable opposition to this before military success made such impositions seem worthwhile. The impact of recurrent outbreaks of plague, however, caused considerable difficulties and, of course, the memories of the victories at Crécy and Poitiers now seemed very dim. In order to address the financial shortfall, Richard's government instituted a series of poll taxes. These would prove to be the catalyst for one of the most spectacular demonstrations of popular unrest in the whole of the Middle Ages.

For a brief moment in the summer of 1381, the Peasants' Revolt threatened to overturn the established social order in England. Although focused on London and the nearby counties of Kent and Essex, the rebellion also enjoyed considerable support elsewhere in the country. While sparked into life by tax demands, discontent had grown over successive decades as a result of various instruments imposed to address what the elite saw as the deleterious financial and social impacts of the Black Death. Labour legislation and sumptuary laws formed part of a raft of measures used to try and prevent social mobility and its appearance. In many respects, the revolt was a movement comprised not of those who were utterly downtrodden and destitute but of those disillusioned with the ruling elite alongside men and women who could see new opportunities and were being prevented from grasping them fully. Many also took advantage of the disruption to settle personal scores. Hence, to think of the 1381 rising as the *Peasants'* Revolt is not entirely helpful given that many who were not from the peasantry became involved and, indeed, the peasantry was far from being a homogeneous group.[5]

There is no doubt that the revolt was extremely violent, but whether it was quite as 'bestial' as some contemporary writers described is difficult to ascertain. Few who wrote about the events of 1381 had any sympathy for the rebels and most saw the rising as a complete and dreadful reversal of the divinely ordained social order.[6] The summer of

1381, however, may be seen as Richard's finest hour. It was no small thing for the fourteen-year-old king to meet with the rebels in person, including those who had butchered Simon Sudbury, the archbishop of Canterbury, in the streets of London, and razed Gaunt's palace, the Savoy. In the second meeting, Wat Tyler, the leader of the revolt, was killed by members of Richard's bodyguard who feared for the king's life. Taking charge of the situation, the young man then presented himself to the rebels and offered to be their 'captain' now that Tyler had fallen and, remarkably, they complied and he led them outside the city walls. As this suggests, one of the most striking aspects of the events of 1381 is the extraordinary faith that those involved in the rising had in the monarchy. They clearly believed both in the ability of the king to right the wrongs that they suffered and that he would do so once he understood the justice of their cause. In reality, Richard would renege on many of the promises made to the rebels, although England would not see another poll tax until the practice was revived by Margaret Thatcher's administration in the 1980s.

Richard II: 1382–1389

Having faced down an attack on his administration by the peasantry, Richard would next have to deal with opposition from a more familiar section of society. The Appellants were a collection of noblemen who sought reform to the royal household and to the general direction of national policy. They included the king's uncle, Thomas of Woodstock, duke of Gloucester; Richard Fitzalan, earl of Arundel and Surrey; and Thomas Beauchamp, earl of Warwick. Later, the group was joined by Henry Bolingbroke, earl of Derby (the future king Henry IV), and Thomas Mowbray, earl of Nottingham (subsequently duke of Norfolk). From early in his reign Richard sought an accommodation with France and he appears to have been considerably more interested in extending English authority within Britain and Ireland than across the Channel. This was not popular with many of the aristocracy raised on tales of glory won at the expense of the Valois. It was around this time that Richard appears to have become keenly aware of the fate his great-grandfather suffered in 1327 and, indeed, he may well have been threatened with deposition during the Appellant crisis in the late 1380s.

However, his awareness of Edward II's fall did not prevent him from making some of the same mistakes. Richard's misuse of patronage is a case in point. His grant to Michael de la Pole of the earldom of Suffolk (in 1385), and creation of Robert de Vere, first as marquis of Dublin (1385) and later as duke of Ireland (1386), formed part of a process that he extended towards the end of his reign, by which the king sought to reshape the peerage and establish a group of his own supporters in the upper ranks of the aristocracy. Edward III had done something similar, but Richard's attempts were sorely mismanaged.

Concerns regarding policy towards France and Ireland and the spiralling expense of the royal household came to a head in the 'Wonderful Parliament' of 1386. Demands by the crown for taxes were met with counter-demands for the removal of the chancellor, de la Pole, and a commission of nobles headed by the king's uncles, York and Gloucester, effectively took control of the government to implement some 'necessary reforms'. Richard sought to oppose these changes, first using legal means, and later his supporters took up arms against the Appellants. But at the battle of Radcot Bridge (1387), de Vere was defeated by Henry Bolingbroke, earl of Derby, the future Henry IV. It may well be that if an obvious successor had been available, the king would have been deposed at this point. Instead, Richard's administration limped on, hamstrung by the Appellants who sought to further undermine the king's position by removing many of his key supporters from positions of influence: the Merciless Parliament of 1388 is well named. Thereafter, in several respects, the reign began again. Richard renewed his coronation oath in 1389 and the nobles, once more, offered oaths of allegiance to the crown. But the rift between the king and the Appellants would never be healed. It is perhaps important to remember that at the time of the Merciless Parliament Richard was only twenty-one years of age.

Richard II: 1390–1399

In 1382, Richard had married Anne of Bohemia, a match which appeared to many contemporaries to offer little political or financial advantage. The author of the Westminster Chronicle complained of the costs associated with *purchasing* 'this little scrap of humanity'.[7] It proved, however, to be a very loving relationship and Richard appears to have been distraught when Anne died in 1394. Moreover, she may have acted as something of a calming and mediating presence at court. Whether or not her death contributed to a changed political atmosphere, there is no doubt that Richard soon adopted a very different approach.

In 1396, he moved to secure a truce with France by marrying the young princess, Isabella. Soon after, and feeling sufficiently secure, he took action against those who had opposed him ten years previously. This final phase of the reign has often been characterised as tyrannical and some historians have suggested that the king was driven by paranoia, narcissism or even schizophrenia. But, equally, this can be seen as a calculated action motivated by the king's wish to systematically rebuild his authority and shaped by a particular notion of royal power. In 1397, three of the leading Appellants, the duke of Gloucester and the earls of Warwick and Arundel, were arrested. Accusations of treason were levelled against them and proceedings that followed were conducted under the watchful gaze of the king's own bodyguard of Cheshire archers. Arundel was condemned to death, Gloucester (conveniently) died in captivity and Warwick was bundled off to imprisonment on the Isle of Man. In 1398, attention fell on Henry Bolingbroke, now duke of Hereford, who found himself banished for ten years following a dispute with the duke of Norfolk. It was this action that would lead to Richard's own downfall.

Bolingbroke's father, John of Gaunt, the duke of Lancaster, died in 1399, and, understandably, Henry wished to take possession of his inheritance. Richard had made what proved to be the disastrous decision to launch a further expedition to Ireland – he had previously visited the lordship in 1394–5. While the king was absent, Bolingbroke grasped the opportunity to invade. It swiftly became apparent that in order to seize the duchy of Lancaster he would have to claim the kingdom as a whole. This, initially, was not difficult: support for the king dissolved and, when Richard returned, he was swiftly taken captive. In parliament on 30 September 1399, he was deposed. The charges laid against him were detailed and extensive and Richard's legitimacy to wield power was called into question as well as his ability to do so in the best interests of the community of the realm. This was necessary because, unlike in 1327, his successor, soon to be crowned as Henry IV, had a claim that was tenuous at best. Richard spent the last months of his life in 1400 at Pontefract Castle. Lancastrian sources suggest that he starved himself to death once the Epiphany Rising – a plot to free him – failed. It is more probable that he was killed on the orders of the new king, his cousin.

Personalities

It is often impossible to describe the appearance of medieval monarchs with any certainty. Heraldic depictions, wall paintings and even funerary effigies rarely provide or even sought to provide realistic impressions of their subjects, although, interestingly, Richard II's memorial may offer us a more reliable indication. For the most part, artists and craftsmen aimed to invoke a sense of majesty, to hint at the qualities the individual possessed or, in the case of tomb sculptures, those qualities which the king or those who came after him wished to suggest that he possessed. This might be especially difficult when the subject in question had been deposed. A usurper did not wish to call into question the office he had now seized, but at the same time he clearly did not wish to exalt the status of the man he had deposed. One answer to this conundrum lay in the location chosen for the monument. Hence, Edward II was laid to rest in Gloucester Abbey (now cathedral) and Richard II was buried first at the friary at King's Langley (Herts.) until Henry V saw fit in 1413 to relocate him to the double tomb at Westminster Abbey, which he now shares with Anne of Bohemia. By that time, the Lancastrian claim to the throne appeared to have been thoroughly secured and the king could be magnanimous to his predecessor.[8]

Edward II

Almost all the contemporary and near-contemporary descriptions that remain of Edward II suggest that he was a fine figure of a man – tall, strong and handsome. Some bemoaned the fact that he did not make better use of his innate qualities and gave himself over to 'rustic pursuits', but others commented on his physical courage, noting, for example, his reluctance to withdraw from the field at Bannockburn. Such differing accounts depended, very much, on the intentions of the author and how he wished to explain the king's deposition and the lessons the author wished his readers to learn from that fall from grace.

The Articles of Deposition of 1327 offer a distillation of the king's limitations and many of them are bound up with an extensive list of character flaws. Alongside the king's inability to maintain his estates in Britain and France and his failure to fulfil his coronation oath, he was said to enjoy a range of hobbies and pastimes unsuitable for a man of his standing. These offer an intriguing insight into his personality. While we must remember that these allegations were made to justify a deposition, Ranulf Higden (d. 1364) offers a similar picture of the king. He tells us that Edward:

> was a handsome man of great strength, but unconventional in his behaviour. For, shunning the company of the nobility, he preferred that of jesters, singers, actors, carters, diggers, oarsmen, sailors and other mechanics. He drank too much, betrayed confidences too easily, struck out without provocation at those standing around him and followed the counsel of others rather than his own. He was extravagant and splendid in his lifestyle, voluble, inconstant, unlucky against his opponents and treated members of his household savagely. However, he was passionately attached to one person [Piers Gaveston] above all, whom he cherished, exalted honoured and showered with gifts. The result of such infatuation was that both the lover and the love were held in odium, the people scandalized and the kingdom brought to ruin.[9]

Edward III

According to the author of the Middle English poem *Wynnere and Wastoure* (c. 1352), Edward was a 'comely king' with a 'berry-brown' beard. The mannequin of the king, made after his death and which remains among the royal memorabilia at Westminster Abbey, suggests he was perhaps 5 feet 10 inches in height – tall by the standards of the time but not remarkably so, especially by comparison with his grandfather, Longshanks. The king's delight in tournaments, hunting and all the courtly panoply of chivalry are well attested. His religious preferences appear to have been conventional even if his relationship with the papacy was often strained. An understanding father, he enjoyed what appears to have been loving relationships with his children and he was also one astute enough to recognise the potential dangers that ambitious sons might pose to a regime, especially when one ruled for as long as he.

Richard II

The appearance of Richard II has been a matter of very considerable discussion, not least because it was clearly a subject in which the king himself took a great interest. In the Westminster Portrait (1390s) (see Figure 16.18) and the Wilton Diptych (c. 1396) (see Figure 16.19), there are two images of the king that we can presume offer us some indication of his appearance. The diptych (a two-panel altarpiece) presents the king as he was (or as he remembered himself to be) at the time of his coronation, while, somewhat awkwardly, the Westminster Portrait shows him as an older man. There are interesting similarities in the latter depiction with Richard's gilt tomb effigy, which may have been begun during the king's lifetime.[10]

The king's interest in the appearance and symbolism of monarchy is well known and he relied heavily on the glamour of kingship to buttress his authority. The Westminster Portrait is the first painting of its kind in England. It was only in the Tudor period – nearly 100 years hence – that this sort of royal imagery became commonplace. Influenced by Valois and other continental rulers and by theoretical works, some of which drew on Roman law to promote an exalted image of royal power, in this and in other ways Richard sought to promote an image of monarchy which hints at the later development of the notion of 'divine right'.

Reputations

The reputations of all three fourteenth-century kings have fluctuated a good deal since their deaths. In their immediate aftermaths, the depositions of Edward II and Richard II needed to be explained and justified. This was an especially acute concern for the fragile Lancastrian regime in its early years, and its propagandists swiftly set to work to sully the late king's memory.[11] For many, however, it is the images given to us in the Elizabethan era which remain most potent. Written in 1592, Christopher Marlowe's *Edward II* (with the full title *The Troublesome Reign and Lamentable Death of Edward the Second, King of England, with the Tragical Fall of Proud Mortimer*) dwells on a homoerotic relationship between the king and Gaveston, developing ideas first advanced by Bishop Adam Orleton (d. 1345) and Thomas Burton, the chronicler of Meaux Abbey (d. 1437). Shakespeare's *Richard II* (1595) has been equally influential. It focuses on the final (tyrannical?) years of the king's reign. We witness the inevitable fall of a foppish, cruel, irresponsible young man but one who, ironically, gains wisdom, a new sense of perspective and a certain philosophical stature just as political power is slipping from his grasp. Both works relied a good deal on Raphael Holinshed's *Chronicles* (1587) for their inspiration. Shakespeare also contributed to *The Raigne of King Edward the Third* (c. 1592), although this play, chiefly because it was only accepted as part of the Shakespearean canon in the 1990s, has had much less of an impact on the king's reputation.

In recent decades, growing interest in all three monarchs has been reflected in and encouraged by major biographical studies authored by Nigel Saul, Seymour Phillips and Mark Ormrod. The anniversary of Richard's deposition in 1999 formed a spur for the first of these, and alongside such works we have seen much greater scholarly attention paid to the fourteenth century as a whole. This has involved the development of new fields of research including studies that have re-evaluated the roles and careers of the queens that reigned in this period. As a result of such works, Isabella, Philippa of Hainault and Anne of Bohemia are no longer bland ciphers or exaggerated caricatures, and the nature of queenship is an evolving area of study which has done a great deal to expand and enrich our understanding of political culture in the later Middle Ages (see Chapter 9).[12] Similarly, a great deal of recent research has explored the three reigns in a wider geopolitical context, bringing to our attention the interrelationships and importance of the wider Plantagenet dominions, most notably Wales, Ireland and Gascony.[13]

As a result of such studies, we now have highly detailed and more finely nuanced impressions of these three fourteenth-century monarchs and the political environments in which they lived. After years of coruscating criticism, Edward II's kingship has been evaluated much more fairly and considered in its appropriate context. While much about the man and his regime is still found wanting, he is now presented to us as not so much worse than many of his contemporaries. As for Edward III, situated between the regimes of his father and grandson, his long reign is now often held up as an exemplar of good kingship. His effective use of chivalry and patronage, his sensitive management of the demands of his family and, most importantly, the military success he enjoyed against the old enemies of France and Scotland are central to this reputation. However, the first and final decades of the reign tell a different story and are an indication of the difficulties of ruling in this tumultuous period.[14] Those difficulties would become very apparent when Richard II came to power. Recently, scholars have explored many facets of the king's character and the nature of his regime. Richard's attitude to royal power, in some respects, presages a later conception of sovereignty and one which did not sit well with many of his contemporaries. His interest in the symbolism and appearance of kingship has encouraged explorations of late medieval masculinity and theories of royal power that have built upon and enhanced classic studies such as Ernst Kantorowicz's notion of the king's 'two bodies'.[15]

The experiences of the fourteenth century refashioned notions of kingship in England. The possibilities of royal power grew in this period as the instruments of government became more sophisticated, access to revenue increased and warfare became an ever more professional business. Theories that underpinned royal authority also developed over the course of the century, buoyed up by facets of Roman law and royal apologists who claimed little less than quasi-divinity for their patrons. Such authority, however, depended on the ability of the monarch to fulfil some very traditional expectations and to ensure he could rely on the support of key power brokers among the community of the realm. If he could not do this, then royal power might prove to be hollow indeed.

Notes

1. *SR*, I, 157–67.
2. I. Mortimer, 'The Death of Edward II in Berkeley Castle', *EHR* 120 (2005), 1175–1214.
3. *Foedera*, III, i, 171.
4. W. M. Ormrod, *Edward III* (New Haven, CT, 2001), 363–84.
5. For some of the rebels' demands, see *The Anonimalle Chronicle*, ed. V. H. Galbraith (Manchester, 1927), 144–5; *Knighton's Chronicle*, ed. G. Martin (Oxford, 1995), 211; Jean Froissart, *Chronicles*, ed. and trans. G. Brereton (Harmondsworth, 1978), 211–13; 'The People of 1381' database, https://data.1381.online/ (accessed 9 June 2025).
6. See, for example, John Gower's account in Book One of *Vox Clamantis: The Major Latin Works of John Gower*, ed. and trans. E. W. Stockton (Seatle, 1962), 49–95.
7. *The Westminster Chronicle, 1381–1394*, ed. and trans. L. C. Hector and B. F. Harvey (Oxford, 1982), 25.
8. J. Burden, 'How Do You Bury a Deposed King? The Funeral of Richard II and the Establishment of Lancastrian Royal Authority in 1400', in *Henry*

IV: *The Establishment of the Regime, 1399–1406*, ed. G. Dodd and D. Biggs (Woodbridge, 2003), 35–54; J. Burden, 'Re-writing a Rite of Passage: The Peculiar Funeral of Edward II', in *Rites of Passage: Cultures of Transition in the Fourteenth Century*, ed. N. McDonald and W. M. Ormrod (Woodbridge, 2004), 13–30.
9. *Polychronicon Ranulph Higden*, ed. J. R Lumby, 9 vols (London, 1882), VIII, 297–9, translation in C. Given-Wilson, *Edward II: The Terrors of Kingship* (London, 2016), 3.
10. D. Gordon and R. Billinge, *The Wilton Diptych* (London, 2015).
11. See P. Strohm, *England's Empty Throne: Usurpation and the Language of Legitimation, 1399–1422* (New Haven, CT, 1998), esp. 4–17.
12. See, for example, L. Benz St. John, *Three Medieval Queens: Queenship and the Crown in Fourteenth-Century England* (New York, 2012).
13. See P. Crooks, D. Green and W. M. Ormrod, eds., *The Plantagenet Empire, 1259–1453* (Donington, 2016) for a selection of essays that consider these territories and their connections to England and to each other.
14. This is suggested by the title of J. Sumption's biography, *Edward III: A Heroic Failure* (London, 2016).
15. E. Kantorowicz, *The King's Two Bodies: A Study in Mediaeval Political Theology* (Princeton, 1997), 24–41; K. Lewis, *Kingship and Masculinity in Late Medieval Europe* (London, 2013); and C. Fletcher, *Richard II: Manhood, Youth and Politics, 1377–91* (Oxford, 2010).

Further Reading

Aberth, J., *The Black Death: A New History of the Great Mortality in Europe, 1347–1500* (Oxford, 2022).
Barber, R., *Edward III and the Triumph of England: The Battle of Crécy and the Company of the Garter* (London, 2013).
Given-Wilson, C., *Edward II: The Terrors of Kingship* (London, 2016).
Goodman, A. and Gillespie, J. L., eds., *Richard II: The Art of Kingship* (Oxford, 1999).
Green, D., *Edward the Black Prince: A Study of Power in Medieval Europe*, 2nd ed. (Abingdon, 2023).
Harriss, G. L., *Shaping the Nation: England 1360–1461* (Oxford, 2005).
Ormrod, W. M., *Edward III* (New Haven, CT, 2011).
Phillips, S., *Edward II* (New Haven, CT, 2010).
Saul, N., *Richard II* (New Haven, CT, 1997).
Sumption, J., *The Hundred Years War, I: Trial by Battle* (Pennsylvania, 1997)
The Hundred Years War, II: Trial by Fire (Pennsylvania, 1999)
The Hundred Years War, III: Divided Houses (Pennsylvania, 2009).

3

Events, Personalities and Reputations
The Fifteenth Century to 1485

To the established causes of conflict (the limits of royal authority, the crown's financial demands and factionalism) a more destabilising dimension was added after 1399: the legitimacy of the ruling branch of the Plantagenet dynasty itself. From 1455 the houses of Lancaster and York, two lines descended from Edward III, contested the throne in a series of civil wars. As Edward Hall put it in 1548, 'All other disorders, divisions and factions flourish to this present day but the old divided controversy between the families of Lancaster and York (were) suspended and appalled in the person of ... Henry VIII and by him clearly buried'.[1]

Henry IV: 1399–1413

Henry of Lancaster, who had returned to England in July 1399 to reclaim his inheritance, decided within a month to take the throne. When Richard II 'abdicated' he claimed it as a descendant of Henry III. The alternative and arguably better claim of the under-age Edmund Mortimer was ignored. He was crowned on 13 October. His accession was smooth but his title weak. He soon faced a series of crises which cost him his early popularity, came close to destroying him and threatened the integrity of the kingdom.

The first challenge came in January 1400 when displaced courtiers of Richard II rose in rebellion. They were easily crushed, but the rising sealed Richard II's fate. To enhance his standing, Henry invaded Scotland in September. The Scots refused to fight and his army returned empty-handed. At the same time an obscure squire called Owain Glyn Dŵr raised rebellion in north Wales. Although Henry marched against him, he too refused to fight. Over the next three years, despite annual royal expeditions, Glyn Dŵr secured control of the whole of Wales and assumed the title of prince of Wales. After 1404 Wales was slowly brought under control by the Lancastrian prince of Wales (i.e. the future Henry V), placed in command in 1403, but reconquest was not completed until 1409.

To make matters worse in July 1403 Henry Percy (Hotspur), heir to the earl of Northumberland, rebelled in alliance with the Welsh with the objective of deposing Henry and installing Edmund Mortimer. The king reacted with characteristic speed and defeated them on the bloody field of Shrewsbury. In 1405, Northumberland himself rose with the support of Archbishop Scrope of York. Northumberland escaped to Scotland, but Scrope was captured and executed. Not until 1407 was the earl defeated and killed on Bramham Moor. The French took advantage to launch attacks on Calais and Gascony, as well as to make war at sea, raid the south coast and in 1405, send an expeditionary force to Wales. Only in 1408 was a truce reached with France. In the meantime the border war with Scotland continued until 1406 when the king of Scots, James I, fortuitously fell into English hands. Moreover the king faced the wrath of his subjects in parliament, particularly angered by the huge costs the king incurred not only in defending his crown but also by his own extravagance. In 1401, 1404 and 1406 the hostile Commons demanded and secured a degree of control over expenditure.

The course of the reign was altered when in the spring of 1406 the king's health collapsed. At the end of the year he stepped back from day-to-day government and accepted the appointment of a continual council. Thomas Arundel, archbishop of Canterbury, presided. His government, aided by the easing of the crises, was able to restore a degree of stability and solvency. But during 1409 tensions between the prince of Wales and his younger brother Prince Thomas, their father's favourite, led to the removal of the archbishop, to be replaced by Prince Henry and his allies. Eighteen months later the prince's government itself fell over a rift in foreign policy: how best to exploit civil war in France between the Armagnacs and Burgundians. Prince Henry favoured taking the Burgundian side; the king and Thomas, by then duke of Clarence, concluded an alliance with the Armagnacs. Infuriated, Prince Henry raised a private army, to assist Burgundy, he claimed, but interpreted by his rivals to depose his father. A reconciliation was achieved, allowing Clarence to invade France and march to Bordeaux, causing havoc as he went. At the end of the year the king's health deteriorated further; he died on 20 March 1413. Prince Henry was at hand to take the crown that he had been impatient to inherit.

Henry V: 1413–1422

The new king set out to heal old wounds and impose his authority. He made his peace with Archbishop Arundel and his brother Thomas, he restored nobles who had rebelled against his father (the Percys had to wait until 1416) and, in an act of atonement, reburied Richard II in Westminster Abbey. He declared that he was determined to enforce the law impartially and manage royal finances prudently. Having established his authority, he announced his intention to recover his rights in France.

The king continued to play Armagnacs off against Burgundians. By the summer of 1414, he was demanding the restoration of Normandy as well as full sovereignty in Gascony for his support. By the beginning of 1415, when the French factions had agreed a truce, it was clear that Henry would invade anyway. By April a formidable army, weapons and provisions, and an armada to transport the troops, were assembled. On the eve of departure from Southampton (31 July) a plot was revealed within his entourage to put Edmund Mortimer, earl of March, on the throne. One of the ringleaders was the earl of Cambridge, married to Mortimer's sister Anne, and brother of the duke of York. The traitors were summarily tried and executed and the expedition set out after a short delay. Henceforth Mortimer, who died childless in 1425, was kept close to the king.

The army landed near Harfleur and laid siege to the town. It fell on 22 September, the English army ravaged by dysentery. Having repatriated the wounded and sick, and leaving a garrison, Henry marched with a much-reduced army to Calais. The French intercepted them after they had crossed the Somme with a much larger and fresher force. On

25 October, Henry won a remarkable victory against the odds and his army made it to Calais and then home to England. The only notable casualty was the childless duke of York. Agincourt did not achieve any territorial gains. On the other hand, it made Henry unchallengeable in England and opened the way for him to invade again.

Harfleur was held against a counterattack, the neutrality of the duke of Burgundy was secured and generous taxation was voted by an enthusiastic parliament. Henry landed on 1 August 1417 and proceeded with the systematic conquest of Normandy which reached a climax with the capture of Rouen in January 1419. In his war with the Armagnacs, Burgundy had taken control of the mentally incapacitated Charles VI in 1418. As Henry continued his conquest towards Paris, negotiations with both sides were renewed. Everything was changed by the assassination of the duke of Burgundy by the seventeen-year-old Dauphin Charles on 10 September 1419. In the aftermath, Philip, the new duke of Burgundy, came to terms with Henry; by the treaty of Troyes (21 May 1420) Charles VI adopted him as heir, agreed the marriage of his daughter, Katherine, to him and entered an offensive alliance to destroy the Dauphin and his supporters.

After campaigning with Burgundy, Henry and his new queen returned to England in February 1421. In his absence the realm had been governed by his brothers John, duke of Bedford, and Humphrey, duke of Gloucester, in turn. They successfully defended the Scottish borders and controlled Wales. His queen was crowned, parliament confirmed the treaty of Troyes and he set off on a royal progress. His progress was cut short by the defeat and death of Clarence (his deputy in France) at Baugé. He crossed back to Calais in June, leaving his queen, who was by then pregnant, in England. Having failed to bring the Dauphin to battle, he turned to a winter siege of Meaux. It took five months to reduce. Dysentery broke out in the English camp, which Henry contracted. He withdrew to recuperate in May 1422, but he could not shake off the disease and died at Vincennes on 31 August.

Henry VI's Minority: 1422–1437

Henry VI was nine months old when his father died. Two months later he succeeded to the French throne. His younger uncle the duke of

Gloucester became head of the minority council in England with the title of protector: his elder, the duke of Bedford, became regent of France. The Lancastrian establishment dedicated itself to the preservation of both inheritances until he came of age. Rule effectively passed to a triumvirate: Bedford, Gloucester and Henry Beaufort, bishop of Winchester soon to be cardinal. Conflict developed between Gloucester and Beaufort in England. They almost came to blows in 1425 and the rivalry erupted frequently thereafter. Bedford acted as peacemaker in 1425-7, when he returned to England and as the king's heir assumed control. In France, English successes continued: Thomas Montagu, earl of Salisbury, at Cravant east of Paris in 1423; Bedford at Verneuil on southern Norman borders in 1424, which opened the door to the conquest of Maine. Thereafter the English advance stalled. In 1428 a new offensive, led by a fresh army recruited in England under Salisbury, was launched to capture Orleans and secure a bridgehead on the Loire. The six-month siege failed; Salisbury was killed in action, the Dauphin, buoyed by the appearance of Joan of Arc, relieved it in May, defeated the retreating English army at Patay in June and was crowned Charles VII at Rheims. The English response, having crowned Henry VI as king of England, was to crown him as the true king of France. A new expedition, with the king nominally at its head, crossed to Calais early in 1430, but it was not until December that the coronation took place in Paris, after which the boy king was hurriedly escorted back to England, leaving Normandy and the Île-de-France more securely in English hands.

The protectorate and regency had ended when Henry was crowned. In England Gloucester continued as chief councillor until June 1433, when Bedford frustrated by the lack of support and Gloucester's scheming against Beaufort, returned once more to assume control of the government. Having secured financial backing for the war, he crossed back a year later. In 1435, on papal and imperial initiatives, a peace conference was convened at Arras. It foundered in September because neither side would surrender the throne. Immediately after the English delegation left, Burgundy switched sides. Two weeks later Bedford died. In the next six months Paris was lost, northern Normandy fell to a French uprising and Rouen seemed likely to fall. A relief army under Richard, duke of York, nephew and heir of the casualty at

Agincourt, landed in June 1436, soon enough to save Rouen. Gloucester independently rescued Calais threatened by Burgundy. By the beginning of 1437 the situation was stabilised.

The minority came to an end in stages. The king began to attend council at the end of 1435, when he was fourteen; in mid 1436 he began to exercise his prerogative in matters of grace. But he did not play a role in formulation of royal policy until November 1437. No declaration was made, but this can be taken as its end. The minority government had largely achieved its aim. Henry began to rule as well as reign.

Henry VI's Majority Rule: 1437–1461

The task facing the sixteen-year-old king was daunting. The crown was still solvent, but only just. Lawlessness had increased, but the council had controlled the worst extremes. Any young king would have struggled, but Henry, uninterested in either fighting or governing, did not try. A man like his father or grandfather would have taken to the field at the head of his troops in 1439, when the earl of Warwick, successor to York in France, died. Instead he focused on the founding of Eton College. It was left to others slowly to recover lost territory in Normandy. Henry was looking to end the war, for which he authorised the release of the duke of Orleans (a prisoner since Agincourt) in the face of Gloucester's opposition. Gloucester was discredited in 1441 by the conviction of his duchess for treasonable witchcraft. Cardinal Beaufort, who since 1439 had been high in the king's favour, withdrew in 1443 and most of the old guard who had dominated the council since 1422 had died or retired. A new faction under William de la Pole, earl of Suffolk, emerged.

War weariness grew. York had returned to Normandy but achieved little. In 1442 Charles VII switched his attention to Gascony; the following year a relief expedition failed disastrously. Both sides were now ready to negotiate. In May 1444, a truce was agree at Tours with Suffolk acting on the king's behalf. By its terms Henry VI was to marry the duke of Anjou's fifteen-year-old daughter, Margaret. The new queen travelled to England in 1445 and was crowned amidst great hopes for the future. There may have been a secret agreement, initiated by the king, to cede Maine, strenuously denied by Suffolk in parliament.

But in 1447 after the arrest and death in custody of Gloucester at Bury St Edmunds, the cession of Maine was announced. Having used the truce to strengthen his armies, Charles invaded Normandy and swept all before him. Rouen fell in the autumn, a relief army was defeated at Formigny the following spring and the last toehold, Cherbourg, fell in August 1450. Gascony fell the following year.

In England in the later 1440s lawlessness grew and royal finances collapsed. In February 1450 Suffolk, by then a duke, was impeached; he was pardoned by Herny VI but murdered on his way to exile. The duke's murder triggered a popular rising in the south-east counties, the most serious since 1381. Cade's Revolt was soon crushed. The duke of York, next in line to the throne since Gloucester's death to the still childless king, and, through his mother, sister to Edmund Mortimer, the heir to his claim, expected to take Gloucester's place. Instead Henry VI turned to Edmund Beaufort, duke of Somerset, who had been in command in Normandy when it fell. Somerset proved more effective than Suffolk in imposing royal authority on the realm. York, who blamed him for the loss of Normandy, endeavoured to force himself on the king, but was outfaced by his rival with the king in his company, at Dartford in February 1452. The new government's standing was strengthened by the recovery of Bordeaux the following October. Moreover the queen was finally pregnant. By the summer of 1453 Herny VI, with Somerset at his side, seemed to have begun to assert his authority.

Disaster then struck. Gascony was lost again, and in August, perhaps at the shock of hearing this news, Henry suffered a total mental collapse. For six months the government of the realm was paralysed. The queen gave birth to a son, christened Edward, on 13 October. Archbishop Kemp, as chancellor, presided over council meetings, but when he died in March 1454, a protectorate was created on the model of 1422. York as the senior nobleman was appointed protector. Somerset had already been imprisoned in the Tower. York did his best to tackle the growing number of aristocratic feuds, but after the king recovered at the end of the year, he surrendered his office; Somerset was released and reinstated.

While he was protector, York had formed an alliance with the powerful Neville Lords; Richard, earl of Salisbury, who was his brother-in-law, and his son Richard, earl of Warwick. They brought with them significant military resources. In May 1455 they intercepted the king's entourage at St Albans, killing Somerset and the earl of Northumberland, and took the king into 'protective custody'. A new parliament was summoned, during which, because the king's health had deteriorated again, York resumed the protectorate. The most significant outcome was the appointment of Warwick as captain of Calais. York stood down as protector in February 1456 but remained the king's chief minister for several more months. In October Queen Margaret, who perhaps already feared for her son's future, emerged as the focal point of a revived court faction. The Yorkists were not yet targeted. Indeed, in 1458, an effort was made to make peace between the victors and victims of St Albans which culminated in a solemn reconciliation at St Paul's Cathedral. It failed.

By the beginning of 1459 both sides were preparing for war. In a hectic nine months from September 1459 to July 1460 first one side then the other was victorious. The Yorkists captured Henry VI at the battle of Northampton and began to rule in his name. York himself, who had been in exile in Ireland, returned to England to claim the throne as the heir to Mortimer. In November, after lengthy debate in parliament, an unworkable compromise was reached that he should be made Henry VI's heir. He was subsequently killed in battle at Wakefield, but his eighteen-year-old son, Edward, on the other hand was victorious against the Lancastrians at Mortimer's Cross. Although Warwick was defeated by the triumphant northern army marching on London at the second battle of St Albans, Edward, joined by Warwick and the remnant of his forces en route, was welcomed by the Londoners who had closed their gates against the Lancastrian army. On 4 March 1461, he assumed the throne by virtue of Henry VI breaking the November award, his superior Mortimer title and election by a hastily gathered assembly of notables.

Edward IV: 1461–1483

Edward IV assumed the crown in the midst of civil war. He had first to defeat the Lancastrians. He pursued them to Yorkshire and was victorious on the field of Towton. Margaret of Anjou, her husband and son escaped to Scotland, leaving many of her principal supporters dead.

After a brief tour to secure the north, Edward returned in triumph to London and was crowned at Westminster Abbey on 28 June 1461.

Edward began his reign with great energy. While his principal enemies were found guilty of treason and had their estates confiscated by process of attainder, he was merciful to some of his erstwhile opponents. He endeavoured to deal with the endemic lawlessness and began to tackle the bankruptcy of the crown. He ruled, at first of necessity, as had Henry IV, through his ducal affinity and the allies who had helped him to the throne, most significantly the earl of Warwick and his relations. But, in the first three years, his most pressing problem was snuffing out Lancastrian resistance in the far north and Wales, as well as facing popular disturbances in western England. Northumberland fell into Lancastrian hands three times between 1461 and 1463. With Scottish and French assistance the Lancastrians held it for almost a year before John Neville, lord Montagu, finally defeated them at Hedgeley Moor and Hexham in 1464. Queen Margaret and her son had slipped away to France; Henry VI was left in hiding with loyal supporters. He was found in 1465 and taken to the Tower for safe keeping. Resistance lasted longer in Wales: Harlech did not fall until 1468.

By 1464, Edward was in command. A truce had been concluded with the Scots and negotiations were in hand for a marriage alliance with France. However, on 1 May the king secretly married Elizabeth Woodville, the daughter and widow of Lancastrians and mother already of two children. The truth did not emerge until the autumn. In the meantime Warwick had been negotiating a French alliance in good faith. The earl had been the young king's mainstay, here, there and everywhere in his service. He accepted the marriage, but their special relationship was damaged. After his marriage, the king became less dependent on the Nevilles and began to rely on a new group of courtiers and servants drawn both from his ducal affinity and the new queen's family, including prominently the queen's father, Earl Rivers. He also began to relax. In 1467, Rivers's son starred in a great tournament at Westminster taking on a Burgundian champion. Behind the façade Edward was busy negotiating an alliance with the Burgundians, while Warwick was in France negotiating with Louis XI. The tournament was cut short when Philip, duke of Burgundy, died. Edward went ahead the following year with a marriage between the new duke Charles and his sister Margaret against Warwick's preference. The rift became open.

The final breach followed when the king refused permission for his younger brother George, duke of Clarence, to marry Warwick's elder daughter Isabel (the earl had no son). In the summer of 1469, Clarence and Isabel were married in Calais (Warwick was still captain), while the earl's agents raised the north in rebellion. The rebels destroyed the king's forces at Edgecote and in the aftermath Rivers and other prominent supporters were hunted down and murdered. The king was briefly the earl's prisoner before an uneasy truce was made. In the spring of 1470 Warwick rebelled again, fomenting a rising in Lincolnshire. This time the king did not fall into his trap. Warwick and Clarence fled to France. There Louis XI engineered a rapprochement between the earl and Margaret of Anjou to restore Henry VI. The seventeen-year-old Edward prince of Wales married Warwick's younger daughter Anne and Warwick undertook to eject Edward IV, release Henry VI and secure the realm in preparation for their return. Warwick and Clarence crossed to Devon in September and on a wave of aristocratic and popular support marched unopposed to London. Edward IV, who had been drawn north by a rising in Yorkshire, was left stranded and fled with but a small company to Holland.

Henry VI was duly restored but now quite incapable of ruling. Warwick took command of the kingdom and prepared for the return of the Queen and the prince. They waited too long and contrary winds further delayed their crossing, while favourable winds blew Edward IV with Burgundian support across the North Sea. In a remarkable two-month campaign Edward recovered the throne. He landed in Holderness on 14 March; marched south gathering support; and persuaded Clarence to abandon Warwick, who declined to engage near Coventry. Edward defeated and killed him at Barnet on 14 April. On the very same day the Lancastrians landed at Weymouth. Edward intercepted them at Tewkesbury on 4 May as they marched to meet reinforcements from Wales. There he won a second and more decisive battle. The Lancastrian cause was destroyed. The young Prince Edward was killed, perhaps after being taken a prisoner; the last Beaufort duke of Somerset was seized from sanctuary in Tewkesbury Abbey and summarily executed; and Henry VI was murdered on the king's orders in the Tower.

Thus did the wheel of fortune turn, assisted by Edward's decisiveness and his enemies' hesitancy. He was now the unchallenged master of England. Moreover his first son, also christened Edward, had been born on 2 November 1470. After mopping up remaining resistance, Edward was in a stronger position than before 1470. He now began to prepare for an invasion of France, constructing an alliance against Louis XI, in which the support of Burgundy was central, negotiating a truce with Scotland, raising taxes to pay for an army and gathering supplies. There were distractions. He had to deal with a threat posed by the earl of Oxford in 1473, who had escaped from Barnet. In the same year he had to defuse a dispute between his brothers, Clarence and Richard, duke of Gloucester, over the division of the spoils. Gloucester, who had been steadfastly loyal to Edward during the years of crisis, married Warwick's widowed daughter Anne in 1472. The two dukes proceeded to quarrel until a partition of the inheritance was agreed in 1474. Edward was finally ready to cross to Calais and attack France in June 1475.

The duke of Burgundy failed to join his brother-in-law on campaign. Edward advanced into France but accepted the offer to negotiate with Louis XI. By the treaty of Picquigny Edward accepted a marriage alliance between his daughter Elizabeth and the Dauphin, a seven-year truce and an annual pension. On his return to England he presented these terms as a great triumph. In 1477, however, the king and Clarence fell out. Clarence who believed his duchess Isabel had been poisoned, took the law into his own hands to punish those he believed were responsible. He thereby challenged the king's authority, and in the ensuing conflict with his brother appeared to cast doubt on his right to the throne. The duke was arrested and imprisoned in the Tower. Ultimately he was tried for treason in a packed parliament in January 1478. The outcome was inevitable. Clarence was condemned and Edward ordered his private execution, rumour soon spreading that he was drowned in a butt of malmsey. After this it was said that Edward ruled as he pleased.

For the last five years of his reign, Edward continued to rule through a narrow group of his own favourites and courtiers, especially the queen's son, Thomas Grey, marquess of Dorset. He could not afford to offend his surviving brother, Gloucester, who had not opposed Clarence's downfall and benefited from it. Gloucester had established his power in the north. It may have been to satisfy Gloucester's ambitions that in 1480 the king sanctioned a war against Scotland. Before his death in 1483, Edward granted him an unprecedented hereditary palatinate in Cumberland and land he could conquer in south-west Scotland.

In the last years of his reign, Edward's foreign policy unravelled as he endeavoured to play Burgundy and France off against each other in securing a lucrative alliance. But when they came to terms in December 1482 he lost his French pension and marriage. Nevertheless when Edward died after a short illness on 9 April 1483 he appeared to have established his dynasty. He left an heir and a spare (Richard of Shrewsbury, born in 1473, created duke of York). He was buried on 29 April in St George's Chapel, Windsor. His twelve-year-old son faced only a short minority and there was no apparent reason to suppose that his brother, Gloucester and other faithful servants would not ensure that in due course the young Prince Edward would take up his inheritance.

Edward V: April–June 1483

Edward, created prince of Wales in June 1471, spent his childhood in Ludlow, under the care of Anthony Woodville, Earl Rivers, where he was residing when his father died. Travelling to London his entourage was joined by his uncle Gloucester and the duke of Buckingham. On 30 May they arrested Rivers and other senior members of his household and took him into their care. On hearing this, the king's mother and her younger son fled to sanctuary in Westminster Abbey. The dukes postponed the coronation which had been fixed for 4 May. On 10 May a council under Gloucester's presidency made him protector, overturning an earlier decision that, following precedent, a protectorate was not needed for a crowned king. The coronation was then fixed for 24 June. On Friday 13 June, at a council meeting in the Tower, Gloucester accused Lord Hastings, who had supported him since April, of plotting against him and had him immediately executed. On the following Monday, after the intervention of the archbishop of Canterbury, Elizabeth Woodville surrendered her younger son to the protector. He joined his elder brother, now accommodated in the Tower, as was traditional for a monarch before his coronation. But the coronation was postponed yet again, as was the parliament summoned to meet afterwards. On 22 June, Ralph

Shaw preached a sermon at Paul's Cross alleging Edward IV's sons' illegitimacy. Two days later after Buckingham had informed the mayor and aldermen of London that Gloucester was the legitimate heir of Edward IV, delegations petitioned him to take the throne. He assented. On 26 June, Edward V was deposed and Richard III became king. The two boys remained in the Tower, but after the elder's attendants were dismissed, they were soon never to be seen again. They may have died that summer: Rivers and his colleagues were executed without trial.

Richard III: 1483–1485

Richard III was crowned king on 6 July and soon afterwards set out on a progress through the west midlands as far as Yorkshire. The culmination was the installation in September of his own son Edward as prince of Wales in York Minster. While still in the north, news came that his erstwhile ally, Buckingham, had rebelled in association with many in the southern counties who remained loyal to Edward V. The king quickly suppressed the revolt; Buckingham was taken and summarily executed in Salisbury. Many other rebels were attainted and their estates and offices distributed to the king's loyal supporters, many from the north. In January 1484 Richard's only parliament formally endorsed his right to the throne on the grounds that Edward's marriage to Elizabeth Woodville was invalid because of a pre-contract of marriage. Not long after parliament had been dissolved, the king learned that his only son had died. He travelled north again where he spent two months, setting in train a truce with the Scots, with whom England was still at war, and reorganising his government of the north through a council.

But he still faced resistance. Henry Tudor, earl of Richmond, who had been in exile most of Edward IV's reign, had come forward as the Lancastrian claimant to the throne through his mother, Margaret Beaufort, descended from John of Gaunt's legitimised line. He had sailed to England in support of the rebellion in the previous autumn, arriving too late. The king sought his extradition from Brittany, and then, after he fled the duchy, from France. At the end of the year Elizabeth Woodville and Margaret Beaufort negotiated a marriage between her daughter Elizabeth and Henry. To add to Richard III's woes, his queen died in the spring of 1485. He was reported to have considered marrying his niece himself but was prevented by his own supporters. The summer was spent preparing the defence of his crown from an expected Tudor invasion. The armies met on 22 August on the field of Bosworth where Richard III was killed. He was subsequently buried in the Franciscan Friary in Leicester. His remains were exhumed in 2012 and now lie in Leicester Cathedral.

Personalities

Henry IV

Henry IV was thirty-three when he came to the throne, a magnate in his own right. He was much admired by his contemporaries as the model of later medieval nobility: a renowned jouster, a crusader, a pilgrim to Jerusalem, patron of poets and an accomplished musician. He was, in the words of Thomas Gower, 'full of knighthood and all grace'.[2] He was also an experienced politician, who had played a prominent role in the opposition to Richard II in the late 1380s. He had not expected to become king. Crafty, ruthless and decisive when it mattered, he was sustained by a Churchillian determination to 'keep buggering on'. He inspired the loyalty of his followers. He remained true to his earlier principles, dealt promptly with treason, but accepted loyal criticism. Often short-tempered, he nevertheless understood that kingship was the art of the possible. He became more irascible when incapacitated but handled his fractious eldest son with forbearance. The manner in which he became king, and the perjury he probably committed, may have troubled his conscience throughout the rest of his life. He was devoutly orthodox and a dedicated husband and father, who appears to have been faithful to his wives. His second marriage to Joan of Navarre in 1402 may have been a love match: there were no children. His effigy in Canterbury Cathedral, possibly based on a death mask, shows a bearded middle-aged man in ruder health than is credible, considering the near-contemporary description of his body being 'adorned only with bones and nerves'.[3]

Henry V

As king, Henry was courteous, a stickler for etiquette, haughty and proud. A man of few words it was said that he would allow no one to look him in the eye. Like his father he was a patron of poets and music. He was an inspiring leader of men, a gifted general, a consummate politician and a master of 'spin'. He adopted the persona of the model medieval monarch: fount of justice, protector of the church and defender of the realm. Behind the mask there lay a man who, as his reign progressed, became increasingly autocratic. There is no truth in the later legend, well established by the end of the fifteenth century, that he had been a riotous wastrel keeping low company. He was pious and chaste. Until his marriage in 1420 he moved in an all-male circle. His hair cut short, clean-shaven, at least until his marriage, he was said to be more like a priest than a soldier in demeanour. He shared the misogyny of the priesthood. His intimate relationship with Richard Courtenay, bishop of Norwich, has led to suggestions that he was gay. Reported to be of above-average height, slim and strong, his face and nose were long but disfigured by the scar of a wound he received at the battle of Shrewsbury. A sixteenth-century copy of an earlier likeness shows him, unusually, in profile and without a scar.

Henry VI

Henry VI, notwithstanding his comprehensive training for kingship, grew to be almost the complete opposite of both his father and his grandfather. He shunned chivalry and all but the most cursory engagement in government. Though highly conscious of his royal status he played little role in formulating policy beyond desiring peace with France and harmony among his subjects. From an early age he devoted himself to religion, more suited to a monastic than a secular life. His lasting legacy was the foundation of Eton and King's Colleges for the training of priests. When he was still sixteen, it was said that he was more religious than the religious orders. He avoided the company of women, disapproving of obscenity and lewd games, yet was modest and approachable. He never fully recovered after his mental collapse in 1453 and was reduced to a pitiful state by 1470. Having planned to be buried in Westminster Abbey, in the event he was first interred at Chertsey Abbey, but subsequently his body was removed to St George's Chapel, Windsor, by Richard III.

Edward IV

When Edward came to the throne at the age of eighteen he had little political experience but was already a successful warrior. He was a man of considerable charm who perhaps relied too much on that charm to defuse political tensions. He was by inclination indolent but could react quickly and decisively when facing crises. He was a gifted general but preferred not to fight. While proclaiming his commitment to the law, he did not hesitate to bend it for the benefit of himself and his family or override it to dispose of rivals. He nevertheless kept a careful eye on his finances and oversaw the government of the realm, leaving the detail to his servants. Often merciful and conciliatory, he could be brutal and vengeful. After the failure of his first reign he ruled more effectively thereafter. In these years he collected an impressive library and promoted the chapel royal as a centre of musical excellence. He maintained a magnificent court which impressed his contemporaries. He was gluttonous and licentious. How many mistresses he had is not known. He was conventionally religious, with a special dedication to St George. St George's Chapel, Windsor, was largely his creation and in it he was buried. He was over six foot tall and as a youth considered handsome. In the surviving image of him, probably based on a likeness made in the early 1470s, he appears to be already going to seed. By the end of his life, when he was only forty-two, he was described as 'very fat and gross'.[4]

Edward V
The twelve-year-old Edward V was described in 1483 as well-educated, dignified in person and good looking, who daily sought remission of his sins because he believed his death was imminent.[5]

Richard III
As duke, Richard III had won esteem for his deeds in arms, his rule in the north in which he had united a deeply divided elite, administered justice (although a commitment to justice did not extend to his own interests) and his piety. He appears to have disapproved of his brother's licentiousness, though it is difficult to distinguish moral outrage from political calculation in 1483. He did not harbour a long-term ambition to become king: his actions in 1483 were opportunistic. It is hard to tell whether he was a brilliant schemer or stumbled from one ill-considered action to another. Undoubtedly he was ruthless and did not hesitate to kill when politically advantageous. He was not physically deformed: he suffered

from scoliosis which was possibly only apparent after he was killed. The condition may have given rise to the false idea that he was hunchbacked. After his death, portraits of him, copied from an original, added this deformity. He was shorter than his brother and said to look like his father.

Reputations

The notion of the fifteenth century being characterised by dynastic conflict began in the reign of Henry VII. Originating as propaganda, justifying his usurpation, it became a powerful historical narrative explaining the whole course of events from 1399 to 1485 in terms of the dire consequences of deposing a divinely ordained monarch. Dramatised with considerable artistic licence by Shakespeare in his cycle of eight history plays, it provided the interpretative framework until the twentieth century.

Henry IV

In this schema Henry IV's reign was perceived only in terms of a deserved sea of troubles. To this was added condemnation for both the execution of Archbishop Scrope and persecution of Lollards, the forerunners of protestants. Very little was written in his favour until in 1878 William Stubbs shifted the focus of debate to his claim that Henry IV was a great king who first steered the kingdom towards a parliamentary monarchy. This assessment held sway until K. B. McFarlane in the mid twentieth century and subsequent historians dismissed it, emphasising the conflict between king and Commons. More recently the pendulum has swung back to a more positive perception of Henry as a man as well as a king. There is a shared, if sometimes grudging, admiration for his achievement against all the odds in leaving a peaceful kingdom to his heir.

Henry V

Immediately after his death the council in England recorded an epitaph which lauded him 'as the most invincible king and the flower of chivalry';[6] it has been so ever since. He was a hero to the Yorkist kings, a hero to Tudor historians and a hero to Shakespeare. He alone escaped the curse incurred by the deposition of Richard II. He has become the quintessential *English* hero. McFarlane in 1954 proclaimed that he was 'the greatest man that ever ruled England'.[7] The leading historians of the next generation agreed that he fulfilled all that contemporaries expected of a king. But since the mid twentieth century there have been dissenting voices who have asserted that Henry's wars were reckless acts of wanton aggression (and not just French historians), that Henry bought immediate glory for himself at the price of eventual bankruptcy for the realm and at home his vindictiveness towards some of his prominent subjects and his rapaciousness to pay for his wars may have led, had he lived longer, to conflict with his subjects. This dissenting perception has cut little ice. His reputation as a great English king remains undiminished.

Henry VI

After his death Henry's simplicity, naivety in worldly affairs and his deep piety came to be seen as virtues, developing into a cult and, in the reign of Henry VII, a campaign for canonisation, abandoned after the Reformation. The perception of him as an incompetent innocent in politics, most memorably expressed in McFarlane's quip that his 'second childhood succeeded the first without the usual interval',[8] remained the consensus among historians until in 1981 both Wolffe and Griffiths published substantial biographies. In assessing the years of his majority until his mental health collapsed, they argued, from the evidence of government records, that he took an active if largely inept part: Griffiths, that he was well-intentioned, and occasionally capable of seeing his wishes realised; and Wolffe that he was vacillating, vindictive and perversely wilful with disastrous consequence. But the notion of an actively engaged king, well-intentioned or not, was in its turn dismissed by Watts in 1996, who argued that while he might have privately expressed certain aspirations, he lacked the assertiveness or capacity to carry them through. As king, he was but a cipher:[9] not a million miles from the traditional view. His reputation remains that he was, even when in full command of his faculties, a man singularly unfitted to be king.

Edward IV

Shakespeare thought so little of the importance of Edward IV that he reduced him to a subsidiary character in his plays about Henry VI and

Richard III. His portrait is not flattering. Two conflicting views on the king and his reign can be found in the memoirs of contemporaries written not long after it ended: the Second Crowland Continuation favourable, and Commynes's Memoirs critical.[10] From the mid sixteenth century Commynes's view dominated. By the eighteenth century he was usually portrayed as immoral, cruel and deceitful; by the mid nineteenth century he was a despot more vicious than any king since John, described in 1909 as 'one of the worst men who ever sat on the throne of England'.[11] It was not until the mid twentieth century that a major revision of Edward's reputation began, reaching a climax in 1997 when Carpenter declared that Edward was one of the greatest of English kings, who came close to perfecting the medieval system of personal monarchy.[12] Few share her enthusiasm, stressing various limitations such as his fitful application, his inability to look beyond the short term, his partisan and factional rule and ultimately the failure to establish his dynasty.

Edward V
Because he was still a child when he disappeared, Edward V will for ever be remembered as an innocent victim.

Richard III
Condemned as a bloody tyrant by his enemies even before he was overthrown, Shakespeare completed his demonisation. In his hands he became evil personified. This reputation lasted with only the occasional challenge until the twentieth century. Few, if any, historians now hold this view. Indeed, the perception has grown of a wronged man and almost faultless king, around whose new burial site at Leicester a cult has emerged. To his modern defenders his title, enrolled in parliament, was rightful; his illegitimate nephews were unharmed by him, others being responsible for their deaths, or even, some believe, living beyond 1485; and Richard's violent road to the throne was justified by the threats he faced from multiple enemies. On the other hand, many historians maintain that he was a usurper, who invented the story that his nephews were bastards, unhesitatingly killed all those standing in his way and probably had the Princes in the Tower murdered. Some are

more sympathetic to his predicament in 1483 than others, but all of this persuasion agree that he had no right to the throne. Thus, Richard III's reputation remains contested.

Notes

1. Edward Hall, *The Union of the Two Illustre and Noble Families of Lancastre and Yorke* (Merston, 1970), fo. 1.
2. Thomas Gower, *Confessio Amantis*, ed. R. Peck (Toronto, 1980), 494–5.
3. *Johannis Capgrave Liber de Illustribus Henricis*, ed. F. Hingeston, RS (London, 1858), III, 110–11.
4. Philippe de Commynes, *Memoirs: The Reign of Louis XI*, trans. M. Jones (Harmsworth, 1972), 414.
5. Dominic Mancini, *The Usurpation of Richard III*, ed. C. A. J. Armstrong (Oxford, 1969), 92–3.
6. *Proceedings and Ordinances of the Privy Council of England*, ed. N. H. Nicolas, 7 vols. (1834–7), III, 3.
7. K. B. McFarlane, 'Henry V: A Personal Portrait', in McFarlane, *Lancastrian Kings and Lollard Knights* (Oxford, 1972), 133.
8. K. B. McFarlane, *The Nobility of Later Medieval England* (Oxford, 1973), 284.
9. J. L. Watts, *Henry VI and the Politics of Kingship* (Cambridge, 1996), 103–11.
10. *Crowland Chronicle Continuations*, ed. N. Pronay and J. C. Cox (Gloucester, 1986), 125–51; Commynes, *Memoirs*, 184, 188, 361, 413–14.
11. W. Edwards, *Notes on British History* (London, 5th ed., 1958), 232.
12. M. C. Carpenter, *The Wars of the Roses* (Cambridge, 1997), 180–205.

Further Reading

Allmand, C., *Henry V* (London, 1992).
Given-Wilson, C., *Henry IV* (New Haven, CT, 2016).
Griffiths, R. A., *The Reign of Henry VI* (London, 1981).
Harris, G. R., *Shaping the Nation, England 1360-1461* (Oxford, 2005).
Hicks, M. A., *Edward V: the Prince in the Tower* (Stroud, 2003).
  Richard III (New Haven, CT, 2019).
Pollard, A. J., *Late Medieval England, 1399–1509* (Harlow, 2000).
Potter, J., *Good King Richard?* (London, 1983).
Ross, C. D., *Edward IV* (London, 1974).
  Richard III (London, 1981).
Wolffe, B. P., *Henry VI* (London, 1981).

Part II

Kingship in Practice

GWILYM DODD

4

Governance and Politics

Central Government and Bureaucracy

To understand the particularities of English governance and politics in the late Middle Ages, we must firstly consider how the structure of government shaped the power of the kings who ruled in this period. By the start of the thirteenth century, England had a well-established and clearly defined central administration. The main departments of state, excluding the central courts of law (see Chapter 6), were the exchequer, chancery and privy seal office. It is often said that England possessed a highly centralised and sophisticated system of government, meaning that the reach of royal authority from Westminster into the localities was both extensive and intrusive. These administrative offices were the most important components of this system. Together, they formed the bureaucratic heart of late medieval English government, and their personnel comprised what could justifiably be described as a medieval 'civil service' (the term is a nineteenth-century invention).

The exchequer was the principal financial office. It was divided into the lower exchequer of receipt, where money was received (such as the proceeds of taxation) and paid out (such as annuities), and the upper exchequer, where accounts were audited and debts pursued. The name given to the exchequer derived from the chequered cloth that covered the table on which much of its business was conducted. The chancery was the main writing office of central government. It issued letters on behalf of the king, as well as his ministers and councillors, communicating orders, information and grants to the king's officers, servants and subjects. The authorisation of these letters was usually by a written 'warrant' or writ that was akin to an internal memo, or order, circulating between the king, his councillors and the officers of state. The privy seal office performed a vital function in this regard, acting as intermediary between the king and his officers by converting the instructions of the king into formal warrants. At the start of our period it acted as the king's personal writing office, but by the end of the thirteenth century it had, along with the exchequer and chancery, become more or less fixed at Westminster, and its previous function as an instrument of the king's personal communication was taken over by the signet seal office. Each of these offices had a seal to symbolise the authority that lay behind the documents issued in their name. Chancery's seal was known as the 'Great Seal', because the most important of the crown's communications were normally issued under the authority of chancery as letters patent (i.e. open or public) or letters close (i.e. to specific recipients).

The combined workload of all these administrative departments was immense. It has been estimated that the three writing offices of chancery, privy seal and signet were issuing in the region of between 30,000 and 40,000 letters a year.[1] Each of them, as well as the exchequer, kept copious records of their business, and in the case of chancery and the exchequer, consolidated registers of transactions were written up onto rolls of parchment to form an extensive and authoritative archive. The vast number of records produced by the late medieval English bureaucracy is the single most tangible measure of the centralised nature of the king's power. The *increase* in the volume of these records, seen especially from the late thirteenth century, is indicative of the expansion of these centralising tendencies.

The treasurer was head of the exchequer; the chancellor was in charge of chancery; and the keeper of the privy seal ran that office. Since the king relied so heavily on these individuals to ensure the smooth functioning of his government, it is no surprise to find that he was usually directly involved in appointments. The chancellor, in particular, was the lynchpin of royal administration, and the key representative of the king, not only when the king was away from Westminster (as he often was) but also when the king needed a spokesman to present the crown's point of view, such as in parliament. In the fourteenth century, treasurers and chancellors were usually high-ranking clerics, and the chancellor was often a bishop and sometimes even the archbishop of Canterbury – a sign of the importance attached to that office. The choice of clergymen for these positions reflected their natural inclination to take on administrative positions, but it was also because full-time bureaucratic posts based in Westminster did not generally appeal to members of the lay elite. Clerical staff were also easier for the king to remunerate in the form of ecclesiastical preferments.

The unsung (and mostly hidden) heroes of the system were, however, the lower-ranking men who ran these administrative offices: it was they who literally made royal government work. They are often referred to, in shorthand, as king's clerks. There were about 100 clerks each in the exchequer and chancery, arranged hierarchically according to their responsibilities and experience. The privy seal office was far smaller, having a staff of around a dozen or so, at all levels. Until the start of the fifteenth century, king's clerks were almost always individuals who had taken holy orders, so they were clerics, as well as clerks; this meant, among other things, that they were not permitted to marry. Their careers were mapped out for them at an early stage, when they entered service as school-leaver apprentices, learning the writing and language skills necessary for their profession – most records were written in Latin or French. This long-term training and a communitarian way of life generated a strong *esprit de corps* and often resulted in individual careers spanning many decades.

In the early fifteenth century the collegiality began to erode as a result of the laicisation of personnel. Permitted to marry, and without access to ecclesiastical remuneration in the form of benefices, lay clerks tended to 'live out' with their families and to seek supplementary sources of income from other types of engagement: they were consequently more inclined to see their employment in the royal bureaucracy as a job rather than a vocation. From 1408, almost all treasurers were laymen. In chancery there were more laymen than clerics by the 1430s. It has been suggested that one of the longer-term consequences of this shift in the profile of administrative personnel was the 'deskilling' of the royal bureaucracy.[2] This left it less equipped than it might otherwise have been – had it remained a closeknit cadre of clerics – to deal with the crisis of governance in the mid fifteenth century. A related development in the fifteenth century was the increasing use in official written communication of the English vernacular in the place of French: Latin, for the most part, held its ground and continued to be the principal language of governmental record.

The royal secretariat deserves the nomenclature 'civil service' because of the extremely high level of professionalism with which its members discharged their duties. It may not have been the most efficient administrative system, and it was certainly dogged by a culture of innovative inertia (witness, for example, the enduring practice of the exchequer and chancery writing up their records on rolls of parchment, rather than in volumes, making storage and information location significantly more challenging), but it nevertheless performed effectively. One especially important feature of its practice was the use of the warranty note that – by recording the authority on which an instruction had been issued – created a valuable 'parchment trail' that, in turn, ensured procedural regularity and accountability.

In other ways too, the king's officers behaved like a civil service. They were, of course, first and foremost, royal servants, and their most pressing duty was to facilitate government in accordance with the wishes of the king. But they were not mere automata. Occasionally, the relationship between the king and his senior ministers could rupture if, for example, the king felt they were not performing their roles with due diligence to his wishes and/or his ministers felt the king was making unreasonable demands. This famously happened in 1340–1 when Edward III had a major spat with his senior administrators. He stormed back from the continent in the middle of the night and unceremoniously sacked them all. One of the most interesting aspects of this episode was the way that the king's main protagonist – John Stratford, archbishop of Canterbury – stood his ground in the face of Edward's onslaught. Edward III learned the hard way that while senior clerics made excellent administrators, their attachment to the church, and the protection this afforded them, could also make them difficult to deal with if they became recalcitrant. Lay chancellors could also stand their ground. In 1382, Sir Richard Scrope was dismissed after some of Richard II's friends complained that he (Scrope) had refused to authorise the king's grants to them: Scrope thought the money was better spent servicing royal debts. As one chronicler scornfully noted, the king 'paid more heed to the false schemes of those tale-bearers than to the loyalty of his faithful chancellor'.[3]

We should not, however, take the civil service analogy too far. If a distinctive feature of a civil service is that its members are apolitical servants of the administration in which they serve, the very opposite set of assumptions seems to have been what prompted the king's aristocratic opponents in 1388 to purge the main departments of state of those who were considered hostile to their political agenda. Similarly, in the aftermath of the usurpation of 1399, Henry IV replaced ex-Ricardian clerks, many of whom were of relatively low status, with more loyal Lancastrian individuals.[4] Personal connections and loyalties still very much underpinned service in the bureaucracy.

How far can the term 'state' be applied to the system of medieval government thus far described? It is another word historians frequently use to describe the mode of government in late medieval England, and is useful shorthand to describe the elaborate and uniform legal, fiscal and bureaucratic structures that were in place to help the king rule without having to do everything in person. It is worth remembering that the king's lifestyle was still remarkably peripatetic; he was almost constantly on the move, travelling between royal palaces and hunting lodges (most of which were located in the south-east of England) and further afield, to wage war, visit sites of pilgrimage and make his presence felt in lawless (and usually more distant) parts of the kingdom. It has been estimated that Edward I travelled 20,000 miles across twelve different years between 1274 and 1305, an average of 1,600 miles each year, or 4.7 miles per day.[5] Map 4.1 shows the extent of his movement across medieval Britain. It was in these circumstances that the main offices of state came to reside more or less permanently at Westminster. There was constant communication between the king and the centre, with the aid of a highly proficient corps of royal messengers; but inevitably a large chunk of the routine business of ruling the realm had to be delegated to the king's ministers. Often, the three main heads of department – the chancellor, treasurer and keeper of the privy seal – would come together, with other people, to form an 'administrative council', whose job it was to free up the king's time of all but those matters that absolutely required his attention.

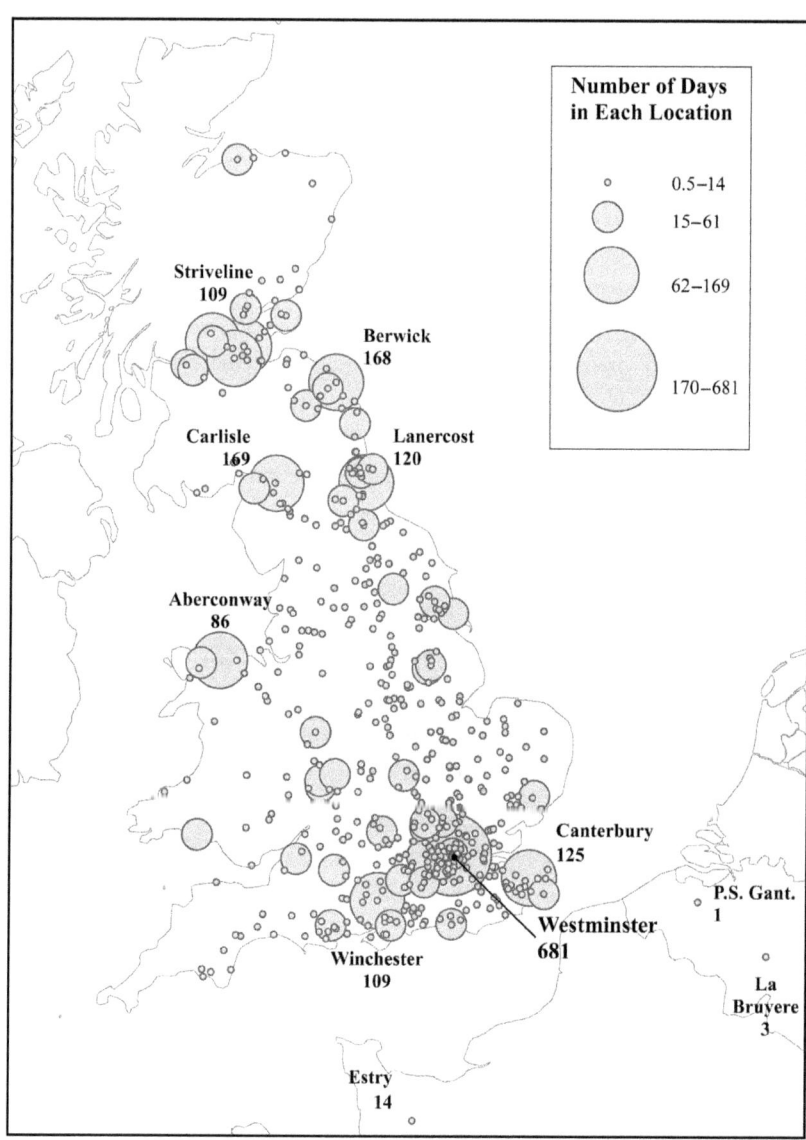

Map 4.1 Locations visited by Edward I, 1291–1307, weighted by cumulative days spent in each location (reproduced with permission from D. Boucoyannis, *Kings as Judges: Power, Justice, and the Origins of Parliaments* (Cambridge, 2021), frontispiece

This, then, was 'the state' in operation at the centre, but it can also be seen in the way that delegated royal authority had an impact in the localities, whether through the implementation of the law, the imposition of taxes, the regulation and adjudication of the land-market or by royal commissions of enquiry (many of these aspects are covered in other chapters). As we shall see in the next section, this was still very much an age of personal kingship, but the quality of governance depended on more than simply the input of the king. Some ministers could make a huge difference: William Eddington, for example, was treasurer in the 1350s and has been credited with the complete transformation of royal finances under Edward III. Talented ministers could not rescue the kingdom from the disastrous consequences of an incompetent monarch, but they could be major assets to kings who knew how to get the best out of them.

Politics and Rule

In a political system based on monarchy it is misleading to equate governance (the active and legitimate exercise of social control) with politics (the public debate surrounding that practice),[6] for the basis of power and authority in late medieval England lay overwhelmingly in the personal rule of the king, and 'public debate' over how he did so was very rarely conducted in the open, though, as we shall see, it certainly could – and did – occur. For most of the time, however, there was very little 'politics' but an awful lot of 'governance'. The basis of a king's right to exercise governance over his subjects lay in the theoretically unimpeachable notion that he had been appointed by God to protect and advance the common interest of the kingdom. To turn this on its head, it was universally agreed that serving and achieving the common interest of the kingdom was the most important goal of governance, and that the best way of achieving this was to place that governance into the hands of a single individual: the king. This, in essence, is what monarchical rule entailed.

In his coronation oath the king swore to protect the church, keep the peace and uphold the law – these were the central planks of the common interest that the king was expected to promote. It was axiomatic of late medieval kingship, and was a basic norm of royal power, that the king should be allowed the freedom to decide himself how best to ensure that these priorities were served. In this, a king was expected to heed advice and counsel, but it was vital to the integrity of monarchical power that royal policy was seen to emanate exclusively from the king's will, for only he could claim to project the public authority that was necessary for all legitimate acts of government. There was thus a strong tradition, in both political thinking and action, that placed emphasis on the importance of safeguarding the personal rule and independence of the king.

From this stemmed two of the most important concepts that defined the unique authority that the king possessed, and that allowed him to sidestep the systems and processes that otherwise circumscribed the actions of everyone else in his kingdom. The first was the royal prerogative. This embodied a set of exclusive rights that specifically pertained to, and expressed, the king's superior sovereignty, and included mobilising an army, assembling a parliament, issuing laws for the better governance of the realm, raising taxation for national defence and exercising a free choice over the appointment of the principal ministers of state, as well as a whole set of fiscal entitlements that derived from the king's position as supreme feudal overlord. Examples of the latter were his rights to wardship (i.e. the custody of the person and estates of the orphaned heirs of tenants-in-chief), scutage (i.e. payments in lieu of military service) and purveyance (i.e. requisitioning goods in local markets to supply the peripatetic royal household). The second concept was royal grace. This allowed the king to override existing customs, systems and traditions. The exercise of royal grace was especially apposite in contexts that required the king's intervention in legal judgements and can be seen in the granting of royal pardons and in his personal reception of petitions from his subjects.

It was thus the king's uniqueness in the polity that made him indispensable to the smooth running of government, and that explains why, even in an age when England had developed a sophisticated, organised and unified 'state', its fate and fortune were still almost wholly invested in the abilities and personal disposition of one individual. The kingdom's unity, stability and prosperity depended, above all, on who sat on the throne. It also explains, on a more practical level, why late medieval English kings still shouldered a massive administrative burden. One mid fifteenth-century commentator recalled how, after dinner, both Henry IV and Henry V would sit themselves comfortably and spend an hour or more receiving requests and complaints 'off whomesoeuer wold come'.[7] As the source of patronage, kings received an unrelenting barrage of solicitation – it has been estimated that Henry IV was on the receiving end of up to 4,000 requests each year: this would have been typical of the age.[8] These did not usually concern matters of state that obviously required the king's attention, but were more mundane matters affecting the individual lives of his subjects. On a petition for financial relief presented in 1348 by the poor people of Finstock and Topples Wood in Oxfordshire, for example, is a note to say that their request had been heard in person by Edward III.[9] In an age of precocious state building, kings were still expected to be accessible, even to their low-status subjects.

The personality of the king, and his suitability for office, counted for everything. Some kings were simply not up to the task: Edward II was famously depicted by one of his own subjects as a wastrel monarch who preferred 'applying himself to making ditches and digging and other improper occupations' to the serious business of kingship,[10] and Henry VI was so unerringly clueless about his regal responsibilities that special measures had to be taken to ensure that petitioners did not take advantage of his vacuousness.[11] To be able to discharge his responsibilities with the common interest of the realm at the forefront of considerations, rather than letting wilfulness or favouritism dictate things was, however, the supreme challenge that every king faced, and severely tested even the most able, fair-minded and far-sighted ruler. It was a challenge because favour and reward were part of the common currency of the exercise of royal power: kings were *expected* to distribute largesse and to show favour. Public authority and private preferment were thus often impossible to disentangle. For the Lancastrian kings, and especially Henry IV who ruled as a usurper king, the challenge was made even harder by the fact that the vast (private) Lancastrian estates they possessed as dukes of Lancaster were kept as a separate entity from the (public) royal domain that fell into their hands when they became king, so they ruled in effect as both king *and* duke. In disputes that involved Lancastrian lands or concerned Lancastrian servants, it was very difficult for the king to claim to be acting as an impartial arbiter.

What mattered, then, was that the king exercised his powers judiciously, prudently and, above all, *representatively*. For the elite this meant principally protection of their property (by the king upholding the rule of law) and the fair distribution of patronage (i.e. grants of favour, lands, money or offices). Patronage deserves a special mention because it used to be considered the essential lubricant of strong government in the late medieval polity, since it was thought that only by offering material incentives could the king be assured of the loyalty of his subjects. This view no longer holds ground, since loyalty to the king derived from a much more complex set of factors, not least, in pragmatic terms, the fact that the landed classes were heavily invested in upholding royal authority because the security of their own positions was usually dependent upon it. They were, in other words, the king's natural allies; their loyalty did not usually have to be bought. But how patronage was distributed still mattered, especially if there was a perception that a small number of individuals were benefiting disproportionately. It was this situation that contributed so significantly to the chronic instability of the reigns of Henry III, Edward II, Richard II and Henry VI. Distributing patronage was not necessarily vital to kings in winning loyalty, but its misuse could be instrumental in their losing it. Good kings used patronage sparingly, not as a means of buying support but to reward service.

In all this, however, it is important to acknowledge that the king, with his ministers and administrators, did not rule alone. He could never have done so even if he had wished to, because the 'state', for all its expansion and growth, was still wholly incapable of supporting the full extent of the reach and centralising ambitions of English governance in the late Middle Ages. Kings had always relied on their nobles as extensions of their power, and it is true to say that the nobility remained the king's foremost collaborators in the matter of governing the kingdom, especially in the localities. Moreover, selected members of the nobility, together with some bishops and the main officers of state, usually formed the core of the royal council that assisted the king in the regular business of ruling the realm from the 'centre'. Occasionally, a king might hold enlarged councils – 'Great Councils' – comprising a much larger selection of nobles and bishops if he wished to consult on specific and/or particularly weighty matters of royal policy. An awful lot of the business of ruling was, however, transacted and determined informally, in now unrecorded conversations between the king and the members of these elites on less prescribed occasions, such as tournaments, hunting expeditions, gatherings at the court (see Chapter 8) or on the king's travels around his kingdom.

One especially important feature of the later Middle Ages is the expansion of the ruling elite to include the gentry and the wealthiest citizens of the towns and cities. Their participation in the governance of the realm pushed even further to the fore the notion that the 'state', that is, the public authority of the crown, was fundamentally underpinned by the private power and private influence of the landed and mercantile elites. It was the emergence of this broader participation in the governance of the realm that has led historians to refer to the existence of a political community. The term aptly describes the common interest that bound its members together, and the spirit of cooperation and mutuality in governance that guided their actions. It emerged only gradually, but the reign of Edward I was a pivotal moment, for these years saw a notable intensification of royal authority in the localities and a concomitant increase in the involvement of local elites in royal commissions and office-holding. It was a perfectly natural corollary that with increased involvement in governance, these groups should also seek a greater say in how the kingdom should be ruled.

In this, parliament was to play a critical function. Parliament had emerged in the course of the thirteenth century principally as an enlarged baronial council (see Figure 4.1). It gave institutional expression to another basic tenet of political life in this period, namely that the king should seek both counsel and consent for royal policies that affected the wider realm. This principle derived from the influential Roman law maxim: *quod omnes tangit ab omnibus approbetur* ('what concerns all should be approved by all'). In time, and especially from the late thirteenth century, parliament increasingly began to take on a fiscal function – that is to say, it was the place where national taxation was granted – and the building-block principles of consultation and consent now had the effect of bringing the gentry and urban elites to parliament on a more frequent basis, for it was they rather than the nobility who were empowered to grant the king taxation in their capacity as representatives of their local communities. The confluence of their greater

Figure 4.1 A fictional depiction of Edward I presiding over parliament, showing the king flanked by Alexander, king of Scots, and Llewelyn ap Gruffydd, prince of Wales. Before him are sat the spiritual and temporal Lords, and royal judges and clerks. The Commons are not depicted. (Wriothesley Garter Book, c. 1530 (RCIN 1047414).) (Photo by DeAgostini/Getty Images.)

involvement in royal government and their role as guardians of the nation's purse strings were the two key factors that propelled them firmly onto the political stage. Parliament was where the king met the political nation, where matters of local, national and international importance were discussed, and where policies were negotiated and agreed upon. Initially, the spiritual and temporal Lords acted as spokesmen for the 'community of the realm' – as it was contemporaneously described – but in the reign of Edward II this function came to be associated primarily with the representatives. It was a moment of great importance: it heralded the emergence of the parliamentary Commons and provided the impetus behind the formulation of the collective requests and grievances, known as common petitions, that they began to submit to the king raising matters of national concern (see also Chapter 12).

Modern scholarship on parliament has for a long time been overshadowed by the legacy of nineteenth-century work that cast the institution into a modern interpretative framework. From this sprang the infamous idea of 'Lancastrian Constitutionalism', that is, the notion that Henry IV and his successors ruled through parliament as 'constitutional monarchs'. The problem with this older scholarly tradition is that it cast parliament into a permanent state of opposition to royal rule and defined its proper functioning primarily in terms of the restraints that it sought to impose on what the king did. This missed the point that parliament was fundamentally the king's parliament, and its primary function was to facilitate royal policy. As the fourteenth century progressed, it is true that the Commons became more and more active in shaping national life, as they skilfully extracted statutory concessions from the king in return for taxation; but this did not automatically result in a lessening of royal power. The king was having to learn to engage with the political community and manage political opinion, and while this emboldened the political classes and got them far more closely involved in the affairs of state, it also considerably extended the basis of royal power, as the king was handed the means to tap into the nation's wealth to fund his wars and was able to regulate public life ever more closely through elaborate programmes of statutory legislation. Kings who managed parliament skilfully, like Edward

III, Henry V and Edward IV, found that it could act as an incredibly efficient tool of royal policy, contributing significantly to the integration of the political classes and to levels of support for royal policy.

As a result of this intense level of engagement, it has sometimes been said that the political system of late medieval England constituted a 'mixed monarchy'; that is to say, that the king and the political community were partners in shouldering the responsibilities of government and reaping the rewards of effective rule. This is a useful conceptualisation and underlines the point that accounts of governance and politics in late medieval England ought to be as much polity-centred as king-centred. But it must be qualified by noting that the king and political community were not *equal* partners. Although much of the legislation enacted by parliament after the 1330s emanated from the mouths of the Commons, it was rare indeed for the Commons to force the king into taking measures that he did not approve of, and the supremacy of royal power was always upheld by that fact that all executive action, whatever its source, was issued by authority of the king. The nobles were closest to the king in social status, but even they were still emphatically subordinated to his will. As 'partners' in the governance of the realm, members of the political community were normally only petitioners and counsellors; it was for the king, with his close advisors, to make the actual decisions.

The mixed nature of the political environment was, nevertheless, recognised by contemporaries. In the mid fifteenth century, Chief Justice John Fortescue famously contrasted the 'regal' rule of France with the 'regal and political' system of England.[12] His intention was to place the public institutions of parliament and the legal system at the heart of the English constitution, and to underline the point that the shape of governance in England was determined as much by upward pressures (from the people) as by downwards ones (from the king). For clarification, the word 'constitution' is used in this sense to signify the customs, structures and ideas that underpinned the norms of government in this period.

Dissent and Deposition

What exactly the 'norms of government' entailed when the king proved less than capable of meeting the high expectations there were of him was a dilemma that frequently confronted the political classes of late medieval England. It was a particularly knotty problem to resolve because there was no formal written constitution, or manual of kingship, to set out what should happen in this eventuality, and also because the 'constitution' itself pointed in different, and sometimes conflicting, directions. On the one hand, the sanctity of royal power was held to be absolute: a king was supposed to be subject to neither correction nor restriction. On the other hand, there was equal insistence that the king had an unqualified obligation to rule for the common interest and to seek counsel and to gain consent for all major acts of governance. The juxtaposition of royal freedom with royal obligation was a dichotomy, even paradox, that was encapsulated in the conviction that the king was both above and also subject to the law. The idea of kingly obligation resided in the belief that while the king enjoyed rights and privileges pertaining to his office, so too the king's subjects had the right to be protected from arbitrary or tyrannical rule. This meant, in essence, that the king was not allowed to exact summary justice on his subjects, nor to impoverish them by extracting taxation without consent. These principles were encapsulated in Magna Carta (1215), a document that was repeatedly cited by the political community throughout the period as a reminder to the king that his rule was more contractual than absolute.

Theoretically the king could not be challenged or resisted, but in practice this was a position that was becoming increasingly untenable in our period as the 'state' expanded and the growing imposition of royal power into the lives of the king's subjects significantly amplified the consequences of bad kingship. At the same time, as we have seen, the intensification of royal power went hand in hand with the increasing involvement of the political classes in the governance of the realm. This gave them a greater stake in how the kingdom was run, and a greater voice at times when things went wrong. The contemporary idea of the 'community of the realm' was an especially powerful conceptual tool in these circumstances for it enabled critics of the king and of royal policy to articulate – in the name of the community of the realm – a vision of what constituted the common interest independent of the king himself. Of even greater significance, however, was the emerging idea that the king could, if necessary, be separated from 'the crown', and that it was to the crown, rather than to the king, that the people ultimately owed their allegiance and loyalty. The principle was famously articulated in 1308, when the barons stated that 'homage and the oath of allegiance are more in respect of the crown than in respect of the king's person and are more closely related to the crown than to the king's person';[13] and in 1450, by the sailors who had captured the duke of Suffolk when they responded to the duke's protestations that he had a safe conduct signed by the king by retorting that: 'they did not know the said king, but they well knew the crown of England, saying that the aforesaid crown was the community of the said realm and that the community of the realm was the crown of that realm'.[14]

The notion that it was possible to separate the king from the crown was so revolutionary, and the implications so potentially catastrophic for the polity, that it was only openly mooted at other times when the king was being deposed (to be discussed shortly), but the underlying idea that the people did not owe the king unconditional loyalty remained implicit in much of the political dialogue of the period, particularly at times of heightened tension. In this sense it could accurately be said that England possessed not only a mixed monarchy but also a limited monarchy: the king's actions were limited by pragmatic considerations (he had no standing army, no professional corps of administrators in the localities, no assured flow of taxation, etc.) and also conceptually, by the customs, norms and principles that defined the scope of acceptable political action.

Political dissent tended to be manifested in three main ways. The first and least threatening to royal authority were political crises generated by fiscal mismanagement. To be sure, a king could be made to feel incredibly uncomfortable when his authority was challenged in these circumstances, but the objectives of his opponents tended to be narrowly defined (i.e. reducing taxation and improving crown finances) and the king's sovereign power was not usually directly threatened. Usually, these episodes were caused when the king taxed his people heavily and had little to show for it. This generated suspicion of misspending (or 'misappropriation of supply', as it was called), peculation and general governmental incompetence. Significantly, two of the kings considered to have been among the most successful of our period – Edward I and Edward III – faced significant dissent when they pushed their realms to breaking point by making huge and unreasonable demands on their subjects for taxation (in 1297–8 and 1340–1). These occasions showed that even politically savvy kings could miscalculate. Other notable political/fiscal crises occurred in the 1380s under Richard II, in the 1400s under Henry IV and in the 1440s/50s under Henry VI – again when the crown's tax demands provoked vociferous criticism.

One marked feature of these episodes was the claim by the political community to have the right to oversee expenditure and to hold the king's ministers to account. These were important manifestations of the idea that taxation was public money, rather than the king's, and that royal ministers were public servants, rather than solely the functionaries of the king. Opposition to the king's tax-raising activities was often successful because the goals were usually limited, because the political community could often effectively invoke the common interest in support of its agenda and because the threat of withholding taxation was a major inducement for the king to cooperate, albeit usually only begrudgingly. Having said all this, however, a king's financial acumen was rarely what ultimately determined his political success: both Edward II and Richard II lost their thrones even though, at the time of their depositions, they were among the richest kings to have ruled late medieval England.

If the political ramifications of fiscal crises were, for the most part, limited and proportionate, the second manifestation of political dissent involved an altogether more direct attack on the king's personal authority. Here, the king's competence to rule was explicitly brought into question, and concrete measures were taken to strip him partially, and sometimes even wholly, of his executive power. Almost always, these political crises were caused by the belief that the king had surrounded himself with the wrong type of people who were leading him astray and destabilising the natural order of royal governance. Often, then, a determination to remove from the king's presence these disruptive elements went hand in hand with a broader set of formal demands for governmental reform that were set out in elaborate constitutional documents that the king was forced to agree to. These are the circumstances that produced Magna Carta (1215), the Provisions of Oxford (1258) and the Ordinances of 1311. In later periods, the focus tended to shift more decisively to simply removing those who were considered to be a bad influence on the king, such as in 1388, when the Appellants purged the royal household of unpopular courtiers, in 1450, when William de la Pole was impeached in parliament and exiled (and then murdered), and in the early 1450s, when Richard, duke of York, sought the removal of his arch rival, Edmund Beaufort, duke of Somerset.

A number of features are worth flagging up. First, all these major challenges to royal authority were led by noblemen. Often they sought legitimacy by appealing to a broader constituency of support, but only noblemen had the military forces to be able to compel the king to agree to their demands – sometimes it simply required the threat of force to carry reforms through. Secondly, the leaders of these reform movements never expressed their aims explicitly in terms of challenging royal authority. This would have been tantamount to treason. Instead, their opposition was packaged as a public service and an act of loyalty to the king, saving him (and realm) from the clutches of self-serving, avaricious sycophants. Finally, these reform movements were almost never successful. While it was possible to resist the king, kill his friends and force through reform, it was never going to be easy to force long-term change on an unwilling and usually hostile monarch. Simon de Montfort (c. 1208–1265) and Thomas of Lancaster (c. 1278–1322) tried to get round this by installing themselves as de facto rulers, in the place of the king, but neither succeeded and both were eventually killed by resurgent royalist forces. The simple truth was that the only legitimate authority in the kingdom was royal authority, and this could never be exercised convincingly by anyone other than the king.

This then largely explains the final manifestation of political dissent in our period: deposition. If kings were resistant to change, and their rule was sufficiently problematic, the next logical step was to get rid of them altogether. In 1386, Richard II had been warned that he would be deposed, as his great-grandfather had been, if he did not heed the reforms demanded of him, for his subjects had the right to replace any king who 'alienates himself from his people, and does not wish to be governed and ruled by the laws of the land and statutes'.[15] On this occasion his opponents stepped back from the brink, but in 1399 Richard II *was* deposed, like Edward II in 1327. On both occasions, the kings were forcibly removed from office, but the proceedings were cynically dressed up as voluntary abdications. Richard is supposed to have said 'I have been and am entirely inadequate and unequal to the task of ruling and governing'.[16] For good measure, like Edward II, all his faults and failings were then laid bare in formal deposition proceedings. The proceedings against Edward II began with the simple, blunt statement: 'because the king is incompetent to govern in person'.[17] In the fifteenth century, further regime changes followed in 1461, 1470/1, 1483 and 1485. If these were strictly speaking usurpations (i.e. the removal of 'false' kings by someone claiming to have a better claim to the throne) rather than depositions (i.e. the removal of kings who were acknowledged to have been kings), the element of judging and castigating the former incumbent on the basis of his inadequacy remained a central part of proceedings. In the act of unmaking an existing king, as well as in making a new one, the participation of the whole political community was vital: those kings who replaced failed ones claimed their new authority above all on their rightful lineage, but the element of popular assent – or acclaim – underlined the important principle that kings ultimately owed their position to the willingness of their subjects to accept them as king.

Whether, after all this turmoil, English kingship was inherently weaker at the end of the fifteenth century than it had been at the start of our period is a complex question to answer. In some ways, there is no denying that more frequent depositions debased the majesty of the royal office, and likely also generated further instability and more depositions. Usurper kings inevitably had to work harder to win the loyalty of their subjects: indeed, it could be said in general of this period that the expectation of English kings to provide good governance had become much more challenging, now that the political community was more closely integrated into the structures of power and was more coordinated in its political action. But monarchy, as a system of political organisation, remained as strong as ever. The temptation to dwell on depositions and political instability must be balanced by acknowledging how tenaciously contemporaries persevered in the face of bad kingship. Henry VI's reign is remarkable for how long the political community put up with a king wholly unsuited to his role. In the event of the long minorities of Henry III, Richard II and Henry VI, the instinct of the political community was not to replace these vulnerable young boys with better qualified adult male relatives but to close ranks and install interim 'caretaker' governments to safeguard their inheritance. The vested interest in maintaining the political status quo usually far exceeded the temptation to make drastic changes. Deposition was thus a last rather than first resort. Nevertheless, the depositions underlined how fragile the medieval political system was, for resting so comprehensively and inflexibly on the personality and ability of one individual. In the closing decades of the fifteenth century the system of governance in England appears to have slowly shifted to address this deep structural flaw: the Tudor dynasty emerged with 'kingship' very much intact, but with a subtle diminution of emphasis on the personal nature of kingly rule and the participatory nature of royal governance.[18]

Conclusion

Kingship was thus a two-sided coin: while it gave a king enormous power, it also entailed huge obligations. The expectation of the king to provide good governance to his subjects was as great as the expectation of his subjects that they should serve him and be loyal. The political system was therefore fundamentally reciprocal in nature: it rested upon a contract between the king and his people that achieved its clearest expression at the coronation, when each acknowledged their sacred obligation to the other. Governance in late medieval England was also overwhelmingly shaped by the sophisticated nature of its central bureaucracy, and by the cooperation and integration of the landed and clerical classes in the structures of power. The centralised nature of the English polity led to a high level of political engagement and a permissive political environment where the line between counsel and criticism was often blurred, and crossed. This integrated and coordinated political structure was a blessing for politically capable kings who were able to harness the considerable power of the state for national enterprises like war. It was a curse for incapable kings, whose failings were intolerable to a political community that had become deeply invested in the well-being of the realm and was often well organised and purposeful. The English system therefore had the capacity to produce both the strongest and the weakest forms of kingship. At the same time, the late medieval English constitution was neither fixed nor clear-cut and contained within it scope to justify both the preservation of and challenges to the political status quo: it could be made to underpin the damaging rule of an overly assertive or incompetent king as much as it could sustain dissent and resistance to that rule by the political community. These contradictions and tensions made the governance of late medieval England an infinitely complex and challenging undertaking, and its politics an often turbulent affair.

Notes

1. A. L. Brown, *The Governance of Late Medieval England 1272-1461* (London, 1989), 52.
2. C. Carpenter, 'Henry VI and the Deskilling of the Royal Bureaucracy', in *The Fifteenth Century IX: English and Continental Perspectives*, ed. L. Clark (Woodbridge, 2010), 1–37.
3. *The Reign of Richard II: From Minority to Tyranny 1377-97*, trans. and ed. A. K. McHardy (Manchester, 2012), 95.
4. D. Biggs, 'A Plantagenet Revolution in Government? The Officers of Central Government and the Lancastrian Usurpation of 1399', *Medieval Prosopography* 20 (1999), 191–211.
5. J. E. Crockford, 'The Itinerary of Edward I of England: Pleasure, Piety, and Governance', in *Journeying along Medieval Routes in Europe and the Middle East*, ed. A. L. Gascoigne, Leonie V. Hicks and Marianne O'Doherty (Turnout, 2016), 231–57 (at 240).
6. Definitions from W. M. Ormrod, *Political Life in Medieval England, 1300-1450* (Basingstoke, 1995), 130.
7. *The Antiquarian Repertory*, ed. F. Grose, 4 vols. (London, 1807–9), I, 314.
8. A. L. Brown, 'The Authorization of Letters under the Great Seal', *BIHR* 37 (1964), 125–56 (at 154).
9. TNA, SC 8/244/12167.
10. H. Johnston, 'The Eccentricities of Edward II', *EHR* 48 (1933), 264–7.
11. *Proceedings and Ordinances of the Privy Council of England*, ed. N. H. Nicolas, 7 vols. (1834–7), VI, 316–20.
12. Sir John Fortescue, *The Governance of England*, ed. C. Plummer (London, 1885), 109.
13. *The Reign of Edward II, 1307-27*, ed. and trans. W. R. Childs and P. R. Schofield (Manchester, 2022), 23–4.
14. R. Virgoe, 'The Death of William de la Pole, Duke of Suffolk', *BJRL* 47 (1965), 489–502 (at 499).
15. *Reign of Richard II*, trans. and ed. McHardy, 153.

16. *Chronicles of Revolution, 1397–1400: The Reign of Richard II*, trans. and ed. C. Given-Wilson (Manchester, 1993), 171.
17. *Reign of Edward II*, trans. and ed. Childs and Schofield, 255–6.
18. J. Watts, '"A New Fundacion of Is Crowne": Monarchy in the Age of Henry VII', in *The Reign of Henry VII: Proceedings of the 1993 Harlaxton Symposium*, ed. B. Thompson (Stamford, 1995), 31–53.

Further Reading

Brown, A. L., *The Governance of Late Medieval England 1272–1461* (London, 1989).
Carpenter, C., 'Resisting and Deposing Kings in England in the Thirteenth, Fourteenth and Fifteenth Centuries', in *Murder and Monarchy: Regicide in European History, 1300–1800*, ed. R. von Friedeburg (Basingstoke, 2005), 99–121.
'Henry VI and the Deskilling of the Royal Bureaucracy', in *The Fifteenth Century IX: English and Continental Perspectives*, ed. L. Clark (Woodbridge, 2010), 1–37.
Gillingham, J. B., 'Crisis or Continuity? The Structure of Royal Authority in England 1369–1422', in *Das Spätmittelalterliche Königtum im Europäischen Vergleich* (Sigmaringen, 1987), 59–80.
Harriss, G. L., 'Political Society and the Growth of Government in Late Medieval England', *Past & Present* 138 (1993), 28–57.
Hicks, M., *English Political Culture in the Fifteenth Century* (London, 2002).
Lander, J. R., *The Limitations of English Monarchy in the Later Middle Ages* (Toronto, 1989).
Ormrod, W. M., *Political Life in Medieval England, 1300–1450* (Basingstoke, 1995).
Walker, S., 'Civil War and Rebellion, 1200–1500', in Walker, *Political Culture in Late Medieval England: Essays by Simon Walker* (Manchester, 2006), 246–62.
Watts, J., '"A New Fundacion of Is Crowne": Monarchy in the Age of Henry VII', in *The Reign of Henry VII: Proceedings of the 1993 Harlaxton Symposium*, ed. B. Thompson (Stamford, 1995), 31–53.
'Ideas, Principles and Politics', in *The Wars of the Roses*, ed. A. J. Pollard (Basingstoke, 1995), 110–33.
'Usurpation in England: A Paradox of State-Growth', in *Coups d'État à la Fin du Moyen Âge? Aux fondements du pouvoir politique en Europe occidentale*, ed. F. Foronda, J.-P. Genet and J. M. Nieto Soria (Madrid, 2005), 115–30.

5

Finance

Crown finance in late medieval England had a lot of moving parts, not all of which fitted together. This chapter looks initially at income and expenditure, before examining the ways in which the financial system was managed, massaged and manipulated.

Income

Medieval English kings had two sources of income: 'ordinary' and 'extraordinary'. The former was the revenue which a king was entitled to receive by virtue of his office and feudal sovereignty. Its chief constituents were (i) the lands held by the crown in demesne ('domainal' lands), which might be either leased out or farmed directly; (ii) the farms of the shires – that is, the annual sums paid at the exchequer by the county sheriffs; (iii) incidental feudal revenues such as reliefs, escheats and the profits of wardship and marriage, plus occasional impositions such as aids and tallages, usually for specific purposes, and forfeitures for treason; (iv) the profits of royal justice, for example fines for contravention of the Forest Laws; (v) the revenues from bishoprics *sede vacante* – that is, between the death of one bishop and the consecration of his replacement, which usually took several months and sometimes years; and (vi) the unquantifiable, often unrecorded, but habitual sweeteners offered by great and small in return for favours such as appointment to offices or tenures in the king's gift, grants of licences or privileges, renewing charters or simply being taken into service; in other words, the profits of royal patronage.

The net value of these ordinary revenues varied considerably, though not inordinately, depending on the familial or political demands made upon them, the diligence with which local officials were supervised and the liberality or restraint with which each king exercised his patronage. For example, a programme of reform between 1236 and 1241, including a systematic revision of the farms of the shires, brought in an additional £2,000 a year net from the sheriffs and the crown lands – an increase of around 10 per cent. Under Edward I, the exchequer reckoned that the crown's ordinary revenues yielded £27,000 a year. Another burst of reform accompanied Edward II's 'tyranny' in the early 1320s, the aim of which was to maximise the profit from the forfeited lands of the lords whom the king had proscribed in 1321-2: as well as managing these lands rigorously, debt-collecting was speeded up, farms were reviewed, allowances were scrutinised and royal rights strictly enforced. By 1324, the value of the shire farms and royal lands (including £8,000 from the confiscated duchy of Lancaster) amounted to £24,000 per annum, nearly double what the sheriffs had collected under Edward I. Following Edward II's overthrow in 1326-7, however, the forfeited lands were mostly restored to their heirs, and it would be another 150 years before the domainal lands were exploited with similar rigour by Edward IV.[1]

Judicial and feudal revenues were by their nature more variable. In the mid thirteenth century, an *eyre* (judicial circuit by royal justices) might yield as much as £20,000. Another option was to mulct the Jews, a popular expedient exploited remorselessly by Henry III in the 1230s and 1240s, when tallages totalling more than £50,000 were demanded from them. The result was to reduce England's small Jewish community to penury and in 1290 they were expelled from the kingdom. Feudal reliefs (payments by heirs to enter into their landed inheritances) had been so punitively exploited by King John that their extent was limited in Magna Carta, but wardships and marriages remained a lucrative source of profit and patronage throughout the Middle Ages, as did fines and forfeitures. One reason why Richard II became wealthy during his last years was the lands and chattels forfeited by his executed or exiled political opponents. Henry V, who exploited his feudal rights methodically, could still in 1415 impose a fine of £6,666 on the earl of March for marrying without royal licence – which was paid almost in full. By this and other means Henry increased his annual income from feudal revenues by some 50 per cent. Yet successful exploitation of the crown's resources required concentration, which not all kings possessed. Moreover, although he had three brothers, Henry did not have a wife or children to provide for until the very end of his reign. A queen would expect to be granted revenues (preferably landed) worth at least £4,000 a year, while a king's sons could hardly be given less than the value of an earldom (a minimum of £1,000 a year) or his daughters married off with dowries which disparaged their status. It was not just personal relationships which came under strain in a large royal family.[2]

Generally speaking, the net value during the late Middle Ages of the crown's ordinary income averaged between £20,000 and £30,000 a year.[3] Even by the beginning of the thirteenth century this was well short of meeting its needs. New – 'extraordinary' – sources of revenue needed to be found, which meant taxation. The key difference between ordinary and extraordinary income is that the latter required consent. A king could not – or at least should not, and usually did not – impose taxation without first securing consent, and consent required evidence of necessity. The demonstration of necessity, the form which consent might take and what the king might be required to concede in order to obtain it were naturally questions which took time to settle, as did the criteria for assessment and collection. Yet if the thirteenth century was an age of experimentation, often fiercely contested, certain principles or at least customs became established quite early: for example, that necessity meant imminent danger to the realm; that laity and clergy would be taxed separately; and that lay taxes would be assessed in the form of fractions on movable goods and clerical taxes on the rental value of their estates. The first real such tax was the thirteenth (of the value of the laity's movable goods) imposed by King John in 1207: based on precedents for feudal aids, its 'necessity' was the 'defence of the realm and the recovery of Normandy' and it was allegedly sanctioned by 'the assent of our council', which in fact comprised little more than John's trusted advisors. In effect, it was an arbitrary imposition, massively unpopular, for which John soon paid a political price.[4]

Nevertheless, the thirteenth of 1207 raised £57,000 and pointed the way forward. In 1225, in return for royal confirmation of the 1215 charters, clergy and laity granted a fifteenth which raised around

£39,000, mostly spent on a campaign to Gascony. It was only at the end of the thirteenth century, however, that direct taxation became a regular contributor to the crown's income. Edward I raised nine lay subsidies, variously assessed at between £34,000 and £116,000 and totalling around £500,000, and £300,000 in clerical subsidies. Like John, he encountered considerable resistance, which he overcame with menace: in 1294, when the clergy refused to grant a subsidy at the exorbitant rate of 50 per cent, Edward threatened to outlaw them all. They capitulated and it raised £101,000, but after 1297, when the king's demands caused a political crisis and a breakdown in Anglo-Papal relations, he was forced to moderate his demands.[5]

It was the following half-century that witnessed the real shift in the structure of English crown finance, heralding a fiscal order based upon principles which would endure for the next 300 years: taxation replaced ordinary revenues as the backbone of government solvency, while forms of taxation and procedures for obtaining consent were settled. Edward I's subsidies were set at a range of fractional rates, from sixths to thirtieths, which meant that each one required a new assessment and collection process. This was cumbersome and open to fraud, and in 1334 it was decided that in future direct lay subsidies would not require new assessments but be based on a standard figure of a tenth (i.e. 10 per cent) from the towns and a fifteenth (c. 7 per cent) in rural areas, with exemptions for the poorest or in counties stricken by war. Henceforward, each 'tenth and fifteenth' reliably raised about £38,000, while clerical tenths, based on valuations made in 1291, yielded about £18,000.

Around 1340, it also became accepted that it was the Commons in parliament, and them only, who had the power to grant lay subsidies, and the clergy in convocation (which usually met simultaneously with parliament) the power to grant clerical subsidies. In return, the Commons – two knights from each shire and two burgesses from each town, who from the 1320s onwards were always summoned to the king's (more or less annual) parliaments – submitted petitions – that is, common petitions – setting out their grievances or requesting new legislation. This set the pattern – fiscal supply in return for representation and redress of grievances – which was to endure for centuries. Parliaments usually began with a request for taxation, following which came weeks of bargaining and discussion, much of it concerning the petitions submitted by the Commons – until, once agreement had been reached, the parliament closed with the king's formal responses to petitions and the Commons' formal grant of taxation, which was binding on their constituents. Very rarely were royal requests for taxation actually refused, although they were frequently modified or granted only once assurances had been received that grievances would be addressed. Similar though less formalised procedures applied in convocation, where the clergy began by drawing up their *gravamina* (grievances), setting negotiations in train.

The result was a significant increase in the crown's income. During the fifty years of Edward III's reign, he received £1,121,000 in lay subsidies (more than twice as much as Edward I in a reign of thirty-five years) and £402,000 in clerical subsidies (roughly equivalent, year on year, to what Edward I had received). Yet at no stage did direct lay or clerical taxation become a royal entitlement, and at times when no necessity – that is, a state of war – could be demonstrated, or when the king was a minor or lacked the authority to press his demands, years passed without any being granted (e.g. the 1360s, 1422–8 and 1454–60). Nevertheless, some leeway developed: periods of truce might be treated as war rather than peace, as might major crises in Wales, Ireland or Gascony.[6]

What really transformed the finances of the late medieval crown, however, was the development of indirect taxation, which, first and foremost, meant taxing wool exports. Medieval England was famous for the abundance and quality of its wool, which was greatly in demand on the continent, especially in the Low Countries. In 1275, when Edward I first imposed a tax of one-third of a pound on each sack of wool shipped from an English port (the value of which abroad was generally around £10), this 'ancient custom', as it came to be called, provoked little opposition, despite raising about £10,000 a year. In 1294, however, when Edward arbitrarily raised the rate to £2 per sack, protest was vociferous, and in 1297 the king had to abandon his *maltolt* ('bad tax') and revert to the ancient custom. Even so, the *maltolt* had raised about £116,000 in three years, once again pointing the way forward.

It was again the first half of the fourteenth century which saw the establishment of indirect taxation as the bedrock of English crown finance. Initially attempts were made, not always successful, to raise the 'ancient custom' to a 'new custom' of ten shillings (half of £1), while grants of tonnage and poundage by parliament allowed taxation of a wider range of goods, including wine imports. Yet wool was always the real prize, and after the Hundred Years War broke out in 1337 Edward III was determined to exploit it. The *maltolt* was reimposed despite once again proving deeply unpopular; monopolistic syndicates to manage the trade on behalf of the crown were established, seizures of wool ordered, embargos decreed. Not until the 1350s did the situation stabilise, but when it did the king emerged triumphant. Between 1327 and 1336, customs revenues had yielded about £15,000 a year, but from 1351 to 1376 they brought in more than £70,000 a year (about £1,750,000 in total). It is in recognition of the primacy of wool in the history of English crown finance that the Speaker of the House of Lords still sits on a woolsack.

What differentiated these indirect customs and subsidies from direct taxation was that, although they too were theoretically subject to parliamentary consent, in practice they became permanent. The breakthrough came in 1362, when, despite peace having been made with France, the Commons agreed to renew the wool customs, and although the rate at which they were levied varied (e.g. foreign merchants usually paid at a higher rate than English merchants), they were in fact always granted, usually for three years at a time. Occasionally (in 1398, 1415, 1453 and 1465) they were even granted to a king for life, although such grants lapsed when he died. Thus, from the mid fourteenth century onwards, the crown could rely on an extraordinary income stream which in reality was as dependable as its ordinary revenues. Between 1360 and 1460, more than half of the crown's total revenue came from indirect taxation. What this golden goose depended on, however, was the maintenance of England's wool export trade, and as war and taxation steadily eroded its profitability and economic circumstances changed, trade declined. By the first quarter of the fifteenth century, as the domestic cloth industry grew, consuming more of England's wool, annual customs receipts were down to about £45,000, and after 1430 they rarely passed £30,000. To have taxed English cloth at a comparative rate would have made it uncompetitive in European markets. Instead, during the later fifteenth century, Edward IV again turned to ordinary revenues: the crown lands (now including the duchies of Lancaster and York) were managed more carefully, some alienated lands were taken back under crown control and feudal rights were strictly enforced. Yet despite the fall in customs revenue, Edward made no demands for direct taxation after 1475 and still died solvent eight years later.[7]

Edward IV also brought his ordinary revenues under his direct control, managing them through his chamber (*camera*). The chamber was both the inner sanctum of the royal household and the king's personal financial department, answerable to him alone, but since it did not generate accounts it is often difficult to calculate its reserves, which at times were clearly enormous. During the 1360s, for example, the vast ransoms demanded from the French and Scottish kings and other great prisoners meant that Edward III's chamber hoard included at least £160,000 in coin locked in chests in the Tower of London. These profits of war were the king's, not the crown's – although in fact, once war with France erupted again in 1369, Edward passed most of it over to the exchequer. When Richard II married the daughter of Charles VI of France in 1396, he was promised a dowry of £133,000, of which £83,000 was received during the next three years. This too went into the chamber, as did the pension of £10,000 a year promised by Louis XI to Edward IV in 1475. These were all times when the chamber was unusually wealthy, but even without the profits of war it kept a healthy reserve, for certain windfalls were routinely paid into it, such as fines, sweeteners, episcopal temporalities *sede vacante*, forfeitures for treason, licence fees and much else. When Edward II fled London in October 1326, he took with him £29,000 from his chamber, in coin carried in barrels. From around 1350 onwards, the chamber also received a *certum* (annual block grant) from the exchequer of between £2,000 and £8,000. Chamber money was spent as the king wished: on jewels, plate, falcons, personal gifts or religious icons. Yet the chamber was more than just the king's pocket money: its occasional great wealth and importance as a reserve hoard which – the king willing – could be called on if needed also made it a pivotal part of the crown's financial system, and its occasional great riches throw a more realistic light on the totality of the crown's income.[8]

Expenditure

In theory, the king's ordinary income was supposed to cover his 'ordinary', or recurrent, expenses, which meant principally the royal household and administration, justice, diplomacy, annuities and retaining fees, upkeep and construction of the king's buildings and the governance of England's 'empire' (Ireland, Wales, Gascony). There were times when it probably did. Edward II, a thrifty as well as rapacious king, reduced his household's costs to below £10,000 a year and left £78,000 in the treasury at his deposition. Yet thrift was a rare quality in medieval kings. The several departments of the royal household, numbering between 300 and 600 persons, rarely cost less than £15,000 and at times absorbed £40,000 or £50,000 a year. The great building projects beloved of rulers consumed enormous sums: Henry III spent £45,000 on reconstructing Westminster Abbey, Edward III some £50,000 on transforming Windsor Castle into the Versailles of its age, Edward I around £80,000 on the ring of castles encircling his newly acquired principality of Wales. This was on top of the constant upkeep needed for the crown's dozens of castles and manor houses. The recurrent expenses of the royal administration (chancery, treasury, judiciary) amounted to around £12,000 per annum, annuities and retaining fees usually about the same, although between circa 1390 and 1410 they rose to more than £20,000, until Henry V cut them back to size. By the later fourteenth century, the defence of Ireland, Gascony, the Scottish Marches and the sea usually required at least £25,000 a year and often much more; the decade-long Welsh rebellion which erupted in 1400 not only cost several thousand pounds a year but also meant that revenues from the principality almost entirely dried up.

Also potentially crippling were the frequent, if episodic, expenses associated with diplomacy and foreign affairs, for no king could afford to appear penny-pinching on the international stage. The duke of Lancaster's embassy to Avignon in November 1354 was accompanied by 500 riders and cost £5,648. To despatch Henry IV's daughter Philippa to Denmark for her marriage to King Erik in 1406 cost more than £4,000, to welcome Margaret of Anjou to England to marry Henry VI, £7,000. Diplomacy was about spectacle as well as substance, and for members of the royal family especially, disparagement was unthinkable.

When Henry III married his sister Isabella to the Emperor Frederick II in 1235, he paid a dowry of £20,000; in 1468, Edward IV paid £41,000 (plus wedding expenses) to Charles, duke of Burgundy, to marry Edward's sister Margaret. And in October 1396, when Richard II met Charles VI of France near Calais for a three-day summit to solemnise the Anglo-French truce and Richard's marriage to Charles's daughter Isabella, it was said that the robes, jewellery, festivities and competitively magnificent gifts which the kings exchanged cost an eye-watering £200,000. This was probably an exaggeration, but £100,000 is far from impossible.[9]

Yet whatever the cost of peace-making, it paled beside the cost of war – and between the 1290s and the 1450s England was almost continuously at war with either France or Scotland or both. By this time, military service as a condition of feudal tenure was becoming obsolete. The English armies sent to France or Scotland during the Hundred Years War (1337–1453) were almost invariably contract armies – that is, armies raised through contracts agreed between the king and his war-captains to serve with a specified number of men for a specified period in return for wages. In turn, the war-captains (usually nobles) recruited agreed numbers of men-at-arms, archers or auxiliaries, promising them the king's wages. Some of these armies numbered 15,000–20,000, although most were 5,000–10,000. Fleets were commandeered under similar terms, with captains and mariners also paid wages. To despatch even a 5,000-strong army to the continent for six months cost £60,000–£70,000. Edward I spent close to £1,000,000 on his wars in France and Scotland between 1294 and 1307, including £165,000 to his allies in the Low Countries. Despite raising unprecedented amounts of revenue from taxation, he died leaving unpaid debts of about £200,000.

The king who came closest to making the English war state of the late Middle Ages a financially sustainable enterprise was Edward III, but once the buoyant wool exports of the mid fourteenth century dropped away, it soon became apparent that England's reach exceeded its grasp. This was not simply because a united France was a larger and wealthier country than England. Nor was it because taxation assessments were still based on century-old precedents, or because by the fifteenth century exemptions had reduced the returns from tenths and fifteenths by about £5,000, or because indirect taxation was no longer targeting the country's real wealth – although all this mattered. Nor was it because the crown had neglected to experiment with different forms of taxation. A tax on parishes in 1371 had raised £50,000, while the combined yield of the first two poll taxes (1377 and 1379) amounted to £49,000, but when an attempt to triple the yield sparked the great revolt of 1381, such manifestly inequitable impositions were abandoned. Early fifteenth-century attempts to levy taxes on land or income at least had the merit of trying to spread the tax burden more equitably between social classes (unlike the exchequer reforms of the 1230s or 1320s, or the poll taxes of 1377–80) but yielded only meagre returns and were quickly abandoned. Meanwhile, more radical solutions were being proposed: partial or even total disendowment of the church was suggested in a number of parliaments (particularly 1404 and 1410), but clerical resistance was fierce and as a policy it became associated with heresy. Resumption of royal grants to lay lords gained more traction, leading to several Acts of Resumption from the 1450s onwards, but the number of exemptions granted reduced their effect (186 recipients of royal grants were exempted from the 1450 act, squandering a potential £3,750 per annum).[10]

The real problem was that by the fifteenth century, despite the enormous social and economic changes following the Black Death, the crown's taxation system had become ossified. While France's Valois monarchy, re-energised from the 1430s, developed a system based on *aides*, *tailles* and the *gabelle*, by which revenue was in effect levied at the king's will in order to support a standing army, English kings remained dependent on parliamentary consent to raise sums which barely covered the contracts for one expedition. It was just about possible to sustain intense military activity on the continent for five or six years, but after this the pressure on the Commons and the accumulation of debts usually resulted in political crisis. Edward III's extravagant military and diplomatic ventures at the start of the Hundred Years War meant that by 1339 crown debts amounted to some £300,000. Thirty years later, when war was renewed and he passed his great Tower coin-hoard to the exchequer, it was swallowed up in less than a year. Henry V raised £300,000 for his invasions of France in 1415 and 1417, but by 1421 resistance in parliament and the country was becoming difficult to contain. He died before the backlash reached crisis point, but during the 1430s the war turned decisively in France's favour, and by 1450, following years of underfunded military ventures and kingly ineptitude, the crown was indebted to the tune of an eye-watering £372,000. What followed was not just military defeat but, before long, civil war and the collapse of the Lancastrian regime.[11]

Bridging the Gap: Begging, Borrowing, Stealing

To summarise thus far, the total annual revenue of the late medieval English crown varied between about £60,000 and £150,000, but collecting it was laborious and it often failed to cover even predictable outgoings, let alone continuous periods of military activity. In the short term, as with modern governments, the gap was bridged by borrowing. Between circa 1270 and 1340, loans on the scale required by English kings could only realistically be provided by the great Italian merchant banks, whose international networks of agents and trading ventures enabled them to provide tens of thousands of pounds at a time in a choice of currencies. In return, they received trading concessions in wool, exemptions from certain dues and rents at peppercorn rates. If they refused to lend, sanctions might follow. Edward I borrowed a total of about £400,000 from the Ricciardi company of Lucca during the first two decades of his reign, of which they were still owed £20,000 in 1294 when, unable to advance any more, their English assets were seized, effectively bankrupting them. The Frescobaldi of Florence, who loaned around £150,000 to the crown between 1298 and 1311, were still owed £25,000 when they were expelled from England during the political crisis of 1311, soon after which they too went bankrupt. They in turn were replaced by the Bardi and Peruzzi companies, both also Florentine, but when Edward III delayed repayment of tens of thousands of pounds of debts to them in the mid 1340s, the primacy of Italian companies as bankers to the crown came to an end and Edward turned to English merchant syndicates.

Between 1337 and 1339, the Hull-born wool merchant William de la Pole – progenitor of a lineage which in time became one of England's noblest – had arranged for native merchants to loan £312,000 to fund Edward's Scottish and continental wars. Much of the money was supplied by Londoners, a pattern repeated so often that by the fifteenth century the city 'had developed into a quasi-bank of England'.[12] Some of these loans were corporate, others were arranged by wealthy citizens such as Richard Lyons in the 1370s or Richard ('Dick') Whittington in the early fifteenth century. Among the free-spending nobility, such liquid wealth was exceptional, although Richard, earl of Arundel (d. 1376) and Cardinal Henry Beaufort (d. 1447), the wealthiest men in England of their respective times, each had enough to advance £20,000 at short notice. In total, over nearly fifty years, Beaufort loaned some £250,000 to the crown, a vital contribution to England's war effort.

These loans were not secured without inducement. In some cases, despite the church's prohibition of usury, it is virtually certain that interest was paid, possibly as high as 33 per cent or even 50 per cent, but there were many other ways for lenders to profit. Like the Italians, they were granted preferential – sometimes monopolistic – access to markets and exemptions from customs duties. There was also the lure of political influence – or, in the case of Beaufort, the threat of royal displeasure: Henry V put great pressure on the cardinal to open his coffers, although after 1422 the minority government lacked the authority to sustain this. Lenders or creditors might also receive pledges in the form of treasure – indeed, this was the main use, apart from ceremonial, to which the royal treasure was put. Stored in the great treasury at Westminster Abbey or at the Tower of London, it was a vast, immensely valuable and readily available hoard of mainly gold and silver crowns, chaplets, cups, plates, candelabra, icons, brooches and other precious objects, often beautifully worked and studded with jewels, many of them received as gifts from foreign kings or nobles at diplomatic summits or ceremonial occasions. An inventory of Richard II's treasure in 1398–9 listed 2,300 items valued at £110,000. Even the most valuable of these, England's 'great crown', worth £33,584, was sometimes mortgaged in return for loans, while Henry V pledged numerous pieces to those who financed or fought on the Agincourt campaign. The access to credit which his treasure afforded the king meant that it too was a vital cog in the crown's financial machinery.[13]

Inducements apart, what lenders needed most was to feel confident that they would, in time, be repaid. What provided that assurance was the wool customs. Many loans to the crown were short-term: after a few days, sometimes even on the same day, lenders would be given tallies (see the section 'Exchequer, Assignment and Public Finance') promising them sums from the customs, which they could then present to the collectors at the ports to secure repayment. And since the wool customs were in effect permanent, they knew that repayment would materialise. Great lenders – Arundel, Beaufort, sometimes the Londoners – went further, insisting that, to guarantee preferential treatment, they be given control of a portion of the seal (*cocket*) without which merchandise could not be exported. But when the crown lost financial credibility, even inducements such as these failed. During the 1450s, the Londoners regularly refused Henry VI's requests for loans. Sixty years earlier, when London refused to loan £10,000 to Richard II, he suspended the city's liberties until the citizens capitulated. Such was the measure of the monarchy's embarrassment by the 1450s. Once Edward IV restored order to the crown's finances, however, the Londoners soon started lending again.[14] Of course, some of those who advanced loans to the crown did so willingly. Lenders on a significant scale – great Italian companies, English wool merchants and city corporations, even wealthy individuals – were, almost by definition, venture capitalists, and the profits they stood to make through interest, economic concessions or political influence were potentially enormous. That there were dangers involved – default, miscalculation, political upheaval – was a risk they were prepared to take.

Quite different were the forced loans and speciously named benevolences sometimes extracted from a wide range of subjects and not always repaid. In 1397, Richard II was accused of sending agents to towns and villages with letters specifying the sum he wished to borrow but only filling in the names of lenders after they had discovered who were the wealthiest citizens. 'Immense amounts of money' were raised, apparently the 'vast majority' of which was never repaid. The Lancastrian kings, despite usually seeking parliamentary sanction before borrowing, were often criticised for their constant demands for loans, which targeted not just the rich but also the 'middling sort' in the shires and boroughs, although the sums raised were modest – for example, £5,000 in 1417, £9,000 in 1421. In 1474, Edward IV began referring to such contributions as benevolences ('goodwill' contributions): raised for military purposes, they were in theory voluntary, but refusal might mean loss of royal favour, potentially more injurious.[15]

Neglecting or delaying repayment of loans was one of many quasi-legal practices employed by the crown to bridge the gap between income and expenditure. The most pernicious was the royal prerogative known as purveyance – that is, the right of the king's scores of purveyors to requisition goods (food, horses, provender, carriage, etc.) in local markets to keep the king's household supplied while moving around the country. Purveyance was practised on an enormous scale, not just by the king and his family but also by nobles and prelates, whose households might number 50 to 100 persons, enough to strip a local market bare. During the early fourteenth century, there were even attempts to extend purveyance to the provisioning of royal armies, but this proved so unpopular that Edward III abandoned it, relying instead on contracts with merchants to supply his troops. In 1362, criticism came to a head and parliament passed the Great Statute of Purveyors, one of whose clauses insisted that 'the hateful name of purveyor' be replaced by 'buyer'. Its chief aims were to limit purveyance to the households of the king and his family and, most importantly, to require purveyors to pay in full at the time of purchase. This they rarely did, instead routinely handing over either tallies or bills issued by the household, theoretically redeemable from a local crown official but in practice frequently discounted and sometimes worthless. As has been pointed out, this was 'little short of theft', but it was not the purveyors' fault: when the exchequer was unable to provide the household with ready cash, as was often the case, purveyors could not pay vendors, yet the king's 400–500 servants still had to eat. It was a problem which never went away. Purveyance remained a running sore well beyond the Middle Ages, but it was really a symptom of deeper malaise in the crown's financial system.[16]

The Exchequer, Assignment and Public Finance

From the eleventh century to the present day, the chief financial department of the English government has been known as the exchequer – or now, alternatively, as the treasury. Between 1290 and 1360, when English kings went on campaign, funds to finance military operations were usually channelled through the wardrobe (*garderoba*), the financial office of the royal household, thus bypassing the exchequer, but after 1360 exchequer supremacy was reasserted. The exchequer's name comes from the Latin *scaccarium* (chessboard), the 3 × 1.5-metre chequerboard with raised edges upon which the chief officers, or 'barons', of the exchequer adjusted counters representing different monetary values. Mirroring its two principal functions, there was an upper exchequer of audit and a lower exchequer of receipt. Twice a year, sometimes more, local accounting officers such as sheriffs and customs collectors were summoned to the upper exchequer to present their accounts – a nerve-racking process, for the barons were renowned for their rigorous scrutiny – following which they would be formally 'quit' and proceed to the lower exchequer to hand over their cash and/or warrants of acquittance.

In practice, however, they often handed over little cash, partly because there was only around one million pounds in coin in late medieval England – a consequence of the bullion shortage throughout medieval Europe – but also because most of the crown's revenue was assigned to creditors in advance. The process of assignment was based on tallies and bills. Tallies were ruler-shaped pieces of wood carefully incised with notches of differing sizes, representing different amounts of money, then split in half. On the side given to the payee (the stock) was written the name of the crown official by whom it was payable (e.g. a sheriff); the other side (the foil) went to the official. For the debt to be paid, they must be matched up, following which the official would present the matching pairs at his next exchequer acquittance. (Many medieval tally-sticks still survive, mainly in The National Archives at Kew.) Bills were IOUs, small sealed pieces of parchment.[17]

This system was entirely rational in conception. If a purveyor requisitioned provisions from traders in, say, Yorkshire, giving them bills or tallies as proof of sale, it made much more sense for them to be able to present these to the local sheriff or customs collector than to have to go to Westminster, where the exchequer was by now almost permanently housed. And, *mutatis mutandis*, the same was true for many crown creditors: lenders, annuitants, soldiers owed wages and so on. Yet it also had two notable disadvantages. Firstly, the fact that most of the crown's revenue never reached the exchequer meant that it was often difficult for the treasurer to provide the cash needed by, for example, household purveyors to undertake their duties, so that they in turn had to issue bills or tallies; in other words, the system became self-perpetuating.

Secondly, it was easy to abuse: faced with mounting debts and clamorous creditors, the exchequer might simply issue yet more tallies, despite knowing that the named local official(s) did not have the resources to redeem them. Thus, a collector in, say, Southampton might receive £2,000 in customs duties in a six-month period but find himself importuned by creditors with tallies worth £4,000 or £5,000 issued against his receipts. At this point, a creditor might return to the exchequer, where a 'bad' tally would be returned, a new one issued and a fictitious 'loan' from the creditor for the same amount created, whereupon the cycle might begin again. In practice, repayment often depended on the creditor's status or political influence, since preference at the exchequer was generally given to magnates, royal servants, household departments or pet royal projects such as building works, with the back of the queue reserved for the less privileged. Faced with delays ranging from the indefinite to the infinite, creditors sometimes had little option but to offload their tallies at a discount. Trafficking in tallies was common, sometimes at a markdown of 50 per cent or more. In 1376, the former chancellor, Bishop Wykeham, was accused before a great council of having at one point removed £6,666 from the treasury to buy back tallies to the crown's profit. Since he had bought tallies worth £100 for £25, or £500 for £133, he should have returned a 'profit' of around £19,000 to the treasury, but in fact returned only £8,300. There was no suggestion that the council saw this as atypical or illegal practice. Wykeham's alleged crime was not making a profit but concealing its extent. For creditors, however, it was, like purveyance, little short of theft.[18]

Yet it was not usually the iniquities of exchequer practice which stirred the wrath of the parliamentary Commons but the wider issue of the crown's failure to 'live of its own' without continually demanding taxation. There is little sign of any consistent effort at budgeting. A number of exchequer memoranda resembling budgets produced in the early 1360s were not in reality evidence of financial discipline but were designed, by disingenuously inflating expenditure over income, to persuade the Commons to renew the wool customs in time of peace. More authentic were the annual attempts made during the years 1407–11 to allocate sums of anticipated revenue to impending items of expenditure, but the recovery to which this contributed soon petered out. In fact, estimates of predicted income and expenditure must surely have been compiled, or at least discussed, frequently, but unforeseen emergencies, royal whim, parliamentary obstinacy or a lack of political will often derailed them, leaving the impression of a scramble for precedence occasionally descending into chaos. The mid 1250s, mid 1290s, late 1330s, early 1380s, early 1400s and, above all, the 1450s were especially chaotic times, all of which led to political as well as financial crisis.[19]

With parliamentary consent needed to raise taxation, the Commons acquired the opportunity to criticise the crown's financial policies – and this they did, persistently, often despairingly and occasionally imaginatively. After all, since the taxation they voted was for the realm's 'necessity', was it not also their responsibility to ensure that it was spent on the necessity for which it was granted, namely the 'public good' or 'common weal'? And when repeated pleas to kings to pull in their horns failed, they devised enforcement measures, such as insisting that taxes should not be received at the exchequer but by special treasurers of war appointed in parliament. Kings hated this, since it deprived them of the ability to spend their income as they pleased, but there were times – the late 1370s, early 1380s and mid 1400s – when it was effectively enforced. Unfortunately, it left a trail of unpaid annuities and household debts. Nevertheless, the call for appropriation of supply had a long future ahead of it, as did other expedients which the Commons periodically advocated, such as auditing of ministerial accounts in parliament or the permanent allocation of specific revenues to specific needs, such as reserving the Calais customs for the town's garrison.

In the long term, the effect of repeated parliamentary intervention, an ever-expanding range of policy proposals and reversals, sanctioned credit operations, experiments and restrictions foreshadowed the shift away from a system of crown finance towards a system of public finance. Take for example the royal household: in theory, it was the king's private domestic establishment, funded by his ordinary revenues. But it was also the royal court, the hub of the nation's political life, and in practice often funded indifferently by a combination of ordinary and extraordinary revenues, which arguably made it a public institution and thus publicly accountable. Parliaments complained repeatedly about the household's 'excessive' and 'outrageous' expenses; ordinances were passed restricting its numbers; its chief officers were periodically dismissed for incompetence; attempts were made, unsuccessfully, to restrict its expenditure to a fixed annual sum (*certum*); conciliar mechanisms were put in place to restrict the king's liberality, such as the Thirty-One Articles of 1406; and commissions of reform with comprehensive powers were set up, most famously in 1310 and 1386. But kings resented being told how to manage their household – in 1397, Richard II threatened anyone who did so with treason – and it was difficult to effect real change without infringing the king's sovereignty.[20]

On the fundamental question of redress of grievances for grants of supply, the Commons rarely blinked and never budged, and in the long term this ritualised exercise in reciprocity was the most important constitutional legacy of the late Middle Ages in England, forming a bulwark against absolutism. Financially, however, the fact that kings still theoretically had the right to dispose of resources as they pleased continued until the late seventeenth century to act as a brake on the development of a system of public finance. There was no permanent mechanism for public accountability, no public budgeting procedure, no public (or 'national') debt. Nevertheless, the many moving parts which ultimately contributed to the evolution of a public financial system, forged in an often charged but fundamentally stable partnership with parliament through a period of protracted war, were one of the keystones of the expanding political society – king, nobility, gentry, merchants – which lay at the heart of the late medieval and early modern English state. The formative century in this process was circa 1260 to 1360 but, despite the political upheavals, ever more frequent financial crises and declining taxation revenues of the century which followed, it proved strong enough to withstand the challenges.[21]

Notes

1. R. Stacey, *Politics, Policy and Finance under Henry III, 1216-1245* (Oxford, 1987), 43-4, 66, 87, 91, 243, 258-9; M. Prestwich, *War, Politics and Finance under Edward I* (London, 1972), 177-203; N. Fryde, *The Tyranny and Fall of Edward II* (Oxford, 1979), 88, 97-9, 102.
2. W. M. Ormrod, 'England in the Middle Ages', in *The Rise of the Fiscal State in Europe, c. 1200-1815*, ed. R. Bonney (Oxford, 1999), 19-52 (at 25); T. B. Pugh, *Henry V and the Southampton Plot of 1415* (Gloucester, 1988), 81, 86-7; G. L. Harriss, 'Financial Policy', in *Henry V: The Practice of Kingship*, ed. G. L. Harriss (Oxford, 1987), 159-79 (at 172).
3. W. M. Ormrod, *Edward III* (London, 2011), 480, calculated £30,000-£40,000 in the 1350s, but that included the 'ancient custom'; B. P. Wolffe, *Henry VI* (London, 1981), 73.
4. S. Church, *King John: England, Magna Carta and the Making of a Tyrant* (London, 2015), 143-9.
5. Stacey, *Politics, Policy and Finance*, 33-6; Prestwich, *War, Politics and Finance*, 177-203.
6. W. M. Ormrod, *The Reign of Edward III* (London, 1990), 204-7.
7. G. L. Harriss, *Shaping the Nation: England, 1360-1461* (Oxford, 2005), 58-66; Ormrod, 'England in the Middle Ages', 40, 47; C. Ross, *Edward IV* (London, 1974), 371-87.
8. C. Given-Wilson, *The Royal Household and the King's Affinity: Service, Politics and Finance in England, 1360-1413* (London, 1986), 85-9; Ormrod, *Edward III*, 373-4, 525-6; Ross, *Edward IV*, 371-87; Harriss, 'Financial Policy', 177-8; Fryde, *Tyranny and Fall*, 105.
9. Fryde, *Tyranny and Fall*, 97-8, 105; Harriss, *Shaping the Nation*, 61-4; Given-Wilson, *Royal Household*, 94; Harriss, 'Financial Policy', 173; R. Griffiths, *The Reign of King Henry VI* (Stroud, 1981), 107-27; K. Fowler, *The King's Lieutenant: Henry of Grosmont, First Duke of Lancaster, 1310-1361* (London, 1969), 136-7; *The St Albans Chronicle: The Chronica Maiora of Thomas Walsingham 1394-1422*, ed. J. Taylor, W. Childs and L. Watkiss (Oxford, 2011), 37-51.
10. Griffiths, *Henry VI*, 310-22; A. Steel, *Richard II* (Cambridge, 1941), 52-7.
11. Ormrod, 'England in the Middle Ages', 38-45; Griffiths, *Henry VI*, 376-95; J. Watts, *Henry VI and the Politics of Kingship* (Cambridge, 1996), 46-50; J. B. Henneman, 'France in the Middle Ages', in *Rise of the Fiscal State*, ed. Bonney, 101-22.
12. C. Barron, *London in the Later Middle Ages* (Oxford, 2004), 13-14.
13. J. Stratford, *Richard II and the English Royal Treasure* (Woodbridge, 2012), 3-11, 57-69, 106, 122-7.
14. Ross, *Edward IV*, 371-87.

15. Harriss, 'Financial Policy', 163–8; *Lay Taxes in England and Wales, 1188–1688*, ed. M. Jurkowski, C. Smith and D. Crook (Richmond, 1998), xlv–xlix; *St Albans Chronicle 1394–1422*, ed. Taylor, Childs and Watkiss, 60–61, 126–7.
16. Given-Wilson, *Royal Household*, 111–13; Griffiths, *Henry VI*, 310–22 (quote).
17. Ormrod, *Edward III*, 113.
18. *The Anonimalle Chronicle 1333–1381*, ed. V. H. Galbraith (Manchester, 1927), 98.
19. G. L. Harriss, *King, Parliament, and Public Finance in Medieval England to 1369* (Oxford, 1975), 470–508; Harriss, *Shaping the Nation*, 65.
20. Given-Wilson, *Royal Household*, 76–141.
21. Ormrod, *Fiscal State*, 46–7; Harriss, *King, Parliament*, 509–17.

Further Reading

Given-Wilson, C., *The Royal Household and the King's Affinity: Service, Politics and Finance in England, 1360–1413* (London, 1986).
Griffiths, R., *The Reign of King Henry VI* (Stroud, 1981), 107–27.
Harriss, G., *King, Parliament, and Public Finance in Medieval England to 1369* (Oxford, 1975).
  Shaping the Nation: England 1360–1461 (Oxford, 2005).
Lay Taxes in England and Wales, 1188–1688, ed. M. Jurkowski, C. Smith and D. Crook (Richmond, 1998).
Ormrod, W. M., 'England in the Middle Ages', in *The Rise of the Fiscal State in Europe, c. 1200–1815*, ed. R. Bonney (Oxford, 1999), 19–52.
  The Reign of Edward III (London, 1990).
Prestwich, M., *War, Politics and Finance under Edward I* (London, 1972), 177–203.
Stacey, R., *Politics, Policy and Finance under Henry III, 1216–1245* (Oxford, 1987).
Stratford, J., *Richard II and the English Royal Treasure* (Woodbridge, 2012).

ANTHONY MUSSON

6

Justice

Introduction

At his coronation the monarch swore to preserve the peace of the kingdom, maintain the laws and customs of the realm and diligently do justice to his subjects. Upholding these tenets underpinned the successful exercise of kingship. Indeed, the quality of the king's rule was frequently judged contemporaneously and historically by his record on justice. Yet, while the king did have personal input and was ultimately responsible for issuing legislative decrees and upholding law and order, operationally this was not something he could do on his own. The enormous task of day-to-day judicial administration was delegated to a mixture of trained judges, lawyers and royal officials, who worked alongside less specialised men of law, shire bureaucrats and a pool of borough merchants and county gentry. These assisted the crown by acting on a variety of local commissions and as constituency representatives in parliament. This chapter explains the nature of that law and its processes in late medieval England and examines both the structure of the legal system and the role of the legal profession. It also considers the operation of the law in areas technically outside the purview of royal justice and reflects on the problems posed by particular monarchs. Their actions (sometimes undermining the system's ideals) in turn shaped public attitudes towards justice and royal rule.

The Common Law

The English common law emerged from the knitting-together of customs and practices existing in Anglo-Saxon and Anglo-Norman times with the considerable administrative innovations occurring in the twelfth century under Henry II. As a body of rules and processes that was authorised by the king, the 'customary law of England' was intended to be applied in standard or 'common' form across the realm to guard against regionality and arbitrariness. Indeed, it was a focus on 'long user' (the duration of particular practices or the extent of time for which rights have been exercised) and the standardisation of its processes that became defining features.

The common law (and 'due process' under it) was underpinned by the writ system, which embodied the essence of the administrative innovations of the twelfth century, providing forms of action originated by a writ of right: that is, a writ available to all free subjects, that was returnable into the king's courts for a hearing of the plea at a specific time and place. The scope and wording of writs were based on frequently recurring cases. To aid litigants and their attorneys, the different types of writs were collected together and classified in registers, which effectively provide an outline of the substantive parameters of the common law in the medieval period. The number of writs or forms of action increased exponentially over time and in turn defined the rights and remedies that were available to litigants. In the early thirteenth century some fifty actions could be initiated by writ. By the start of the next century this figure had risen to 900. Further writs were added to the registers thereafter with the result that by the early sixteenth century the total number stood at 2,500. Since the defendant was given an opportunity to answer the action initiated by the writ and counter the claims, exchanges between the parties in court promoted an adversarial system. The legal principles that were developed as a result of arguments and judgements in the courts became part of the 'common learning', guarded by the judges and passed down within the legal profession. Common law could be clarified or altered by statute, a directly enforceable adjunct body of rules decreed by the sovereign, usually with the assent of the Lords and Commons in parliament.

Legal Codification

Statutory law provided a second tier to the common law. Although it frequently codified royal initiatives, legislation could also arise from single cases in the courts or as a result of petitions submitted to the crown (see 'Recourse to Extra-curial Procedures'). The extent to which in practice it was driven by the king's personal engagement as opposed to the internal logic and momentum of government is open to speculation. In practice, legal experts and other members of the king's council played a decisive role in formulating written law, but certainly by the fourteenth century, the making of legislation was influenced by the concerns of parliamentary representatives, even if these usually reflected the agenda of the privileged classes. In gauging the effect of statutory law no reign should be viewed in isolation, nor should any piece of legislation necessarily be seen as the finished product. Edward I's reign was significant for its statutes setting out the substantive law, while Edward III's witnessed a number of 'establishments' (statutes) in the areas of judicial administration and procedure that were important to contemporaries who were experiencing the law in action. Although Richard III's brief reign is remembered for its conspicuous legislative initiatives, many were reversed or adapted by Henry VII or his successors. Like the common law, legislation must adapt to society and so is rarely totally frozen in time: judges can override or attenuate its effect, while legislators may abolish it or tinker with it to suit the prevailing conditions. Labour legislation, first issued in 1349 and still being adjusted in the 1490s, is a remarkable case in point.

The introduction or preamble to a statute set out the reasoning behind the legislative action and became an increasingly important pragmatic device. By prefacing significant pieces of legislation with rhetoric that highlighted the inadequacy of the system in times past, rulers were able to point to novel solutions and thus present themselves as reformers addressing the needs of their subjects. Magna Carta, for example, begins with a justificatory preamble that uses language of correction and reform. The trend was again set by Edward I's legislation, notably the Statute of Winchester (1285), which provided a swingeing denunciation of the state of the peace – complaining that daily there were more crimes committed than formerly – and then proceeded to offer a combination of measures designed to rectify the problem. The tradition was extended and the propagandist stance utilised particularly effectively under Edward III and Richard II, during whose reigns the preambles tended to increase in length and verbosity.

The prolonged passage preceding the statute of 1378, for example, not only maintained that the 'people ... who conspire' did so without 'consideration to God, the laws of Holy Church, or of the land, or to right, or justice ... refusing and setting apart all processes of law', but stressed their actions were to the 'great mischief and grievance of the people and the hurt of the king's majesty and against the king's crown'.[1] Acknowledging the different hierarchies of law and need for due process, this preamble also unites the interests of crown and people. Preambles to numerous statutes strategically employ the discourse of amending the law for the 'common profit of the realm', suggesting the phrase had become not only standardised in form but a necessary tag in the minds of legislative draftsmen. It was a phraseology which equally gained currency outside royal circles. From the early fourteenth century it was adopted by the parliamentary Commons in petitions (particularly those relating to fiscal and economic matters), thereby demonstrating an appreciation of the textual precedents as well as asserting their moral right to speak for the welfare of the kingdom.

From 1297, a special place in the legislative canon was reserved for Magna Carta. Following Edward I's confirmation of the charters, the 'Great Charter of Liberties' was formally absorbed into the common law and, however ambiguous technically, took on the mantle of the pre-eminent statute of the realm. Magna Carta continued to receive endorsement in parliamentary legislation up to Henry VI's reign and was so embedded that a formula was included in the chancellor's (or chief justice's) opening speech to parliament until at least 1435. Confirmation of the liberties of the church 'by authority of parliament' continued into the sixteenth century, even if endorsement of the full import of Magna Carta was no longer considered necessary.

The effectiveness of royal legislation depended entirely upon its interpretation and enforcement by the courts. Texts invoking or referencing Magna Carta and statutory law (e.g. the parliament rolls, private petitions, chronicles, readings and moots of the Inns of Court together with the records of cases appearing in the law courts) provide a significant insight into the development and influence of legislation as well as evidence of its practical application. Such texts also 'help to construct discourses of royal justice and grace that both responded to a particular historical moment and continue to resonate over time'.[2]

They are invaluable sources therefore for the diversity of royal law's reception within medieval society. More particularly, they demonstrate the continued applicability of Magna Carta's chapters to a variety of legal, social and economic circumstances, though paradoxically, the Great Charter itself became less overtly visible since supplementary legislation elaborated on its substantive clauses and its principles became absorbed into the fabric of the legal system.

Court Structure

Common law was administered through the system of royal courts. Parliament stood at the apex of the judicial system, acting as a high court in addition to its legislative, fiscal and various political and constitutional responsibilities. It provided the venue for state trials, especially high-profile cases of treason or official wrongdoing; it acted as a 'court of appeal' (though not in the modern sense), receiving notice of errors made in other courts and as a forum for the resolution of difficult cases. These could be referred to it either on petition to the king in parliament by individuals or directly by the court concerned if a legislative remedy were required. In such instances the king himself might be consulted or called upon to adjudicate (see 'Recourse to Extra-curial Procedures').

At a national level there existed the *curia Regis*, though by the late thirteenth century, owing to a gradual increase in business, what had previously been an omnicompetent court had separated out responsibility for particular forms of litigation and in effect split into three distinct judicial organs. The earliest of these was the exchequer, which was concerned with financial administration. By the early thirteenth century it was accepting debt litigation from private individuals, but its jurisdiction was later curtailed and channelled into another tribunal, referred to as 'the bench' or (as it was later known) the court of common pleas. This body was responsible for a whole range of civil litigation or 'common pleas' (personal suits in which the king had no interest). The establishment of this court 'in some fixed place', in accord with Magna Carta, originally meant pleas should be heard only in established centres of royal government rather than necessarily a single permanent location, but increasingly the direction became identified with a particular site, namely Westminster Hall. This did much to enhance the court's accessibility to litigants and thus increase its judicial business. The viability of bringing actions in this forum was sustained by the fact that parties did not have to attend in person (proxies or 'attorneys' were permitted to represent plaintiffs and defendants) and by the practice of transferring cases out of Westminster to be heard (though not brought to judgement) locally.

The court of common pleas had probably the most significant impact on the development of the common law during the medieval period. This can be measured, albeit crudely, by the sheer bulk of the rolls recording its proceedings, which doubled in size over the course of the fourteenth century as a result of the volume of litigation. The voluminous official records of its proceedings, beginning in the 1190s but providing an unbroken series from the 1270s onwards, are complemented by unofficial law reports (dating from the second half of the thirteenth century) in recording the dialogue of the legal arguments. Since these were not preserved in the truncated and summarised version of proceedings in the plea rolls, they yield an insight into not only legal thinking but what actually went on and was said in the medieval courtroom.

The other superior court that emerged, the king's bench or court *coram Rege* ('before the king'), retained, as its name suggests, a particular association with the sovereign and maintained responsibility for upholding his rights at law. Although the court of common pleas initially shared some areas of jurisdiction with the court of king's bench, the latter was distinct from the former in three particular ways. First, it could not entertain common pleas but instead had special jurisdiction over criminal cases, especially treason and felony. It could also instigate actions of trespass brought not by writ but by written petition or oral bill. The court's acceptance of bill procedure enabled it to act as a court of first instance (one entertaining a complaint normally made in a lower court) when visiting the localities during the fourteenth century, usually to quell disturbances or carry out investigations in areas that required direct assertion of royal authority. Although not an appellate court in the modern sense, the king's bench was accorded a certain superiority and dignity within the judicial hierarchy by the fact it could hear cases brought on writs of error from any court of record and that cases could be removed to it for further legal discussion (by virtue of writs of *certiorari*). By the fifteenth century it was also common for cases brought before justices of the peace to be transferred into the king's bench for trial and judgement demonstrating its role as a superior criminal court.

The higher national courts were in session during the four legal terms of Michaelmas, Hilary, Easter and Trinity. Depending upon the dates of movable religious feasts, this meant a total of about four months' work a year, interspersed with three short vacations and a much longer break between early July and early October. From the late thirteenth century, during vacation periods it was usual for commissions of assize and gaol delivery to travel out to the provinces, operating on prescribed circuits of counties, ensuring that disputes concerning the 'possessory assizes' (actions relating to the possession of land) were heard and that prisoners arrested for criminal offences committed within a particular shire were tried at the corresponding local gaol. These commissions originally supplemented the work of the general eyre, which had periodically travelled the country on defined circuits of counties from the twelfth century onwards. The eyre entertained both civil and criminal cases on the basis of elaborate 'articles of the eyre', questions put to local juries. From the mid thirteenth century it had concentrated its inquiries on the usurpation of royal rights (including investigation of the warrants by which jurisdictional franchises were held by lords) and the conduct of royal and seigneurial officials. An expansion in business highlighted the limitations of the eyre, and its scrutiny of goings-on in the localities made it unpopular. Following suspension in 1294, owing to the outbreak of war with France, its visitations were never fully resumed on a countrywide basis. Instead, over the course of the early fourteenth century, the focus for complaints of trespass and breach of the king's peace, which had also been brought before the eyre justices, were channelled into peace sessions, proceedings held four times a year that were presided over by justices of the peace: a mixture of assize justices, local 'men of law' and members of landed society. At shire level, too, the county court, and below that the administrative subdivision of the hundred, provided the forum for much day-to-day civil litigation, petty criminal cases and the initial stages of more serious criminal offences reserved for the crown.

The role of the justices of the peace, the method of their appointment (often via recommendations from influential members of the church or the nobility as members of their affinity) and influence over proceedings coming before them in their quarterly sessions are often regarded as contentious. As royal judicial representatives and the principal form of local government, they had authority to hear and determine serious crimes and misdemeanours committed in their county as well as possessing an ever-expanding list of statutory powers covering both judicial and administrative matters. Often regarded as enforced in the interests of the landed classes, tasks included implementation of labour legislation, punishing participation in unlawful games and causing public nuisances (such as health hazards and blocked highways) as well as failure to maintain public amenities or engaging in poaching. Indeed, a perceived association between sedition and poaching gained traction during the fifteenth century as the latter became increasingly conflated with the networks of sedition and organised demonstrations of rebels and protesters attacking parks and warrens from the 1440s until at least the 1490s.

The size of peace commissions themselves grew exponentially from the later fourteenth century onwards, often including non-residents and honorific members. Membership was a significant status-marker, but its composition, though ideally supposed to reflect the balance of political interests within a particular shire, was frequently targeted amidst concerns about illegal retaining and the subversive practices of bastard feudalism. Comparatively few records of county sessions survive, however, making it difficult to discern which commissioners were 'active' and how dynamics were affected by divided loyalties during periods of civil war. Historians have usually underestimated the substantial number of 'men of law' amongst those appointed (in addition to the assize justices on the *quorum*) and thus confuse who was justifiably retained and overemphasise the extent to which landowning 'amateurs' dominated or manipulated proceedings.

A Plethora of Jurisdictions

Historians of English law have concentrated predominantly on the relentless expansion of royal justice and the jurisprudence of the common law. While the common law was predominant as the law of the land, other types of law and their administrative systems operated within the realm, notably the law of the forest (which stood apart from the common law in having an arbitrary element), mercantile law (a body of traders' customs applicable internationally and based on natural law principles), ecclesiastical law (canon law and diocesan decrees operating in the church courts) and customary law (underpinning the work of urban courts and the private feudal courts of the honour and the manor). As legal entities dispensing the 'custom of the manor' and setting local bye-laws, the latter were crucial in the organisation of agrarian life and society but interpreted 'custom' according to local convention and so, unlike the common law, judgements were not standardised across the realm. These territorial units were nevertheless accepted as constituent parts of the broader legal system by contemporaries for whom the advantages of their locality and specialist nature were apparent.

The legal and constitutional ramifications of private jurisdiction have been largely overlooked. Indeed, the complexity of the English judicial system and the vitality of customary law, though long recognised, have still to be satisfactorily evaluated across the Middle Ages, with the result that the jurisdiction of the local courts and their relationship with the common law courts (both central and at shire level) remain imperfectly understood. This has implications for our understanding of periods of breakdown in law and order and in the management of property disputes and relationships between communities. Although their jurisdictions were seriously eroded by the growth of the common law, the crown lacked the vision, incentive and resources to become the sole determinant of dispute settlement and there remained discrete areas both geographically and jurisdictionally that maintained their customs and judicial autonomy: notably the enclaves permitted to exercise varying degrees of authority as franchises (from palatinates and honours to liberties and boroughs).

Theoretically, the royal courts were open only to free men (and free women who were widowed or unmarried). Those who were designated unfree on account of their birth or because they were tenants of customary or servile land were barred from suing at common law and had to settle their disputes in the manor court, unless they could show they had privileges arising from their relationship with the crown as so-called tenants of 'ancient demesne'. While serfs or villeins often sought (and were occasionally awarded) emancipation by their lord, the disadvantages and restrictions that were bound up with servile tenure became burning issues that erupted during the Peasants' Revolt of 1381. Although the charters of freedom obtained by duress from the young Richard II were later cancelled and servile status continued, this could be overturned if it were proved judicially that they had been a litigant or served on a jury in the royal courts.

English courts even claimed international jurisdiction. The wars waged by the English in France led to the need for tribunals that could deal with disputes that arose on land or sea, beyond the reach of the common law, resulting in judicial bodies that both procedurally and (arguably) substantively operated in accordance with continental traditions. Invoking international principles that formed the law of the sea, the court of admiralty controlled naval discipline and regulated the supplying of ships and levying of sailors. It also handled cases of piracy and disputes concerning the capture of enemy ships and their cargoes. Although the centrally based court was the venue for and oversaw the judicial administration of a variety of shipping-related disputes, admiralty jurisdiction was also devolved to individual ports. Indeed, possession of authority to hear cases involving seafaring matters locally was a distinct administrative advantage in avoiding procedural delays but equally a privilege eagerly sought or claimed by maritime locations. Under the presidency of the constable and marshal of England, the court of chivalry heard cases that arose out of acts of war, including disputes over rights in prisoners and their ransoms as well as about rights to particular coats of arms. It also took cognisance of appeals of treason, in which battle was offered by the appellant. Perceptions of the court of chivalry as an arbitrary body were influenced by the lack of differentiation between that judicial forum and the king's council/parliament as a venue for treason trials.

Treason Trials

Westminster Hall was probably by convention the venue for state trials for treason despite the lack of a specific trial venue or procedure stated in any ordinance, though in practice hearings could be convened elsewhere as circumstances dictated. 'Treason' as espoused during the later Middle Ages depended on the prevailing ideology and style of kingship adopted. As the most heinous crime on the statute book, 'high treason' (as distinct from 'petty treason' levelled against a servant for killing his master) could be an offence directed against both the king's person and the realm in that it contemplated raising war against the king (riding with banner unfurled), counterfeiting the Great Seal and the currency and murdering high officials of state when in session. It embraced accroaching on royal power, infringement of royal rights and waging private war but more broadly included attempting to kill the monarch's consort or heir and the rape of his consort or eldest unmarried daughter or his heir's wife. Plotting treasonous acts was taken as seriously as actually carrying them out and so any alleged conspiracy 'imagining and compassing' the king's death could be brought within its ambit. The legislative basis for the crime, still the 1352 Statute of Treasons, was expanded incrementally over ensuing reigns as dictated by new fears over the safety of the king's person (owing to various forms of sedition and the use of magic arts) and to the kingdom (by undermining truces and protections and clipping or washing coins). Even after the offence was given a statutory basis, an arbitrary element remained procedurally in that a summary trial could be instigated by public repute 'on the king's record', without the need for the formalities of indictment and appeal or trial by jury. Furthermore, in addition to the legally defined crime punishable at common law, 'traitor' had a range of more general meanings, including an evildoer, an untrustworthy or malicious person, a violator of responsibilities or an oathbreaker. This conflation of meanings and the strength of accusation by public clamour often led in times of political disturbance to 'informal' retribution carried out on individuals by a dissatisfied mob.

Even though its jurisdiction was theoretically distinct, cases heard by the court of chivalry sometimes overlapped with those voiced in parliament or brought before the king's council. This confusion was not assisted by the fact that sessions of the court of chivalry frequently took place in the Painted Chamber of Westminster Palace or in the more intimate setting of the White Chamber, where the parliamentary Lords and king's council usually met. The issue was also that of trial by combat itself, a lawful procedure within the court of chivalry, but one which sometimes resulted in what have been referred to as 'slippages between knighthood and treason' in the treatment of persons of high status accused of treasonous behaviour. A blurring of the lines occurred noticeably in the Merciless Parliament of 1388, where not only was the constable, Thomas of Woodstock, one of the presiding peers but knights of the Order of the Garter, such as Sir Simon Burley, were tried for treason. This was also the case with the challenge to armed combat between Henry, duke of Hereford, and Thomas Mowbray, duke of Norfolk, which was proffered in full parliament at Shrewsbury in 1398 but deemed to be resolved 'according to the law of chivalry'.[3]

In 1399, at the start of Henry IV's reign, in the wake of continued use of its procedures for accusations of treason occurring within the realm, the court of chivalry, as opposed to parliament, was confirmed as the proper venue for treason trials and combat on appeal of treason was common during Henry VI's reign. Yet, even after the 1399 statute ought to have made things more distinct, there was clearly some overlap. For example, peers in parliament heard the tenor of the case against Henry Percy, earl of Northumberland, and Thomas, Lord Bardolf, for their part in the uprising of May–June 1405 even though it was already in progress in the court of chivalry. Since it was declared that this case seemed to be one of treason and that the correct procedure should be followed, the latter's procedure was then resumed and both men were summoned to appear to answer the charges. Since neither nobleman appeared, they were later judged to be traitors *in absentia* in the parliament of December 1406.

The politically charged nature of the offence can be seen in the closely related procedures of impeachment and attainder but also in the treatment of high-profile figures (such as Andrew Harclay, Thomas of Lancaster and the Despensers) in the 1320s and in the large number of cases appearing between the 1460s and the 1480s (during the Wars of the Roses) where harsh punishments were meted out to those Yorkists or Lancastrians deemed traitorous. Overseen directly by members of the king's council, cases were frequently delegated to commissions of oyer and terminer comprising a mixture of high-ranking courtiers and lawyers. Their proceedings, however, though flexible, were not as novel and unacceptable as made out by partisan contemporary chroniclers and even some modern historians. These tribunals might be charged to try the case 'summarily and plainly without noise and show of judgment on simple inspection of fact',[4] yet provided it was not a time of peace they were not 'unconstitutional' if they followed the accepted legal formulas of the court of chivalry and the law of arms. Moreover, the occasion of summary adjudication itself allowed for the king to alter his stance and magnanimously exercise his prerogative of mercy, as Edward IV did in 1465 when a young esquire was found guilty of fighting within Westminster Palace. Equally, although Edward may not have been quite so merciful in the aftermath of the battles of Barnet and Tewkesbury (1471), an occasion when he made examples of traitorous nobility and gentry alike, insurgents in other contexts could at least be given an alternative: face financial ruin through the imposition of a substantial fine rather than face a gruesome death and the forfeiture of lands and goods that befell a traitor.

Recourse to Extra-curial Procedures

Despite the precociousness of English royal justice, litigants found that certain matters could not satisfactorily be resolved at common law, either because there was as yet no remedy available, or on account of the difficult issues of procedure or substantive law involved, or because justice had been denied, or it was feared the circumstances were such that it could not reasonably be obtained. Methods of dispute resolution other than formal adjudication are now recognised by historians as part of a continuum of complementary judicial remedies. Both parliament and the courts fostered arbitration and mediation where appropriate. Indeed, negotiation and private treaties were actively encouraged to settle disagreements among the gentry and nobility and were also widely employed by merchants as a means of achieving compromise in commercial disputes. Far from being mutually exclusive resorts, a willingness to combine litigation and arbitration as part of a coherent strategy is a significant feature of this period. In carrying out negotiations and reaching mediation, judges and lawyers usually played as significant a role as they did in the processes of formal court pleadings and adjudication.

Matters could also be referred directly to the king in parliament or to the king's council (the inner circle of ministers and judges who undertook the routine work of government) by means of written petition requesting the king's 'grace', or in other words, the exercise of his royal discretion. From around the mid fourteenth century petitions in a similar vein (particularly with regard to 'uses', the holding of land by a group of feoffees on trust for the benefit of another) began to be addressed to the chancellor, extending the jurisdiction of the chancery from being largely an administrative body, issuing instructions and dealing with common law judicial process, to become a 'court of conscience', thereby dispensing royal grace and exercising an equitable jurisdiction. Remedying situations for which there was no existing recourse or which the common law was prevented by its own strictures from adequately redressing, the court of chancery (as it became known), essentially existed outside of the common law both jurisdictionally and procedurally. By the late fifteenth century supplications were being made to the sovereign's court of requests, which was specifically intended to provide inexpensive justice for poor people.

Procedure by bill originated in the thirteenth-century general eyre as a way of encouraging less affluent litigants by circumventing the need for the legal and linguistic formalities of a writ. Bills/petitions usually had input from 'men of law' or scriveners and could be formulated with an eye on future litigation. Yet the format enabled individuals to couch their grievance on their own terms, which if the complaint did not fit within the spectrum of common law remedies meant pushing conceptual boundaries. In many instances the focus was access to justice, either through unnecessary delays, the costs involved, evidential difficulties, conflicts in jurisdiction (often between the customary and common law courts or the ecclesiastical ones) or as a result of feared or actual intimidation. While their substance should not necessarily be taken wholly at face value, they demonstrate an important means of voicing complaint and achieving redress. Equally, in terms of perceptions of royal justice, it is significant how the rhetoric of petitioners sometimes reveals a desire to link their purely personal interest in ensuring their individual 'droit' (right) is upheld with a more extensive concern for maintenance of the sovereign's rights and duties in respect of the welfare of the realm and for safeguarding the common course of the law 'in salvation of the royal jurisdiction of the king'.[5]

Legal Profession

The peculiar development of the common law rested largely on the rise of a distinct legal profession. Unlike their continental counterparts, English common lawyers of the later medieval period did not derive their legal education from attendance at one of the two universities (Oxford and Cambridge). From the late thirteenth century onwards judges and advocates in the higher courts were predominantly laymen, and although some were familiar with aspects of Roman law and ecclesiastical law, they were no longer truly versed in the 'learned laws'. Their sense of identity and professional standing was increasingly underpinned by legal education in England's 'third university'. This was primarily a practical, skills-based, 'on-the-job' form of training, for which the provision made for education in the Inns of Court (and for the secretariat, the Inns of Chancery), situated equidistant between Westminster and the city of London, came to be highly significant as a marker of professional status and of the common law tradition itself. Lectures ('readings') and mooting took place in the hall after the communal dinner. Their vocational exercises were complex, often extensive, problems involving oral pleadings rather than points of law, intended to imitate real cases as if the participants were acting in the court of common pleas. Education in the common law therefore was less formal and more practically oriented than could be gained at university. This distinguished them not only from lawyers practising in the ecclesiastical courts but also from the majority of the secretariat, who at least until the early fifteenth century were university-educated members of the clergy and hence imbued with a very different legal tradition, which left its mark on the procedures of the developing prerogative courts of chancery, chivalry and admiralty.

The English legal profession (versed in the common law as distinct from the continental *ius commune* tradition of canon law and Roman civil law) witnessed both the development of its own identity as a body of practitioners (with its own distinctive costume, rules of conduct and avenues of promotion) and an expansion of the profession itself. The intense litigiousness of medieval society fuelled a demand for legal advice, advocacy assistance and the drafting of legal instruments, which in turn offered the burgeoning profession ample opportunities for employment in various capacities and at differing levels. The emergence of a cadre of senior judges, specialist pleaders and attorneys focused mainly on the central royal courts was complemented by a corresponding body of 'men of law' based in the provinces. Developments within the judicial system and 'consumer demand' thus had a significant effect on the profession in terms of its recruitment and in formation of its identity.

Advances in the provision of legal education and training in the common law, together with a corresponding demand for professional literature covering substantive law and procedure, marked it out as a book-learned profession at every level. In addition to formal lectures and practical learning exercises for those who attended the nascent Inns of Court and Chancery, legal knowledge and private reference was aided by treatises by senior judges and lawyers on various jurisprudential topics and manuals providing precedents on modes of pleading or bringing an action in court. In addition to practitioner treatises by royal justices (such as the thirteenth-century *On the Laws and Customs of England* attributed to Henry de Bracton and Sir Thomas Littleton's late fifteenth-century land law compilation *New Tenures*),[6] Sir John Fortescue's writings *On the Law and Governance of England* and *In Praise of the Laws of England* were particularly influential not just in legal circles but in contemporary political thought.[7]

The legal profession (strictly defined) was not the only 'consumer' of legal literature. Concomitant with a more documentary culture and in line with expanding levels of literacy, a pragmatic desire for legal knowledge took hold amongst non-lawyers, fostered by a mixture of litigiousness, growing familiarity with record-keeping and increasing participation in the proliferating court system. Informal instruction by word of mouth and practical experience was supplemented by handbooks on how to hold local courts and manage estates as well as templates for potential administrative and judicial encounters. Some literature even catered for women who required assistance in managing their estates in their husband's absence. An awareness of significant statutes and current legislation was particularly crucial for landowners serving as justices of the peace, while locating the correct legal remedy was also paramount. From the marginal annotations and indications of ownership, it is clear that consumers of this legal literature included public officials, male and female lay landowners, merchants, estate stewards, ecclesiastical corporations and urban corporations (in addition to lawyers) and they were clearly genuinely used for the purposes for which they were compiled.

The King's Personal Role in Justice

The monarch's responsibility for justice was eloquently symbolised in the two images on the obverse and reverse respectively of the Great Seal: the sovereign enthroned in majesty bearing the sword of justice; and as a knightly warrior on horseback with shield in one hand and outstretched sword in the other. This image highlights the monarch's constitutional proprieties, which were set out in his coronation oath and embodied his personal obligations to the realm. He undertook to the best of his ability to preserve peace and concord for the sake of God's church, clergy and people, maintain, defend and uphold 'the just laws and customs which the people shall have chosen' and 'in all your judgments see that right and impartial justice is done in mercy and truth'.[8] It was a potent image that echoed the Roman law maxim: 'clothed with arms; armed with laws' and accompanied the execution of royal commands.

The conventions of medieval administrative kingship meant that although the king was, in theory, the fount of justice, in actual practice he delegated trials to the professional judiciary and only occasionally intervened in a case or sat in his court in person. The king's personal involvement in justice was nevertheless still a historical reality, with extant evidence for judicial interventions of varying types though, as one might expect, any such involvement was usually to enhance law enforcement drives and give royal attention to serious offences or disputes involving high-status parties. Edward I, for example, was said to have intervened in person in several disputes, including a case in the court of king's bench and one heard in parliament involving the countess of Aumale. A 'hands-on' approach to the exercise of justice was adopted when the circumstances dictated, especially when the king was in the vicinity and wrongdoing was brought to his attention. At various points during his reign Edward II summoned into his presence knights and others alleged to have behaved traitorously and disloyally and dealt directly with them himself or sent them to be tried in the courts. While on campaign in France, Henry V ordered the hanging of a soldier who was alleged to have stolen a gold pyx from a nearby church during an interdict of peace. In civil matters, Henry was also not averse to using coercion to induce parties to compromise, reportedly telling two knights whom he had summoned to Windsor that he expected agreement by the time he had eaten his oysters or they would be hanged.

The granting of a royal pardon for serious offences and serial offending as well as letters of protection reveals tensions inherent in the judicial system. On one hand, it highlights the power of the royal prerogative of clemency and how the reputation of the king as a just arbiter rested on how effectively he dealt with difficult cases. On the other, the comparative ease of obtaining a pardon or 'grith' (protection) was perceived as making a mockery of the law and undermining law enforcement. The king could be petitioned for pardon by an individual after a serious offence had been committed, but equally such pardons were eagerly sought (following payment of a fee) as a form of insurance against conviction. Although the crown periodically agreed to statutory limitations on pardons, no monarch seems to have felt constrained by them and it remained a live issue in parliamentary debates into the fifteenth century.

For those unable to make the journey to London or Westminster, the king's itinerary around the country provided an opportunity for the monarch to be seen and his personal presence felt in the regions. Sessions of the court of king's bench normally coincided with his visits to a particular location. By the thirteenth century, however, it was a legal fiction that proceedings were actually held in the king's presence. From the late thirteenth century to the 1360s the court was stationed at York or convened in a provincial centre (such as Lincoln, Nottingham, Norwich or Carlisle), irrespective of the king's whereabouts, and from the late fourteenth century onwards it mostly remained at Westminster with occasional sojourns such as to Shrewsbury in 1413. The king's visibility nevertheless remained a potent factor as he continued to visit various regional royal residences on his progresses. The monarch's accessibility to petitioners seeking justice was noticeably enhanced in the late fifteenth century when informal complaints from a broad spectrum of people were channelled through the court of requests, a judicial committee which travelled around with the king when visiting the shires. While it had its antecedents in the informal justice-giving of previous monarchs, the acceptance of 'requests' in this manner was instituted under the much-maligned Richard III, who openly invited petitions from his subjects when away from the capital and who by late 1483 was celebrated for the fact that many 'a poor man that suffred wrong [was] relevyd and helpyd by hym and his commands in his progresse'.[9] It is unlikely that the king dealt with all 'requests' personally, but he may at least have been in the vicinity, thereby giving the appearance of dispensing equitable jurisdiction.

The balance between order and disorder was very much dependent upon the king's unchallenged authority and noticeably deteriorated when his reputation as an impartial provider of justice was called into question by serious lawlessness and armed revolt (as in the cases of Edward II and Henry VI). Confidence in the system was therefore closely connected to the whereabouts of the monarch and his own personal involvement in justice. Law enforcement initiatives, particularly those led by the itinerant court of king's bench to target specific regional trouble spots (as in 1323 and 1413), reflect the continued notion that 'the king's actual physical presence in a defined spatial context could still provide a very important determinant to the operation of justice'.[10] Edward III explicitly commanded that those charged as a result of the 1332 royal commissions investigating serious crimes (especially those alleged to have been committed by the outlawed Folvilles and Coterels, criminal gentry who had murdered one royal judge, Roger Beler, in 1326 and kidnapped the chief justice of king's bench, Richard Willoughby, in 1332) were to be arrested and brought to Nottingham Castle. The king also personally presided over court sessions held under these commissions at Stamford later that year. Edward IV, similarly, took a personal interest in judicial matters, supervising treason proceedings against various individuals in 1461, 1468 and 1474 and undertaking judicial progresses with the two chief justices during the 1460s and 1470s.

As well as his physical presence and visibility to his subjects, it was considered important to have access to the sovereign or be able to approach him indirectly through the mediation of his queen (see Chapter 9). Indeed, queenly intercession was a strategic and often powerful means of influencing matters of justice and mercy in a political context. While some of these instances are anecdotal, purely ceremonial or stage-managed interventions (as with Queen Philippa's in 1347 and Queen Anne of Bohemia's public displays in 1384 and 1392), the actions of contemporaries in their continued routine submission of private petitions for the king's or queen's grace embody the strongly held belief in the efficacy of their personal intervention. This further underlines the notion that while such petitions could be delivered at a session of parliament, supplication to the king or queen personally either by way of an audience or via the written word was perhaps a more effective way of communicating their personal issues and obtaining justice. Indeed, the desire on the part of the rebels participating in Jack Cade's rebellion in 1450 to have free access to the king in order to seek justice ('every man might have his due by coming in due time to [the king] to ask justice or grace as the cause requires')[11] suggests this perception of the king as the fount of justice still remained a deep-seated one in the mid fifteenth century.

Conclusion

The judicial ideals of accessibility, impartiality and efficiency enshrined in Magna Carta were supported by a growing cadre of professionals 'learned in the law' operating within the framework of an ever-evolving common law and national court system. The judicial hub at Westminster theoretically provided certainty and due process while the accessibility of royal justice regionally through the advent of the assizes and peace commissions was enhanced by its personal coordination and dispensation by the king when in the provinces. Yet the precociousness and reach of royal justice was nevertheless tempered by factors that highlight the complexity of the picture. The system, its processes and personnel were inevitably affected by the personal qualities, abilities and inclinations of the king. Moreover, the king's courts only formed part of a judicial continuum, which included multifarious overlapping jurisdictions and informal or extra-curial methods of dispute resolution. Finally, despite all its real advances, the judicial system was (and remains) subject to the court of public opinion: a combination of perceptions and attitudes fuelled by anecdote and rumour, heightened expectations and unfortunate experiences.

Notes

1. *SR*, II, 9–10.
2. P. Brand, 'Edward I and Justice', in *La culture judiciaire anglaise au Moyen Âge*, ed. Y. Mausen (Paris, 2017), 118–22.
3. *PROME*, parliament of September 1397 (pt. 2), item 11.
4. L. W. V. Harcourt, *His Grace the Steward and Trial of Peers* (London, 1907), 409–10.
5. TNA, SC 8/20/985.
6. *The Formation and Transmission of Western Legal Culture: 150 Books That Made the Law in the Age of Printing*, ed. S. Dauchy, G. Martyn, A. Musson, H. Pihlajamaki and A. Wijfels (Berlin, 2016), 31–3, 55–7.
7. Sir John Fortescue, *On the Laws and Governance of England*, ed. S. Lockwood (Cambridge, 1997).
8. *PROME*, parliament of October 1399 (pt. 1), item 17.
9. *Christ Church Letters: A Volume of Medieval Letters Relating to the Affairs of the Priory of Christ Church Canterbury*, ed. J. B. Sheppard, Camden Society, New Series 19 (London, 1809), 46.
10. W. M. Ormrod, 'Law in the Landscape: Criminality, Outlawry and Regional Identity in Late Medieval England', in *Boundaries of the Law: Geography, Gender and Jurisdiction in Medieval and Early Modern Europe*, ed. A. Musson (Aldershot, 2005), 7–20 (at 9).
11. *Historical Manuscripts Commission*, 8th Report, appendix, 266.

Further Reading

Brand, P., *Origins of the English Legal Profession* (London, 1992).

Butler, S. M., 'Even a Compensation Culture Has Its Limits', *Journal of Legal History* 44 (2023), 127–58.

Dodd, G., *Justice and Grace: Private Petitioning and the English Parliament in the Late Middle Ages* (Oxford, 2007).

Harding, A., *Medieval Law and the Foundations of the State* (Oxford, 2002).

Haskett, T., 'The Medieval English Court of Chancery', *Law and History Review* 14 (1996), 245–313.

Hyams, P. R., *Rancor and Reconciliation in Medieval England* (Ithaca, NY, 2003).

Johnson, T., *Law in Common: Legal Cultures in Late-Medieval England* (Oxford, 2020).

Lacey, H., *The Royal Pardon: Access to Mercy in Fourteenth-Century England* (York, 2009).

McKelvie, G., *Bastard Feudalism, English Society and the Law: The Statutes of Livery, 1390–1520* (Woodbridge, 2020).

Musson, A., *Medieval Law in Context: The Growth of Legal Consciousness from Magna Carta to the Peasants' Revolt* (Manchester, 2001).

Musson, A., with E. Powell, *Crime, Law and Society in the Later Middle Ages* (Manchester, 2009).

Musson, A. and Ormrod, W. M., *The Evolution of English Justice: Law, Politics and Society in the Fourteenth Century* (Basingstoke, 1999).

Ormrod, W. M., 'The Use of English: Law, Language and Political Culture in Late Medieval England', *Speculum* 78 (2003), 750–87.

Powell, E., *Kingship, Law and Society: Criminal Justice in the Reign of Henry V* (Oxford, 1987).

Summerson, H., 'Attitudes to Capital Punishment in England, 1200–1350', in *Thirteenth Century England VIII*, ed. M. Prestwich, R. Britnell and R. Frame (Woodbridge, 2001), 123–32.

ANDY KING

7

Warfare and Chivalry

Kingship and Knighthood

> Oh ye knights of England where is the custom and usage of noble chivalry that was used in those days, what do you now, but go to the brothels and play at dice?[1]

So wrote William Caxton in an epilogue to *The Book of the Ordre of Chyualry*, published in 1484, the year following Richard III's usurpation of the throne. The book was an English translation of a French text of Ramon Llull's Catalan original, but Caxton's epilogue was his own addition, bemoaning the current debased state of English chivalry. Exhorting his readers to peruse the 'noble volumes' recording the deeds of 'that noble king of Britain king Arthur' and his Knights of the Round Table (in which volumes he had a certain vested interest, as a printer of Arthurian literature), he further directed them to consider the deeds of 'king Richard Coeur de Lion, Edward the first, and the third, and his noble sons' and 'that victorious and noble king Harry the fifth, and the captains under him, his noble brothers', along with other English captains 'whose names shine gloriously by their virtuous nobility and acts that they did in honour of the order of chivalry'.

Chivalry, the martial ethos of knighthood, with its emphasis on honour and prowess, shaped contemporary perceptions of the proper conduct of war; and war – properly conducted – was a key component of medieval kingship. Writing during Edward II's reign, the author of the *Vita Edwardi Secundi* quoted a letter sent to the king's confessor (and presumably circulated more widely): 'a king is so styled from the fact of ruling, as one who should rule his people with laws and defend them with his sword from their enemies'.[2] This summed up a commonplace view of kingship, a duality reflected in the iconography of the kings of England: since the reign of William the Conqueror, the Great Seal had depicted the king enthroned in majesty on the front (Figure 16.15); and on the reverse, armed, mounted on a charging warhorse, wielding a sword – the very image of chivalric knighthood. And the Great Seal was (apart from the coinage) one of the most widely distributed images of the king in the realm. It is then entirely fitting that Caxton's principal exemplars of chivalry should be kings.

Penning a literary portrait of Edward I shortly after his reign, the chronicler Nicholas Trevet highlighted the link between kingship and knighthood, commenting that:

> He was a man of proven judgement in conducting business, and dedicated to the practice of arms from adolescence, through which he had gained for himself a reputation for knighthood far surpassing all the other rulers of his time across Christendom.[3]

A century later, in a brief verse history of the kings of England, the poet John Lydgate summed up Henry V as 'of knighthood [the] lodestar'.[4] And in 1472, a similar link between knighthood and kingship was made in the text of a grant of taxation in parliament, when the Commons lauded Edward IV's intention to set out 'in your princely and knightly courage ... to resist the said malice conspired by your and our said enemies'.[5] Caxton's roll call of chivalric honour made no distinction between kingship and knighthood; the qualities of bravery, prowess and prudence were held to be paramount for both knights and kings. And, of course, every king *was* a knight.

Knightly qualities of prowess and bravery on the battlefield were lauded even in kings who were otherwise held to be tyrannical or inept (or both). Thus, a St Albans chronicler commented that at Bannockburn in 1314, Edward II had fought like a lion, 'and, like a spirited knight, spilled the blood of many with his brandished sword', before being reluctantly dragged away from the battlefield by his bodyguards.[6] Similarly, while the contemporary historian John Rous compared the reign of Richard III to that of no less than the Antichrist, he had still felt compelled to add:

> For all that, let me say the truth to his credit: that he bore himself like a noble soldier and despite his little body and feeble strength, honourably defended himself to his last breath.[7]

Kings at War

Virtually all of the kings of late medieval England personally led armies in the field, albeit some more frequently, and indeed more successfully, than others. Henry III was by temperament a comparatively pacific king who did not relish campaigning, and was not particularly good at it; nevertheless, over the course of his fifty-six-year reign, he campaigned in Wales, in 1228, 1241, 1245 and 1257; led expeditions to Poitou, in 1230 and 1242; and twice led armies against English rebels: Richard Marshal in 1233 and Simon de Montfort in 1264, the latter of which ended disastrously in defeat at the battle of Lewes. By contrast, his son, Edward I, was particularly warlike, conquering Wales in two campaigns in 1276–7 and 1282–3 and putting down a rebellion there in 1294–5. He conquered Scotland in 1296 and led an army to Flanders in 1297. He had to lead another army to Scotland in 1298, winning a victory at the battle of Falkirk, before reconquering Scotland between 1300 and 1304. He led yet another expedition there after Robert Bruce's rising of 1306 and died on the Scottish border at the head of his army in 1307, at the age of sixty-eight.

Edward II led armies to Scotland in 1310–11; again in 1314, when he was catastrophically defeated at Bannockburn; in 1319, when he failed to recapture Berwick; and in 1322, when he was nearly captured by the Scots on his way back south. His only successful military endeavour was the campaign he led against his own subjects in the civil conflict of 1321–2. In 1327, at the age of fourteen, Edward III was nominally in command of Roger Mortimer's Weardale campaign against the Scots, which ended in ignominy. He personally commanded a rather more successful expedition in 1333, winning a resounding victory over the Scots at Halidon Hill, and he led armies to Scotland in 1335, 1336 and again in 1341. He led an army to Flanders in 1338–40, winning a naval battle at Sluys; and invaded France in 1346–7, winning the battle of

Crécy. He personally defeated a French attempt to recapture Calais in 1349, won another naval victory at Winchelsea in 1350 and led expeditions to France and Scotland in 1355–6 and another expedition to France in 1359–60.

Coming to the throne at the age of ten, Richard II was much less militarily active but still led armies to Scotland in 1385 and to Ireland in 1394–5 and 1399. Henry IV seized the throne by force of arms in 1399 and led an expedition to Scotland in 1400. He led expeditions against Welsh rebels led by Owain Glyn Dŵr and against English rebels led by Henry Percy, defeating the latter at the hard-fought battle of Shrewsbury in 1403. He led an army to the Anglo-Scottish Marches in 1405 to put down another rebellion, but his military career was then curtailed by chronic ill health. His son, Henry V, renewed the war with France in 1415, winning the battle of Agincourt; thereafter, he campaigned relentlessly in France, spending more of his reign there than in England. Edward IV also seized the throne by force of arms in 1460–1, fighting battles at Northampton, Mortimer's Cross and Towton; and he had to repeat the exercise in 1471, fighting battles at Barnet and Tewkesbury. He did lead an expedition to France in 1475, but he was bought off after a short campaign. Richard III reigned too briefly and insecurely to lead armies abroad; he had, however, gained a reputation for martial deeds during his brother Edward's reign, campaigning successfully against the Scots and recapturing Berwick. And as king, Richard died fighting on the battlefield at Bosworth, defending his right against a rival claimant to the throne.

The exception to this long catalogue of hardy military endeavour was Henry VI. The only time he campaigned in France was at the tender age of ten, when he was taken on a military expedition which ended with his coronation as king of France at Paris in 1431. He did lead an expedition against the Scots in 1448 but only got as far as Durham, framing the exercise as a pilgrimage to St Cuthbert. He was present at a number of battles in the civil war of 1459–61, but more in body than in mind, and he played no significant part in any of them.

Kingship and Martial Prowess

Success on the battlefield was the key to a chivalric reputation. The *Book of Chivalry*, written in the early 1350s by the renowned French knight

Sir Geoffroi de Charny, a councillor of Philip VI and John II, included the often repeated refrain: 'He who does best is most worthy.'[8] Edward I, Edward III and Henry V, the kings singled out by Caxton in 1484, all personally led armies to victory in battle, at Falkirk; Halidon Hill, Sluys and Crécy; and Agincourt respectively. And victory in battle was a signal mark of God's favour, and therefore prima facie evidence of the justness of their cause. Notably, these were victories over national enemies rather than the victories against English rebels won by Henry IV at Shrewsbury in 1403 and Edward IV at Towton in 1461. Kings did not gain the same honour and prestige from defeating their own rebellious subjects as they did from the defeat of national enemies – not least because from the reigns of Edward I and II, taking up arms against the king was, from the crown's point of view, held to be fundamentally illicit; and so civil conflicts (or 'internal' or 'inward' conflicts, as they were referred to by contemporaries) came to be framed by the crown not as war but as the suppression of treason.[9]

A king's prowess on the battlefield against his own subjects might well be described in admiring terms by contemporary commentators; thus, the *Historie of the Arrivall of Edward IV* described how Edward, fighting the Lancastrians at the battle of Barnet, 'manly, vigorously and valiantly assailed them in the midst and strongest of their battle, where he, with great violence beat and bore down before him all that stood in his way ... so that nothing might stand in the sight of him'.[10] However, the *Arrivall* was written to justify Edward's actions; and royal victories in internal wars frequently provoked a more ambiguous response, as some commentators (and their readers) might sympathise with the rebels. Thus the *Brut Chronicle*, describing the routing of Edward II's opponents at Boroughbridge in 1322 (though Edward was not himself present), lamented: 'Alas, what shameful dishonour the noble order of knighthood received at this defeat.'[11]

Internal war was – self-evidently – divisive; yet 'outward war', against the king's external enemies, was seen as a means of bringing the realm together, especially when led by the king himself. Armies for expeditions led by the king were usually recruited on a massive scale, substantially larger than for those not led by the king in person, and constituted some of the largest forces recruited in Britain before the period of the seventeenth-century civil wars. They thus amounted to some of the biggest gatherings of the king's subjects in this period, brought together from across the realm (and indeed, from across all of his dominions; royal armies frequently included forces raised from Wales, and sometimes from Ireland and Gascony, and, after 1417, from northern France). When Edward I besieged Caerlaverock Castle in Dumfriesshire for a week, in 1300, the siege camp accommodating his army of perhaps 11,000 men, plus numerous camp followers, would have been – however briefly – one of the largest settlements in the British Isles. Even after repeated outbreaks of plague had decimated the population, Richard II led some 13,500 men into Scotland in 1385; Henry IV about 13,000 to Scotland in 1400; Henry V around 12,000 to France in 1415; and Edward IV 13,000 to France again in 1475. These armies provided a point of personal contact between the king and his subjects. For many men recruited in areas remote from the centres of royal power, such as Devon and Cornwall in the south-west, Lancashire and Derbyshire in the north-west, and Wales, such occasions may well have been the only time they ever set eyes on their king.

A speech in parliament in 1472, justifying Edward IV's proposed expedition to France, referred back to the 'trouble this realm has suffered' (an obvious, if euphemistic, reference to the internal conflicts of the previous years), deploring 'many a great sore, many a perilous wound left unhealed', exacerbated by the crimes committed by 'idle and misruled persons' who were perpetuating these divisions.[12] The most honourable and expedient solution was to employ these persons in 'outward war' under the guidance of the king, for – it was claimed – it was evident from history that there had been justice, peace and prosperity in England only when its kings made outward war. This was an unusually explicit appeal to the notion of external war as a means of unifying the nation behind its king after a period of internal conflict; but similar thinking probably influenced Henry IV when he invaded Scotland in 1400, after usurping the English crown in 1399; and probably also Henry V's decision to go to war with France in 1415, after succeeding as the son of an usurper in 1413. And since the reign of Edward I, kings of England had regularly recruited large numbers of criminals and troublemakers for military service in exchange for pardons, which did at least have the practical value of removing them from their localities for a while.[13]

Failure in war, however, was liable to have direct, and sometimes dire, political consequences for kings. The failure of Henry III's campaigns against Llywelyn ap Gruffydd was one of the factors leading to the overthrow of his government in 1258, sparking a protracted political crisis which culminated in the Barons' War of 1264–5. And Edward II's authority was so undermined by the disastrous defeat at Bannockburn that over the following two years he was forced effectively to cede control of his own government to his cousin – and bitter opponent – Thomas, earl of Lancaster (though in the event, Lancaster proved so politically inept that Edward was able to wrest control back again). In 1327, the third of six 'articles of accusation' justifying Edward's deposition referred specifically to his martial failings: 'Also, through lack of good government he has lost the realm of Scotland and other lands and lordships in Gascony and Ireland, which his father left him in peace.'[14] The failures of Richard II's government against the French and the Scots, and in particular the threat of a French invasion of England in 1386, led to the impeachment in parliament of Richard's chancellor, Michael de la Pole; and this provided the opportunity for the Appellants (a faction of noblemen opposed to the king) to seize effective control of the government the following year.

Nevertheless, despite some initial successes, the Appellant regime proved no more successful in war, and they were discredited in turn by the defeat in battle inflicted by the Scots at Otterburn in Northumberland in 1388, enabling Richard to reassert his authority. Similarly, the collapse of English rule in Normandy in 1449–50 immediately provoked a fierce political reaction in England. Even before the last English garrison had surrendered, the leader of Henry VI's government, William de la Pole, duke of Suffolk, had been banished, and then murdered on his way into exile. On a more personal level, the defeat of an English expedition at Castillon in July 1453, leaving Calais as the only English holding in France, may have helped to bring on Henry's mental collapse in August, precipitating the chain of events which led to the Wars of the Roses, and the loss of his throne.

Criticisms of a king's lack of martial bearing could penetrate every level of society. Shortly after Bannockburn, Robert le Messager, one of the king's messengers, held forth to the villagers of Newington in Kent, explaining how the king had lost the battle because, instead of hearing

Mass, 'he wasted time busying himself with making ditches, and digging, and other unbecoming things'.[15] And perceptions of military failure among the wider population could have serious political consequences: high tax demands to pay for a very visibly failing war effort sparked the Peasants' Revolt of 1381, while defeat in France in 1450 was the catalyst for John Cade's rebellion, a large-scale popular rising in the south-east which broke out even as the defeat was unfolding.

Imperatives for War

According to contemporary religious and political theory, no Christian king should fight a war of aggression, but only a just war: that is, wars to defend against aggression or wars to recover lands or rights which had been unjustly taken or withheld. From a dynastic viewpoint – a viewpoint shared by the entire landowning classes – there was a strong social imperative to ensure that the crown inheritance was passed on to the next generation whole and entirely unimpaired. But the kingship of England came with hereditary lands in France and claims to overlordship in Britain. The dynastic and chivalric imperatives to preserve the lands and rights of the crown, and to recover those which were lost, so preserving the crown's honour, thus impelled successive kings into long-running conflicts with France and Scotland which they lacked the resources to win.

The kings of England were also the dukes of Aquitaine; and under the terms of the treaty of Paris in 1259, Henry III had agreed that he and his heirs would do homage for the duchy to the kings of France. A series of disputes over the exercise of the French kings' overlordship of Aquitaine followed; when the duchy was declared forfeit by the French, in 1294, again in 1324, and once again in 1337, this was, from the viewpoint of the kings of England (in their capacity as dukes of Aquitaine), a wrongful seizure of their lands.[16] The respective wars which followed were therefore clearly just wars – though just to be sure, the threat to England was emphasised; both Edward I and Edward III claimed that the French were bent on eradicating the English language.[17] Conversely, the kings of England had long claimed to be the overlords of Scotland; and in 1292, Edward I had obtained the unequivocal homage of John Balliol, king of Scots, for his kingdom.

From the point of view of the English, this created a cast-iron precedent – a precedent which Edward took great care to record, bolstering his case with additional precedents from British history (or at least, a version of British history derived from Geoffrey of Monmouth's immensely influential, but largely fictional, *History of the Kings of Britain*). The overlordship of Scotland was thus cast as an integral part of the rights of the English crown; and so any war to enforce that overlordship was, from the viewpoint of the king England, *ipso facto* a just war.[18]

In 1340, at Ghent, Edward III transformed English claims in France, formally proclaiming his right to the French kingship, as the rightful heir through his mother Isabella, daughter of Philip IV, king of France (r. 1285–1314). He may have been driven at least in part by the need to provide a legal basis for the men of Flanders to come into his allegiance without breaking their allegiance to the French crown. Nevertheless, he emphasised that the claim had 'devolved upon us divine disposition', and that he was taking up the rule of France 'lest we should seem to neglect our right the gift of heavenly grace, or to be unwilling to conform the force of our will to the divine pleasure'.[19] In other words, Edward (or his advisors) argued that it was his Christian duty to wage war to pursue a claim that had descended to him by God's providence.[20] Similarly, in 1414, when Henry V justified his war plans to parliament, saying that he would 'strive for the recovery of the inheritance and right of his crown outside the realm, which has for a long time been withheld and wrongfully retained', he cited the authority of the Bible that 'unto death shalt thou strive for justice' (Ecclesiasticus 4:33).[21] Indeed, it was a common feature of the preparation for a royal expedition for the king to order his bishops to have prayers for its success to be recited in churches throughout their dioceses – a process aided by the fact that many of the bishops were also ministers (or ex-ministers) in the king's government, and so were (or had been) personally involved in the administration of the king's wars.[22] These prayers served to publicise the king's campaigning and were usually couched in terms which demonstrated that the war was indeed just.

But once such claims had been established in so definitive a manner, it was very difficult to abandon them. In 1328, in the aftermath of the failed Weardale campaign, the young Edward III reluctantly agreed a treaty with Scotland in 1328 (i.e. the treaty of Northampton/ Edinburgh), abandoning his claims to overlordship and recognising Robert Bruce as a sovereign ruler. Yet, despite the background of years of abject military failure, during which northern England had been subject to a series of devastating invasions, the treaty was widely denounced as a 'shameful peace'.[23] Such concessions were problematic even (or perhaps especially) for a king as successful as Edward III, whose cause had been vindicated by God-given victories at Sluys, Crécy and Poitiers. The treaty of Brétigny, in 1360, gave Edward full sovereignty over an enlarged duchy of Aquitaine in return for renouncing his claim to the kingship of France. The status of Aquitaine had been a continual cause of conflict between England and France, and the treaty promised to solve the issue entirely in Edward's favour. Yet, in a society that had now become highly militarised, some of his subjects, buoyed by the astounding martial feats achieved by English arms, regarded this as a dereliction of his duty. Under the treaty's terms, English captains were ordered to surrender to the king of France towns and castles which had not been ceded to the English; and a contemporary English chronicler lamented that this was:

> to the great loss and injury of the King of England and his heirs for all time, as nearly all of the community of France was in subjection and ransom to them, and the said [English] captains and their men could easily have conquered the kingdom of France in a short time, to the benefit of the King of England and his heirs, if he had been willing to allow them.[24]

War and Taxes

This imperative to wage war drove developments in how English kings recruited and paid their armies. The raising of armies by feudal summons, whereby those holding lands by knight service were obliged to serve for forty days when summoned, had always been hopelessly inadequate for prolonged campaigns and fell into disuse after 1327 (with the exception of the feudal summons issued for Richard II's Scottish campaign in 1385, which may have been primarily a financial measure). Edward I, Edward II and Edward III all experimented with various methods of extending military obligation; but paying captains to raise retinues, under contracts in the form of indentures, proved to be the most practically convenient – and the least politically contentious – means of raising armies. Such contracts were first regularly used for recruiting royal forces by Edward I, for raising garrisons for Scotland; and they had become the norm for raising all English forces by the renewed outbreak of war with France in 1369. This period also saw the development of new tactics, integrating men-at-arms and archers in a defensive formation, which proved so successful that English kings became convinced that, on any battlefield with the right terrain, they would probably win – a conviction borne out by spectacular victories such as Halidon Hill, Crécy and Agincourt (these developments have been hailed by military historians as a 'military revolution'; or for those more au fait with current American military doctrines, as a 'revolution in military affairs').[25]

War with Scotland and France required armies of a size which the English crown could not afford to fund out of its own resources, so the king's just wars had to be paid for through taxation. Edward I was particularly successful at raising vast sums through taxes, invoking the Roman law doctrine of necessity, by which the subjects of a prince (a sovereign ruler) were obliged to provide assistance in cases of urgent need. However, he still needed to obtain consent for taxation, which he did using the developing forum of parliaments; and it was during his reign that the principle became established that taxes could not be raised without the consent of the Commons in parliament – a principle which would have a lasting impact on the kingship of England.

Military success tended to beget success in gaining such consent – Edward I, Edward III and Henry V were all remarkably successful tax-raisers (unlike Henry III, Edward II and Henry VI). Even so, Edward I faced an acute political crisis in 1297, when opposition came to a head over his excessive demands for taxes, military service and purveyance (the forced purchase of supplies). He was able to defuse the crisis partly because he was a skilled politician who knew when to back down – but also in part because of his previous triumph in conquering Wales and (apparently) Scotland. And so when a Scottish rebellion culminated in a humiliating defeat for the English at Stirling Bridge, while Edward was in Flanders pursuing an unpopular war with France, the political community rallied round, and he returned to lead a huge army into Scotland to win a major victory at Falkirk in 1298.[26] Similarly, Edward III faced an acute political crisis in 1341, over the failure of his enormously expensive and unpopular expedition to Flanders; and again, he was able to defuse it, in part because of the prestige and respect he had gained by his spectacular victories over the Scots (at Halidon Hill in 1333) and the French (in the naval battle of Sluys in 1340). Conversely, in 1376, after the renewed war with France had been going very badly, Edward was much less able to defuse criticism of his government in the 'Good Parliament', which saw the impeachment of several of his ministers.

The problem was that the defence of lands won to such acclaim involved English kings in the expenditure of yet more money. Once Edward I had invaded Scotland in 1296, it became necessary to install permanent garrisons to try to enforce English rule. The loss of all his Scottish lands meant that this ceased to be a problem for Edward II; but with the renewed English occupation of southern Scotland in the 1330s, garrisons had to be maintained once more, notably at Roxburgh (until it finally fell in 1460) and at Berwick (until the Union of the Crowns in 1603). Similarly, English garrisons were established in France at various times; in particular, Calais had to be protected by a large permanent garrison after its capture in 1346. Gascony, Ireland and the English Marches against Scotland also all required standing forces to be maintained for their defence. Such standing forces, and the fortifications required to house them, were colossally expensive; in the parliament of 1378, the chancellor claimed that the garrison of Calais alone cost more than £24,000 a year.[27] And these garrisons had to be maintained even during times of truce (albeit usually at a reduced strength), in case the truce broke down. Yet the Commons were loath to grant taxation except when war was imminent or had already broken out; a plea of necessity was difficult to justify during a truce, when – by definition – war had been suspended. The problem became particularly acute in the long period of truce after 1389. The garrison of Calais eventually mutinied over pay arrears in 1407; and the walls of Berwick remained in a state of collapse for years after Henry IV had been obliged to bombard them in 1405, when it was held against him by English rebels.

Chivalric Theatre

For any medieval king, it was vital to gain the support of the political classes for his wars – and, in particular, the support of the nobility and the gentry, as it was proportionately the men of these classes who served most consistently in the king's armies (at least, until the fifteenth century) and whose political influence was vital for the procurement of the necessary money and resources. As a martial ethos, which provided the nobility with its cultural identity, chivalry could provide a powerful means of linking the nobility with the king's wars, as a shared chivalric adventure; and the trappings of chivalry could be employed to great political effect. Royal tournaments, for instance, were a means of celebrating a shared martial culture; but they also served as potent theatre, carefully orchestrated to highlight victory in war. Thus Edward I held an Arthurian-styled round table in 1284 at Nefyn in north Wales (a former centre of native Welsh government) 'to mark the triumph achieved against the impudent Welsh'.[28] The round table, which still survives today at Winchester, may have been constructed for a similar event in 1285, also celebrating Edward's conquest of Wales, evoking – as would Caxton, some two centuries later – comparison with King Arthur, the great exemplar of chivalric kingship (at least, in the English tradition).[29] His victory over the Scots at Falkirk in 1298 was commemorated with another round table there in 1302. And as Arthur had, according to most contemporary historiography, established his overlordship over Britain (and indeed over France), these events also served to emphasise the longevity of the kings of England's claims, as the (self-proclaimed) heirs to the kings of Britons. Edward went on to mark the knighting of his son Edward in 1306 with the Feast of the Swans, inviting all those across the realm who wished to take up knighthood to come to be dubbed alongside him, in the expectation that they would be thus inspired to serve against the Scots.

Edward III, perhaps the most enthusiastic tourneyer of any medieval English king, held a grand tournament at Smithfield in London in 1357, where his prisoners John II, king of France, and David II, king of Scots, were ostentatiously presented as the principal guests. Such occasions served to emphasise not only the divinely vindicated justness of the king's wars but also that the contributions made by his subjects, in the form of military service and taxation, had been put to good use – with the corollary that future demands for such contributions would similarly bear fruit. Edward also contemplated forming a standing round table as a company of knights based at Windsor Castle, framing his palace as a new Camelot, and himself as a new King Arthur. In the event, he modified his plans, founding the Order of the Garter instead, to celebrate and memorialise his great victory at Crécy. As such, membership was a coveted honour, a reward to those knights and noblemen (irrespective of social precedence, or indeed nationality) who had shown the most prowess in Edward's wars – though after Edward's reign, membership gradually came to be granted more on the basis of straightforward political favouritism, or as a diplomatic sweetener to current or potential allies. This changing emphasis was marked by the admittance of Ladies of the Garter from 1375.[30]

Richard II was not himself an enthusiastic tourneyer, but he did sponsor tournaments, notably including two held at Smithfield in 1390. These were grand chivalric occasions, where Richard himself appeared under arms, attracting knights from across western Christendom; and they were used to good diplomatic effect: the duke of Guelders, and William of Ostrevant, son of the count of Hainault and Holland, both potential allies of the English, were inducted into the Order of the Garter during the first and second tournaments respectively.[31] But while patronage of tournaments undoubtedly served to burnish a king's martial and chivalric credentials, it was not, of itself, sufficient to create them; Richard II's tournaments could not win him a reputation for chivalry, for they were not buttressed by successful martial endeavour – indeed, the Smithfield tournaments were held shortly after the sealing of the truce of Leulinghem, which had brought the Anglo-French war to a temporary close. Richard's great-great-grandfather Edward I, his grandfather Edward III and his father Edward the Black Prince all owed their chivalric reputations to their undoubted prowess on the battlefield. By contrast, Richard had presided over the loss of most of the French lands won by his grandfather and father. His only successful military venture was his expedition to Ireland in 1394–5, when he obtained the submission of a number of prominent Gaelic lords; but Ireland was regarded by most of his subjects as an uncivilised backwater, so it could not bring him the prestige which a successful campaign in France, or even Scotland, would have done – particularly as his campaign was won by low-key raiding and negotiations, rather than by a signal success in battle.

Henry V took a decidedly austere approach to jousting. When a tournament was arranged at Troyes in June 1420, to celebrate his wedding to Katherine Valois, daughter of Charles VI of France, he refused to attend, announcing his intention instead to go and besiege Sens, held by supporters of the Dauphin: 'there may we all tilt and joust and prove our daring and courage, for there is no finer act of courage in the world than to punish evildoers so that poor people can live'.[32] Nevertheless, Henry was alive to the benefits of publicising his triumphs; his victory at Agincourt was followed by an elaborately orchestrated ceremonial entry to the city of London, accompanied by the most prominent of the prisoners taken at the battle, and featuring a number of edifying *tableaux vivants*, emphasising the hand of God in providing that victory.[33]

Unsurprisingly, there was little royal interest in tournaments under Henry VI, but royal sponsorship of jousting was revived by Edward IV. This was motivated in part by the need to keep up with the fashions set by the culturally dominant Burgundian court. More importantly though, it was a means of projecting an image of the renewal of English chivalry under his kingship, as part of his ongoing efforts to restore the authority of the monarchy after the civil wars of 1459–69 and 1470-1. And Caxton proposed that Richard III should revive the chivalric ethos of former days by holding a regular series of tournaments at which the English gentry and nobility might compete, hoping thus to 'cause gentlemen to resort to the ancient customs of chivalry, to great fame and renown'.[34] However, it was not until the reign of Henry VIII that England would again have a king who was personally an active and enthusiastic tourneyer.

Chivalry in Decline?

From the viewpoint of Richard III's reign, it is perhaps not surprising that William Caxton should have considered that English chivalry was in decline, after years of – albeit intermittent – internal strife, following the ruin of the English cause in France. Nevertheless, it was perhaps in the reign of Henry V, the last of Caxton's exemplars of royal chivalry, that the seeds of that defeat had been sown. Henry's spectacular victory at Agincourt had enabled him to obtain repeated grants of taxes from the Commons to fund his sustained campaigning in France, culminating in the treaty of Troyes of 1420 by which Charles VI recognised his right to the French kingship, making Henry his heir. This had marked perhaps the zenith of his reign – yet it also served effectively to help to undermine the English war effort. English taxpayers, as represented by the Commons in parliament, were prepared – up to a point – to fund the wars of the king of England in pursuit of his claim to the kingship of France; once, however, that claim had been made good, they were much less willing to fund any of his further wars as the king of France – particularly as they were determined to ensure that the kingdoms of England and France should remain entirely separate entities, even if under the same king. The suppression of rebellions against English kings of France was a matter for the kingdom of France, to be paid for by French taxpayers, particularly as France was famously wealthy.[35]

This increasing detachment of the English political community from the war in France was heightened by a change of strategy introduced by Henry V. During the fourteenth century, the English had conducted war with France mainly by means of vastly destructive (and hugely profitable) large-scale and far-ranging raids, known as *chevauchées*, intended to undermine the authority of the kings of France by demonstrating their inability to defend their subjects, and so forcing them to come to terms. This paid off in 1360, with the treaty of Brétigny – though in the event, Edward III could not bring himself to ratify the treaty's provision requiring him to renounce his claim to the French kingship, leading to its collapse nine years later.

In 1417, however, Henry V embarked on an invasion of Normandy aimed at its permanent occupation, methodically besieging towns and installing garrisons once they had been captured. While this was not a complete break with previous English strategy – some permanent garrisons had been maintained in France in the fourteenth century, while *chevauchées* remained an English tactic during the fifteenth century – the change was sufficient to radically alter patterns of military service. *Chevauchées* required English armies to serve in France for only a limited period, usually a few months, or no more than a year, before returning to England. This enabled the majority of the English gentry to serve under arms on an occasional basis, while maintaining their interests in England.

By contrast, Henry's occupation of northern France required the maintenance of large numbers of permanent garrisons along with standing armies in the field, which meant a long-term commitment to military service. English armies also relied increasingly heavily on archers, generally recruited from the yeomen (the wealthier peasantry), with far fewer knights and men-at-arms, generally drawn from the more politically influential gentry. For much of the fourteenth century, a large part of the political community of the realm had personally served in the king's wars and so had a personal stake in them. This was no longer the case in the fifteenth century, partly because of the twenty-five years of peace after the truce of Leulinghem; while the nobility and peerage remained heavily engaged in the war in France, the gentry became increasingly demilitarised and increasingly disengaged. Yet, while they were ever less willing to participate in, or pay for, the wars in France, the loss of Normandy and Aquitaine was still regarded as a national disgrace, for which Henry VI and his government were squarely blamed.

This served to highlight the fundamental link between perceptions of good kingship and successful leadership in war. Later kings looked back to the loss of France and continued to make sporadic efforts to reverse it; in particular, Henry VIII would embrace the image of himself as a chivalric warrior king in the mould of Henry V and invaded France, albeit to no great effect.[36] And so while the claim to English overlordship of Scotland was ultimately resolved with the Union of the English and Scottish Crowns in 1603, James I/VI inherited the English claim to the French kingship; and notwithstanding Scotland's previous record of alliance with France, it was not until 1800 that the British crown formally renounced the claim, eight years after the establishment of the first French Republic.

Notes

1. For this and the following quotes (here paraphrased in modern English), see *The Book of the Ordre of Chyualry*, ed. A. T. P. Byles, EETS, original series, 168 (1926), 122–4.

2. *Vita Edwardi Secundi*, ed. W. R. Childs (Oxford, 2005), 129.
3. *Nicholai Triveti, Annales sex regum Angliae*, ed. T. Hog (London, 1845), 281.
4. J. Lydgate, *Minor Poems*, ed. H. N. McCracken, EETS, original series, 192 (Oxford, 1934), 716 (English modernised).
5. *PROME*, parliament of October 1472, First Roll, item 8.
6. 'Johannis de Trokelowe Annales', in *Johannis de Trokelowe et Henrici de Blaneforde chronica et annales*, ed. H. T. Riley, RS, 28 (London, 1866), 86.
7. 'John Rous's Account of the Reign of Richard III', in A. Hanham, *Richard III and His Early Historians 1483-1535* (Oxford, 1975), 123.
8. *The Book of Chivalry of Geoffroi de Charny*, ed. R. W. Kaeuper and E. Kennedy (Philadelphia, 1996).
9. A. King, '"War", "Rebellion" or "Perilous times"? Political Taxonomy and the Conflict in England, 1321-2', in *Ruling Fourteenth Century England: Essays in Honour of Christopher Given-Wilson*, ed. J. Bothwell, R. Ambühl and L. Tompkins (Woodbridge, 2019), 113-32; J. G. Bellamy, *The Law of Treason in England in the Later Middle Ages* (Cambridge, 1970).
10. *Historie of the Arrivall of Edward IV in England*, ed. J. Bruce, Camden Society, 1st series, 1 (London, 1838), 20.
11. M. L. Maxwell, 'The Anglo-Norman Prose "Brut": An Edition of British Library MS Cotton Cleopatra D.iii', unpublished Ph.D. thesis (Michigan State University, 1995), 545.
12. *Literae Cantuarienses: The Letter Books of the Monastery of Christ Church, Canterbury*, ed. J. B. Sheppard, RS, 3 vols. (1887-9), III, 274-85 (English text modernised). For the date of the speech, see C. L. Scofield, *The Life and Reign of Edward the Fourth, King of England and of France and Lord of Ireland*, 2 vols. (London, 1923), II, 44n.
13. L. J. A. Villalon, '"Taking the King's Shilling" to Avoid "the Wages of Sin": English Royal Pardons for Military Malefactors during the Hundred Years War', in *The Hundred Years War (Part III): Further Considerations*, ed. L. J. A. Villalon and D. J. Kagay (Leiden, 2013), 357-435.
14. *The Reign of Edward II, 1307-27*, trans. W. R. Childs and P. R. Schofield (Manchester, 2022), 256.
15. H. Johnstone, 'The Eccentricities of Edward II', *EHR* 48 (1933), 264-7 (at 267).
16. M. Vale, *The Origins of the Hundred Years War: The Angevin Legacy, 1250-1340*, 2nd ed. (Oxford, 1996).
17. A. Ruddick, *English Identity and Political Culture in the Fourteenth Century* (Cambridge, 2013), 161-3.
18. A. King and C. Etty, *England and Scotland, 1286-1603* (Basingstoke, 2015).
19. 'Robertus de Avesbury de gestis mirabilibus regis Edwardi Tertii', in *Chronica A. Murimuth et R. de Avesbury*, ed. E. M. Thompson, RS, 99 (1889), 309.

20. A. King, 'War and Peace: A Knight's Tale. The Ethics of War in Sir Thomas Gray's *Scalacronica*', in *War, Government and Aristocracy in the British Isles, c.1150–1500*, ed. C. Given-Wilson, A. Kettle and L. Scales (Woodbridge, 2008), 148–62.
21. *PROME*, parliament of November 1414, item 2.
22. W. R. Jones, 'The English Church and Royal Propaganda during the Hundred Years War', *JBS* 19 (1979–80), 18–30; A. K. McHardy, 'Some Reflections on Edward III's Use of Propaganda', in *The Age of Edward III*, ed. J. S. Bothwell (Woodbridge, 2001), 171–92.
23. 'Adæ Murimuth continuatio chronicarum', in *Chronica*, ed. Thompson, 56.
24. *The Anonimalle Chronicle, 1333 to 1381: From a MS. Written at St. Mary's Abbey, York*, ed. V. H. Galbraith (Manchester, 1927), 49.
25. C. J. Rogers, '"As if a new sun had arisen": England's Fourteenth-Century RMA', in *The Dynamics of Military Revolution, 1300–2050*, ed. M. Knox and W. Murray (Cambridge, 2001), 15–34.
26. A. King, 'Crisis? What Crisis? 1297 and the Civil War That Never Was', in *Edward I: New Interpretations*, ed. A. King and A. Spencer (Woodbridge, 2020), 163–84.
27. *PROME*, parliament of October 1377, item 15.
28. 'Annales de Waverleia', in *Annales monastici*, ed. H. R. Luard, RS, 36, 5 vols. (1864–9), II, 402.
29. M. Morris, 'Edward I and the Knights of the Round Table', in *Foundations of Medieval Scholarship: Records Edited in Honour of David Crook*, ed. P. Brand and S. Cunningham (York, 2008), 57–76.
30. R. Barber, *Edward III and the Triumph of England: The Battle of Crécy and the Company of the Garter* (London, 2013); H. Collins, *The Order of the Garter, 1348–1461: Chivalry and Politics in Late Medieval England* (Oxford, 2000); S. Mitchell, 'Ladies of the Garter: Edward III; Richard II; Elizabeth II', *Court Historian* 22 (2017), 151–67.
31. J. L. Gillespie, 'Richard II: Chivalry and Kingship', in *The Age of Richard II*, ed. J. L. Gillespie (Stroud, 1997), 115–38.
32. *A Parisian Journal, 1405–1449*, trans. J. Shirley (Oxford, 1968), 151.
33. N. Coldstream, '"Pavilion'd in Splendour": Henry V's Agincourt Pageants', *Journal of the British Archaeological Association* 165 (2012), 153–71.
34. *Book of the Ordre of Chyualry*, ed. Byles, 124 (English text modernised).
35. G. L. Harriss, 'The Management of Parliament', in *Henry V: The Practice of Kingship*, ed. G. L. Harriss (Oxford, 1985), 137–58.
36. C. S. L. Davies, 'Henry VIII and Henry V: The Wars in France', in *The End of the Middle Ages? England in the Fifteenth and Sixteenth Centuries*, ed. J. L. Watts (Stroud, 1998), 235–62.

Further Reading

Barber, R., *Edward III and the Triumph of England: The Battle of Crécy and the Company of the Garter* (London, 2013).

Barron, W. R. J., ed., *The Arthur of the English: The Arthurian Legend in Medieval English Life and Literature*, 2nd ed. (Cardiff, 2001).

Bell, A. R., Curry, A., King, A. and Simpkin, D., *The Soldier in Later Medieval England* (Oxford, 2013).

Dodd, G., 'English Politics and the Hundred Years War', in *The Hundred Years War Revisited: Problems in Focus*, ed. A. Curry (London, 2019), 1–32.

Keen, M. H., 'The End of the Hundred Years War: Lancastrian France and Lancastrian England', in *England and Her Neighbours, 1066–1453: Essays in Honour of Pierre Chaplais*, ed. M. C. E. Jones and M. G. A. Vale (London, 1989), 297–311.

'Chivalry and English Kingship in the Later Middle Ages', in *War, Government and Aristocracy in the British Isles, c. 1150–1500*, ed. C. Given-Wilson, A. Kettle and L. Scales (Woodbridge, 2008), 250–66.

King, A., 'Chivalry in the Hundred Years War', in *The Hundred Years War Revisited: Problems in Focus*, ed. A. Curry (London, 2019), 133–52.

Pollard, A. J., 'English Chivalry and the Decline of Strenuous Knighthood in the Later Fifteenth Century', in *Prowess, Piety, and Public Order in Medieval Society: Studies in Honor of Richard W. Kaeuper*, ed. C. M. Nakashian and D. P. Franke (Leiden, 2017), 140–58.

Prestwich, M., *Armies and Warfare in the Middle Ages: The English Experience* (London, 1996).

Rogers, C. J., *War Cruel and Sharp: English Strategy under Edward III, 1327–60* (Woodbridge, 2000).

Saul, N., *For Honour and Fame: Chivalry in England 1066–1500* (London, 2011).

Sumption, J., *The Hundred Years War*, 5 vols. (London, 1990–2023).

MATTHEW HEFFERAN

8

The Royal Court and Household

The Royal Court and Household: What and Who?

While later medieval England enjoyed an increasingly sophisticated array of governmental institutions that helped kings to rule, kingship itself remained a fundamentally personal and personality-driven enterprise. Consequently, space was needed where the 'personal side' of politics could take place and where each monarch's domestic needs could be met. It was the royal court and household that provided space for both of these things. Despite the importance of each, defining them, and their relationship to one another, is not easy. The royal court (not to be confused with the courts of law, discussed in Chapter 6) has proven particularly problematic to historians because it lacked a clear structure or boundaries. Even contemporaries were not entirely sure how to define it: as Walter Map famously commented in the late twelfth century, 'in the court I exist and of the court I speak, but what the court is – God knows – I know not!'[1] This uncertainty has led some historians to question the extent to which we can see the court as a coherent and meaningful element of late medieval kingship.[2]

But we need not be too pessimistic. For one thing, despite suggestions to the contrary, it seems beyond doubt that those at the time knew that the royal court existed, and most probably understood (albeit not always precisely) where its boundaries lay. Indeed, Map's comments were intended for rhetorical effect: given that he went on to liken the court of Henry II to hell in his work, it is evident that he understood well enough what the court was in practice. Moreover, individuals were frequently described as being 'in court' (*in curia* in Latin, *à la court* in French) while they were with the king and 'out of court' when not. In January 1355, for example, John de Staunton was retained as a knight of the king's chamber, to hold the position 'when absent from court' as well as 'when present'.[3] While a definitive definition is not possible, then, we can have some confidence that at its most basic the royal court represented the physical space around the king and the people who occupied that space – his entourage, his 'courtiers'.

What of the household? The relationship between the court and household (commonly rendered *hospicium*, *hostel* or *domus* when talking about the institution, or *familia* when talking about the people who staffed it) was a very close one and the overlap in personnel between the two was considerable. But they were not the same thing. While the court was a broad, fluid and ill-defined group, membership of which was often only loosely conferred, the royal household was a more structured body around which the court could function, the personnel of which were usually specifically employed within it. In the words of Malcolm Vale, it provided the 'backbone' of the court.[4] While there were countless changes to the precise structure and organisation of the royal household in this period – many of which were set out in formal 'ordinances', such as the famous Household Ordinances of 1318 and the so-called Black Book of Edward IV, containing ordinances of 1478 – some generalisations can be made.

Throughout our period it consisted of two main parts, usually described as the 'above stairs' (*domus magnificencie*) and 'below stairs' (*domus providencie*), a reflection of the fact it was both a governmental institution and a domestic establishment. The responsibility of the below stairs of the household – which typically numbered anywhere between 200 and 1,000 individuals and slowly grew over the period – was to look after the daily needs of the king and those at his court. This included providing food and drink, clothing, jewels, cutlery and crockery, bedding, candles, parchment, quills and so on. All this had to be sourced and stored, and in the case of meals, prepared and served. It was an enormous operation carried out under the direction of the controller, who oversaw a variety of sub-departments including the buttery, pantry, kitchen, wafery, spicery, bakehouse, chandlery and laundry. Each of these departments had its own designated staff and within the household were retained minstrels, physicians, surgeons, tailors, almoners, a royal hat-maker, keepers of the king's horses, dogs and falcons and many more besides. While these individuals were not 'courtiers' as such, without their considerable efforts it would not have been possible for the household or court to function.

The so-called above stairs encompassed the governmental side. It contained several important officials, such as the steward (who had overall control of the household), the chamberlain (who controlled physical and written access to the king), the keeper of the privy seal (through which the king could validate his personal commands, to be sent to the chancery and other government departments), the keeper of the wardrobe (also known as the treasurer of the household, in charge of finances) and the cofferer (who assisted the keeper and was in charge of the money itself). These officials were leading figures both at court and in government and frequently advised the king.

Alongside these officials were the knights and esquires of the household who, while part of the above stairs of the household, in a sense formed a distinct 'military' arm that sat alongside the administrative one. They fought with kings on military campaigns and carried out a variety of tasks both in and away from court. Like the officers of the household, they also provided the king with counsel and advice on a day-to-day basis and played a crucial if often informal role in shaping royal policy, though some also sat on the royal council too. Like all members of the household, they were granted livery of robes twice a year, the style and quality of which varied dependent on one's rank, which would have been worn to differentiate themselves from others at court. On average, between thirty and fifty household knights were retained in any given year, and a similar if slightly greater number of esquires, although this fluctuated dramatically. The number of household knights retained in any given year, for instance, routinely fell to around 20 when the king was not militarily active but could rise to more than 60 in years of heavy campaigning and even topped 100 in 1314.

While household knights and esquires were a mainstay of the household before the 1360s, things changed after this date. Thereafter, a much smaller number of men (rarely more than a dozen) called 'chamber knights' were retained in their place. This was a reflection of the fact that the king's 'chamber', the most intimate part of the household, slowly came to take precedence over the larger, more public-facing 'hall' during the course of the fourteenth century. These chamber knights were, from the later fourteenth century onwards, joined by ranks of 'king's knights' and 'king's esquires' who, though sharing many similarities with the earlier household knights, do not appear to have been as regularly in court as their predecessors. Instead, they formed a 'royal affinity', which extended the king's influence outwards across the realm (see Chapter 12). By the mid fifteenth century there were also knights and esquires of the king's body within the household. Finally, the above stairs of the household also contained the royal chapel, which comprised around twenty chaplains, ten choristers under a dean, and the king's personal confessor, who had care of the king's spiritual well-being.

The personnel of the above stairs of the household offered a steady stream of courtiers. But they were not alone. The queen's household, which was ordinarily separate to the king's (although it was common for men to move between the two establishments), provided another contingent when the king and queen were together. Alongside the household courtiers were others who stayed at court for shorter durations, such as while attending parliament, celebrating a religious festival or for a special occasion such as a coronation, jubilee or royal marriage or birth. Chief among these occasional courtiers were the leading magnates of the realm, who, though too busy managing their own estates and aiding the king in his foreign wars to reside at court for lengthy periods, were keen to spend time there when they could. Leading members of the church were likewise often too busy with their own business to be regularly resident at court but might attend larger gatherings. Merchants also sometimes found their way to court. In their case, entry to court could mark an important moment in their social advancement and was often in recognition of financial aid they had rendered to the crown, usually in the form of loans. An example of this can be seen in the career of William de la Pole, a merchant who initially made his fortune in the Gascon wine trade alongside his brother Richard, before turning his hand to government work as a collector of royal customs. During the first half of Edward III's reign, William used his deep pockets to provide loans to the English crown and by October 1339 the king had incurred debts to de la Pole amounting to £111,156. In return, de la Pole acquired various estates, including the lordship of Burstwick worth £1,000 a year. He was also raised to the rank of knight banneret and summoned to parliament. His heirs would go on to be raised to earldoms, now firmly a family of courtiers.[5] When all got together, the numbers at court could thus be vast, numbering many hundreds, perhaps more than a thousand on special occasions such as coronations.

It is also important to recognise that the court had a strong international contingent, with many courtiers coming from beyond the borders of England. During the 1240s and 1250s, there was a strong contingent of Provençals and Savoyards, a result of Henry III's marriage to Eleanor of Provence in 1236, as well as Lusignans from Poitou, following his mother's marriage to Hugh de Lusignan. Similarly, in the early years of Edward III's reign several men from the Low Countries (most notably Walter Mauny) established a place for themselves at court as a result of the king's match with Philippa of Hainault. Other international courtiers were there on diplomatic business, residing at court while conducting negotiations. Sometimes, these men were retained as part of the household, particularly if they were to remain there for extended periods. Peter of Castile, the future king of Spain (known to history as Pedro the Cruel), appears among a list of household knights in 1346, a decade during which there was ongoing Anglo-Castilian negotiations.[6] Not all international guests were there of their own accord: English kings also enjoyed showing off their high-profile prisoners of war at court. The pinnacle of this undoubtedly came in the later 1350s when Edward III was able to flaunt the captive kings of Scotland and France, David II and John II respectively, in front of his court. The presence of so many foreign nobles at the English court reminds us that this was not an insular body, cut off from the wider world: it was an outward-looking, international gathering.

The Royal Court and Household: Where and When?

Neither the court nor the household had a fixed home in this period. Rather, because they were so closely connected to the person of the king, they moved around as the king did, and late medieval English kings, while not quite as mobile as their Angevin predecessors, were rarely static: they regularly spent extended periods abroad in the pursuit of their foreign ambitions or managing their overseas dominions, and frequently travelled around England in the exercise of government or in pursuit of kingly leisure activities such as hunting (see Map 4.1). It has been estimated that on average kings moved residences between 50 and 100 times in a year in the fifteenth century, figures that are matched in the thirteenth and fourteenth centuries. It was therefore uncommon for the court to be in the same place for more than a few weeks at a time.[7]

The process of travelling (or, 'removing', as it was called) presented an immense logistical challenge, yet would have been completely familiar to the court and household in this period. Indeed, the household was a well-oiled machine in this respect. A designated group travelled a day ahead of the king to prepare the way. Within this group were the 'harbingers', in charge of securing lodgings. Sometimes, a royal palace, castle or hunting lodge provided a place to rest. On other occasions, larger abbeys or the residences of the king's magnates/prelates could be utilised (the archbishop's palace in York was, for example, a popular stopping point for kings moving to and from the north of England/Scotland). Such comfortable lodgings were not always available and sometimes while on the move kings had to make do with the best house that could be found in the town through which they were passing, leaving the rest of the household to camp outside. Alongside the harbingers were the 'purveyors', who had the right to compulsorily purchase food and other victuals for the king's court, often at very low prices and/or with promises of later payment. Needless to say, it was a frequent source of complaint, with under- or non-payment a common problem.

The king would usually follow on from this advanced party a day or so later with his private bodyguard and a select group of advisors and servants. The main bulk of household personnel then brought up the rear, pulling the many carts containing the household's equipment and baggage. An ordinance of 1279 ordained that the wardrobe should have three 'long' carts to transport its goods and personnel, while the pantry, buttery and kitchen were each designated one 'long' and one 'short' cart.[8] Other departments also had their own carts, and the total number of carts kept by the royal household has been estimated at around a dozen in the 1280s.[9] Each of these would have needed horses to pull them. Additional pack horses were also kept specifically to transport the most valuable goods, such as the royal robes. Where feasible, as much was transported by river as possible to ease some of the burden. Despite the scale of the enterprise, the household could move an average of fifteen miles per day, which could be extended to up to twenty-five miles a day when speed was required.

While the court and household rarely remained static, there were places where kings chose to stay more frequently than others. Partly, this was dictated by the personal preferences of each monarch. Henry III favoured his royal palace at Westminster. David Carpenter has calculated that he spent roughly 49 per cent of his lengthy minority there, and about 28 per cent of his time between 1234 and 1252.[10] Edward I preferred his smaller hunting lodges, such as Clipstone (Notts.), Woolmer (Hants.), Banstead (Surrey) and Geddington (Northants.). Edward I's successors, meanwhile, spent an increasing amount of their time at a small number of royal palaces in the south-east of England, especially those within a day's ride of Westminster, where government was becoming settled. Windsor Castle and the royal manors of Sheen (now Richmond Palace, London) and Eltham (Kent) became particular favourites.

These larger royal residences usually played host to important religious festivals such as Christmas, Easter, All Saints' Day, Candlemas, St George's Day and Whitsun. Henry IV, Henry V and Henry VI spent virtually every major religious holiday at either Eltham, Sheen, Westminster or Windsor.[11] Considerable sums of money were also spent on these residences to increase their suitability as homes for the court. At Sheen, Edward III ordered the construction of nine new private apartments between 1358 and 1370, all of which probably had their own fireplaces and private latrines.[12] Similar developments were undertaken at Eltham during his reign. But it was at Windsor that the most extravagant building programme took place. Edward III spent more than £51,000 developing Windsor between 1350 and 1377, £40,000 of which went on a series of new royal apartments along the north side of the upper bailey between 1357 and 1365. This included a new great hall and chapel for the use of the court and household, as well as seven chambers – one of which, the 'great chamber', was for the king's use – a closet (a private area to which the king could retreat for some peace and quiet) and a private chapel. Edward III's building work

Figure 8.1 The great hall built at Eltham Palace, c. 1470s. (Photo by Print Collector/Getty Images.)

at Windsor, Eltham and Sheen was continued by his successors, who further enhanced their size and splendour. Edward IV, for instance, oversaw the construction of a new great hall at Eltham (Figure 8.1). Most of our kings also invested significant sums of money into building projects at Westminster Abbey and Palace, important centres of royal power (see Chapter 16). Even so, the court never became fixed in one place during the late Middle Ages. It was only in the early modern period that royal courts became static and that grand new royal palaces, such as Versailles in France, allowed monarchs to stage-manage their 'court societies' on a scale hitherto unknown.

Ceremony and Opulence

The royal court was heavily steeped in ceremony and ritual. Indeed, it has been described as 'a stage', and courtiers as 'actors'.[13] Certainly, there was a performative element to just about all aspects of court life. This began each day as soon as the king rose. His clothes were brought to him by yeomen and grooms of the household, and he was dressed by his esquires. Mealtimes were similarly choreographed. A treatise on court ceremonial known as the *The Rydalle Book*, which has been dated to the reign of

Henry VI, outlines in detail just how this might have unfolded.[14] According to this, the king mostly took his meals in the great chamber (though, earlier in this period, this would have taken place in the hall), where the main officers of the household also dined, along with the queen and any important magnates, prelates or foreign dignitaries in residence. At the beginning of the meal, a towel was presented to the king so that he could wash his hands. Then, meat was brought in and carved by the knight carver and served by knights and esquires of the household. Henry V apparently insisted on being served only by those of knightly rank. Following the meal, the king would once more wash his hands, before retreating to hear vespers (evening prayers) privately. He would then return to the great chamber (or hall) for wine, spices and conversation – a period of time referred to as the void. Richard II was peculiar here in that he apparently preferred to remain at a distance during this more intimate part of proceedings, seated away from the masses but always observing.[15] At the end of the void, the king retreated to his private chambers to relax before heading to bed. Even here, however, royal grooms, yeomen and esquires were once more required to prepare the royal bed (a process that involved jumping up and down on the litter, hitting the feather mattress and pillows and shaking out the blankets), undress the king and bring in the queen if she was to share the king's bed that night. The king's servants would then retire, though some would sleep outside the king's door for his protection.

While such unceasing formality may seem an unwelcome hassle to us, it reminds us of one of the core functions of the court: to highlight the splendour, honour and dignity of the monarchy. This was achieved in a myriad of other ways. Sermons, ceremony and prayer in the royal chapel were ideal ways of reminding people of the sacred nature of kingship. Similarly, there is evidence to suggest that during the second half of the fourteenth century, and particularly the reign of Richard II, new forms of address – perhaps inspired by developments at the French court, which had a considerable influence on all aspects of the English court in this period – emerged, which saw kings increasingly styled 'prince' and addressed as 'your majesty' or 'your highness', far loftier terms than had previously been used.[16]

The food and drink served at court also signalled its power and opulence. According to a surviving kitchen account from 1291 at

Christmas that year Edward I's court consumed a substantial quantity of veal alongside 1,742 chickens, 22 pheasants, roughly 200 partridges, a similar number of mallard duck and 72 plover (a small wading bird).[17] This would have been seasoned with expensive spices, available to few at the time: pepper, saffron, caraway and cumin. Gallons of mustard and vinegar were also provided, as was bread and cheese. Drink was also needed. Ale could be sourced from local brewers, but wine came from further afield, often Bordeaux. As a result, it tended to be purchased in bulk. In 1289/90 the royal butler, Matthew de Columbers, bought 1,858 tuns of wine at a cost of £3,827. This was needed: during the Christmas celebrations a few years earlier, some 13 tuns (nearly 15,000 litres) had been consumed by the court!

The clothing and jewels that the king wore further reinforced his dignity. Multiple tailors were kept within the royal household and the most lavish cloths (fine wools, sindon, silks, samite, cloth of gold) were purchased for them to turn into the finest garments for the king. If the Evesham chronicler is to be believed, Richard II spent as much as £20,000 on one robe that was lined with precious stones.[18] Such finery would have been everywhere one looked: in the wall-hangings that kings had placed in their halls and chambers, the cutlery and crockery used, and so on. Nor did kings keep all this luxury for themselves. The giving of expensive gifts to courtiers was also popular. These were often distributed at important festivals, such as New Year, and/or to distinguished guests, such as foreign ambassadors.

Past Times and Court Culture

What did people do when attending court? And to what extent can we talk of a defined 'court culture' in this period? Physical pursuits played a crucial role in court life. Hunting was particularly popular. Kings owned vast hunting parks full of deer, boars, hares and foxes. They employed men within their households to look after their hunting dogs and birds of prey (which were commonly given as gifts to kings) and routinely purchased bows, arrows, hunting swords and spears with which to hunt. Many of the kings in our period were also lovers of tournaments: Edward I, Edward III and Edward IV all frequently organised and participated in them. The exact format of the late medieval tournament is not always entirely clear, but it usually involved a mêlée between two 'teams' in a small enclosure. In this respect, it represented something of a midway point in the transition from the expansive mock-battles of the twelfth and thirteenth centuries that covered many miles to the one-on-one jousts of the later fifteenth and sixteenth centuries, although jousts between individuals were enjoyed in this period too. For martially inclined kings, tournaments provided an excellent forum in which they could not only have fun but bond with like-minded members of the nobility while showing off their wealth and chivalric prowess.

Usually, royal tournaments included the knights of the household, but others were regularly invited to join too. Edward III's round table tournament of 1344 saw 300 knights from all across Europe invited for three days of action. After 1348, the Order of the Garter celebrations in April each year provided the ideal occasion on which the chivalric classes of England could gather to indulge such passions. The 'round table' event and annual Garter celebrations were also opportunities for Edward III to publicly align himself with the figure of King Arthur, tales of whom were popular at court in this period. He even had a physical 'round table', which had been constructed for his grandfather Edward I, hung on the wall of the great hall of Winchester Castle. Moreover, the pageantry that surrounded such occasions, which often mirrored famous Arthurian tales, allowed Edward and those at his court to actively engage with the ideals of 'courtly love', a popular literary construct that offered a highly romanticised notion of how male and female courtiers should act and interact (in a non-sexual way) with one another. This required courtiers to speak lovingly towards one another and for men to carry out valiant deeds in honour of the ladies at court, who in turn encouraged and often judged their efforts. It was in a bid to demonstrate a commitment to the ideals of courtly love that, on the first night of the 1344 round table tournament, Edward III 'gave a solemn feast' during which 'the great hall of the castle was filled by all ladies, with just two knights among them'.[19]

Not all our kings were as enthusiastic about tournaments as Edward III. Edward II, Richard II and Henry VI showed little interest in them and their courts were decidedly less militaristic in nature. There were still many pastimes available for them to enjoy, however. Chess was popular and often played for money. Edward I's financial records reveal that he was forced to pay out three times in 1278 after losing games. Whether or not he got any better we do not know, but he was seemingly still interested in the game in 1300, when he is recorded as owning an ornate chess set made of crystal and jasper.[20] Similarly, most of our kings owned books and commissioned works of literature. Henry III's patronage was directed towards poems and saints' lives, while Edward I, though generally unenthusiastic about literature, showed at least some preference for French romances – a reflection of how closely entwined Anglo-French literary culture was in the thirteenth and fourteenth centuries.[21] Edward II had more eclectic tastes, which included books of romances, primers and prayer books, copies of the lives of St Edward, St Anselm and St Thomas (the latter two of which were contained in one volume that he borrowed from the library of Christ Church, Canterbury, but failed to return), a didactic text called *De Regimine Principum* ('On Royal Rule') and even a collection of Welsh poetry. Finally, Edward IV has been credited as the first English king to accumulate a substantial royal library, which contained a number of beautifully illuminated chivalric romances as well as some early printed material courtesy of William Caxton's new printing press, established in the vicinity of Westminster Abbey in 1477.

Yet it is the court of Richard II that is most famous for its literary enthusiasm. During the middle years of his reign several famous and talented English poets became popular at court. The most famous was Geoffrey Chaucer, who first appears as a household esquire under Edward III in the late 1360s, around which time his first major work, *The Boke of the Duchesse* (c. 1368–9), was completed. It was during the 1380s when Chaucer really rose to prominence, however, with the publication of the *House of Fame*, the *Parlement of Foules*, *Troilus and Criseyde*, and *The Legend of Good Women*. After circa 1387, his attention turned to his most famous work, *The Canterbury Tales*. Writing at the same time as Chaucer, with whom he was acquainted, was John Gower, who authored a variety of works in English, Latin and French, the most famous of which was his *Confessio Amantis*. Also of note were the talented chamber knights John Clanvowe, author of the *Boke of Cupide*, and John Montagu, none of whose works survive but who received plaudits for his writings during his own lifetime.[22] Scholars have, however, been rightly cautious about linking these broad literary developments too closely to the court. Little evidence survives to suggest that Richard himself was directly involved in the patronage or production of these works, and it would be wrong to overlook the important influence that the gentry had on this cultural phenomenon. Indeed, while Clanvowe and Montagu had clear links to the court, it was in the rural manors of the county gentry and city houses of the urban elite that a great deal of this work was produced and popularised. Nevertheless, the Ricardian court clearly provided a keen audience (and perhaps source of encouragement) for these writers and their work.

Music – which was closely connected to literature and poetry in this period given the fact that texts were frequently set to music and performed in the form of ballads – was another area of great interest for the royal court. The Household Ordinances of 1318 note that 'there shall be two trumpeters and two other minstrels, sometimes more, sometimes less, who shall perform their minstrelsy before the king whenever he pleases'.[23] In practice, numbers usually far exceeded this. A livery roll from 1328 shows that a young Edward III had eleven minstrels on the books, while at Christmas in 1287 Edward I was entertained by some 125 minstrels.[24] Similarly, at the wedding of Henry V to Katherine of France in 1420 a vast host of trumpeters and minstrels walked in front of the coach carrying the new queen of England, who later in the celebrations performed on the harp herself. What she played we do not know, but one suspects it would have been something French. This seems likely because not only was Katherine herself French but, as has already been noted, French culture had a considerable influence on English court culture in this period. Her performance would no doubt have pleased Henry V, who took an active interest in music and is credited with bringing together a talented group of composers within the royal chapel, who were widely praised for their work with a new polyphonic style.

Courting Controversy

While the extravagance and exclusivity of the royal court played an important part in curating an image of power and prestige for the late medieval English monarchy, it also meant it was sometimes a target for criticism. Some of this criticism was localised, with the communities through which the court travelled voicing discontent, especially over the unpaid bills of unscrupulous purveyors. In 1362, Edward III attempted to address the problem by enacting the Great Statute of Purveyors.[25] While some abuses lessened thereafter, the issue of non-payment and underpayment remained and people continued to complain. Purveyance was not the only negative experience of the royal household that many endured. The trampling of crops by the royal hunt, or the killing of animals by royal hunting dogs, also featured among grievances. The 1318 Ordinances also claimed that daily complaints were made about a mass of people who followed the royal court, including women of ill-repute and other undesirable figures. Courtiers themselves were also capable of unsavoury behaviour and were regularly accused of serious crimes, including homicides and violent assaults, down to minor infringements such as failure to pay debts.

From the 1290s these crimes fell under the jurisdiction of the 'court of the verge', usually presided over by the steward of the household, which had jurisdiction over just about all crimes committed within a twelve-mile radius of the royal household (or the person of the king if he was not with his household, as happened on occasion). The steward had long since possessed special judicial powers, but as with many aspects of the royal household, these were formalised under Edward I. The court of the verge, which usually convened every other day, was not only about enforcing household discipline, however. Among other things, it punished crimes committed against household officials (such as resistance to purveyors) and the king's peace more generally (even where they did not involve a member of the court or household) and ensured that the markets from which the household was buying its goods were using correct weights and measures.

Important though local grievances were, kings were generally more concerned when they faced criticism of their court and household that was political in nature. Often when such criticism emerged it centred on household finances, which could be very considerable. On several occasions in this period ordinances were introduced in an effort to constrain household expenditure. For the most part, these were predicated on the idea that 'ordinary' royal expenditure (i.e. money spent on the royal household, the administration of justice, diplomacy and the maintenance of the crown's estates) should be covered by the crown's 'ordinary' income (drawn from its demesne lands, the farms it received from the shires, feudal incidents such as the profits of warships and marriages, the profits of royal justices and a few lucrative gifts), which has been estimated at £20,000–£30,000 a year in this period (see Chapter 5). Complaints of this nature were common throughout the later Middle Ages, although they were particularly prevalent during the reign of Richard II. Remonstrances were made in parliament during the early years of Richard II's reign and in November 1381 the king was asked to pass new ordinances regulating household expenditure, which had sat at roughly £15,000–£20,000 a year during the 1370s.[26] Measures were agreed in 1383 and by 1386–7 the king's living expenses were down to roughly £12,000 for the financial year. This was one of the lowest amounts for the whole of the fourteenth century, which rarely, if ever, fell below £10,000 per year. While this did not altogether stop complaints, they were far less common thereafter until the late 1390s, by which time expenditure was on the rise once more, climbing to nearly £37,000 for the year 1396–7. In response, in February 1397 Thomas Haxey presented a parliamentary bill on behalf of the Commons that criticised the king for running a household that was too extravagant, too expensive and unable to cover its own living expenses and asked the king to address this. Richard reacted angrily, arguing that the Commons had no business meddling in his personal affairs and Haxey was convicted of treason, though his life was spared at the request of the prelates at parliament. Richard's household expenses continued to soar thereafter, peaking at more than £37,000 for 1397–8, and remained at near enough that level until his deposition in 1399. His successor, Henry IV, succeeded in reducing his living costs to roughly £20,000–£25,000 a year in the early 1400s, yet he still faced recurrent attacks from parliament regarding his personal finances and in 1406 (by which time he had racked up debts of more than £25,000) he was forced to agree to meet with a newly appointed council who would help decide a suitable sum to be set aside for household expenses.[27]

Some observers – usually clerical ones – were also worried about the morality of a court that indulged too heavily in luxury and excess. As Christopher Fletcher has shown, concepts such as 'decorum' and 'constancy' were important to the reputations of medieval rulers: these required medieval rulers and their courtiers to demonstrate qualities such as truthfulness, loyalty, logic, reasoning and self-mastery, and to shy away from excess.[28] A common target for these moral critiques was the clothing that courtiers wore. During the 1340s and 1350s new trends saw tunics becoming shorter and clothing generally more elaborate. In response, one French author wrote that the nobility now 'have robes so short that ... when they bend to serve a lord, they show their underwear, and that which is within, to those who are behind them'.[29]

Such criticism was often linked to broader concerns about excessive lust and sexual activity, which could be used as a way of attacking the court or king. One of the most famous incidents in this regard came in the 1350s, when Edward III was accused of violently raping the countess of Salisbury, the wife of one of his leading courtiers. While the story was almost certainly not true – part of a French smear campaign aimed at discrediting the English king – it highlights the importance of proper sexual conduct to maintaining a morally reputable court. This was something that Edward III ended up falling foul of in the latter years of his reign when he took one of the queen's *demoiselles* (a type of lady-in-waiting), Alice Perrers, as his mistress. She became hugely unpopular with the English nobility and was banished from the realm following the Good Parliament of 1376, though she was back at the king's side when he died the following year.

Alice Perrers was so unpopular because she enjoyed unparalleled influence and acquired a substantial landed estate. She was far from alone in this and is emblematic of a much wider concern that the political community had in this period regarding royal 'favourites' (see Chapter 11). Indeed, Perrers was just one key figure in a clique of royal favourites who dominated court in the 1370s. Alongside her were William Latimer, John Neville of Raby and Richard Sturmy, all of whom were attacked by the Good Parliament for being 'evil counsellors and evil doers'.[30] They were not the first to have such criticisms levelled at them: Henry III was accused of placing too much stock in the Lusignans at his court, while Edward II was attacked for the closeness of his relationship with first Piers Gaveston and later Hugh Despenser the Younger. Nor were they the last: Richard II faced the wrath of the so-called Merciless Parliament in 1388, which declared that twelve of his twenty-three chamber knights were 'undesirable' figures,[31] while Henry

VI kept about him an influential and unpopular group of courtiers in the late 1430s and 1440s (led by William de la Pole, the duke of Suffolk and including Ralph Boteler, Adam Moleyns, Edmund Beaufort, Roger Fiennes, James Fiennes, Thomas Tuddenham and many other household retainers) on whom he showered generous grants of royal patronage.

We might ask, however, how fair all this criticism was. The demonising of 'evil counsellors' was certainly a useful trope for condemning the poor performance of government without running the risk of criticising the king directly. Likewise, while some courtiers were undoubtedly self-serving and used their privileged position for personal gain, to suggest that all were so inclined would be unfair. If we look at the Merciless Parliament of 1388 from the other direction, for instance, we might note that eleven of Richard's twenty-three chamber knights were *not* considered 'undesirable' figures. Indeed, when serious criticism was aimed at the court, it was often focused on a few 'bad apples', rather than challenging the court as a whole. Even the vehemently anti-court rhetoric of John Cade's rebellion in the 1450s was keen to stress that 'we blame not all the lordys, ne all tho that is about the kyngs person'.[32] This is important for it reminds us that at no point was it suggested that the court should not exist, only that it should perhaps be smaller, less expensive, and that a few unsavoury individuals should be compelled to leave it. Its place in late medieval kingship was not up for debate.

Conclusion

The royal court and household underwent several important changes during the later Middle Ages. A small number of royal residences in the south-east of England became increasingly popular as homes for English kings. The great chamber came to take preference over the hall as the king's main social space. Household knights gave way to chamber knights, king's knights and, later, knights of the king's body. And ordinances were passed in an attempt to regulate the size, structure and cost of the household (with varying degrees of success), often following criticism from the wider political community.

Despite these changes, the core function and character of both remained broadly consistent across the period. The court represented the environment and people around the king. It offered a space in which he could interact with his nobility and international visitors, and it played a crucial role reminding the world of the monarchy's unique dignity and splendour. But it lacked a defined structure: it had no fixed home, no fixed membership and no rule book on how it should operate in this period. In some ways, it existed in the mind as much as in reality. By contrast, the household was a more formal body, containing important offices and officials above stairs, whose job it was to advise the king and help him run his kingdom, and a range of departments below stairs that met the monarch's domestic needs. This offered all-important structure around which the court could operate.

The court and household were thus central to the exercise of late medieval kingship. This was not just the case in England. Indeed, all rulers in Europe – kings, emperors, popes – kept a court and household around them in this period. In late medieval England, as elsewhere, the court and household were key components of the king's ability to project his authority and create an aura of majesty around his person. To this extent they made positive and vital contributions to his position as king; but when they were mismanaged and attracted criticism the court and household could undermine his power and weaken his standing. The court and household were, like many aspects of late medieval kingship, double-edge swords.

Notes

1. Walter Map, *De Nugis Curialium*, ed. M. R. James, revised ed. (Oxford, 1983), 248.
2. J. Watts, 'Was There a Lancastrian Court?', in *The Lancastrian Court: Proceedings of the 2001 Harlaxton Symposium*, ed. J. Stratford (Donington, 2003), 253–71.
3. *CPR, 1354–58*, 173.
4. M. Vale 'Courts', in *Government and Political Life in England and France, c.1300–c.1500*, ed. C. Fletcher, J.-P. Genet and J. Watts (Cambridge, 2015), 24–40 (at 35).
5. E. B. Fryde, 'Pole, Sir William de la', in *ODNB*, https://doi.org/10.1093/ref:odnb/22460 (accessed 23 September 2024).
6. M. Hefferan, *The Household Knights of Edward III: Warfare, Politics and Kingship in Fourteenth-Century England* (Woodbridge, 2021), 76.
7. G. L. Harriss, 'The Court of the Lancastrian Kings', in *Lancastrian Court*, ed. Stratford, 1–18 (at 14–15).

8. T. F. Tout, *Chapters in the Administrative History of Mediaeval England* (Manchester, 1920), 163.
9. M. Prestwich, *Edward I* (New Haven, CT, 1997), 162.
10. D. Carpenter, *Henry III, 1207–1258: The Rise to Power and Personal Rule* (New Haven, CT, 2020), 351.
11. Harriss, 'Court of the Lancastrian Kings', 16.
12. For this and what follows, see C. Given-Wilson, *The Royal Household and the King's Affinity: Service, Politics and Finance in England, 1360–1413* (London, 1986), 30–33.
13. S. Gunn and A. Janse, *The Court as a Stage: England and the Low Countries in the Later Middle Ages* (Woodbridge, 2006).
14. Harriss, 'Court of the Lancastrian Kings', 9–10.
15. '*Continuatio Eulogii*', in *Chronicles of the Revolution, 1397–1400: The Reign of Richard II*, ed. C. Given-Wilson (Manchester, 1993), 68; N. Saul, *Richard II* (New Haven, CT, 1997), 340.
16. N. Saul, 'Richard II and the Vocabulary of Kingship', *EHR* 110 (1995), 854–77; G. Dodd, 'Kingship, Parliament and the Court: The Emergence of "High Style" in Petitions to the English Crown, 1350–1405', *EHR* 129 (2014), 515–48.
17. Prestwich, *Edward I*, 158.
18. *Historia Vitae et Regni Ricardi Secundi*, ed. G. B. Stow (Philadelphia, 1977), 156; Saul, *Richard II*, 355.
19. A. Murimuth, *Continuatio Chronicarum*, ed. E. M. Thompson, RS (London, 1889), 155–6.
20. Prestwich, *Edward I*, 114–15.
21. M. J. Bennett, 'France in England: Anglo-French Culture in the Reign of Edward III', in *Language and Culture in Medieval Britain: The French of England, c.1100–c.1500*, ed. J. Wogan-Browne (York, 2009), 320–33.
22. M. J. Bennett, 'The Court of Richard II and the Promotion of Literature', in *Chaucer's England: Literature in Historical Context*, ed. B. Hanawalt (Minneapolis, 1992), 3–20.
23. T. F. Tout, *The Place of Reign of Edward II in English History* (Manchester, 1914), 303–4.
24. TNA, E 36/201, f. 52.
25. *SR*, I, 371–8.
26. For figures, see Given-Wilson, *Royal Household*, appendix 1.
27. G. Dodd, 'Unanimity, Anonymity and Immunity: Thomas Haxey and the Form of the Common Petition in Fourteenth-Century England', in *Petitions and Petitioning in Europe and North America: From the Late Medieval Period to the Present*, ed. R. Huzzey, M. Janse, H. Miller, J. Oddens and B. Waddell (Oxford, 2024), 219–38.
28. C. Fletcher, *Richard II* (Oxford, 2008), 45–59.
29. *The Battle of Crécy: A Casebook*, ed. and trans. M. Livingston and K. DeVries (Liverpool, 2015), 133.

30. 'The *Anonimalle Chronicle*', in *EHD, 1327–1485*, 121.
31. Given-Wilson, *Royal Household*, 163.
32. 'Stowe's Memoranda', in *Three Fifteenth-Century Chronicles with Historical Memoranda by John Stowe*, ed. J. Gairdner (London, 1880), 96.

Further Reading

Binski, P., *Westminster Abbey and the Plantagenets: Kingship and the Representation of Power, 1200–1400* (New Haven, CT, 1995).

Carpenter, D., *Henry III: 1207–1258, The Rise to Power and Personal Rule* (New Haven, CT, 2020), ch. 7.

Given-Wilson, C., *The Royal Household and the King's Affinity: Service, Politics and Finance in England, 1360–1413* (London, 1986).

Gunn, S. and Janse, A., *The Court as a Stage: England and the Low Countries in the Later Middle Ages* (Woodbridge, 2006).

Harriss, G. L., *Shaping the Nation: England 1360–1461* (Oxford, 2005), ch. 2.

Horrox, R., 'Caterpillars of the Commonwealth? Courtiers in Late Medieval England', in *Rulers and Ruled in Late Medieval England: Essays Presented to Gerald Harriss*, ed. R. E. Archer and S. Walker (London, 1995), 1–16.

Prestwich, M., *Edward I* (New Haven, CT, 1997), ch. 6.

Saul, N., *Richard II* (New Haven, CT, 1997), ch. 14.

Scattergood, V. J. and Sherbourne, J., *English Court Culture in the Later Middle Ages* (London, 1983).

Stratford, J., ed., *The Lancastrian Court: Proceedings of the 2001 Harlaxton Symposium* (Donington, 2003).

Vale, M., *The Princely Court: Medieval Courts and Culture in North-West Europe, 1270–1380* (Oxford, 2001).

  'Courts', in *Government and Political Life in England and France, c.1300–c.1500*, ed. C. Fletcher, J.-P. Genet and J. Watts (Cambridge, 2015), 24–40.

J. L. LAYNESMITH

9

Queens and the Royal Family

Of the eleven kings under discussion in this volume, only two were married at their accession. Four of the others were still children, but those who had reached adulthood were expected to marry as soon as possible. There were practical reasons for this – the need for an heir to guarantee stability and the opportunity to create a diplomatic alliance that would strengthen a new regime. There were also ideological reasons. Medieval literature, chronicles and reports of gossip all demonstrate that a queen was an integral part of the medieval ideal of stable, mature kingship. This sense of a need for a feminine element in sovereignty was similarly apparent in the elevated position of the Virgin Mary who had been celebrated as queen of heaven from at least the sixth century. Just as medieval kings were Christ's representatives, so the ideology of late medieval queenship drew inspiration from His idealised mother. Yet kings often ruled without a queen consort, especially at the beginning of their reign. So the structures underpinning queenship had to be repeatedly dismantled then reimagined and reconstructed.

Queen-Making

For most of this period, the first priority in selecting a queen was usually to protect English-held territories in France. If, like Henry III's marriage to the well-connected Eleanor of Provence, it offered potential influence with the papacy and the Holy Roman Empire too, these were significant additional attractions. Only after all of England's French lands except

Calais had been lost, in the mid fifteenth century, and amid the struggles of the Wars of the Roses, did priorities change. Edward IV's council looked primarily for an alliance that would cut foreign aid to his Lancastrian opponents.

Royal councillors expected to be fully involved in the king's choice of bride. They were consequently outraged in September 1464 when Edward IV revealed that he had secretly wed a Northamptonshire gentlewoman – Elizabeth Woodville – who was the widowed daughter of one of his own council members. Contemporary responses to this marriage reveal much about the expectations and superstitions surrounding late medieval royal matrimony. Both Elizabeth's social status and the fact that she was not a virgin were given as reasons that the marriage should not have taken place. Kings had married widows before, but virginity was considered to be a spiritually superior condition, especially for women. Second marriages always risked opprobrium and priests were not supposed to grant them the nuptial blessing that was part of the usual wedding ritual. The desire for a virgin queen also had practical aspects to it. It was assumed that a younger queen's character could be more easily moulded to her new country's manners (assuming she was a foreign princess) and to her husband's ways, and there was a reasonable concern about the possible impact that children from an earlier marriage might have on the political structure. Following Edward IV's early death, his brother, Richard, duke of Gloucester, was able to build on the earlier sense of Elizabeth Woodville's unfitness for queenship. Asserting that she had never legally been married to Edward IV because hers was not the first secret contract King Edward had made, Richard III's parliament declared: 'After the ungracious pretended marriage [between Edward and Elizabeth] the order of all politic rule was perverted' and England descended into lawlessness.[1] This sense that if the king's marriage was unpleasing to God the entire kingdom would suffer had its roots in Old Testament prophetic works and frequently appeared in chronicles and romances.

The queen's physical appearance was also considered when choosing a royal bride. Ambassadors brought back portraits or detailed descriptions of potential queens. Giles of Rome, in his widely read volume *The Governance of Kings and Princes*, optimistically advised that a fair wife should be chosen 'to avoid fornication'.[2] It was probably more important that her admirable appearance would reflect well upon the king and his court, yet if she was so beautiful that she was thought to be distracting the king from the business of government this too would be an occasion for criticism.

Most queens travelled to England for their wedding, usually after receiving the security of a proxy wedding in their home country. The future queen's journey gave a king opportunities to demonstrate the ideals and strengths of his kingship to a wide audience, showing off the impressive resources at his disposal. The wedding generally took place within a few days of the bride's arrival in England: Eleanor of Provence and Margaret of France both arrived at Dover and married Henry III and Edward I respectively at Canterbury Cathedral. Canterbury was the kingdom's spiritual capital, paralleled with the political centre at Westminster where they would be crowned. Henry IV, having recently usurped the throne, chose to marry Joan of Navarre at Winchester, which was a more ancient political capital, associated with exemplary kings Alfred and Arthur, as well as being a more convenient location for a bride travelling from Brittany. Edward IV's decision to marry in secret, in order to force his council's hand, meant that he had lost the opportunity for these displays and affirmations. Demonstrating the perennial flexibility of queenship, he instead arranged for a formal acceptance of their union in the church at Reading Abbey, where his council was meeting, so that she could be 'openly honoured as queen by the lords and all the people'.[3]

The wedding ceremony traditionally occurred at the church or cathedral door but was followed by a Mass at the high altar and an appropriately lavish feast. Typically the service was performed by the archbishop of Canterbury. When Edward III's queen, Philippa of Hainault, arrived in late 1327 there was a vacancy at Canterbury, so she was escorted to the northern province for the archbishop of York to perform the ceremony at York Minster. This was followed by festivities 'scarcely less ostentatious than the king's coronation a year earlier'.[4] In a telling break from tradition, there was no coronation for Philippa herself in the immediate aftermath of her wedding. Her mother-in-law, Isabella of France, who had overthrown her own husband months earlier, remained the only crowned and anointed queen in the realm until 1330. It seems likely that Isabella only permitted Philippa's coronation in February that year because the young queen was by then five months pregnant. The idea that a queen's coronation affected the throne-worthiness of her offspring probably similarly explains Edward I's decision not to crown his second queen, Margaret of France. Edward thereby reduced the potential for the children of this marriage to undermine the heir of his first who had been born before Edward himself became king. For Henry IV, as a usurper king, such considerations were presumably of less importance than the symbolic value of arranging a sumptuous coronation for his only queen, Joan of Navarre. The association between children's throne-worthiness and the timing of their parents' coronation probably waned as a result of the upheavals of the fifteenth century.

The earliest recorded anointing of an English queen was a ritual intended to protect the status of the Frankish princess Judith at the court of her much older husband, Æthelwulf of Wessex, in 856. The purpose, form and ideology of such rituals evolved over the centuries. Unlike the liturgy for a king's coronation, there was little change in the words used for the queen's rite between the twelfth-century 'Third Recension' of the Coronation ordo and the 'Fourth Recension' used in 1308 and thereafter. However, the wider form and function of the ritual developed considerably. As it became more elaborate, and there was sometimes a significant delay between wedding and coronation, it became less a celebration of her legitimacy as the king's wife and more of an affirmation of her status as an integral part of the workings of kingship: inclining the king to mercy, generosity, piety and peace, and making his earthly court a reflection of that in heaven.

Earlier coronations were so firmly an extension of the wedding celebrations that Matthew Paris described the feast after Eleanor of Provence's coronation as 'the king's nuptial festivities'.[5] But it developed as an opportunity for the three estates of the realm to demonstrate their assent to the queen's new status. The, often fiercely contested, right to perform most of the roles and services at the coronation had become hereditary – by blood or by office. The earliest record of a court of claims to determine this is from Eleanor of Provence's coronation and it provides a valuable description of the ceremony. The king, crowned and in royal robes, walked from the palace of Westminster to the abbey with his regalia carried before him and the queen followed after him, even when it was only the queen who was to be crowned. The banquet which followed was almost as important as the service in the abbey: a secular, aristocratic celebration affirming the new status quo. Claims to sit at certain tables at the feast, or to serve the royal table, were contested as eagerly as the rights to hold regalia.[6]

The late fourteenth-century innovations in kings' coronations – a procession from Blackheath to the Tower of London, a ceremony creating knights of the Bath and a formal procession from the Tower to the palace of Westminster next day – were adopted for queens' coronations too, contributing to a popular perception of greater similarity between the two rituals than the carefully composed differences in liturgy intended. Joan of Navarre, consort of Henry IV, was probably the first queen given centre stage at her coronation by her husband's absence, a practice that was continued throughout the fifteenth century. The increasingly elaborate pageants created for queens' routes through the city enabled the citizens of London to work with the king's council in presenting their own commentary on queenship. Verses accompanying the pageants displayed to Margaret of Anjou focused on her role as peacemaker. Her recent marriage was woven into extended metaphors comparing her bridegroom, Henry VI, with Christ the bridegroom and London with the heavenly Jerusalem.[7] After the abbey ritual and banquet, the final stage of the queen's coronation celebrations throughout the later Middle Ages was one that brought the queen firmly back into the world shaped by the secular nobility: a tournament.

Income

A key element of most royal marriage treaties was the financial settlement that the king promised to provide for his new queen. This generally included discussion of her income as queen consort but centred on the value of lands and fees that would be assigned to enable her to maintain her status if widowed: her dower. Dower was distinct from the dowry which was the money and/or lands traditionally given to a couple by the bride's family. In practice a number of kings waived their right to dowry in exchange for their father-in-law's or brother-in-law's recognition of their rights to contested lands or because the alliance itself was considered reward enough. Dower arrangements changed according to the financial priorities of kings and the expectations of queens' families. Specific properties were often allocated some years into the marriage as appropriate lands became available to the king or in response to the births of children, and arrangements could prove complicated if a queen dowager were still alive at the time of the king's marriage or when there were two queen dowagers.

Twenty-six years into her marriage, after four previous assignments, the value of Eleanor of Provence's dower lands was finally set at £4,000 a year. Commitments for the queen's dower remained in this region, more often £4,500, until 1396 when Richard II promised his child bride Isabella of Valois 10,000 marks (£6,666 13s. 4d.). Lancastrian kings, anxious not to appear less dignified and solvent than the regime overthrown in 1399, attempted unsuccessfully to maintain this tradition. Edward IV, free from the constraints of foreign in-laws' expectations, re-established £4,500 as the appropriate sum for a queen's dower. This enabled him to demonstrate his commitment to more sound financial management than his predecessor as well as his policy of kingship modelled on Edward III's.

During their husbands' lifetime, queens relied on a range of income sources to maintain their household and lifestyle, and to fund their religious and artistic patronage. These sources changed across the period and often with the queen's lifecycle. In the thirteenth century, young queens were typically financed at the king's discretion with grants from the exchequer to the keepers of her wardrobe. A substantial portion of their income came from queen's gold. This was a 10 per cent levy on 'voluntary' fines that had been paid to the king. The Jewish community were especially vulnerable to these levies which were also applied on that third part of every Jew's possessions which were forfeit to the crown on their death. Queen's gold appears to have originated in the moneys paid to early medieval queens in return for persuading their kings to grant certain privileges.[8] By the later twelfth century the percentage had been regularised and it seems active intervention by the queen was no longer required, but the range of fines to which it should be applied was regularly a matter of dispute. Following the expulsion of the Jews in 1290, and as a result of the considerable resentment provoked by queen's gold, this became an increasingly unpredictable source of revenue.

The most reliable element of Eleanor of Provence's income came from grants of wardships (i.e. the custody of the person and estates of the orphaned heirs of tenants-in-chief). This provided her not only with income but also with responsibilities and opportunities for influence on the estates of significant landholders. Inevitably she retained these only for as long as the landholders were minors. Eleanor of Castile, supported by her husband, Edward I, sought greater stability by purchasing lands for herself. She was also granted *amobr* fines which were customarily paid in Wales when a woman married or was found guilty of sexual misconduct. Until the end of the fourteenth century these fines were part of each queen consorts' income.

Edward I's decision to allow Margaret of France, his second queen, to access the revenues of some of her dower lands in her lifetime reintroduced a practice that seems to have fallen into abeyance in the twelfth century. This resource became more significant throughout the later Middle Ages. Both Margaret of Anjou and Elizabeth Woodville controlled all of their dower lands from the first months of their marriage. These were not merely a source of revenue and opportunity for patronage but also places in which loyal affinities were built up: in the tempestuous mid 1450s, the Lancastrian court frequently retreated from the hostile capital to Margaret of Anjou's Midland estates. In more peaceful times the renovations they made to their properties could enhance their queenly image and express their sense of identity, as Rachel Delman has demonstrated in a study of Margaret of Anjou's designs and decorations at Greenwich.[9] Queens were dependent upon the king's good will for their financial solvency. At the outbreak of the War of Saint Sardos in 1324, Edward II confiscated Queen Isabella's West Country estates, claiming there was a risk of a French landing there. The grant he gave her in compensation was much less than their annual value.[10] In 1419, in order to help finance his war with France, Henry V seized his stepmother Joan of Navarre's dower, claiming that she had been complicit in sorcery directed against him. More positively, when Philippa of Hainault's debts were out of control, in 1360, Edward III absorbed much of her household and administration into his.

Household and Administration

Unlike other married women, queens held land in their own right and were expected to manage the finances of their household, with support from their own council. There is ample evidence in letters and financial accounts that they actively engaged with their councils, estate officials and tenants as any other landholder did. The queen's ministers and officials enjoyed a degree of political immunity in comparison with those of other lords because only the king could authorise investigations into their actions and this proved particularly contentious in the thirteenth century.

The queen's council was drawn primarily from her household and her estate administrators and seems to have met daily. The council had a permanent headquarters for storing its records and for meeting when practical. This was initially in London, possibly, by the mid fourteenth century, at the queen's wardrobe at La Reole in Vintry Ward. Joan of Navarre's council and her successors' were based at the New Tower in the palace of Westminster, within easy reach of other royal administrators. As well as advising the queen and working on the day-to-day administration of her estates, this council also, at least by the fourteenth century, had jurisdiction over any disputes involving the queen's tenants. In the 1450s Margaret of Anjou was employing a team of eleven lawyers to support her administration. A sample of the sorts of business dealt with is given in a surviving memorandum by her clerk to the council that refers to a blocked highway, illegal fishing, a coroner absconding with his fee without giving a verdict and pasture rights. As well as appointing many of the officials on their estates, queens often had responsibility for presenting clergy to livings or to senior positions in religious houses. Occasionally this resulted in conflict when locals objected to her choice or the right was contested.

Queens cannot have been involved in all the administrative decisions that their councils carried out, but letters were always phrased as expressions of the queen's will and were presumably understood as that by officials and tenants. Like other noblewomen and churchmen in the high Middle Ages, queens initially adopted vesica-shaped (pointed oval) seals on their letters. Whereas kings were typically depicted seated on thrones or on horseback, queens stood facing the viewer, cloaked and with their hair loose beneath their crown as it was at their coronation. Eleanor of Provence's earliest seal depicts her holding elaborate rods or sceptres.[11] Much has been written about the possibility that queens' sceptres were seen as emblems of their intercessory role, yet the various styles of rod or sceptre that appear in images of kings, queens, princes, God and the Virgin Mary are so interchangeable that this could not have been effective. It is more likely to have been an emblem of divinely sanctioned authority (like Aaron's rod), especially when depicted on seals. Philippa of Hainault was the last queen to use this style for her great seal and the vesica shape was already somewhat old-fashioned in England by then. Her privy seal was round and bore a shield of the arms of England quartered with those of Hainault. Shields of arms had been appearing within queens' seals since Margaret of France's administration and they now became the dominant image, celebrating not only the queen's status as consort in England but also her natal lineage.[12]

Eleanor of Provence was the first queen with an independent wardrobe to deal with her household accounts.[13] The structure of the queen's household was much like the king's in miniature (100–180 personnel), designed to mesh with his when the king and queen were together yet operate independently as needed. The most obvious difference between their households was the queen's closest attendants: between twelve and thirty women, often collectively described as 'ladies' but also officially divided between ladies (noblewomen), damsels (gentlewomen) and lesser female attendants (under-damsels/night-watchers/chamberers). The largest groups were the damsels, including women who had travelled with queens from their home country. Some of these gentlewomen served successive English queens. It was not uncommon for a man to see his career prospects in royal service improve through marriage to one of the queen's damsels. In her detailed surveys of Isabella of France and Philippa of Hainault's attendants, Caroline Dunn notes that these women were not provided with salaries, only room, board and livery, but that good service was rewarded with annuities, pensions and corrodies.[14] By the mid fifteenth century, attendants could expect a regular salary appropriate to their status with principal ladies receiving the same salary as the queen's chamberlain.[15]

This community of women added to the theatre of monarchy on formal occasions like civic entries and tournaments. Just as important were the staged 'informalities' such as a carnivalesque Easter Monday tradition in which Edward I and his son permitted their queens' ladies to catch them in bed and demand a ransom.[16] At times of crisis, the political potential of these women becomes apparent. Caroline Dunn argues that several of Isabella's women were significant in achieving her coup against Edward II in 1326 and were well rewarded for this.[17] When Margaret of Anjou brought an army to the gates of London, the women sent by the city authorities to negotiate with her included Ismanie, Lady Scales, who had been Margaret's principal attendant. The other women in the queen's household were the nurses and governesses, some of whom later became queen's damsels. Even when the queen had no royal children of her own, important royal wards were often brought up in her household. Those in Joan of Navarre's care included Richard Despenser, whose father had been executed for rebellion against Henry IV.[18]

Queens commonly employed men in their household and on their estates who also held offices in the king's service or in the church. This was probably often with the king's encouragement, helping him to build up certain men's careers in particular areas. It also enabled queens to extend the potential for their influence. Finding opportunities for promotion for these men was an expectation of good ladyship. Some of the church livings acquired for these servants, like the 'church worth thirty marks' that Eleanor of Provence asked the archbishop of York to provide for her clerk of the wardrobe in 1243, were essentially sinecures that enabled the queen to fund her staff from sources outside of her own income.[19] Others influenced the relationship between church and court more profoundly: Margaret of Anjou's chancellor, Laurence Booth, went on to become keeper of the privy seal and one of the prince of Wales's council members as well as bishop of Durham. He was a key supporter of the queen's interests throughout the turbulent 1450s.

Patronage

Considerable evidence survives of the genuine affection between queens and their household members. Isabella of France (Edward II's queen), having decided she would be buried near her aunt Margaret at the Greyfriars in London, began paying for some of her attendants to be buried in this space that had previously been the preserve of 'super-rich' former benefactors of the Franciscans.[20] Many of the churches and guilds supported by queens had clearly been brought to their attention by household members. It was Philippa of Hainault's chaplain, Robert de Eglesfield, who founded Queen's College, Oxford and drew her patronage to the project.

Religious benefactions were also inspired by queenly tradition – Eleanor of Provence controversially wrested the patronage rights of the hospital of St Katherine's at Westminster from the priory to which it had been given by its founder, Matilda of Flanders, and then ensured subsequent queens enjoyed the same rights. Queens' generosity reflected contemporary fashions – Eleanor of Castile and Isabella of France were described as 'mothers' of, respectively, the Dominican and Franciscan orders in England, whereas late fifteenth-century queens showed more devotion to Carthusians and Bridgettines. Queens commonly undertook pilgrimages and the shrine at Walsingham (Norf.) appears to have been a particular focus for those, like Anne of Bohemia, struggling to conceive an heir.

Artists, musicians and writers also looked to queens for patronage. The extent to which some of these queens were personally active in such commissions is contested, although there can be no doubt that, for instance, Eleanor of Castile was responsible for arranging copies and original compositions to be created as well as purchasing 'off the shelf' books of various genres, or that Margaret of France commissioned a eulogy for her husband, Edward I.[21] Queens also spent hundreds of pounds every year on jewellery and plate, most of it to give away at diplomatic occasions, social visits, in the course of pilgrimages and, especially, at New Year. There was a strict etiquette matching the value of the gifts with the status of the recipients from the lowliest members of the queen's household to royal dukes and the king himself.

Relationships

Most kings grew up knowing that their marriage would be arranged for political reasons and that they would need to work at the relationship if it was to be an affectionate marriage. They were also aware that love in marriage was a social expectation and that a harmonious royal marriage was considered necessary for the good of the kingdom. This can make it difficult to be certain whether the signs of loving relationships between kings and queens should be accepted at face value or were merely the acting out of idealised kingship. In most cases, it does appear that positive relationships developed. Mark Ormrod observed that the many small gifts of fresh meat, hawks or horses that Philippa of Hainault and Edward III sent to each other when they were apart are more telling evidence of their affection than the lavish presents exchanged at religious festivals and family events. He also noted that they were 'avid letter-writers' and that Edward called his queen *douce cuer*, 'sweetheart'.[22] Edward I's grand gesture of grief at Eleanor of Castile's death – two tombs and twelve magnificent memorial crosses along the route taken by her funeral cortège (see Figure 16.17) – was clearly a response to the nine stone crosses (*montjoies*) recently set up between Paris and Saint-Denis celebrating Louis IX's sacred kingship.[23] This does not mean that Edward's mourning was not genuine. Richard II and Anne of Bohemia were exceptionally close and their households were rarely apart. After she died at the manor of Sheen he ordered its destruction. In all three of these relationships the queens' deaths were followed by political friction and, arguably, a deterioration in kingship which suggests these women had been providing the supportive and moderating influence hoped for in ideal queens. Eleanor of Provence and Henry III survived some very public fallings out but Edward II's marriage to Isabella of France was the only union that broke down entirely. The consequences were catastrophic for Edward.

Even loving marriages were not necessarily faithful ones, yet royal mistresses in England at this period did not achieve the levels of influence found in medieval France or early modern England. The outstanding exception is Alice Perrers and even she did not emerge as a public figure until after Philippa of Hainault's death. She was the daughter of a London goldsmith and widow of one of the king's jewellers. It was presumably Edward III who appointed her as one of his wife's damsels. Alice's avaricious influence at the heart of a hated court clique is described by Laura Tompkins as 'inverting queenship'.[24] After Edward III's death, Alice's goods and lands were confiscated as punishment for political corruption and she died still trying to reclaim them. Their son, Sir John de Southeray, had been permitted to retain the £100 annuity that his father had granted him and, like many royal bastards, pursued a military career.[25]

Both before and after his love match with Elizabeth Woodville, Edward IV's licentiousness was the subject of public comment, but his mistresses had no discernible political influence, other than Elizabeth Shore/Lambert's possible involvement in opposing Richard III's coup in the summer of 1483. Elizabeth Shore was from the same social milieu as Alice Perrers whereas others of Edward IV's mistresses were from minor gentry families. These probably included the mother of Arthur Plantagenet who was acknowledged by Edward IV, permitted to grow up in the royal nursery as 'the lord bastard', joined the household of his half-sister (Henry VII's queen) and enjoyed a distinguished career in Henry VIII's service, until he fell out with Thomas Cromwell. Elizabeth Woodville may have had little choice about Arthur's presence in her children's household but the fact that Edward IV's bastard daughter Grace was one of her attendants at her death suggests a pragmatic attitude to her husband's infidelities.[26]

Intercession

The 'inverted queenship' that Tompkins identified in Alice Perrers's behaviour focused on her abuse of her potential to persuade the king to attend to other's needs and desires: intercession. The significance of queens' roles as intercessors has been the focus of considerable scholarship. As Paul Strohm demonstrated, Philippa of Hainault's appeal for the lives of the condemned burghers of Calais and Anne of Bohemia's mediation between Richard II and the citizens of London in 1392 captured contemporary imaginations. They were written up in exaggeratedly gendered accounts that presented these women's self-abasement as a means of moderating and balancing the necessary imposition of royal justice. Both incidents were probably staged to allow the king to change his mind or be conciliatory without appearing weak.[27]

As both Anthony Musson and Lisa Benz St John have demonstrated, intercession (the receipt and presentation of petitions) was just as much a feature of male lordship as it was of queenship. The language of humble supplication to the king or chancery that was used by queens was the same as that used by other lords. Through the fourteenth century the majority of queens' recorded acts of intercession were not direct appeals to the king but requests addressed to chancery. Margaret of France's appeals were just as successful when her husband was in Scotland as when they were together, but queens' standing in the kingdom clearly shaped their capacity for influence with the chancellor: Isabella of France's intercessions were reduced dramatically during the rise of the Despensers, but in 1327–30 they significantly exceeded those of her daughter-in-law Philippa. As Benz St John observes, it is likely that queens' direct appeals to their husband usually occurred in person with no necessity to create a written record.[28]

Some petitioners to the queen did construct the intercession they hoped for in gendered terms, mentioning pregnancy or recent childbirth, or using quasi-Marian language to address her.[29] As Philippa of Hainault and Anne of Bohemia's most famous acts demonstrated, the queen's unique status as a woman at the heart of power could be used in the theatre of sacred kingship, but most of the time intercession was part of the queen's 'workaday, business-like role'.[30] Queens were intercessors not because of their gender but because the privilege of proximity to the king required it, just as noblemen's proximity to the king did, and because it was part of the wider culture of reciprocity in medieval lordship.

The dark side of intercession was the potential to assist favourites to dominate the court or to encourage the king to make poor political decisions. Eleanor of Provence and Eleanor of Castile both came in for particular criticism for their promotion of foreigners, to the extent of Londoners hurling missiles and insults at Eleanor of Provence's barge on one occasion. Edward IV's queen became the focus of the earl of Warwick's justification for rebellion on the grounds that she had 'always exerted herself to aggrandise her relations ... and had brought things to such a pass that they had the entire government of this realm'.[31] Queens as 'evil counsellors' were a safer target for criticism than kings themselves and rhetoricians had no shortage of examples to draw on in encouraging the king's subjects to mistrust female influence.

The question of how much power queens genuinely exerted continues to be debated. Christine de Pisan's *Treasure of the City of Ladies* assumed that queens would offer advice to their kings, ideally counselling peace and conciliation. Occasions for more direct influence were more commonly determined by personalities and political circumstance than by defined roles within the office of queenship. In 1253, Henry III appointed Eleanor of Provence as his regent in England while he quelled rebellion in Gascony, but she eventually joined him on the continent, leaving his brother to continue government. Indeed, it was much more common for king's brothers to take up this role (as 'keeper of the realm') than for queens. Yet on several occasions Edward III named one of his infant sons as 'keeper', leaving Queen Philippa unofficially presiding over the actions of his council in the king's absence. For most of the time, queens' authority and influence bore strong similarities to that of other major landholders with access to the king, including occasional ambassadorial roles to foreign courts. Surviving letters also reveal queens encouraging noblewomen to persuade their husbands to acquiesce to requests from the king or to support the queen's own patronage. At times of crisis they could step into the breach left by a captive or incapacitated king. Eleanor of Provence's diplomatic skill and networking were essential to bringing about the defeat of Simon de Montfort in 1265. It may not have been until 1460 that Margaret of Anjou truly became the 'arch-defender and decision-maker of the Lancastrian cause' but her right to do so was accepted by Henry VI's loyalists from then on.[32] What most clearly set queens apart from every other political player was their potential role in guaranteeing dynastic security for the realm.

Royal Children

On 31 March 1485, in front of the mayor, aldermen and many citizens of London in the Hospital of St John of Jerusalem, Richard III publicly denied that he had arranged for his queen to be poisoned so that he could marry his niece.[33] That this rumour had become so widespread and serious was almost certainly because Queen Anne's recent death appeared all too convenient for a king whose only legitimate child had died the previous year. The experiences of Edward II and Henry VI had demonstrated that producing a male heir could not in itself protect a king from deposition, but there can be no doubt that male heirs were as much a part of ideal kingship as the queen who would bear them. Three years after Margaret of Anjou's marriage, a farm labourer was accused of claiming that 'Oure Quene was none abyl to be Quene of Inglond ... because that sche bereth no child, and because that we have no pryns in this land'.[34]

The birth of a royal child was naturally greeted with considerable celebration – Matthew Paris recorded that for Edward I's birth the citizens of London arranged 'bands of dancers, with drums and tambourines' who continued to perform through the night by lantern light. 'Costly presents' were sent from across the kingdom.[35] The queen herself was absent from any celebrations and from the child's baptism because, like any new mother, she was expected to remain in the privacy of her rooms for several weeks after the birth until the ceremony of purification (churching). Senior noblewomen from across the country were invited to attend this ritual and join a formal procession from the queen's chamber to the church which enabled a wider audience to view the proceedings.

Royal children were provided with a small number of servants as soon as they were born: a wetnurse or two, at least one more senior woman to oversee the nursery and a couple of men to manage the logistics and finances. David Carpenter suggests that the use of English nurses helped ensure royal children grew up able to understand English as well as the French that was spoken at court.[36] Whereas the first three Edwards seem to have seen little of their parents when they were very young, Henry III, Edward of Woodstock (Edward III's heir), Edward of Lancaster (Henry VI's heir) and Edward V had establishments more closely attached to their mothers' for their first few years.[37] For most of these boys, the fragile political situation and need to keep the heir safely close to the centre of power was probably as much of a factor in this as their mothers' personalities. This was not the case for Edward of Woodstock, but James Bothwell has noted the exceptional level of affection that Edward III seems to have lavished upon his children, all of whom were depicted on his tomb.[38]

The heir to the throne usually began to be given a more independent household from the age of three or four and typically was eventually provided with estates worth in the region of £4,000 which would increase considerably if he married in his father's lifetime. It was common to place other noble and gentry boys in these households, some of whom grew up to be their king's most loyal adherents. The men chosen to oversee their education usually had considerable military experience and were often closely linked with the boys' mothers: Edward II's master, the Gascon knight Guy Ferre, had served in Eleanor of Provence's administration and accompanied Eleanor of Castile to the Holy Land.[39] Eleanor of Castile is known to have sent one of the scribes from her personal scriptorium into her eldest son's household and from the fourteenth century evidence survives of the increasing importance of books in the education of future kings.[40] Vegetius's treatise on military strategy, mirrors for princes, histories and romances seem to have made up most young princes' reading matter along with the prayer books which were probably the first texts they learned to read from.[41]

Queens' status and authority were immediately enhanced by becoming the mother of the heir to the throne. Only in exceptional circumstances, like Margaret of Anjou's court in exile, were they very closely involved in these boys' administrations for long. Daughters and younger sons, however, often remained with their mothers for much longer and queens were more commonly closely involved in the arrangements for their weddings, whether those had been arranged to support the king's foreign policy, to win over powerful but troublesome magnates or to draw the estates of a major heiress into royal administration. Eleanor of Provence spent much of each year with her younger children at Windsor but would leave trusted staff with them for months at a time when she needed to travel. Temporary households of 50–100 staff were sometimes established for younger children while a queen accompanied her husband on campaign, but such separations seem to have become increasingly uncommon.

Unlike in France, no tradition of dowager queens running regency governments for their young sons developed in England. This was perhaps a consequence of the combinations of political circumstances and personalities involved in the first few minority governments. Kings' mothers, even if they had never been queen, were still usually significant figures in their sons' regimes. Cecily, duchess of York, mother of Edward IV, was recommended to papal nuncio Francesco Coppini for her influence over the king and Joan of Kent secured pardons from Richard II for murderers and debtors as well as mediating in high-profile disputes.[42] As Katherine Lewis has suggested, in the fraught climate of Henry VI's minority it appears that Cardinal Beaufort sought to manipulate this potential by (unsuccessfully) pressuring the young dowager queen, Katherine of Valois, to marry one of his own nephews.[43] Katherine may have hoped to avoid destabilising the political community by marrying an obscure Welsh squire instead. However, the consequence of her marriage to Owen Tudor, in the person of their grandson Henry, would ultimately have even greater impact on English politics than that of the unpopular de Lusignans, the children of Isabella of Angoulême's second marriage, whose influence with Henry III was so resented that it provoked rebellion.

Death of the Queen

Not every queen outlived her king to take up these opportunities. According to the fifteenth-century *Liber regie capelle*, a queen's funeral should follow exactly the same form as a king's. This tradition may have been established by Eleanor of Castile's remarkable exequies. Her body's interment in Henry III's recently rebuilt Westminster Abbey marked the abbey's new role as the Plantagenet mausoleum: Edward I commissioned two gilt-bronze effigies for her tombs (her bowels were buried at Lincoln) at the same time as arranging one for his father. As can be seen on her effigy at Westminster (Figure 9.1), Eleanor is depicted with loose hair beneath her crown. The pageantry of the funeral procession and her burial in royal robes with replica regalia similarly echoed her coronation. Some queens were involved in planning their tomb designs. These typically evoked their natal family lineage as well as that of English royalty. Philippa of Hainault's realistically plump white marble effigy was an innovation in portraiture. Anne of Bohemia seems to have been the first queen whose coffin was graced with a funeral effigy, a practice introduced for Edward II's burial.

Figure 9.1 Tomb effigy of Queen Eleanor of Castile, Westminster Abbey, c. 1291–3. (Photo by Angelo Hornak/Corbis via Getty Images.)

Most dowager queens were buried beside their husbands. This was not always at Westminster since deposed kings and those launching new dynasties were generally buried elsewhere. There was often competition between religious houses for such prestigious burials. Eleanor of Provence reversed an earlier commitment to Westminster Abbey for burial at Amesbury where she had become a nun. Isabella of France eschewed Edward II's burial site but was interred in her scarlet wedding mantle with her deposed husband's embalmed heart.

Conclusion

As the number of qualifiers in this chapter indicates, there is almost always at least one woman who has to be excepted from any general statement about queenship. It was a flexible institution, repeatedly reshaped by varying personalities and political situations. It was also a balancing act with impossible requirements: making use of valued continental connections without allowing foreign family and friends to inspire disruption; appearing resplendent and generous without living beyond her means or developing a reputation for acquisitiveness; being the king's most trusted confidant without provoking resentment for her influence. A queen could be the decisive figure in her husband's downfall, but more often she was a loved and respected companion who facilitated kingship in myriad ways.

Notes

1. *PROME*, parliament of 1484, item 1[5].
2. Giles of Rome, *The Governance of Kings and Princes*, ed. D. C. Fowler, C. F. Briggs and P. G. Remley (London, 1997), 189.
3. *Letters and Papers Illustrative of the Wars of the English in France*, ed. J. Stevenson, 2 vols., RS 22 (London, 1861–40), II, 783.
4. W. M. Ormrod, *Edward III* (New Haven, CT, 2013), 70.
5. *Matthew Paris's English History from the Year 1235 to 1273*, trans. J. A. Giles (London, 1852), 8.
6. L. G. W. Legg, *English Coronation Records* (Westminster, 1901), 57–65.
7. G. Kipling, 'The London Pageants for Margaret of Anjou: A Medieval Script Restored', *Medieval English Theatre* 4 (1982), 5–27.
8. K. Geaman, 'Queen's Gold and Intercession: The Case of Eleanor of Aquitaine', *Medieval Feminist Forum* 46 (2010), 12–33.

9. R. M. Delman, 'The Queen's House before Queen's House: Margaret of Anjou and Greenwich Palace, 1447–1453', *Royal Studies Journal* 8 (2021), 6–25.
10. S. Philips, *Edward II* (New Haven, CT, 2010), 482.
11. F. Sandford, *A Genealogical History* (London, 1677), 57.
12. Ibid., 124, 239.
13. H. Johnstone, 'The Queen's Household', in *Chapters in the Administrative History of Medieval England*, ed. T. F. Tout, 6 vols. (1920–33), V, 231–89 (at 235).
14. C. Dunn, 'All the Queen's Ladies? Philippa of Hainault's Female Attendants', *Medieval Prosopography* 31 (2016), 173–208.
15. A. R. Myers, *Crown, Household and Parliament in Fifteenth-Century England* (London, 1985), 181–2, 287–8.
16. C. Dunn, 'Serving Isabella of France: From Queen Consort to Dowager Queen', in *Royal and Elite Households in Medieval and Early Modern Europe*, ed. T. Earenfight (Leiden, 2018), 169–201 (at 188).
17. Ibid., 191.
18. T. B. Pugh, *Henry V and the Southampton Plot* (Gloucester, 1988), 78–9.
19. Johnstone, 'The Queen's Household', 235.
20. C. Steer, 'The Patronage of Queen Isabella (d. 1358): Monuments of the Royal Household at Friars Minor London', in *Creativity, Contradictions and Commemoration in the Reign of Richard II*, ed. J. A. Lutkin and J. S. Hamilton (Woodbridge, 2022), 249–68.
21. *The Court and Household of Eleanor of Castile in 1290*, ed. J. C. Parsons (Toronto, 1977), 13–14.
22. W. M. Ormrod, 'Philippa of Hainault: Dignity, Duty and Display', in *Later Plantagenet and the Wars of the Roses Consorts*, ed. A. Norrie et al. (Cham, 2023), 49–66 (at 53).
23. N. Coldstream, 'The Commissioning and Design of the Eleanor Crosses', in *Eleanor of Castile 1290–1990*, ed. D. Parsons (Stamford, 1991), 55–67.
24. L. Tompkins, 'The Uncrowned Queen: Alice Perrers, Edward III and Political Crisis in Fourteenth-Century England', unpublished PhD thesis (University of St Andrews, 2013), 217–30.
25. C. Given-Wilson and A. Curteis, *Royal Bastards of Medieval England* (London, 1984), 138–42.
26. *The Royal Funerals of the House of York at Windsor*, ed. A. F. Sutton and L. Visser-Fuchs (London, 2005), 73.
27. P. Strohm, *Hochon's Arrow: The Social Imagination of Fourteenth-Century Texts* (Princeton, NJ, 1992), 95–119.
28. L. Benz St John, *Three Medieval Queens: Queenship and the Crown in Fourteenth-Century England* (New York, 2012), 35–46; A. Musson, 'Queenship, Lordship and Petitioning in Late Medieval England', in

Medieval Petitions: Grace and Grievance, ed. W. M. Ormrod, G. Dodd and A. Musson (York, 2009), 156–72.
29. J. C. Parsons, 'The Queen's Intercession in Thirteenth-Century England', in *Power of the Weak*, ed. J. Carpenter and S. B. MacLean (Urbana, IL, 1995), 152–5.
30. Musson, 'Queenship, Lordship and Petitioning', 161.
31. *Calendar of State Papers and Manuscripts in the Archives and Collections of Milan 1385–1618*, ed. A. B. Hinds (London, 1912), 131.
32. M. Hicks, *The Wars of the Roses* (New Haven, CT, 2012), 126.
33. L. Lyell and F. D. Watney, *Acts of Court of the Mercer's Company 1453–1527* (Cambridge, 1936), 173–4.
34. *Fifth Report of the Royal Commission on Historical Manuscripts* (London, 1876), 455.
35. *Paris's English History*, 172.
36. D. A. Carpenter, *Henry III: The Rise to Power and Personal Rule, 1207–1258* (New Haven, CT, 2020), 3.
37. Ibid., 2–3; R. Barber, *Edward Prince of Wales and Aquitaine* (Woodbridge, 1996), 18.
38. J. Bothwell, 'An Emotional Pragmatism: Edward III and Death', in *Monarchy, State and Political Culture in Late Medieval England: Essays in Honour of W. Mark Ormrod*, ed. G. Dodd and C. Taylor (York, 2020), 39–70 (at 54–64).
39. Philips, *Edward II*, 54.
40. Ibid., 57; Ormrod, *Edward III*, 13–14.
41. N. Orme, *Medieval Children* (New Haven, CT, 2003), 247–70.
42. J. L. Laynesmith, *Cecily Duchess of York* (London, 2017), 85.
43. K. Lewis, 'Katherine of Valois: The Vicissitudes of Reputation', in *Later Plantagenet Consorts*, ed. Norrie et al., 123–144 (at 132–41).

Further Reading

Benz St John, L., *Three Medieval Queens: Queenship and the Crown in Fourteenth-Century England* (New York, 2012).
Crawford, A., 'The Queen's Council in the Middle Ages', *EHR* 116 (2001), 1193–211.
Howell, M., *Eleanor of Provence: Queenship in Thirteenth-Century England* (Oxford, 1998).
Laynesmith, J. L., *The Last Medieval Queens: English Queenship 1445–1503* (Oxford, 2004).
Norrie, A., Harris, C., Laynesmith, J. L., Messer, D. R. and Woodacre, E., eds., *Norman to Early Plantagenet Consorts: Power, Influence, and Dynasty* (Cham, 2023).

eds., *Later Plantagenet and the Wars of the Roses Consorts: Power, Influence, and Dynasty* (Cham, 2023).

Ormrod, W. M., 'The Royal Nursery: A Household for the Younger Children of Edward III', *EHR* 120 (2005), 398–415.

Parsons, J. C., *Eleanor of Castile: Queen and Society in Thirteenth-Century England* (London, 1994).

Tingle, L., *Chaucer's Queens: Royal Women, Intercession, and Patronage in England, 1328–1394* (Cham, 2020).

Part III

The King and His Subjects

ALISON K. MCHARDY

10

The Clergy

General Background

The clergy were important to the crown because they were (compared with today) very numerous – historians have described the country as 'swarming with clerics' and their 'vast numbers' as 'one of the surprises of medieval history';[1] collectively they were very rich, owning perhaps 20–30 per cent of England's landed wealth; many had skills which few laymen possessed; and, most importantly, they could, through their performance of religious ritual, send souls to paradise or perdition – hell – in the everlasting world to come. Clergy were of two kinds: the seculars, who lived in the world, serving parishes and collegiate churches; and regulars (also called 'the religious') who lived under a Rule, and were monks, nuns, canons and canonesses regular and friars. Religion was the way that medieval people made sense of the world; it was not an optional extra in life but affected all aspects of society. Everyone was a church member. The farming seasons and the liturgical year were entwined together, and church feasts and saints' days – not days of the month – were the points for fixing future dates, for example, in legal business. Oaths, sometimes made while touching gospel books, were used to cement agreement; now we use signatures. The oaths taken by witnesses in law courts today are the last remnants of the practice. The church was an immensely powerful, multinational institution with wide powers; for example, in England it had control over testamentary and matrimonial matters.

The English church was a highly structured organisation. The basic unit was the parish (c. 9,000 of these). These were grouped into archdeaconries, which, in turn, were grouped into bishoprics, also called dioceses, or sees (see Map 10.1). The holders of those twenty-one sees mattered to all our kings. The northern province, headed by the archbishop of York, contained three bishoprics: York, Carlisle and Durham. Canterbury province, headed by the archbishop of Canterbury,

Map 10.1 Dioceses of late medieval England and Wales

contained the remaining dioceses, including the four in Wales. The map shows how unevenly sized bishoprics were. They also varied greatly in wealth; though Lincoln was the largest diocese, Winchester was the richest. Rochester and Ely were both tiny, but Ely was proportionally very rich. All the Welsh dioceses were poor. Monastic houses – abbeys and priories – were scattered over the whole country, and like bishoprics, varied greatly in wealth. The clergy were legally distinct from laymen, but they were not a united body. The higher clergy, namely bishops, and rich abbots were distinct not only economically but also politically in the minds of kings.

The existence of two legal systems – on the one hand church courts dispensing canon law, with a hierarchy going up to the pope, and on the other hand secular, that is, common law administered by the kings' judges – could cause conflict with English kings. Yet church and crown were natural allies, for both relied on intangible power to enforce their wills, and both believed in obedience to authority and in the rule of law. Unglamourous as cooperation was, it was the norm in crown–church relations, even if low-level friction was often evident. This underlying harmony of ideals did not prevent conflict, especially between kings and some senior clerics. Every subsequent dispute took place under the shadow of the Henry II versus Thomas Becket contest of the 1160s. Becket's murder in 1170, at Henry's instigation, the king's subsequent humiliating punishment and Becket's canonisation formed a warning to all parties not to carry conflict to extremes. This restrained the contestants during Edward I's struggles with archbishops of Canterbury Pecham and Winchelsey between 1270 and 1297 and in archbishop Stratford's dispute with Edward III in 1340 over the funding of the king's wars. Only in 1405, with the execution of Richard Scrope, archbishop of York, was this gentlemanly convention breached.

Crown–clergy relations can be studied at three levels: the personal and private devotional lives of kings; the political interactions of kings with senior English clergy and with the papacy; and the daily life and routine work of government. This subject is best approached analytically, rather than chronologically, but underlying this is the importance of Edward I's reign, when crown–church relations were at their worst for any time between the late twelfth century and Henry VIII's breach with Rome, when government made a great leap forward in complexity and ambition and when significant legislation was passed.

Christian Kingship

Kings were spiritually distinct from their subjects; the anointing which they received at their coronation, which was (and still is) a religious ceremony conducted by senior clerics, made them *quasi* priests. One manifestation of this was their supposed power to cure a disease, scrofula, by touch, for which the best evidence comes from the reigns of the first three Edwards.[2] All our kings were ostentatiously pious, and an essential part of their daily lives was attendance at religious services. Henry III was an enthusiastic churchgoer who engaged in competitive Mass-going with his brother-in-law Louis IX of France ('I went to more Masses than you did'). Henry, essentially a man of peace, was an extravagant almsgiver who also revived the cult of Edward the Confessor and rebuilt Westminster Abbey.[3] Edward I, a former crusader, tried to attend Mass daily and gave extra alms when he failed. An enthusiastic visitor to Marian shrines, he also founded the Cistercian abbey of Vale Royal in Cheshire. Edward II founded the Dominican friary of King's Langley, Hertfordshire. Edward III founded two colleges of secular priests, St George's, Windsor, which was to be the 'headquarters' of the Order of the Garter, and St Stephen's, Westminster. Following the Black Death he founded St Mary Graces, London, a Cistercian abbey, whose increased endowment was one of the cares of his last months.

No king has left so vivid a picture of his beliefs as Richard II. The Wilton Diptych shows (Figures 16.19 and 16.20), on the left-hand panel, King Richard supported by his three patron saints, John the Baptist, Edward the Confessor and St Edmund. On the right are the Virgin and Child surrounded by angels who all wear Richard's white hart badge; clearly, they are members of his affinity. There are eleven angels, and their gestures and stances indicate that they are recommending Richard II to be the twelfth member of the angelic company. Much about this work is still mysterious, but it was surely commissioned to be part of the furnishing of the king's most private chapel and designed to accompany him when travelling. Richard's staunch orthodoxy gave him the erroneous belief that he had crushed religious dissent.

All our kings hitherto had employed Dominican friars, the most theologically highly trained order of clergy, as their confessors. The house of Lancaster, however, had traditionally favoured Carmelites friars, so both Henry IV and Henry V had Carmelite confessors.[4] Henry IV founded (Shrewsbury) or refounded (Fotheringhay) several colleges and showed conventional enthusiasm for relics and pilgrimages.[5] Henry V fiercely confronted heresy and aimed to reinvigorate the church with his monastic foundations at Sheen (Carthusians) and Syon (Bridgettine nuns). The piety of Henry VI was proverbial and found dramatic expression in founding educational colleges at Eton (Berks.) and Cambridge (King's College). Edward IV's contributions to church life were less notable, but he was conventionally pious and regularly heard sermons.

Monarchs were, however, detached from the clerical estate in not putting members of their family into holy orders. Only Edward III and Henry IV had 'spare' sons, and they used these as generals, rulers of dependencies and as diplomatic marriage tools, while no king after Edward I sent any daughter to a nunnery.[6] Instead, kings and their immediate kinsmen, concentrated on securing bishoprics for their ablest servants, a policy in which they competed with baronial families who sought high preferment for their sons.

Clergy, Politics and International Affairs

Relations between kings and their clerical subjects were complicated by clergy who were not English subjects but whom monarchs could not ignore: popes. Popes were the ultimate authority in all matters of theology and patronage and were the last court of appeal in ecclesiastical disputes. Papal power was greatest in the thirteenth century, and of our kings, Henry III was most deferential to papal ambitions. Most later kings regarded popes with a mixture of reverence, fear, irritation and contempt, but they could not ignore them. Papal developments during the thirteenth century affected relations between English kings and their clergy. The Fourth Lateran Council (1215) enacted measures to boost church observance and to raise the standard of clergy; the reformers were keen to detach individual clerics from secular pursuits, including crown service. Robert Grosseteste, the formidable bishop of Lincoln

(1235–53), was a great advocate of retreat from worldly employment, and John Pecham, archbishop of Canterbury (1272–92), under the influence of the Council of Lyons (1274) aspired to the same policy.

Papal power was diminished after 1300 by events on the continent. First, between 1309 and 1377, the popes, after their expulsion from Rome, took refuge in Avignon and fell under strong French influence. Then came the Great Schism of 1378–1417, when there were two, sometimes three popes, and when the European powers chose which line to support; England followed the Roman line, France those at Avignon. The Roman popes were anxious to retain English support, which made them compliant with requests arising from political events. Thus in 1388, and again in 1397–8, they agreed to translate, that is, move, prelates from one bishopric to another, to suit the faction in power. Dramatically, in 1405 when Henry IV executed Richard Scrope, archbishop of York, for rebellion, Pope Innocent VII excommunicated those responsible for Scrope's death, *but not by name*, so allowing Henry to obtain papal absolution (forgiveness) for this outrage by an exchange of letters. The high point of English royal strength against papal weakness came after Henry V's victory at Agincourt (1415) which gave the English delegation at the church Council of Constance (1414–18) power to heal the schism. All our kings, and their successors too, felt it was important to have amicable relations with popes.

The lessening of papal authority, combined with rising English nationalism, lay behind legislation in the fourteenth century designed to curb papal powers over ecclesiastical patronage (Statutes of Provisors: 1351, 1390) and to restrict appeals to the papal court (Statutes of Praemunire: 1353, 1360, 1390, 1393). Parliament complained that England was being flooded by papal appointments to benefices, whose holders never exercised pastoral care but drained the country of revenues. Yet many looked to popes for church advancement: poor men without influential patrons, and worthy university graduates. The problems posed by papal power were not as great as were widely believed; there was a difference between reality and the perceptions and complaints as aired in parliament. The anti-papal legislation of the 1350s and 1360s may be seen as 'playing to the gallery'[7] by Edward III, though it was not a dead letter under Richard II,[8] and this legislation was useful for Edward's successors to hold in reserve, witness Henry V's threat to use *praemunire* legislation against Henry Beaufort, bishop of Winchester, in 1419 over Beaufort's wish for enhanced powers.[9] At this level of crown–church relations there was a three-way tension between king, popes and clergy, but in matters of dispute or friction, English clergy and popes were not always on the same side, for many English churchmen were as patriotic and competitive as laymen.

The Upper and Lower Clergy

Many bishops were chosen from the ranks of senior king's clerks. This was not surprising as these men had skills and political experience which made them indispensable. It was over promotions to bishoprics and archbishoprics that kings were most likely to come into conflict with the papacy. Monarchs were understandably anxious to have loyal men in important bishoprics, but popes could promote any individual who happened to be at the papal court (the *curia*) when the vacancy occurred, and they could raise anyone to the rank of cardinal, which compelled that man to live at the *curia*. The vacancy caused by the promotion of the archbishop of Canterbury Robert Kilwardby as cardinal in 1278 was followed by the papal appointment of the Franciscan friar and distinguished academic John Pecham (1279–92), who was at the *curia* at the time, to succeed him. By contrast Robert Winchelsey (1294–1313) was apparently advanced by a free vote of the Canterbury monks.[10] Both were staunch defenders of clerical rights and supporters of papal plans for reform. Edward I was unable to secure any more prestigious see for his favourite Robert Burnell than that of Bath and Wells (1275–92), perhaps because of Burnell's scandalous private life. But even Edward III, at his most powerful, sometimes struggled to secure the promotions of favourite candidates, with tussles to secure, first, the huge see of Lincoln and then Winchester, most valuable see of all, for two favourite and senior king's clerks.[11] When Simon Langham, archbishop of Canterbury 1366–8, was made a cardinal Edward lost a financially able minister.

Under Richard II the promotion and transferring of bishops from one see to another became largely a matter of lay politics, aided by a compliant papacy, anxious lest England desert the Roman popes and transfer allegiance to the rivals in Avignon. This is evident in the changing about of bishops in the political upheavals of 1388, 1397 and 1398, when the Roman popes, Urban VI and Boniface IX, obediently transferred prelates from see to see at the behest of whoever wielded political power in those years. In contrast, the early Lancastrians had two powerful prelates as pillars of their regime: Thomas Arundel, archbishop of Canterbury (1396–1414), and, for most of his life, Henry Beaufort, one of John of Gaunt's children by Katherine Swynford, bishop of Winchester (1404–47).

The character of the episcopate changed in the fifteenth century, when bishops were no longer recruited overwhelmingly from the ranks of professional crown administrators but were more likely to be graduates, whether theologians or lawyers. This did not necessarily make them better bishops, or even resident in their dioceses. Promotions to bishoprics reflected political realities, so Henry V favoured men with diplomatic skills whom he employed to further his continental ambitions, while under Henry VI episcopal patronage reflected the power of factions at court, when the king was forced to compete with aristocratic councillors, and even with Queen Margaret, in his attempts to advance his own candidates.[12] Those men did not stand aloof from political disputes and were unable to act as effective peacemakers.

From its earliest days parliament included a clerical element.[13] All bishops, and a varying number of the heads of religious houses, were summoned by individual writs, as spiritual peers. Archdeacons and cathedral deans were also supposed to attend in person, as were representatives of cathedral chapters and of diocesan clergy. The total of secular clergy, had they all attended, was 169. Numbers of abbots summoned to parliament varied widely. Under Henry III these were large, approaching 100, while under Edward I they fluctuated at between 67 and 80. Subsequently, numbers fell and hovered between the high twenties and low thirties. In most other countries, including Scotland, the clergy formed a separate 'estate', but in England, as parliament developed during the early fourteenth century, they were contained within the two houses – Lords (including clerical peers) and Commons – which explains why their presence has been so neglected by parliamentary historians.

There were good reasons for kings to call their clerical subjects: some had great wealth and were the social and economic equivalents of earls and barons, while many had the experience which kings drew on for political decision-making and to staff diplomatic missions. The lower clergy, either in person or represented by proctors, fulfilled Justinian's maxim that 'what concerns all should be approved by all' and, as the clergy had been taxed by the crown from the late twelfth century, by about 1200 lawyers understood this to mean, effectively, 'no taxation without representation'. Even when clerical tax-voting moved into the clerical assemblies called convocations in the early fourteenth century, the clergy still needed to give consent to such national matters as making war and peace and approving new legislation. The lower clergy ceased to be directly summoned by the crown in 1340, but bishops still warned their lower clergy to send representatives. This warning, known as the *praemunientes* clause, continued to be included in bishops' parliamentary summonses until 1969. Yet even when lower clergy gradually ignored this clause, during the early decades of the fifteenth century, there were still many who served the crown and attended in their capacities as royal servants, so there was no danger of the lower clergy being unrepresented in parliament under the Yorkists.

Lower clergy too had their grievances against the crown. Though less dramatic than the confrontations between kings and archbishops there were the occasions when the clergy collectively addressed lists of complaints to their rulers. These complaints, called *gravamina*, are evident from the late thirteenth century and the first two decades of the fourteenth. They were not always identical, and they encompassed many subjects, including the oppressive burden of providing hospitality to kings and magnates, the negligence of sheriffs in responding to requests for help from bishops, many allegations that the lay courts were encroaching on the power of ecclesiastical courts, and requests that religious houses were not to be burdened by excessive financial demands by the crown.[14] The results of these complaints were unsatisfactory for the clergy; either the king promised to amend his ways – promises always unfulfilled – or there was no response at all. In such matters the clergy did not speak with a united voice, for too many, especially the bishops, were members of the royal council and were 'establishment men'. When the granting of clerical taxes moved from parliament into convocation, the brief minutes of those proceedings very occasionally (as happened in 1356)[15] recorded lists of complaints which it was hoped the crown would address before a tax was granted.

Taxation

The greatest effect on crown–church relations from the 1290s to the 1460s was the almost constant foreign wars which kings waged. The result was that the most important aspect of their relations with the clergy was finance. Englishmen were taxed since the 1180s,[16] and from the 1220s occasional taxes were imposed by popes on the clergy alone to support their crusading ambitions. In the 1250s Henry III allowed popes to tax the clergy heavily to support his unrealistic ambition to secure the throne of Sicily for his younger son.[17] Under Edward I these taxes became more common and more burdensome, and, although 'the crusades' were the ostensible objects, in practice most money ended in crown coffers.

Taxation of the clergy followed several distinct phases. The 1290s were the pioneering years and the time of greatest confrontation. In 1291 papal agents assessed the wealth of the English church: a combination of landed endowments and income from parishioners as tithes (essentially an income tax) and fees, and the resulting document, the *Taxatio Ecclesiastica*, became the tool for taxing the English church, by kings as well as popes, until the *Valor Ecclesiasticus* of 1535. Only the destruction by Scottish raiders forced some reassessments of the northern province (the *Nova Taxatio*, 1318, 1327–8). Edward I's reign saw the greatest crown–church conflicts since those of Henry II against Becket and until Henry VIII versus the papacy in the 1530s, and its cause was taxation. Resistance to heavy clerical taxation was led by the strong-willed Robert Winchelsey, archbishop of Canterbury, 1295–1313. In 1295, Edward savagely imposed a tax of 50 per cent on his clerical subjects, but they were not his only disaffected subjects. The clergy were saved because the English baronage also objected to the king's financial demands to support his foreign warfare. One solution to the problem of obtaining consent for taxation of the clergy was to ask the pope to impose a subsidy, ostensibly for some papal cause. The popes got the blame for these, but English kings took most of the money. Popes were sometimes generous in imposing taxes, at the rate of one-tenth of income per year, over several years; for example, seven papal tenths were granted in 1305, six in 1312 and six in 1333. But there were drawbacks too: though kings took most of the sums raised they did not take all; if the pope died mid collection, his grant became invalid; and when the popes moved to Avignon in 1305 it was felt, rightly, that English clerical taxes were supporting the French war effort.

A second phase of clerical taxation runs from circa 1300 to circa 1330. During this period the 'papal route' of obtaining grants was quietly abandoned, and from the early 1330s the standard procedures of both granting and collecting clerical taxes were established. In these years of parliamentary development, the clergy's tax-granting forum shifted from parliament to their two convocations of York (the dioceses of York, Carlisle and Durham) and Canterbury (the rest of England and all of Wales), which voted taxes based on a tenth of the 1291 valuation. The mechanism for collecting clerical taxes was established then: bishops appointed the collectors, and they chose mostly the heads of religious houses.

Phase three, which lasted until 1396, saw the link between clerical taxation and England's foreign warfare strongly established. In seeking such taxes, the crown had to make a case for its military ambitions and became skilled at advertising its successes. Thus, in the 1350s war heroes, including the Black Prince, appeared in the Canterbury convocation to encourage the granting of generous sums. During this phase the clergy, like laymen, were the subjects of a decade of experimental taxation from 1371 to 1381, in the clergy's case granted in their convocations of Canterbury and York. These culminated in a poll tax granted in 1380 (by clergy and laity separately, as always) but at higher rates than before.[18] After the great revolt of 1381 the traditional pattern of clerical, as of lay, taxation was re-established. A new phase began after Richard II concluded a twenty-eight-year truce with France in 1396. Hitherto, tax grants were demanded for foreign warfare, yet both he and Henry IV, when technically at peace, continued to demand subsidies, citing 'imminent perils' as the reason; and as the 1396 agreement was a truce, not a peace treaty, it could be imagined that England was still at war. The Anglo-French war was restarted by Henry V, and during the fifteenth century taxes were voted by the northern province at the rate of one grant almost every three years, and by Canterbury province almost one every two years. Taxation of the southern province was especially heavy under Henry IV, which probably reflects the influence of his very close friend and supporter Archbishop Thomas Arundel, who invested much clerical authority in the survival of the new regime, while the longest intervals between grants, in both provinces, came in the later 1450s, reflecting the loss of royal power.

Far from escaping the burden of taxation which was laid on the laity, the clergy actually paid proportionally more heavily. The standard rate for most of the laity (boroughs and the royal demesne excepted) was at a fifteenth of their wealth, which usually raised about £36,000. By contrast, the clergy paid a tenth which was worth about £18,000. Whatever proportion of the population was clerical – historians' estimates are between 3 per cent and 5 per cent – this meant that the clergy were expected to pay more than 30 per cent of England's taxes. This tax burden fell most heavily on the clergy of the much richer southern province, and though Wales was part of this, collecting taxes in Wales was always difficult and, after Owain Glyn Dŵr's rebellion, impossible.

The clergy resisted this constant fiscal oppression in several ways, but only once, in 1373, did a bishop protest about crown taxation in principle; William Courtenay, young, aristocratic, well-educated, and a man never scared to speak truth to power, spoke on behalf of his clergy's poverty in the face of crown impositions.[19] However, the clergy often made tax grants reluctantly and with bad grace; the convocation record will often say, 'they discussed for some days and finally they made a grant'. They could make less generous grants than were demanded, typically voting half-tenths instead of tenths, as was especially true in Richard II's later years when the war was going badly. They could impose conditions – such as, 'the king must campaign in person' (1383), or 'he must campaign in France' (1385) – and specify exemptions. Bishops had a traditional right to request exemption of named clergy from a tax grant on account of poverty, a privilege which was sparingly used and always respected. But from 1385 the blanket exemption of 'poor nuns' was increasingly demanded to protect them from the crown's demands.

During the fifteenth century the practice of granting taxes with named exemptions developed markedly, so that, for example, in the northern province almost every religious house was exempted, and even rich collegiate establishments, like York Minster, were sometimes excused payment. This was the clergy's way of shielding individuals, and whole groups, from tax burdens, without risking offence by the outright refusal to vote a subsidy. It was probably no coincidence that this practice gathered momentum during the time when the crown was comparatively weak. Bishops, however, continued to take their role in collecting clerical taxes seriously, and in the fifteenth century, when the standard of record-keeping in bishop's chanceries declined, the one subject which they conscientiously enregistered was clerical taxation material.

Servants of the Crown

As well as being constant taxpayers in support of foreign wars, the clergy were also occasionally ordered to be armed for home defence. Nine times, from 1369 to 1418, the command was issued to all male clergy, aged from sixteen to sixty, to equip themselves according to their income and parade before inspectors chosen by their bishop.[20] Kings employed this command only when they thought the realm was at risk of invasion and made no mention of the theoretical authority behind it. There is evidence from several dioceses that the bishops obeyed: Rochester, Chichester, Winchester, Exeter, Lincoln and Durham; but (hardly surprising) their commands were not always well observed in inland areas. Some clergy, however, were conspicuous in defending the realm; in the summer of 1377 the defence against French raids on the south coast was led by the abbots of Battle (Sussex) and St Augustine's, Canterbury, and, most heroically, by the prior of Lewes, in Sussex, himself a Frenchman. On foreign military expeditions there was always a clerical element, both for administration, such as the disbursement of money for saying Masses, and, crucially, for the spiritual welfare of the combatants, such as hearing confessions, granting absolution and performing last rites. Henry V took his chapel royal choir with him in 1415 when its skilled and elaborate singing demoralised enemy prisoners.[21]

Domestic propaganda was even more fundamental. When kings were planning foreign wars, they needed to create a favourable climate of public opinion, which was very necessary both for recruiting soldiers and for raising taxes from laymen and clergy alike. For this the clergy were essential. Every parish church, every collegiate church, even monasteries, provided perfect forums for spreading propaganda. Churches were more all-encompassing than the county courts, which were the other centres for spreading information. Our kings inherited a tradition of clerical intercession on their behalf, dating from before the Conquest, and occasional examples of prayers being offered for political purposes occurred under Henry III, but it was from Edward I's reign, and especially from 1294, that prayers were regularly ordered in support of military expeditions.[22] From then until the 1440s the people of England, through their clergy, were ordered to attend special services, say prayers and make liturgical processions in support of the war effort and other national emergencies, such as plague, and for members of the royal family in sickness and after death. In return, the bishops would grant indulgences, that is, remission from sin, usually of forty days' duration, to anyone who took part. The Masses and prayers used on these occasions were not specially composed, but the reasons why they were being ordered were set out in the preambles to writs which were sent to the bishops. Bishops forwarded them to archdeacons and others of their flock. The reasons for these efforts were, the writs stipulated, to be explained in English, and in this way the vernacular was introduced into church services and almost into the liturgy.

For most of our period the work of government and the implementation of kings' wishes were carried out by crown 'civil servants' called king's clerks. These were men in holy orders who had literacy, financial and often legal skills to run the royal administration. Under Edward I their numbers increased greatly as the crown sought to keep a record of every official letter it despatched. Edward I and his growing number of king's clerks were opposed to papal ideas of reform which aimed to detach clerics from worldly concerns. Edward and his successors relied on the income from church benefices to pay their clerical servants, the more successful of whom held such benefices not singly but in plurality. In 1279 a royal clerk said that, as he and his colleagues effectively ran the country, they should ignore papal rules against pluralism.[23] King's clerks were numerous into the fifteenth century. The balance between the number of clerical and lay crown administrators tipped towards the latter only during the years 1425–50, perhaps as the result of Henry V's enthusiasm for using English in official documents. Since much of their payment came in the form of church benefices – in parish churches, colleges and cathedrals – control of church patronage was, until the later fifteenth century, a matter of great importance to kings.

At the highest level of the 'civil service', the three leading officers of state, chancellor, treasurer and keeper of the privy seal, were normally senior bishops and archbishops. Immensely powerful and richly rewarded, these men, 'duly qualified for the service of God in church and state', were the lynchpins of crown administration in normal times. As their close associates they gave counsel to living monarchs; many were named executors of their wills. In life they lived lavishly, and many were generously charitable in life and after death. William of Wykeham (bishop of Winchester 1366–1404; chancellor 1367–71, 1389–91; and founder of Winchester College and of New College, Oxford) is a famous example.

More everyday was the crown's use of bishops to act as unpaid servants performing many governmental tasks in the localities. From the late thirteenth century bishops received royal commands – writs – in such numbers that they kept them in special collections, and these enable us to observe crown–church cooperation or interaction in detail. The orders ranged over many aspects of law and administration, but it should be stressed that these commands, even those chancery writs which conclude *Teste me ipso* (Myself as witness), were not of personal concern to kings but were routine, and their language was in common form. Commands included to receive the oaths of local officials; to recover money from debtors to the crown; to cause those involved in private debt claims to appear in court; to discover who was the patron of a particular living; and to enquire into individuals whose status was being challenged in the king's courts, usually in connection with inheritance disputes, with such questions as, 'is she a nun?' or 'is he a bastard?' If the answer to either was 'yes' the individual was ineligible to succeed to the disputed property.

The Church and Patronage

The orders which had potential to cause friction between the two powers of crown and church were the writs which, far from telling a bishop to do something, ordered him *not* to do something: not to admit a man to a benefice pending litigation or not to hold a particular case in a church court – specifically, not to hold a patronage case. Disputes over which jurisdiction should hear patronage cases had loomed large in Henry II's quarrels with Becket. Henry won. So, disputes about ownership of the right to present to a church benefice – the word is advowson – were to be held in lay courts; if the word 'advowson' was uttered in a church court, proceedings had immediately to be halted. Patronage cases were often surprisingly complex, with multiple parties laying claim to present to one benefice.

Kings had a variety of ways, beside direct taxation, of making money from the church. One was by selling licences to evade the Statute of Mortmain (1279). Kings and nobles had, for twenty years previously, been concerned that gifts of land to the church deprived the donors' social superiors of the benefits they gained when a tenant died, such as the wardship of minors and patronage of churches in their gift. The church, by contrast, never died, so its dead hand – mortmain – lay on the gift, to the overlord's permanent disadvantage. Edward I was perhaps prompted to legislate in 1279 by the request of the master of the Temple for a definitive ruling on the subject, which explains the date.[24] Only in 1299 did Edward realise that he could make money by selling licences to evade the statute. This income source was unreliable, depending on his subjects' wish to increase the endowment of religious houses, or to found new institutions, but the patent rolls record many such gifts and licences, with their costs, in the succeeding centuries.[25]

Those clergy which the statute most affected were the religious, mainly the Benedictines and Cistercians. Collectively they controlled a great amount of church patronage, which kings were able to exploit when the headship of a house was vacant. But kings also demanded financial benefits, called corrodies, for every kind of crown servant, including humble members of the household, the stable, building workers and some more elevated employees, like doctors. This was done by foisting individuals on to religious houses, to grant them 'maintenance'.[26] Traditionally these grants were thought to be old folks' lifetime gifts of board and lodging for those in retirement. This may once have been true, but, if it ever was so exclusively, the great famine of 1314 to 1316 drove the crown to desperate measures to support its servants. From then on, we can be sure that corrodies included annual pensions, as well as gifts in kind. The grants, which are recorded on the Close Rolls, would say, 'to X, to have such maintenance as Y used to have', because once a house had accepted one crown pensioner it was fated to receive a succession. Many of those servants are known to have continued in crown employment while receiving such a 'maintenance', thus disproving the idea that they had 'retired'. Some received several corrodies concurrently. Crown corrodies can be detected from the late thirteenth century, and their heyday was in the fourteenth, with a revival under Edward IV; they continued to be imposed on monasteries to 1500 and beyond. Less common, but nevertheless burdensome, was the obligation to provide hospitality to kings and courtiers, but this usually affected only a few large abbeys, like Reading, St Albans, Bury St Edmunds and Canterbury.

What Kings Did for the Clergy

Kings saved clerics from execution if found guilty of a felony, felonies being serious crimes of violence and theft. This privilege, called benefit of clergy, had been won by Thomas Becket in his contest with Henry II. Guilty criminal laymen were not imprisoned; they were hanged. But guilty clergy escaped this fate if they could prove their clerical status, and then were handed over to their bishop and imprisoned. Every bishop owned a prison. During the thirteenth century this process underwent change in that royal justices insisted that accused clerics should be subjected to a form of trial, so that it should be known what their alleged crime was. Later, the proof of clerical status changed. Originally it was by being tonsured (with a shaven head), but, probably in the early fourteenth century, this was abandoned as being too open to abuse: the accused could bribe their gaolers to shave their head. The later proof of clergy was by having an ability to read. The same biblical passage was chosen every time, which came to be known as 'the neck verse': 'Have mercy upon me, O God, after thy great goodness, according to the multitude of thy mercies do away mine offences.'[27] In the fourteenth and fifteenth centuries many of those claiming benefit of clergy had no pretension to clerical status but were merely laymen who passed this same reading test. Benefit of clergy was a thus ramshackle system which was resented by kings and by their lay lawyers who tried to encroach on this privilege. How long a convicted cleric spent in custody was very random, often bearing no relation to the seriousness of his crime. Some restrictions were placed on this privilege in the course of the fourteenth and fifteenth centuries (high treason was excluded, for example), but the privilege was not finally abolished until 1827.

Kings also supported the authority of the higher clergy in enforcing ecclesiastical discipline upon both laity and clergy. Bishops could inform the royal chancery about people who, after excommunication, remained unrepentant for more than forty days. After receiving their names, the chancellor passed the details to the local county sheriff ordering him to capture and imprison the miscreants until they repented. This procedure was most used in the late thirteenth century, though with some revival between 1350 and 1400.[28] A similar mechanism was used by the heads of religious houses to recapture runaway members of their community, and this continued to be employed into the sixteenth century.[29]

A judicial mechanism in which crown and church cooperated was in the use of churches and churchyards as places of sanctuary. A person accused of a serious crime could take refuge there and remain in safety for up to forty days. Then the fugitive could either abjure the realm, that is, promise to go abroad or elect to stand trial in the lay court, where conviction rates were very low. This ancient procedure was designed to stop tit-for-tat feuding and prevent mob rule. The two powers cooperated to enforce this arrangement: the church punished sanctuary-breakers with excommunication; lay law regarded sanctuary-breaking as a felony. Though things could go wrong at every stage of the process the cases of sanctuary-breaking were comparatively few, and the procedure endured into the early seventeenth century. The concept of sanctuary now forms the basis of contemporary rules about diplomatic immunity.

Clergy also had the same rights as laymen to appeal to the king for favours or the redress of wrongs, and here the activities of the religious, usually from individual houses, are notable.[30] A subset of these petitioners were women: nuns and canonesses.[31] There are seventy-seven extant petitions from women religious, most not from individual nuns but from abbesses and prioresses seeking to protect their house's property from unscrupulous neighbours. One subject on which kings and clergy were agreed was the need to eradicate heresy. The originator of English heresy was the Oxford academic John Wycliffe (d. 1384).[32] Wycliffe not only called for church reform and inveighed against church wealth but maintained that at the Mass the bread and wine were not turned into the actual body and blood of Christ but remained as symbols of Christ's passion. Performance of this miracle, called transubstantiation, was the theory that underpinned clerical authority, so this opinion was revolutionary. Wycliffe and his followers, nicknamed Lollards, also denied the efficacy of rites performed by sinful priests and scorned the usefulness of pilgrimages and the veneration of saints' images. Wycliffe's opinions might have been considered merely a university problem, or even a church problem, as his attractive, and revolutionary, ideas began to leak out of Oxford University in the late 1370s. What changed lay perception of heresy was the revolt of 1381, for many believed it was caused by Wycliffe's seditious teachings. Whether true or not, contemporaries *thought* there was a link, so the equation of Lollardy with sedition became fixed in the minds of kings, as well as the church hierarchy. This was reinforced by Sir John Oldcastle's revolt in 1413–14, and there is emerging evidence of the links between proscribed religious belief and disorder, if not downright rebellion, in the 1420s and 1430s.

Conclusion

Medieval people were not ourselves in fancy dress but had a different mindset. Yet the status of the clergy changed during our centuries as they became less of a distinctive international caste and, mainly under the pressure of long wars, much more like ordinary English citizens. Clerical powers were also challenged by wider societal changes, especially by the rising numbers of lay lawyers, administrators and university graduates. Yet religious beliefs, opinions and practices remained of central concern to English people and their rulers, and did so for centuries to come.

Notes

1. J. R. H. Moorman, 'The Medieval Parsonage and Its Occupants', *BJRL* 28 (1944), 137–53 (144–5). He cites the phrase 'swarming with clerics' from A. Jessup, *The Coming of the Friars* (London, 1888, repr. 1930), 83.
2. M. Bloch, *The Royal Touch*, trans. J. E. Anderson (London, 1973).
3. D. Carpenter, *Henry III: The Rise to Power and Personal Rule 1207–1258* (New Haven, CT, 2020), ch. 6.
4. C. Given-Wilson, 'The King's Confessors and the Royal Conscience in Late Medieval England', in *Fourteenth Century England XII*, ed. J. Bothwell and J. S. Hamilton (York, 2022), 1–28.
5. C. Given-Wilson, *Henry IV* (New Haven, CT, 2016), 380–2.
6. Mary, who was sent to the Benedictine abbey of Amesbury (Wilts.), where she ran up large gambling debts: M. Prestwich, *Edward I* (New Haven, CT, 1988), 128.
7. W. M. Ormrod, *Edward III* (New Haven, CT, 2011), 367.
8. D. Martin, 'Prosecution of the Statutes of Provisors and Premunire in the King's Bench, 1377–1394', in *Fourteenth Century England IV*, ed. J. S. Hamilton (2006), 109–23.
9. K. B. McFarlane, 'Henry V, Bishop Beaufort and the Red Hat, 1417–21', *EHR* 60 (1945), 316–48; repr. in McFarlane, *England in the Fifteenth Century* (London, 1981), 79–113.
10. All the medieval bishops of England, though not all of Wales, have entries in *ODNB*.
11. John Buckingham, keeper of the privy seal, to Lincoln (1363–98) (see A. K. McHardy, 'The Promotion of John Buckingham to the See of Lincoln', *JEH* 26 (1975), pp. 127–35), and William of Wykeham, chancellor, to Winchester (1367–1404) (see J. R. L. Highfield, 'The Promotion of William of Wykeham to the See of Winchester', *JEH* 4 (1954), 37–54).
12. L.-R. Betcherman, 'The Making of Bishops in the Lancastrian Period', *Speculum* 41 (1966), 397–418.
13. *Proctors for Parliament: Clergy, Community and Politics, Vol. 1, c. 1248–1377*, ed. P. Bradford and A. K. McHardy, Canterbury and York Society, 107 (2017), xi–xvii, and references.
14. J. H. Denton, 'The Making of the *Articuli Cleri* of 1316', *EHR* 101 (1986), 564–99.
15. *Records of Convocation III: Canterbury 1313–1377*, ed. G. Bray (Woodbridge, 2005), 269–270.
16. For all taxation information, lay as well as ecclesiastical, the freestanding E 179 database is essential. See TNA, E 179 Database, www.nationalarchives.gov.uk/e179/ (accessed 20 August 2024).
17. Carpenter, *Henry III*, 527, 549–54, 260–1, 289–90, 629–35, 646, 685.

18. *Clerical Poll-Taxes of the Diocese of Lincoln 1377–1381*, ed. A. K. McHardy, Lincoln Record Society, 81 (1992).
19. R. Swanson, 'Courtenay, William (1341/2–1396), archbishop of Canterbury', *ODNB*, www.oxforddnb.com/view/10.1093/ref:odnb/9780198614128.001.0001/odnb-9780198614128-e-6457 (accessed 20 August 2024).
20. B. McNab, 'Obligations of the Church in English Society: Military Arrays of the Clergy, 1369–1418', in *Order and Innovation in the Middle Ages: Essays in Honor of Joseph R. Strayer*, ed. W. C. Jordan, B. McNab and T. E. Ruiz (Princeton, NJ, 1976), 293–314.
21. A. K. McHardy, 'Religion, Court Culture and Propaganda: The Chapel Royal in the Reign of Henry V', in *Henry V: New Interpretations*, ed. G. Dodd (York, 2013), 131–56.
22. D. W. Burton, 'Requests for Prayers and Royal Propaganda under Edward I', in *Thirteenth Century England III*, ed. P. R. Coss and S. D. Lloyd (Woodbridge, 1989), 25–35.
23. Prestwich, *Edward I*, 250.
24. Ibid., 251.
25. S. Raban, *Mortmain Legislation and the English Church 1279–1500* (Cambridge, 1982).
26. For this paragraph, see A. K. McHardy, '"Such maintenance as . . . .": Corrodies of the Crown', in *Fourteenth Century England XII*, ed. Bothwell and Hamilton, 29–46.
27. Psalm 51:1, in the Authorised Version translation.
28. F. D. Logan, *Excommunication and the Secular Arm in Medieval England* (Toronto, 1968).
29. F. D. Logan, *Runaway Religious in Medieval England, c. 1240–1540* (Cambridge, 1996).
30. G. Dodd, *Justice and Grace: Private Petitioning and the English Parliament in the Late Middle Ages* (Oxford, 2007), 243–54.
31. W. Mark Ormrod, *Women and Parliament in Later Medieval England* (London, 2020), 64–66.
32. A. Hudson and A. Kenny, 'Wyclif [Wycliffe], John [called Doctor Evangelicus] (d. 1384), Theologian, Philosopher, and Religious Reformer', *ODNB*, www.oxforddnb.com/view/10.1093/ref:odnb/9780198614128.001.0001/odnb-9780198614128-e-30122 (accessed 20 August 2024).

Further Reading

Carpenter, D., *Henry III: The Rise to Power and Personal Rule 1207–1258* (New Haven, CT, 2020).

Denton, J. H., *Robert Winchelsey and the Crown 1294–1313* (Cambridge, 1980).

Dobson, R. B., ed., *The Church, Politics and Patronage in the Fifteenth Century* (Gloucester, 1984).

Heath, P. *Church and Realm 1272–1461* (London, 1988).

McFarlane, K. B., *John Wycliffe and the Beginnings of English Nonconformity* (London, 1952).

McHardy, A. K., 'The English Clergy and the Hundred Years War', *Studies in Church History* 20 (1983), 171–8.

'Kings' Clerks: The Essential Tools of Government', in *Ruling Fourteenth-Century England: Essays in Honour of Christopher Given-Wilson*, ed. R. Ambühl, J. Bothwell and L. Tompkins (Woodbridge, 2019), 59–76.

Thomson, J. A. F., *The Early Tudor Church and Society, 1485–1520* (London, 1993).

11

The Nobility

In every human relationship there is a tension, or perhaps better say a dynamic, between what is and what is desired by the parties involved, and in this the relations between medieval kings and the upper nobility were no different. When these factors coincided, the relationship tended to work well; when they did not, it could break down. Both at the time and since, debates have arisen about what was the most profitable state of affairs in a monarchical form of government, as defined by kings and nobles, by parliaments and other councils, and by contemporary theorists.[1] In more recent times, historians have engaged in an intellectual push and pull between concepts of a constitutional, or at extreme idealised, outlook on the royal/noble relationship in the English Middle Ages on the one hand and a personalised, or, more basely, self-interested, view on the other.[2] To understand how this relationship played out between medieval English kings and their nobilities, we first need to understand how the structure of that relationship evolved. We can then examine how it manifested itself in areas such as the king's role in maintaining the nobility, service and cooperation between kings and his nobles, the interplay of ideas of wealth and power, favouritism, political instability and in some cases the removal of monarchs.

Kings and the Positioning of the Nobility

At the beginning of the thirteenth century, there were still only two recognised noble titles under the English king: baron and earl. The barons were the more numerous, normally between 150 and 200 at any one time, and held lands worth, on average, some £200 per annum.[3] They initially held lands by barony, sometimes referred to as an honour;[4] that is, a collection of knights fees (i.e. land held in exchange for homage and service to a lord) and/or manors held directly of the king (a status known of as tenancy-in-chief) and inherited by a single owner (e.g. the honour of Pontefract held by Edmund de Lacy, earl of Lincoln, in the mid thirteenth century). These baronies were almost always partitioned and partitioned again as the generations, and marriages, came and went. Both barons and earls (the latter of which numbered around ten in our period) are often referred to under the general term 'baron' (e.g. 'King John's barons'), while the term 'magnate' would come to indicate earls, or at the very least the richest of barons, and usually those closest in wealth and power to the king. As both earls and barons traced their English titles only back to the Norman invaders of the eleventh century, any further ideas of rank beyond size of estate, especially by way of antiquity, was a fine distinction, at least at the beginning of our period.

Thereafter, there were two key elements which helped position the nobility more firmly within the polity, and the kingdom as a whole: knighthood and royal blood. Concerning the former, by the end of the twelfth century at the latest, mainly as a result of the expectation of military service inherent in the Anglo-Norman system of feudal land tenure, it was accepted that most nobles holding land directly of the monarch would raise knights and other fighting men for the king's army, and so would usually be knights themselves.[5] Knighting would normally take place at the age of twenty-one, but at whatever age it happened, it helped further mark the noble off from the major landholders who remained, by either choice or necessity, unknighted.[6] For the highest levels of the nobility, including the royal family, the knighting ceremony itself was usually done at coronations, the royal court or some other important public setting. Richard Beauchamp, the future earl of Warwick (d. 1439) and later one of the most famous warriors of his generation, was knighted at Henry IV's coronation in October 1399.[7] Even the further promotion of a noble would frequently be connected with what was in effect an enhanced knighting ceremony (though with a lance rather than a sword) in parliament – for example the 1362 creation of three of Edward III's sons, Edmund, Lionel and John, as earl of Cambridge, duke of Clarence and duke of Lancaster.[8] Aside from being a rite of passage, such public acts also re-emphasised the military responsibilities of the noble to the monarch and the kingdom. Not all knights were noble, but it was an expectation that nobles, and especially those inheriting land, position and responsibilities, would have been knighted.

The other issue, royal blood, again helped delineate a select few of the nobility from the rest of medieval society, as well as making clear the different levels within the nobility. The rationale for monarchs ensuring that eligible members of the royalty were included in the titled nobility was twofold. First, there was the reinforcement of the elite status of the reigning royal family by distributing titles among them, usually a costly process for the monarch but one which helped shore up royal authority at the top of the polity.[9] While this was particularly important after 1066, as well as following various dramatic events connected with the royal succession (e.g. 1327, 1330, 1399, 1461), for any king, however secure he felt on the throne, to make clear the pre-eminence of the royal line was crucial for both his political control and longer-term dynastic security. Secondly, while there were aberrations, such as Prince Edward's brief acceptance of the governance of Simon de Montfort in the spring of 1265, on the whole, having one's offspring, and especially one's direct heir, prominent in the higher nobility not only buttressed the king's power but also influenced noble behaviour more broadly. The Black Prince is perhaps the most famous such case, but even Prince Henry, the future Henry V, played the loyal son until the last couple of years of his father's reign. This is not to say that royal family members would be listened to any more than other nobles, especially if they were not believed to have the experience, competence or track record for good advice. There would, though, always be the awareness of their royal blood, being in essence an extension of monarchical power, when such individuals made their presence felt, whether inside or outside formal and informal small and great councils, or in parliament itself.

Stratification of the English Nobility

As the relationship between monarchs and nobles developed over the later Middle Ages, these less structured delineations were supplemented by a more clearly and officially tiered system under the king. To start with, there was the proliferation of new titles conferred by the monarch starting in the mid fourteenth century, in part as a means of reward for past or future service but also of control inherent in the process of ranking. As noted, earl and baron were the only titles in post-Conquest England. However, in 1337 we have the first new type of title, namely the first English royal duke (Edward, first son of Edward III), followed in 1351 by the first non-royal duke when Henry of Grosmont was made duke of Lancaster. In 1385 the first marquis was created, the marquis of Dublin (Robert de Vere), one of Richard II's favourites, and in 1440 Robert de Beaumont became the first viscount in English history. All three new titles (duke, marquis, viscount) were also notably of continental origin, possibly indicating some desire by monarchs to make the social hierarchy of the nobility more compatible with their ambition to unite the English and French thrones. Alongside these, there was the development of titles of duchess and viscountess, which, with that of countess, denoted some of the most powerful women in the kingdom – for example, Margaret of Brotherton, duchess of Norfolk (c. 1320–99), and Marie de St Pol, countess of Pembroke (c. 1304–77). Below these ranks came the baronage, and then the gradations within the gentry of knights, esquires and gentleman, and with each such development, an ever clearer positioning of the nobility within the social hierarchy.

It was not just the development of new titles which solidified the reality of noble rank under the king; there was also the peerage's rise as the upper chamber of parliament, and their role within the assembly as a source of royal counsel and as judges in prominent state trials.[10] Up until the later thirteenth century, membership of the Lords (another name for the parliamentary peerage) could fluctuate from one session to the next, depending on the king's whim and the needs of that particular parliament. Thereafter, starting in Edward I's reign, there developed the idea of semi-regular individual parliamentary summons, normally for the greatest and/or most powerful landowners in the kingdom, though also intermittently connected with the 'shadowy' idea of tenure of land by barony.[11] Over the next half-century, due to repeated copying of the parliamentary summons list, the royal writs calling these individuals to attend parliament became standardised and by extension hereditary, so that a son or next male heir could normally expect to have a summons if a father had received one, whether the heirs of the Beauchamp earls of Warwick or the Grey barons of Rotherfield. This in turn helped stabilise the parliamentary peerage's membership, though it still ultimately remained subject to the king's will due to his pivotal role in presiding over the renewal and replenishment of noble ranks (see next section). By the early fifteenth century, some historians refer to a closed peerage,[12] which meant in turn an even more conscious effort needed on the monarch's part to get new members included within its ranks.

The emergence of a stabilised parliamentary peerage in turn influenced the delineation of noble rank under the monarch in two further areas. First, in practice it separated out those landed individuals not considered well enough off in terms of property, only allowing those with a certain amount of landed wealth to be allowed a place within the peerage. In the *Modus Tenendi Parliamentum* – a tract written in Edward II's reign outlining how parliament should operate – a minimum level of landed income was set at 400 marks (£266 13s. 4d.) per annum for barons and £400 per annum for earls.[13] This estate income for barons appears to have been within the reach of most otherwise acceptable candidates, for when the next monarch, Edward III, started granting lands to sustain new titles, he ranged mainly from 100 marks (£66 13s. 4d.) to £200 per annum, with only a few specially needful individuals such as Reginald Cobham given amounts closer to those in the *Modus*.[14] However, for Edward's earldom promotions in 1337, because of the greater expectations of individuals holding the title, the king arranged a massive 1,000 marks (£666 13s. 4d.) per annum in land and/or annuities for William Montagu and Henry Grosmont to enable them to sustain their new ranks of earls of Salisbury and Derby respectively, far beyond the minimum of £400 per annum.[15] Nevertheless, such amounts as laid out in the *Modus* would remain a baseline for peerage incomes for the rest of the Middle Ages.

Secondly, and equally importantly, the development of the peerage within parliament, and the growing importance of later medieval parliament more generally, created a national communal setting to ratify and assent to the creation of the new forms of title by the king. It is perhaps no accident that the expansion of grades within the nobility (i.e. dukes, marquesses and viscounts) came during the gradual solidification of the parliamentary peerage's membership in the fourteenth and early fifteenth centuries. In other words, parliament was now one of the places where the king could find counsel but also wider affirmation for his reshaping of the nobility. Furthermore there gradually developed a system whereby those holding such titles had the right of trial by their peers in parliament,[16] as well as, if less useful for the king, a forum for nobles to come together legitimately as a group. Both developments would give the nobility more coherent power at times but also a way for the monarch to deal with the nobility en masse, allowing him to make policy decisions which were seen to have been acknowledged by, if not necessarily ultimately binding on, the greatest men in the kingdom.

The King's Role in Maintaining a Noble Class

The English monarch had an ongoing interest in replenishing the developing noble hierarchy in order to help him govern England and fight wars both at home and abroad. Therefore, throughout the later Middle Ages numbers in the upper reaches of the nobility were sustained and augmented by the king in response to death on the battlefield, political miscalculation and, more importantly, natural wastage, especially in the male line.[17] This was done mainly through the redistributing of lands which had returned to the king through lack of any legal heir (escheat); confiscation and forfeiture of estates (regularly due to criminal/treasonous activity); end of entailed, life and shorter property tenures; and the exercise of royal rights over wardships and marriages of minors. Thousands of such royal grants were made throughout our period to this end, as recorded in the charter, patent, close and fine rolls. For instance, in September 1334, Richard Fitzalan, earl of Arundel, was granted by Edward III the castle, manor and town of Chirk, lately of Roger Mortimer, earl of March's forfeited estate.[18] In May 1382, Richard II granted to Michael de la Pole, later to be made earl of Suffolk, the manors of Dedham and Benhall (Suffolk) from the escheated estate of William Ufford, the last earl of Suffolk.[19] Such patronage, as well as the further authority and/or economic power offered by royal grants of various offices and monetary fees, could in both short and longer term build up or bolster established noble families and 'new men' alike.

Perhaps the monarch's most publicly visible role in maintaining the noble class was the ceremonial around promotions such as that of Andrew Harclay, hero of the battle of Boroughbridge, to the earldom of Carlisle in March 1322, when Edward II himself was said to have girded Harclay with the belt of earl.[20] However, while high medieval kings had frequently created or promoted nobles by such use of the royal prerogative, perhaps most notably during the Anarchy (1138–53), by the fourteenth century such actions were nonetheless beginning to cause criticism, at least in part due to the growing power of parliament. When Roger Mortimer, the lover of Queen Isabella, was made earl of March in 1328, the concern among the established nobility was not only that the earldom itself was a novel title but the manner in which Mortimer's ennoblement seemed to be forced on parliament, an institution becoming less and less accepting of the minority government's behaviour.[21] Unsurprisingly, then, when the young Edward III took independent control of the throne a couple of years later, he made every effort to ensure that his promotions into, or within, the nobility were done with parliamentary approval, most notably with his creation of six earls in the March parliament of 1337, the largest such group of promotions to date.

The backing of parliament increasingly became the *sine qua non* of such creations after this point, and kings circumvented its authorisation at their peril. During the first crisis of Richard II's reign, when John Beauchamp of Holt was made a baron by letter patent (i.e. by royal command) on the authorisation of the privy seal in late 1387 rather than in parliament or another important occasion,[22] there was a considerable degree of disquiet among the political community. Richard's numerous promotions during his 'tyranny' of the late 1390s, including those referred to as 'the duketti', were again back to being made in parliament, though a parliament that was now very much controlled by the king.[23] By the time of the creation of Thomas Beaufort (a career soldier and one-time royal chancellor but also the bastard, if now legitimised, of John of Gaunt) as duke of Exeter by Henry V in the October 1416 parliament,[24] such authorisation was both hardening procedure and common sense. Kings not only created and maintained the noble class; they also were increasingly expected to interact with the wider elements of the polity to do so.

Service and Cooperation

If the nobility could expect to receive largesse and position from their relationship with the king, the king in turn expected to receive service and cooperation from his nobles. Such ideas of mutuality were evolving throughout the later Middle Ages, but they are primarily visible in three main areas – war and defence, local administration and royal counsel.

At the beginning of our period, circa 1215, service in war – both foreign and in defence of royal rights within the kingdom – was still firmly linked to feudal obligations of tenants-in-chief to serve the king in return for holding lands from the crown. Thereafter, due to sub-infeudation (the dividing up of feudal knight service attached to land through either inheritance or grant), the sometimes questionable quality of fighting men raised (because property holding rather than martial ability had become the most important qualification for knighthood) and the need to keep the king's armies in the field for greater amounts of time, over the fourteenth century there developed a new method for raising troops. Under the contract system, the king would pay large sums to, usually, titled or otherwise higher nobles, who would in turn subcontract to other nobles and gentry, who would thereby raise the required men. Most noble families were involved in this system, especially after the outbreak of the Hundred Years War in 1337 and the requirements of the on again/off again nature of continental campaigning.[25] In this way, not only could quality be controlled, with the choice of men based mostly on individual ability, but the contract system also allowed the monarch to raise and keep an army in the field for as long as the royal finances, or access to credit, would allow.

Similarly, as the English royal administration grew in size and complexity over the later Middle Ages, spurred on by the continued development of offices of state and the expansion of royal record-keeping,[26] so too did the monarch's need for competent individuals to fill posts not just at the centre of government in Westminster but also in the localities. Occasionally, nobles were appointed as justices of the peace, and even sheriffs, such as the baron Walter Lacy, appointed sheriff of Herefordshire from 1216 to 1222.[27] Increasingly, though, formal county office-holding was expected to be performed by members of the gentry.[28] Rather, instead of manning such posts themselves, the nobility tended to fill local roles more closely connected with the king's immediate needs. Titled nobles can be found on royal commissions of oyer and terminer and various other judicial commissions looking into the more serious transgressions in the localities. This can be seen in the appointment in May 1365 of Hugh de Courtenay, earl of Devon, and the barons Guy Brian, John Mowbray and Henry Percy, to look into an attack on one of the king's officers responsible for the examination of gold and silver exports from Devon.[29] Ultimately, the presence of such a powerful mix of individuals at this level, especially if they or their families or immediate lords were firmly loyal to the king, was invaluable to royal interests in both peace and war. This presence, along with the expectation that nobles were to use their own power in the localities in the form of family and informal networks, influence and intimidation, usually helped keep the localities, and the realm as a whole, in reasonable order if not always free from tension.

Then there was the vital role which nobles played as the king's councillors. Throughout our period, of course, the monarch could find counsel through private engagement with his nobles, especially on more sensitive matters. When a larger, more formal forum was needed, there was the king's small/personal and, later if less frequent, great councils which comprised a mixture of administrators (e.g. chancellor, chamberlain, etc.), established nobles, and trusted individuals and favourites, to which others would be invited on an ad hoc basis. This mixture of personnel was ideally meant to temper royal interests with the practicalities of a situation, a formula championed by, among others, John Fortescue (d. 1479), a chief justice of the king's bench and later commentator on the laws of England.[30] By the mid fourteenth century, however, when an even broader consensus was deemed necessary, especially in connection with public finance, formal counsel and assent from the gentry were increasingly voiced through the Commons in parliament, while responses coming from the higher nobility were made either in the Lords or through associated councils or committees. In the parliaments of 1376 and 1385, both driven at base by the issue of war finance, we see the Lords offering counsel, in the form of critical instruction, to Edward III and Richard II.[31]

During our period such noble advice offered to monarchs can basically be broken down into that given by those close to the king with this closeness sometimes being the deciding factor in its acceptance; advice given by royal administrators and officers, whose knowledge of the realities of the situation could be tempered by their own career ambitions; advice given by council, parliament or larger assemblies for the sake of the kingdom, or at the very least its own power; and guidance given by a variety of individual nobles from dukes to barons, again usually with something of an eye to their own interests. These four areas were obviously not mutually exclusive, either in terms of personnel or outlook; each ideally played into the level of cooperation between the king and the nobility at any given time, especially if both parties were firmly enough aware of, and confident in, their own rights and needs concerning an issue.

Wealth and Power

The wealth and power, landed and financial, of a noble was another important part of his overall status throughout the Middle Ages, one which attempted to emulate, on a lesser scale, that of the monarchy. Whether it be families such as the Mowbray dukes of Norfolk and the Fitzalan earls of Arundel towards one end of the noble economic spectrum or the Bassets of Sapcote and the Beauchamps of Bletsoe towards the other, the size of landed estates was how nobles emphasised their position and was a key determinant of their power.[32] Overall noble incomes, and household staff (including the steward, marshal and chamberlain) dependent on them, could also give a general sense of position, with gross incomes for Edward II's higher nobility ranging from £2,500 per annum for the baron Hugh Audley the Younger, with a household size of 96, to Thomas, earl of Lancaster, with a gross income of £11,000 and a total size of 708.[33] At the other end of the scale, income of lesser nobles, going from a tax raised early in the reign of Henry VI, could range as low as £175 per annum for someone like Thomas, Lord Clifford.[34] As a result households tended to be considerably smaller. Size mattered in the later Middle Ages, and the more wealth, and the greater number of household staff a lord had, the more likely he was to be taken seriously by his monarch, his peers and his subordinates.

Even so, beyond crude indicators of wealth and status, there also needed to be other ways that an ambitious nobleman could distinguish himself from the landholding herd, while also positioning himself ever closer to the monarchy. In the high Middle Ages, due to the unsettled nature of the countryside in the century or so after the Norman Conquest, noble residences were built mainly as utilitarian military strongholds, such as the early versions of the castles of Kenilworth (Warwickshire) and Alnwick (Northumberland). However, by the later medieval period, as a result of greater stability, if not peace, within the kingdom, there was a gradual shift to noble residences built more to impress such as at Tattershall Castle (Lincolnshire) and Wingfield Manor (Derbyshire).[35] In connection with this, the lifestyle of noble families was transformed to reflect both individual aspirations and the changing styles of the monarchy and aristocracy above them (e.g. in terms of diet, dress and decor).[36] Indeed, while high medieval noble lifestyle has been likened more to that of 'rugby clubs than Camelot',[37] by the later Middle Ages, though the amount of food, clothing and other expressions of material wealth probably did not vary greatly, the refinement, and therefore cost, of such goods did. Whether it be the artistic tastes of the duke and duchess of Bedford evidenced in the patronage of their fifteenth-century Book of Hours; the translation, and composition, of poems and other tracts by individuals ranging from John Montagu, earl of Salisbury (d. 1400), and the duke of Lancaster (d. 1361) to Earl Rivers (d. 1469) and the duke of York (d. 1415); or even the effigy of Richard Beauchamp, earl of Warwick (d. 1439), the good things in life, and death, were meant to be appreciated and emphasised, both for the sake of social prestige and the ease of the family. After all, the latter part of our period saw the refinements of the Renaissance starting to seep in from the continent, as well as the growth, if still in its infancy, of a trend towards university education for noble sons.[38] These changes in turn would further distinguish English noble families' wants and needs socially and culturally, as well as intellectually, from most members of the thrusting gentry and mercantile classes.

Developments in noble landed estates and material environment, then, overlain by a more refined aristocratic lifestyle, reinforced a noble's power and status below the monarch at both a national and a local level, furthering his ability to recruit a retinue or affinity and dominate a geographical sphere of influence. The regular sight of liveried retainers in all their finery of the Houses of Lancaster and York in the fifteenth century, with their 'esses' and red and white roses, and with knowledge of the power and prestige that lay behind them, was enough to both cow most local critics and encourage potential followers. However, just as the king's ability to raise and maintain contract armies in the field was highly dependent on the exchequer's resilience rather than the royal household's magnificence, so too for a later medieval nobleman his resources also needed to be able to take the financial strain of a large domestic retinue for peace and war, as well as a wider affinity of administrators and other officers. The gradual development of 'bastard feudalism', where money replaced land as the medium of exchange in return for service, meant that the larger a noble's financial resources, the more substantial his following could be – it is, therefore, of little surprise that among the largest retinues of the later Middle Ages were those of the dukes of Norfolk and Lancaster (both died 1399), with 70 and 200 knights and esquires respectively.[39] The size and health of such retinues in turn played into how monarchs treated and related to such nobles, and how much clout the latter potentially had at court, especially as kings were as concerned about control within the counties of England as beyond its borders. At their most extreme, 'overmighty subjects' were as much an issue in the localities as on the national political stage, as seen during the Wars of the Roses.

Favourites and Political Instability

Despite much bad publicity, the idea of the noble royal favourite was not necessarily a negative thing: all medieval kings valued their close friends, allies and confidantes and were expected to reward them as such. And so long as the king was seen to be generally in control of his nobility, contemporary comment tended to be limited, although rarely entirely absent. All the same, the idea of the royal favourite dominating the monarch, or being given too much in the way of royal resources, was a far more common trope both at the time and in modern discussions of medieval politics.[40] Whether an individual was also romantically connected with the king, as was probably the case of Piers Gaveston for

Edward II or possibly Robert de Vere for Richard II, or those whose relationship was primarily in a more political vein such as Henry III's Savoyards and Poitevins, ideas of the overly powerful courtier were ever present.

At a local level, problems came about as a result of the granting of property to royal favourites which had usually previously been held, or at least claimed, by other, often aggrieved, parties. Some grants to favoured individuals arose simply from the routine functioning of the feudal system, in particular, as we have seen, the return of lands to the king either through simple escheats, wardships or the end of tenures such as leases, and so tended to be little contested. However, large amounts of property usually became available as a result of more problematic, and often controversial, events such as forfeitures (e.g. with the Despensers' demise in 1326 or the Appellants in 1397), ends of entails and/or grants in expectancy (basically a future grant of a piece of property 'expectant' upon the failure of a line or end of tenure). As such these properties also frequently had a number of previous claimants who could cause local tensions and initiate court cases at the highest levels of the judiciary. For instance, there were the cases of the manor of Marston Maisey (Wiltshire), claimed at various times during the first half of the fourteenth century by Hugh Despenser the Elder, earl of Winchester, the baron John Darcy, as well as the Maisey and de Veel families; and the whole of the honour of Denbigh (Wales), which within the course of a decade had moved from the control of the earls of Lancaster to the Despensers and then to the Mortimers.[41] Both properties would ultimately be granted by Edward III to favoured individuals in the 1330s to build up royal control of the nobility. Moreover, the fact that new noble landowners or their representatives were habitually taking over such properties with little knowledge of the estate itself or the individuals they were dealing with could also cause further stress. Even annuities and other money payments could cause problems when used as royal patronage to nobles, especially when there were several claimants to most streams of revenue.[42] It is little surprise to find that unless kings were careful, and noble recipients of such grants very tactful, there were going to be complications, both of a minor and major variety, connected with how and where such grants were made.

At the centre of power, domination of royal favourites at court, and by overmighty subjects in general, could cause yet more instability. Part of this was down to the behaviour of individuals. Piers Gaveston was famously recorded as giving established nobles caustic nicknames (e.g. Guy Beauchamp, earl of Warwick, was called 'Warwick the dog'), no doubt to poke fun at them and undermine their standing.[43] Gaveston, in line with other favourites, was seen as not knowing his place within medieval society, as were individuals such as Michael de la Pole, the son of a Hull wool merchant, made earl of Suffolk by Richard II in 1385.[44] When, then, during Edward III's reign, a statement was made in the 1341 parliament by John de Warenne, earl of Surrey, and a member of a long-established titled family, that there were those present in the peerage chamber who should not have been present,[45] he was basically restating the long-standing criticism that the natural order within the polity was once more being tampered with. That said, the more active favourites were, especially in important matters of state, the greater the chance that they would upset not only the established nobility but also the country as a whole. We need only to look again to the Despensers of Edward II in the 1320s and the 'duketti' of Richard II in the 1390s, or Edward IV's Woodville in-laws in the 1470s, for such evidence of widespread popular disdain for powerful individuals considered upstarts and imposters. In each of these cases, ill-feeling eventually turned into outright opposition to the king. Even when a favourite was trying to do the right thing, as when the duke of Somerset attempted to keep the kingdom functioning during Henry VI's bouts of madness, he nevertheless was often depicted as an essentially malign influence.[46] Whatever the truth of individual cases, the more general perception of royal favourites in our period as self-seeking interlopers into the highest reaches of the king's government made them a problematic, or at the very least, concerning element for the rest of the political community, if not the entire kingdom.

Opposition and Role in King's Deposition

Nobles were, of course, not the natural opponents of kings. Indeed, as we have seen elsewhere in this chapter, their default position was usually to hold a strong bond of common interest with the monarchy and so they were naturally inclined to support the sitting monarch wherever possible. However, there were areas where friction could arise. Favouritism was one element that could create serious tensions within the medieval polity, though there were others. Opposition could come from inside or outside the royal court, within parliament or from the localities, but almost always with disaffected nobles taking a prominent position of leadership. More often than not, conflict began in the localities but could often lay the groundwork for more widespread opposition to the king. Examples include Hugh Despenser trying to gain control over the lordship of Gower in south Wales in the early 1320s in the face of stiff opposition from the earl of Hereford, Roger Mortimer of Wigmore and others, who eventually turned against the king himself; and the running dispute between the Nevilles and the Percies on the Scottish border throughout the later Middle Ages, sometimes spilling over into outright rebellion against the king.[47] Similarly, when the issue was one which affected the whole of the kingdom, such as noble opposition to Edward I's financial exactions for French campaigning in the late 1290s, or the rise of an aggressive court party in the middle of Henry VI's reign,[48] the monarchy could face mounting opposition which might develop into violence against the king himself. In such instances, however, it did not necessarily follow that the nobles wanted to remove the king. Instead the opposite was usually the case, with the king being seen as the keystone of the medieval political and social structure, a point strongly emphasised in numerous political tracts which called for the reform of the royal government rather than the removal of the monarch (e.g. Magna Carta, 'Paper' Constitution of 1244, Remonstrance of 1297, Ordinances of 1311, etc.). A secure monarch acting in the interests of the nobles was a far more useful asset to the nobility than one with the weakness of being newly placed on the throne, whatever his actual abilities were.

When it did come to the ultimate act of political rebellion in the Middle Ages – the deposition (or at the very least forced abdication) of a monarch – dissatisfied members of the nobility could play a variety of roles, depending on their stance prior to the deposition and what they could expect to get out of a change of monarchs. The nobilities of some reigns had a hands-off approach to events surrounding changes of king. The nobility of Edward II's reign, while generally supporting the outcome of Queen Isabella's invasion of 1326 and the toppling of Edward's government in favour of the heir apparent, took a mainly passive role in proceedings, letting themselves be led by the force of Isabella's will.[49] Similarly, when the young Edward III deposed Isabella and Mortimer's minority government in 1330, it was Edward himself who organised the coup.[50] In both cases, in other words, nobles looked to the queen and her son, or king in his majority, as their ultimate lead and/or justification for action. On the other hand, when it came to the later depositions of monarchs in 1399, 1461 and 1485 (i.e. those of Richard II, Henry VI and Richard III), it is notable that in each case it was basically a nobleman who was the main driver behind events (Henry Bolingbroke, Richard of York, Henry Tudor). This was, then, in dramatic contrast not just to the 1320s and early 1330s but also to an earlier age when the nobility still tended to back in rebellion the candidacy of an individual close to the king in blood (such as a son, daughter or sibling) who could easily have inherited anyway, as with William Rufus and Henry I (Robert Curthose), Stephen (Matilda) and Henry II (the Young King Henry). In other words, by the close of the Middle Ages, the upper nobility seem to have been far more willing to countenance the possibility of deposing a sitting king and replacing him with an individual from among their own ranks.

Conclusion

The relationship between later medieval English kings and their nobility was thus in both a static and a flux state. On the one hand, this relationship remained the principal way in which kings related to the wider kingdom, in terms of either governance, control, defence or wealth extraction. On the other, as we have seen, with the growing definition and self-awareness of the nobility as a class, not only did their lifestyle, and the way they engaged with the political life of the kingdom, change but also their relationship with the monarch, up to the point where they felt they could question his right to rule. Nonetheless, there are also some fundamental questions which historians have yet to fully answer. If, as is now thought, for the most part the later medieval English monarchy and nobility rubbed along, and if on the whole it can be seen to bear out the idea of an organic, if not always symbiotic, polity, why were there so many violent upheavals involving the nobility, including at least one major civil war in each of the centuries of our period? Why so many attempts to place restrictions on royal governance (e.g. 1244, 1258, 1264, 1297, 1311, 1316–18, 1340–1, 1376–7, 1386–8, 1406 and 1450) if the body politic was essentially a healthy organism? And why so many depositions? Part of the answer to these questions lies in the fact that, while the king held ultimate power in the realm, he still depended on the cooperation and good will of his nobles to rule effectively – and those nobles often had sufficient power to make life difficult, and sometimes *very* difficult, for their king if his rule was deemed to be damaging to their interests. More though would come from the type of individuals such a system produced. Figures such as Simon de Montfort and Richard, duke of York, stood out from their contemporaries not just in their knowledge of their own importance but in their firm conviction in how relations between the nobility and monarchs should be and how hard they should push change in pursuit of that ideal. Whether or not they were right will probably remain an open question, but examining such issues in more detail is important for understanding both noble and royal behaviour and for seeing in much broader terms how later medieval England was governed.

Notes

1. Starting with John of Salisbury for the later medieval period: *Policraticus*, trans. C. J. Nederman (Cambridge, 1990).
2. See C. Carpenter, *The Wars of the Roses: Politics and the Constitution in England, c.1437–1509* (Cambridge, 1997), ch. 1; R. Horrox, 'Personalities and Politics', in *The Wars of the Roses*, ed. A. J. Pollard (Basingstoke, 1995), 89–109; M. Keen, 'English Political History of the Late Middle Ages, 1272–c.1520', in *A Century of British Medieval Studies*, ed. A. Deyermond (Oxford, 2007), 51–69 (at 56–63).
3. C. Given-Wilson, *The English Nobility in the Late Middle Ages* (London, 1987), 11–14.
4. For debate around both terms, see J. E. Powell and K. Wallis, *The House of Lords in the Middle Ages* (London, 1968), 303–15; D. Crouch, *The Birth of Nobility: Constructing Aristocracy in England and France 900–1300* (Harlow, 2005), 280–92.
5. For knightly status, see D. Crouch, *The English Aristocracy 1070–1272: A Social Transformation* (New Haven, CT, 2011), 3–20.

6. Those eligible men who avoided knighthood by choice faced forced submission or fining: S. L. Waugh, 'Reluctant Knights and Jurors: Respites, Exemptions, and Public Obligations in the Reign of Henry III', *Speculum* 58 (1983), 937–86.
7. C. Carpenter, 'Beauchamp, Richard, Thirteenth earl of Warwick (1382–1439)', *ODNB*, www-oxforddnb-com.ezproxy3.lib.le.ac.uk/view/10.1093/ref:odnb/9780198614128.001.0001/odnb-9780198614128-e-1838 (accessed 14 September 2024).
8. *PROME*, parliament of October 1362, item 36.
9. For the double-edged nature of such policies, see W. M. Ormrod, 'Edward III and His Family', *JBS* 26 (1987), 398–422.
10. As we are dealing here with the secular nobility, we are also dealing with the secular peerage: the ecclesiastical peerage's development has far more to do with the church's relationship with the monarchy than the monarchy's relationship with the nobility, for which see Chapter 10.
11. Given-Wilson, *Nobility*, 60–2.
12. E.g. Powell and Wallis, *House of Lords*, 436–7.
13. *Parliamentary Texts of the Later Middle Ages*, ed. N. Pronay and J. Taylor (Oxford, 1980), 81.
14. *CPR 1334–8*, 346.
15. Given-Wilson, *Nobility*, 37.
16. *PROME*, parliament of April 1341, introduction; cf. Magna Carta, clause 39.
17. K. B. McFarlane, *The Nobility of Later Medieval England* (Oxford, 1973), 142–76.
18. *Calendar of Charter Rolls 1327–1341*, 318–19.
19. *CPR 1381–5*, 122–3; N. Saul, *Richard II* (New Haven, CT, 1997), 108.
20. H. Summerson, 'Harcla, Andrew, Earl of Carlisle (c. 1270–1323)', *ODNB*, www-oxforddnb-com.ezproxy3.lib.le.ac.uk/view/10.1093/ref:odnb/9780198614128.001.0001/odnb-9780198614128-e-12235 (accessed 15 September 2024).
21. W. M. Ormrod, *Edward III* (New Haven, CT, 2011), 74–5.
22. *CPR 1385–9*, 363.
23. *PROME*, parliament of September 1397, item 35.
24. *PROME*, parliament of October 1416, item 13.
25. S. Gunn and A. Jamme, 'Kings, Nobles and Military Networks', in *Government and Political Life in England and France, c. 1300–1500*, ed. C. Fletcher, J.-P. Genet and J. Watts (Cambridge, 2015), 41–77 (at 53, 60).
26. M. Clanchy, *From Memory to Written Record: England 1066–1307*, 3rd ed. (Oxford, 2012).
27. C. Leach, *Lordship in Four Realms: The Lacey Family 1166–1241* (Manchester, 2014), ch. 6.
28. E.g. R. Gorski, *The Fourteenth-Century Sheriff: English Local Administration in the Late Middle Ages* (Woodbridge, 2003), 70–2.
29. *CPR 1364–7*, 148.

30. J. Fortescue, *On the Laws and Governance of England*, ed. S. Lockwood (Cambridge, 2002), 114–17.
31. Ormrod, *Edward III*, 551–5; *PROME*, parliament of October 1385, appendix.
32. For later medieval estate size/income, see G. Holmes, *The Estates of the Higher Nobility in Fourteenth-Century England* (Cambridge, 1957).
33. C. Woolgar, *The Great Household in Late Medieval England* (New Haven, CT, 1999), 12.
34. H. L. Gray, 'Incomes from Land in England in 1436', *EHR* 49 (1934), 607–39 (at 618).
35. G. Harriss, *Shaping the Nation: England 1360–1461* (Oxford, 2005), 108.
36. L. Kjoer, 'Magnates, Ritual and Commensality at Royal Assemblies: Bogo de Clare and Edward I's Easter Parliament, 1285', in *Edward I: New Interpretations*, ed. A. King and A. M. Spencer (Woodbridge, 2020), 66–83 (at 83).
37. R. Bartlett, *England under the Norman and Angevin Kings, 1075–1225* (Oxford, 2000), 237.
38. J. T. Rosenthal, 'The Universities and the Medieval English Nobility', *History of Education Quarterly* 9 (1969), 415–37 (at 434).
39. Given-Wilson, *Nobility*, 79.
40. Recently, H. Bagerius and C. Ekholst, 'Kings and Favourites: Politics and Sexuality in Late Medieval Europe', *JMH* 43 (2017), 298–319.
41. J. Bothwell, *Edward III and the English Peerage: Royal Patronage, Social Mobility and Political Control in Fourteenth Century England* (Woodbridge, 2004), 119–20, 122–3.
42. G. L. Harriss, 'Preference at the Medieval Exchequer', *BIHR* 30 (1957), 17–40.
43. *Vita Edwardi Secundi: The Life of Edward II*, trans. W. Childs (Oxford, 2005), 16–17, 45.
44. A. Tuck, 'Pole, Michael de la, First Earl of Suffolk (c.1330–89)', *ODNB*, www-oxforddnb-com.ezproxy3.lib.le.ac.uk/view/10.1093/ref:odnb/978019 8614128.001.0001/odnb-9780198614128-e-22452 (accessed 18 September 2024).
45. *Croniques de London*, ed. G. J. Aungier (London, 1844), 90.
46. J. Watts, *Henry VI and the Politics of Kingship* (Cambridge, 1996), 282–98.
47. N. M. Fryde, *The Tyranny and Fall of Edward II, 1321–1326* (Cambridge, 1979), 43–9; C. J. Neville, *Violence, Custom and Law: The Anglo-Scottish Border Lands in the Later Middle Ages* (Edinburgh, 1998).
48. Though how serious was the threat of civil war has been questioned: A. King, 'Crisis? What Crisis? 1297 and the Civil War That Never Was', in *Edward I*, ed. King and Spencer, 143–62; R. A. Griffiths, *The Reign of King Henry VI: The Exercise of Royal Authority, 1422–1461* (London, 1981), chs. 13 and 14.

49. J. R. S. Phillips, *Edward II* (New Haven, CT, 2010), 504.
50. Ormrod, *Edward III*, 90–1.

Further Reading

Crouch, D., *The English Aristocracy 1070–1272* (New Haven, CT, 2011).
Davies, R. R., *Lords and Lordship in the British Isles in the Late Middle Ages* (Oxford, 2009).
Fletcher, C., Genet, J.-P. and Watts, J., eds., *Government and Political Life in England and France 1300–1500* (Cambridge, 2015).
Given-Wilson, C., *The English Nobility in the Later Middle Ages* (London, 1987).
Hicks, M., *English Political Culture in the Fifteenth Century* (London, 2002).
McFarlane, K. B., *The Nobility of Later Medieval England* (Oxford, 1973).
Rigby, S., *English Society in the Later Middle Ages* (London, 1995).
Thompson, B. and Watts, J., eds., *Political Society in Later Medieval England: A Festschrift for Christine Carpenter* (Woodbridge, 2015).
Ward, J., *English Noblewomen in the Later Middle Ages* (Harlow, 1992).
Woolgar, C., *The Great Household in Late Medieval England* (New Haven, CT, 1999).

12

The Gentry

The relationship between the crown and the gentry was multifaceted. It encompassed both military needs and civilian offices. It could be both direct and indirect, involving personal service – in the royal household for example – on the one hand or indirect in helping to maintain royal rule across the realm. It involved central organs of government – attendance at parliament most particularly – and, crucially, power and influence in the provinces. The relationship was by no means a static one. It evolved and shifted focus over time. Before exploring this relationship, however, we need first to define what we mean by gentry.

Definition

Gentry, it has to be recognised at the outset, is not a term of constant social usage but is a historian's 'construct', a tool of analysis. Some take it to mean simply lesser landowners or those who lay claim to gentility, and proceed to delineate the gentry of their chosen time and place. However, when we come to define the gentry we recognise other characteristics: it is a territorial elite, with a tendency to form social gradations; it seeks to exercise control over the populace; and it has a collective identity. Most importantly, in the present context, it exercises public authority on behalf of a central authority which requires the services of a local elite but which is unable to support a paid bureaucracy in the localities. So defined, the gentry was formed, it has been argued, in an accelerating process from the middle of the thirteenth century to the mid fourteenth.[1] Naturally, a proto-gentry did not suddenly emerge. To understand the origins and evolution of the gentry we need to take a long view, concentrating on the phenomenon of knighthood.

Knighthood and Service to the Crown

For John of Salisbury, the scholar who wrote his *Policraticus* in 1159, the primary purpose of knighthood was service to the prince chosen by God. Hence the great lords and other tenants-in-chief of the crown were obliged to send their quota of knights to the royal host, the so-called *servitium debitum* established after the Norman Conquest. The Angevin legal reforms which created the common law during the second half of the twelfth century drew on this status and sense of service and enhanced them further.[2] A prominent feature of these reforms was the grand assize. Introduced in 1179, it dealt with the right to land and substituted a jury of twelve knights from the locality where the disputed property was located in place of trial by battle. It was thus a solemn procedure and it required the status of knighthood. This and other deployments of knights within the judicial system can be seen in operation with the survival of plea rolls from the central courts from the 1190s onwards. Some of them were lords with several manors; others possessed only one.

A striking fact, however, is that there were still many knights in society with comparatively little land, indicating that the *milituli* or 'knightlings', a term used contemptuously by contemporaries, still persisted in early thirteenth-century England.[3] Landless knights in households or employed as stipendiaries, however, could not be called upon unless they had some stake, that is, property, in society. Lords still held their honour courts with an obligation upon their knights to attend, even if these courts had had their wings clipped somewhat by the onward march of the royal courts. Many knights continued to spend part of their time in retinues and in households, and magnates employed them as ministers in the burgeoning seigneurial administration. In addition, the king called upon some of the secular landowners, essentially knights, as agents of the crown in various matters, including gaol delivery, where they acted as justices, and as taxers. There were also local offices which largely drew on knights. Although these roles persisted, by the 1240s knighthood was changing rapidly, with important consequences in terms of the relationship between knights and the crown.

During the late twelfth and early thirteenth centuries chivalry was transformed into an exclusive ideology.[4] The class consciousness it embodied was aimed at the exclusion of those born of peasant stock, men of urban life and origins and mercenaries. The elaboration of the knighting ceremony and the diffusion of chivalric manners were prominent manifestations of change. In England, the shift was undoubtedly spearheaded by the nobility and it led to a retreat from knighthood by those who had not the wherewithal or social position to support it. The number of knights in England thinned spectacularly and by the 1240s this phenomenon was in full sway. Knights were now called *dominus* (sir) in charters and their documents were validated by heraldic seals. Those who ceased to be knights were overwhelmingly the *milituli* and the less-endowed county knights. Social pressure and cost were the key factors in the decline. Knighthood was now a matter for the higher nobility, their greater tenants and followers, and men associated with the crown or the court. The crown itself adopted the process of distraint of knighthood in an attempt to stem the haemorrhaging and to force those who qualified to take up arms, but with limited effect. The new situation is revealed in the grand assize, where knightly jurors were now drawn from across the county and no longer from the narrow locality where the disputed property was located. The crucial decades were the 1240s and 1250s. From somewhere around 5,000 at the beginning of the century the number of knights in England fell to around 1,250 by the time they can be estimated at the beginning of the fourteenth century.

In consequence the knights became a lesser nobility, sharing their way of life with their superiors. During the mid thirteenth century they were drawn into parliament (initially a forum for ministers and tenants-in-chief) and increasingly during the reign of Edward I (1272–1307) knights were summoned there as representatives from the counties.[5] They played a major part in the king's wars, especially during Edward's attempt to conquer Scotland.[6] Given his manpower concerns he sought to summon lesser landowners directly and not only through the service owed by the magnates. The future lay, however, in contracts drawn up with the higher nobility to provide mounted warriors. Central to the lives of many of these knights were magnate retinues to which they were indentured for peace and war.[7] With its spirit of exclusivity, knighthood might seem to have been coming to delineate a caste nobility.[8] That the future did not lie in this direction has much to do with service to the crown.

During the first half of the reign of Edward I knights continued to function in the counties as royal justices of gaol delivery, as occasional taxers and the like, but there were not very many high-status tasks requiring their input. This was to change, however, in the second half of the reign with the explosion of commissions resulting largely from the king's wars.[9] Taxation on personal property became increasingly common as the reign progressed, with more than a score of subsidies between 1294 and 1340. Most of the personnel involved were knights. The taxation necessitated calling knights to parliament more often so that subsidies could be approved. When it came to the armies themselves, the knights constituted the backbone now and throughout the period of study. However, it was not only cavalry that was required but also infantry. By the end of Edward's reign commissions of array, established to draw upon wider manpower resources in the counties, were being manned by magnates and knights with military experience. With regard to justice, the later thirteenth century and early-to-mid fourteenth century saw the rise of keepers, later justices, of the peace. As a result, the counties came to be ruled by amateur magistrates, drawn from the landowners.

By 1307, the percentage of knights participating in prestigious offices and commissions of array was very high – more than 80 per cent. The crown was drawing upon the pre-existing status of the knights in society, and in consequence these men began to see themselves not merely as crown officials but as essential partners in government. It is not surprising, therefore, that in parliament the Commons became a serious political force. During the 1320s and 1330s, we begin to see the emergence of a Commons policy.[10] It was naturally the knights of the shire who took the lead, as opposed to the burgesses from the towns. Moreover, we begin to see a relationship between the assembly of representatives at the centre and the counties, in particular, as constituencies. With the opening of the Hundred Years War and the need for heavy taxation, the 'knights of the shire' were able to exert considerable pressure.

The Formation of a Graded Gentry

The term 'knights of the shire' is used advisedly. The knightly domination of the role of member of parliament for a county was not sustained. As early as 1322 there were men who were of sub-knightly stock. They were known as *valetti*, employing a term that had long been in use to describe men who were of gentle stock but were not knights, both in civilian and in military contexts.[11] Many were local landowners, some were men of law, a few were of urban origin. You could now be a knight of the shire without actually being a knight. The same is true of royal taxers as we look across the second quarter of the fourteenth century. On the judicial side, knights worked in tandem with men of law. We are seeing the development of a wider county elite, and the gentry is being born.

This graded gentry took some time to achieve and to understand the process we need to examine contemporary terminology.[12] The word *valettus* (French *vadlet*, *valet*) meant in origin 'little vassal' and it had strong service connotations. From the mid thirteenth century it was used of non-knightly household retainers. Consequently, it was employed in a military setting. In 1297, for example, Sir John Bluet retained William Martel, *seon valet*, for life. In addition to his fee, William was to receive two robes annually and to be provided with food and drink as a *gentil homme*. He undertook to serve John loyally as a valet in the current war between the kings of England and France and in any future war. In Latin documents one is more likely to encounter the word *armiger* (in origin armour-bearer), translatable into French as esquire. Esquire, too, it should be noted had strong service connotations. In origin it denoted a knight's servant with particular responsibility for his horse and armour. Some esquires were trainee knights, as shown in romance. But many were not men of breeding. In fact, esquire like valet could be used of quite menial servants.

By the middle of the fourteenth century, however, esquire was ousting valet to denote the retainer and was well on the way to becoming a genuine social category. This had been achieved by the time of the national sumptuary legislation of 1363, which spoke of esquires and all manner of *gentils gentz* below the level of knight. The graded poll tax of 1379 identified three levels of esquire, each being taxed at different rates. We can pin down the change a little more. Although it occurs sporadically before, it became commoner for esquires to seal their documents heraldically from the 1340s onwards. By 1370 we have evidence of the existence of a heraldic roll containing esquires as well as knights. By the turn of the century, we find esquires on sepulchral monuments.

How, then, do we explain the development of this social gradation? It would be tempting to do so solely in terms of war, both directly and indirectly, that is to say in terms of service and manpower needs. The Hundred Years War solidified a powerful military culture and created what has been called a military community, formed by means of recruitment to and service within retinues. However, we should be careful not to erect a dichotomy between the military or retinue dimension to life on the one hand and the civilian dimension characterised by public service on the other.[13] Kings needed both. In all of this we are dealing with elevated social status, a factor which unites the worlds of retinue and office. Esquires functioned alongside knights within the warrior elite. They also tended to live alongside knights as landowners and as participants in the duties and opportunities that that involved. It was natural that they should enter the heraldic world of display.[14] A further factor was the upward mobility that increasingly involved lawyers and lawyer/administrators as well as wealthy men of urban origins. There was a need for a second tier of gentility to encompass these, and it was achieved by means of the elevation of the word esquire.

However, the gradation of the emerging gentry does not end there. The sumptuary legislation indicates that there were others who were assumed to be, or assumed themselves to be, gentle, in addition to esquires. After a period of uncertainty and tension over social status, parliament passed the Statute of Additions in 1413 which announced the arrival of the estate of gentleman. As this solidified, the three-tiered gentry of knights, esquires and gentlemen, and their female counterparts, came to fruition. There was now a fundamental divide in English society between the gentle and the rest, that is to say, yeomen and below. Once again the new status of gentleman had heraldic connotations. This time, however, it was decoupled from military service. A period of demilitarisation during the late fourteenth and early fifteenth centuries was followed by one of consolidation when one can perceive the many and varied routes to social success. Indeed, the military changes which brought the mounted archer to the fore, and the mixed retinues of mounted archers and men-at-arms, led not to further widening but to a clamping down on men assuming heraldic arms: the military community was becoming too socially diverse to be encompassed within the world of gentility. On 2 June 1417, Henry V instructed sheriffs to have it proclaimed that men should not assume *cotearmures* on the basis of their participation in military campaigns unless they had an ancestral right to them, or they had been granted by someone with authority to do so. The exception was those who had actually fought at the battle of Agincourt in 1415, where the king achieved his greatest victory against the French.

But the break on assuming heraldic arms was not the result of top-down action alone. Social acceptance was crucial to the achievement of gentility, and military service as a lever clearly had its limitations. Examination of the qualities required for recognition as a gentleman in the fifteenth century shows that it was essentially a matter of 'general repute' or 'common fame', and that this rested on five qualities: gentle blood or ancestry; livelihood, that is, income from land held freely; the holding of office; kinship or association with 'worshipful gentlemen'; and honourable service, typically in war, administration or a noble household.[15] In short, the formation of the gentry results from the interplay of various forces and impulses, among which royal needs played a major part.

The most convenient entrée into the numbers of gentry is the income tax of 1436.[16] H. L. Gray calculated from the returns that after 51 lay barons there were 183 non-baronial landholders which he called 'greater knights' with an annual income in excess of £100. These were followed by a further 750 'lesser knights' whose income was £40–£100 per annum. Then came the esquires, of whom 1,200 had £20–£39 and were followed by 1,600 others with £10–£19. At this point we have therefore 933 'knights' out of a total gentry of 3,733. These are followed by another 3,400 landholders with £5–£9 per annum.[17] These are rough figures only and the tax returns, and Gray's treatment of them, are somewhat problematic.[18] Nonetheless they are indicative. They have been equated with the social gradations, the £5–£9 being the yeomen who were below the level of gentility.[19] The number of actual belted knights had been steadily falling for some time and was subsequently to decline even further. The number per county varied considerably. It remained a mark of social distinction. Even so, some like Thomas Chaucer, son of the poet, five times Speaker in parliament, chose to remain esquires, underlying the growing equivalence in status between these grades. Knighthood was losing its cohesive force, as it became identified with a narrow elite. The elite had more in common with the baronage than with the gentleman; indeed, the prevailing climate of social aspiration meant that each grade saw itself as a pale reflection of that above and sought to distance itself from that below. While as a class the gentry possessed a preponderance of landed wealth within the shire, the steeply graded economic and social differentiations within it reinforced the hierarchical nature of society.

King, Gentry and Parliament

The gentry had a collective identity and collective interests which necessitated the existence of a forum for their articulation. This was provided by the Commons in parliament.[20] It is understood that from the mid 1310s onwards the Commons, that is to say the knights, took over the right to speak in the name of the 'community of the realm' and that by the late 1320s they were the primary authors of those petitions that were designated as 'common'. In 1315, petitions were presented by the community alone, that is, not by the barons and prelates. One of the petitions of this year, in fact, accuses the great lords of subverting justice. At some point between 1316 and 1322 the MPs began to gather their common grievances and present them as a single schedule. Although the impetus for this came from the Commons, it must have had the support of the crown. The parliament of January 1327 was the moment when the crown allowed that the common petitions could form the basis of legislation. In other words what we are now seeing is the bringing of collective pressure on the crown and its advisors. Moreover, the king was soon to find himself in a difficult financial position at the outset of the Hundred Years War and felt obliged to redress the Commons' grievances in return for direct taxation. Although we should be wary of exaggerating the power of the Commons in initiating government policy, there can be no doubt of its new-found ability to press for legislation and to influence the crown.

The common petition continued to develop.[21] From the 1370s the Commons began to 'avow', that is to say, adopt, those private petitions they considered to have a sufficiently broad application to be presented as common petitions. What this indicates is a growing perception of the Commons as a political authority in its own right. It is shown by the appearance of private petitions which were addressed to the Commons themselves. From the mid 1370s the common petitions began to include requests that were specific and reflect local or sectional concerns. At the Good Parliament of 1376, for example, there was a flood of petitions concerned with more local issues that would previously have been considered as private. Common petitions concerning a particular locality were presented in the name of a county or borough constituency, implying that they were submitted by the MPs themselves. In other words, in the last quarter of the fourteenth century it was not the content that governed a common petition but who was supporting it.

These developments had consequences. The members of the Commons and the local elites they represented had become part of the political and social establishment. Petitions were becoming increasingly socially exclusive, and some were actually aimed at the lower orders. This was the case with the sumptuary legislation following a petition from the Commons in October 1363. Then there were the petitions and legislation which followed the Black Death, involving wage control. From 1376 onwards we encounter legislation against vagrancy and vagabonds, reflecting a change in attitude towards poverty and the advent of the concept of the 'sturdy beggar'. The lack of effective outlets for the widespread discontent that ensued from the class-orientated actions of these years must have been a contributory factor to the conflagration known to historians as the Peasants' Revolt of 1381. Urban revolts were also a feature, and it has been quite plausibly suggested that the parliamentary bias towards the elites in towns, as shown by the petitions, is likely an explanatory factor here too.

By the last years of the reign of Edward III, the knights and wealthier esquires had virtually monopolised membership of the Commons as was true of the major offices of sheriff and justice of the peace.[22] This was to continue to be the case through the fifteenth century. Various statutes were passed that reinforced this.[23] Hence, historians talk of upper, greater or county gentry, as opposed to lesser or sometimes, if less accurately, parish gentry.[24] Nor should one forget the administrators and others who tended to dominate in the towns and have been referred to as 'urban gentry'.[25] The wealthier knights had wider political horizons and social contacts than the majority of the local gentry. The elite were appointed to the more prestigious royal commissions. The lesser gentry were largely confined to more minor offices such as coroners and tax collectors and to commissions dealing with purely local matters. As officers in royal and seigneurial service their household livery was a mark of gentility, as was service in arms, chivalric behaviour and social bearing in their lifestyle.

Bastard Feudalism, Gentry and the Crown

There is, however, a further dimension to gentry life, which historians call bastard feudalism. The term was employed by K. B. McFarlane as a 'label to describe the society which was emerging from feudalism in the early part of the fourteenth century'.[26] Around the cash nexus a new world of retinues and indentures, of liveries and affinities 'occupied the centre of the stage' for two centuries following the death of Edward I. According to this view, a key role was played by a new form of recruitment to royal armies based on contracts, pioneered by Edward I within a wider context of service to magnates and gentry clientage. For McFarlane and the highly successful school which he spawned, bastard feudalism was a force for stability and social cohesion and its institutions allowed for magnate control of the localities under the aegis of the king. When instability occurred, it was due not to bastard feudalism but to the failure of inadequate kings.

There is, however, an alternative interpretation of the origins and meaning of bastard feudalism.[27] This argues that the origins are to be found in magnate reaction to the growth of central government, more specifically to the possibilities that were latent within the more direct relationship between the free subject and the crown which developed out of the Angevin polity and the Angevin legal reforms. Men came increasingly into contact with the central government during the thirteenth century and in a whole variety of ways. The potential threat to magnate power caused them to react in a series of reflexes. Initially the emphasis lay on the development of local franchises, that is to say, through extending the impact of their privatised public authority and on the exclusion of royal officials from their domains. By the mid thirteenth century, however, they were also retaining judges and other officials. Increasingly they penetrated royal courts and sought to bind lesser landowners to them, and indeed others who were likely beneficiaries of the development of the direct, public relationship to the crown.

What we see in this second view, then, is a series of important developments during the late thirteenth and early fourteenth centuries, including the ending of the judicial eyres and the substitution of the more locally influenced commissions of oyer and terminer, the appointment of sheriffs drawn from the local community, and the rise of the keepers and ultimately justices of the peace. As they grow, baronial authority permeates all of these. The more direct binding of the lesser to the greater begins to find its fullest expression in the highly developed indentured retinue. In the end, magnate power in the localities not only survived but was strongly reinforced. There can be no doubt that magnates sought the rule of the areas they wished to dominate and in some cases they certainly achieved this. Looking more closely at magnates' affinities, what we see is 'a sea of varying relationships'.[28] At the top were feed retainers followed by those in receipt of annuities, and then an outer circle of well-wishers attached more loosely to a lord.[29]

The development of the bastard feudal affinity brought a reaction from the crown. An important study deals with the development of king's knights and king's esquires.[30] During the twelfth and thirteenth centuries knights retained by the king had been restricted to household knights whose role was essentially military. By the mid fourteenth century this system had broken down, due largely to military inactivity on the king's part, and the household knights were replaced by a small number of chamber knights (see Chapter 8). At the beginning of the reign of Richard II we find the appearance of king's knights, operating outside of the royal household, attached to the king by indentures and recruited for their local significance. From 1377 to 1413, some 290 men are referred to as *milites regis*. They were granted annuities at the exchequer, mostly of £40 per annum. There were also 'king's esquires', receiving 20–40 marks per annum. There were about 280 under Richard II and about 140 under Henry IV. If, however, we exclude the years 1397–9, when Richard was recruiting heavily from Cheshire, the numbers are similar in both reigns.

During the last quarter of the fourteenth century, therefore, the crown was moving towards a system of retaining that mirrored that of the higher nobility. In the first part of Richard's reign these men were largely former followers of Edward III and the Black Prince. After the crisis of 1387–9 the king set out to build his own following among the gentry. Two features stand out. One is the wide geographical spread of this retaining. The other is the concentration upon the upper layer of the gentry. The king was utilising existing power structures. During the early part of his reign, when he was most vulnerable, Henry IV followed the same policy. At a council meeting in February 1400 the king was advised that:

> in each county of the realm a certain number of the more sufficient and well-respected (*de bone fame*) men should be retained by the king and associated with the said commissions (of the peace), and charged also diligently and carefully to save the estate of the king and his people in their localities ... And that all those of the said retinue should receive a grant from the king annually, as much as shall please the king, a reasonable sum according to their estate.[31]

Henry was following not only Richard's example but also that of his father, John of Gaunt, 'a great retainer of men'.[32] Both men tried to balance their support geographically, Richard adding northerners to his southern heartland, Henry adding southerners to the Lancastrian core in the north and north midlands. The figure of 250–300 knights and esquires retained by Richard and Henry can usefully be compared with the estimated norm of 60–80 followers whom the greatest members of the English nobility seem to have retained at this time. It is probably true to say that the number of knights and esquires retained by Richard II and Henry IV was between four and eight times greater than the number retained by most dukes or earls. The policy stemmed from a recognition of the crucial role played by the gentry, and of the consequent need for the king to harness their skills and influence to his cause. What is significant here is the kings' attempts to secure direct royal influence within the counties. A recent study argues that the king 'used his own affinity, of both nobility and gentry, deliberately to undermine the power and influence of [the earl of] Warwick and to replace him with men he thought he could trust'.[33] The methods used included appointments to the shrievalty, of justices of the peace and justices of oyer and terminer and of other officers. In other words, the king used against the earl the very means by which the earl's own local power functioned. This interpretation has sparked controversy about not only the wisdom but also the significance of what the king was trying to do in dealing more directly with members of the gentry.[34]

What emerged from all of this was essentially a three-cornered polity, comprising crown, magnates and gentry.[35] For the most part, the system worked tolerably well, although there were flashpoints. Unsurprisingly, petitions, when they raised concerns or complaints, generally did not come anywhere near challenging the political and social order. On the rare occasions when they did, they failed and have become famous in their failure. One of these arose from the Commons' obsession with law and order. At the parliament of October 1377, in addition to petitioning against maintenance, where a defendant's relationship with a lord was used to browbeat a plaintiff pursuing an action at court, the Commons raised concern about abuses committed by retinues. A statute was duly enacted. This, however, was just the opening salvo. At the parliament of April 1384, the Commons complained bitterly about lords' retinues. The request for a statute governing this was met with strong opposition from the lords in parliament, prompting the duke of Lancaster's well-known retort that 'every lord was competent and well able to correct and punish his own dependants for such outrages'.[36] The Commons were cowed into silence and dropped the matter; for now. When they returned to the attack, they requested that all liveries should be abolished. The king referred the matter to his council, and the result was the Ordinance on Livery and Maintenance issued by king and council in May 1390. Henceforth only dukes, earls, barons and bannerets should give livery and only then to those retained for life by indenture and not to those below the level of esquire unless they were servants living in their household. Although this might appear on the surface to be a victory, albeit a limited one, it was in reality a defeat for the Commons.[37] They continued to petition for the rest of the reign and beyond and the statute does not appear to have had much impact. It was a poor result for all the effort the Commons had put in.[38]

As regards rule in the provinces, however, there were different permutations. There were counties under a single great lord: Lancashire under John of Gaunt, Devon under Courtenay, Warwickshire under Beauchamp and East Anglia under de la Pole.[39] There were counties of multiple lordship, where ties between magnates and gentry functioned to strengthen the cooperation of the governing class, although rivalry between lords could cause disruption as in the Bedford 'riots' in 1437 and 1439 between the factions of Lord Fanhope and Lord Grey.[40] There were also areas where the crown had considerable wealth, Staffordshire for example, where the Lancastrian estates lay in some concentration allowing the king to act as a surrogate magnate. Direct or indirect royal influence could also alter the structure of power. There were counties such as Lancastrian Nottinghamshire where the greater gentry had considerable sway.[41] The absence of greater gentry in some areas permitted the lesser to assume the trappings of lordship and status.[42] All of this had important implications for the functioning of the shire as a political community and the exercise of the magistracy within it.

The Issue of Gentry Independence

The question of the independence of the gentry has given rise to more controversy. Some historians see a high degree of self-rule and play down magnate power, allowing for a more direct relationship between the gentry and the crown. This argument rests on the relative wealth and influence. If the overall wealth of the gentry was greater than that of the magnates and the latter were unable to afford to retain the majority of the gentry, it is argued that their power to direct the gentry would necessarily have been limited. It follows that the magnates, where they exercised exclusive or shared control, must have worked with the grain of local opinion and not against it.[43] A counter view is that this misunderstands how magnate power worked.[44] What the magnates tended to do was to attract the greater among the gentry, thereby bringing others on board and giving the great lord control and direction. There seems little doubt that this was what magnates strove for and in many cases achieved.

A concomitant of this view is the belief that it was the relationship between the higher nobility and the gentry that created the local stability that most landowners sought. It is true that there was sometimes conflict between rival nobles, as in East Anglia during the 1440s when the dukes of Norfolk and Suffolk battled for control, a situation revealed graphically by the Paston Letters. This needs to be set against those areas where a single magnate dominated. An allied debate is the significance of the county community. That this existed as a concept is beyond doubt. How far and in what circumstances it existed in reality is another question.[45] An alternative approach to gentry society is to look for networks of power and influence.[46] Whatever the variations, wherever we look there is a gentry elite whose views had to be taken into consideration. Helen Castor has shown how both the Pastons and the soldier Sir John Fastolf, investing in Norfolk during the 1440s, encountered strong opposition from more established gentry who were members of the crown/duchy of Lancaster network.[47]

In basic terms a gentry landowner sought to maintain his own and his family's position, and to further this where he could. It was therefore a competitive world, one in which men would naturally take advantage of opportunities that came their way. What they needed above all was safety and stability. As regards the greater gentry, in particular, this came in part from the crown and the positions they held in relation to it. It could also come very often from attachment to great lords and from a great lord's rule over the 'country' in which their lands were located.

The attitude towards law and order was nonetheless ambivalent. G. L. Harriss put the situation succinctly: 'Gentry society, rooted as it was in landed power, was held in a volatile balance of cooperation and rivalry.'[48] The frequent property disputes often involved violence. Most often, however, such violence was tactical and occurred within a process. Litigation and force were not by and large opposing methods but were often combined. Disputes, moreover, were often settled by arbitration, sometimes by great lords and sometimes within the gentry community.[49] There were episodes of violent disorder. When this occurred, retinues could easily become gangs. One was the 1320s when the failures of central government resulted in the lawlessness of the Folville brothers and the Coterel gang.[50] Naturally, this phenomenon created problems for the crown as it held ultimate responsibility for keeping the peace. For the most part, however, the crown, the magnates and the gentry had a vested interest in maintaining general law and order, in which to function. This meant in practice sustaining social equilibrium.

Such equilibrium was severely tested by the Wars of the Roses. The gentry, in particular, were threatened by the breakdown of the three-cornered polity. Christine Carpenter writes: 'At almost every phase of national crisis, the scale of local conflict and attack on local property rose alarmingly. Throughout the period, uncertain or inadequate kingship was accompanied by increasing local discord.'[51] The lack of stability and direction was especially damaging to the gentry because the lives of even the greater gentry were essentially lived on a local scale compared with those of all but the most meagre nobles. As Carpenter suggests: 'It is the landowners' responses, in trying to maintain some kind of normality in this lengthy period of distorted politics, especially the worst years from 1450 to 1471, that may hold the key to the emergence of the new monarchical style towards the end of the century.'[52] Once the magnates were deprived of their leadership in the shires and the gentry looked to their own salvation, it was possible for the king to work more directly with the latter.

The result was the Tudor polity, 'a court-centred polity' where the gentry ruled the shires 'at the command of the monarch'.[53] This development had been latent within the English polity since the early fourteenth century but was prevented by the stranglehold of the higher nobility, upholders of traditional loyalty and subservience. They failed ultimately because 'cumulative wealth and access to political authority gave the broad class of landowners independence from the nobility as mediators of patronage and power'.[54] From here it is but a short step to the oft-expressed view that the efficacy of Tudor monarchy was due, at least in part, to the establishment of direct crown–gentry relationships. These relationships, however, were built upon varieties of service and a general rapport that had been evolving over the past three centuries.

Notes

1. P. Coss, 'The Formation of the English Gentry', *Past & Present* 147 (1995), 38–64.
2. P. Coss, *The Knight in Medieval England, 1000–1400* (Stroud, 1993), ch. 3.
3. P. Coss, *Lordship, Knighthood and Locality: A Study in English Society c. 1180–c.1280* (Cambridge, 1991), chs. 6 and 7.
4. P. Coss, 'The Origins and Diffusion of Chivalry', in *A Companions to Chivalry*, ed. R. W. Jones and P. Coss (Woodbridge, 2019), 7–38.
5. J. R. Maddicott, 'Parliament and the Constituencies 1272–1377', in *The English Parliament in the Middle Ages*, ed. R. G. Davies and J. H. Denton (London, 1981), 61–87.
6. D. Simpkin, *The English Aristocracy at War: From the Welsh Wars of Edward I to the Battle of Bannockburn* (Woodbridge, 2008).
7. 'Private Indentures for Life in Peace and War 1278–1476', ed. M. Jones and S. K. Walker *Camden Miscellany XXXII*, Camden Society 5th series 3 (1994), 1–190.
8. P. Coss, 'Knighthood, Heraldry and Social Exclusion in Edwardian England', in *Heraldry, Pageantry and Social Display in Medieval England*, ed. P. Coss and M. Keen (Woodville, 2002), 39–68.
9. P. Coss, *The Origins of the English Gentry* (Oxford, 2003), ch. 1.
10. W. M. Ormrod, 'Agenda for Legislation, 1322–c.1340', *EHR* 105 (1990), 1–33.
11. Coss, *Origins of the English Gentry*, 196–7.
12. P. Coss, 'Knights, Esquires and the Origins of Social Gradation in England', *TRHS*, 6th series 5 (1995), 155–78; repr. in Coss, *Origins of the English Gentry*, ch. 9.
13. P. Coss, 'Andrew Ayton, the Military Community and the Evolution of the Gentry in Fourteenth-Century England', in *Military Communities in Late Medieval England: Essays in Honour of Andrew Ayton*, ed. G. P. Baker, C. L. Lambert and D. Simpkin (Woodbridge, 2018), 31–49.
14. M. Keen, *Chivalry* (New Haven, CT, 1984); M. Keen, *Origins of the English Gentleman: Heraldry, Chivalry and Gentility in Medieval England, c. 1300–c.1500* (Stroud, 2002); C. Carpenter, *Locality and Polity: A Study of Warwickshire Landed Society, 1401–1499* (Cambridge, 1992), ch. 3.
15. Carpenter, *Locality and Polity*, 76–7.
16. S. Payling, *Political Society in Lancastrian England: The Greater Gentry of Nottinghamshire* (Oxford, 1991), ch. 1.
17. H. L. Gray, 'Incomes from Land in England in 1436', *EHR* 49 (1934), 607–39.
18. T. B. Pugh, 'The Magnates, Knights and Gentry', in *Fifteenth Century England, 1399–1500*, ed. S. Chrimes, C. Ross and R. Griffiths (Manchester, 1972), 67–128; J. M. W. Bean, 'Landlords', in *The Agrarian History of England, Vol. 3: 1348–1500*, ed. E. Miller (Cambridge, 1991), 526–42.

19. G. L. Harriss, *Shaping the Nation: England 1360–1461* (Oxford, 2005), 137–8.
20. J. R. Maddicott, 'The County Community and the Making of Public Opinion in Fourteenth-Century England', *TRHS*, 5th series 27 (1978), 27–43; J. R. Maddicott, *The Origins of the English Parliament 924–1327* (Oxford, 2010), ch. 6; G. Dodd, *Justice and Grace: Private Petitioning and the English Parliament in the Late Middle Ages* (Oxford, 2007), ch. 5.
21. Dodd, *Justice and Grace*, ch. 5.3.
22. Payling, *Political Society*, 112–13; N. Saul, *Knights and Esquires: The Gloucestershire Gentry in the Fourteenth Century* (Oxford, 1981), 126.
23. Payling, *Political Society*, 109–10.
24. C. Moreton, 'A Social Gulf? The Upper and Lesser Gentry of Later Medieval England', *JMH* 17 (1991), 255–62.
25. R. Horrox, 'The Urban Gentry in the Fifteenth Century', in *Towns and Townspeople in the Fifteenth Century*, ed. J. A. F. Thomson (Gloucester, 1988), 22–44.
26. K. B. McFarlane, 'Bastard Feudalism', in McFarlane, *England in the Fifteenth Century: Collected Essays* (London, 1981), 23–4.
27. P. Coss, 'Bastard Feudalism Revised', *Past & Present* 125 (1989), 27–64.
28. G. A. Holmes, *The Estates of the Higher Nobility in Fourteenth-Century England* (Cambridge, 1957), 79.
29. C. Carpenter, 'The Beauchamp Affinity: A Study of Bastard Feudalism at Work', *EHR* 95 (1980), 514–32 (516).
30. C. Given-Wilson, 'The King and the Gentry in Fourteenth Century England', *TRHS*, 5th series 37 (1987), 87–102. See also M. Hefferan, 'Household Knights, Chamber Knights and King's Knights: The Development of the Royal Knight in Fourteenth-Century England', *JMH* 45 (2019), 80–99.
31. Given-Wilson, 'King and the Gentry', 96–7.
32. S. Walker, *The Lancastrian Affinity 1361–1399* (Oxford, 1990).
33. A. K. Gundy, *Richard II and the Rebel Earl* (Cambridge, 2013), 159.
34. See G. Dodd, 'Tyranny and Affinity: The Public and Private Authority of Richard II and Richard III', in *Rulers, Regions and Retinues: Essays Presented to A. J. Pollard*, ed. L. Clark and P. W. Fleming (Woodbridge, 2020), 1–16.
35. Although one must not forget the existence of an urban dimension.
36. J. Rose, *Maintenance in Medieval England* (Cambridge, 2017), 274–5.
37. N. Saul, 'The Commons and the Abolition of Badges', *Parliamentary History* 9 (1990), 2–15.
38. For recent work on the underlying phenomena, see J. Rose, *Maintenance in Medieval England* (Cambridge, 2007), and M. J. Ward, *The Livery Collar in Late Medieval England and Wales: Politics, Identity and Affinity* (Woodbridge, 2016).

39. Walker, *Lancashire Affinity*, ch. 5; M. Cherry, 'The Courtenay Earls of Devon: The Formation and Disintegration of a Late Medieval Affinity', *Southern History* 1 (1979), 71–99; Carpenter, *Locality and Polity*, ch. 10; H. Castor, *The King, the Crown and the Duchy of Lancaster: Public Authority and Private Power 1399–1461* (Oxford, 2000), ch. 4.
40. Harriss, *Shaping the Nation*, 167–8; P. Maddern, *Violence and Social Order* (Oxford, 1992), 206–25.
41. Payling, *Political Society*, ch. 4; S. M. Wright, *The Derbyshire Gentry in the Fifteenth Century* (Chesterfield, 1983), chs. 1 and 5.
42. Harriss, *Shaping the Nation*, 139.
43. Payling, *Political Society*, 11, 108.
44. C. Carpenter, *The Wars of the Roses: Politics and the Constitution in England, c. 1437–1509* (Cambridge, 1997), 57–63.
45. For a recent review of the controversy, its historiography and its parameters, see G. Dodd, 'County and Community in Medieval England', *EHR* 134 (2019), 777–820.
46. C. Carpenter, 'Gentry and Community in Medieval England', *JBS* 33 (1994), 340–80.
47. Castor, *King, Crown and Duchy*, 128–55.
48. Harriss, *Shaping the Nation*, 187.
49. E. Powell, 'The Settlement of Disputes by Arbitration in Fifteenth-Century England', *Law and History Review* 2 (1984), 21–43; C. Rawcliffe, 'The Great Lord as Peacemaker: Arbitration by English Noblemen and Their Councils in the Late Middle Ages', in *Law and Social Change in British History*, ed. J. A. Guy and H. G. Beale (London, 1984), 34–54.
50. E. L. G. Stones, 'The Folvilles of Ashby-Folville, Leicestershire, and Their Associates in Crime, 1326–1347', *TRHS*, 5th series 7 (1957), 117–36; J. G. Bellamy, 'The Coterel Gang: An Anatomy of a Band of Fourteenth-Century Criminals', *EHR* 79 (1964), 698–717.
51. Carpenter, *Wars of the Roses*, 262.
52. Ibid., 263.
53. Ibid., 264.
54. G. L. Harriss, introduction to McFarlane, *England in the Fifteenth Century*, xxvii; Given-Wilson, 'King and Gentry in Fourteenth Century England', 87.

Further Reading

Carpenter, C., *Lordship and Polity: A Study of Warwickshire Landed Society, 1401–1499* (Cambridge, 1992).

The Wars of the Roses: Politics and the Constitution in England, c. 1437–1509 (Cambridge, 1997).

Castor, H., *The King, the Crown and the Duchy of Lancaster: Public Authority and Private Power 1399–1461* (Oxford, 2000).
Coss, P., *The Origins of the English Gentry* (Oxford, 2003).
   'The Origins and Diffusion of Chivalry', in *A Companion to Chivalry*, ed. R. W. Jones and P. Coss (Woodbridge, 2019), 7–38.
Dodd, G., *Justice and Grace: Private Petitioning and the English Parliament in the Late Middle Ages* (Oxford, 2007).
Given-Wilson, C., 'The King and the Gentry in Fourteenth Century England', *TRHS*, 5th series 37 (1987), 87–102.
Harriss, G. L., *Shaping the Nation: England 1360–1461* (Oxford, 2005).
Keen, M., *Origins of the English Gentleman: Heraldry, Chivalry and Gentility in Medieval England, c.1300–c.1500* (Stroud, 2002).
Maddicott, J. R., 'The County Community and the Making of Public Opinion in Fourteenth Century England', *TRHS*, 5th series 27 (1978), 27–43.
Payling, S., *Political Society in Lancastrian England: The Greater Gentry of Nottinghamshire* (Oxford, 1991).

ELIZA HARTRICH

13

Citizens

Introduction: Who Was a 'Citizen'?

Twenty-first-century readers perhaps associate the word 'citizen' with nations and states. The inhabitants of England in the later Middle Ages, however, were subjects of the king, not citizens of a nation. The word 'citizen' did exist in late medieval England, but it referred to cities and towns rather than nations, realms or states. A citizen was someone who swore an oath to be a member of an urban political community: a person who paid taxes to the local urban government, took up municipal office when called upon and contributed towards the defence of the city. In return, the citizen received the right to practise a trade within the city and to be tried by the city's own law courts. Male citizens attended municipal assemblies, where civic officials were elected and where key business pertaining to the town (for instance, about levying taxation) was discussed. Women could become citizens, but they were allowed only the economic benefits of citizenship and rarely accorded political rights. Technically speaking, only a city could have citizens. In the Middle Ages, a city was defined as an urban settlement with a cathedral. Population size was not especially relevant. Wells, the seat of the bishop of Bath and Wells, was a city with citizens even though population estimates derived from tax records suggest it was the forty-fourth largest urban settlement in England in 1377 and the seventy-fourth largest in 1524–5. Colchester, ranking tenth and ninth in the same datasets, had a population at least double the size of Wells's but, lacking a cathedral, was not a city.[1] Colchester was, instead, designated as a borough or town. It, too, had residents with the same privileges and responsibilities as citizens of a city, but in Colchester they were called burgesses. This chapter uses the word 'citizen' interchangeably with 'burgess', as the terminology did not affect the relationship between privileged inhabitants of towns and the English monarchy.

Each town had its own eligibility criteria for citizenship. Typical routes in larger towns were to inherit the status from a parent, complete an apprenticeship with a member of a trade guild or make a payment to the civic government. In some towns, burgess status was tied, instead, to property-holding: specifically, to those in possession of a long and thin strip of land called a burgage plot which, unlike other kinds of property, could be sold or rented out without securing an overlord's permission. The percentage of a town's residents who were citizens varied, from around a quarter of adult males in late medieval London to a much more restricted elite in Exeter.[2] The citizens of a town typically included merchants (traders and distributors, who tended to dominate high civic office), artisans (producers of textiles and other consumer goods) and victuallers (bakers, butchers, fishmongers, brewers and others involved in the provision of food and drink). In addition to these stereotypically 'urban' professions were gentlemen and lawyers. The latter, in particular, proved useful advocates for civic interests in royal law courts, and by the early fifteenth century many municipal governments employed local lawyers as 'recorders' to fulfil these duties of legal representation and lobbying.

Citizens, while a heterogeneous group, notably excluded children, Jews, most women, journeymen (individuals trained in a trade but who did not run their own shop), servants, migrant labourers from the countryside and vagrants – even though all these people lived in towns, contributed to urban economies and were subject to municipal laws. Recent work has stressed that 'citizenship' was a legal category invented in the thirteenth century, and that thereafter many people who were not 'citizens' in a legal sense were nevertheless active participants in urban politics.[3] In this chapter, I examine the uniquely privileged legal relationship of urban citizens to the English crown but I shall also consider the much broader range of non-citizens who lived in English cities and towns. Simply by living in more densely populated spaces, town dwellers were in a position to act as audience for and critics of the monarchy in ways less accessible to residents of the countryside.

Towns and Cities in England, 1215–1485: An Overview

By 1215, there was already a dense network of towns across much of southern, central and eastern England. The thirteenth century, fuelled by commercial prosperity and a demographic boom, saw the extension of England's urban system into the south-west and north-east. Around fifty places in England were newly designated as towns between 1215 and 1368.[4] Many of these would hardly seem more than villages, with populations in the hundreds rather than thousands. The vast majority were speculative seigneurial boroughs founded by bishops, religious houses and aristocrats eager to stimulate trade on their estates – often unsuccessfully. Edward I also embraced town plantation in an attempt to develop ports in militarily strategic locations – most notably in north Wales during the 1270s to 1290s but also in England at Hull (Yorkshire), Newton (Dorset) and New Winchelsea (Sussex). The arrival of the Black Death in England in 1348, and the subsequent reduction in England's population and economy, brought an almost complete stop to new urban foundations.

Throughout the later Middle Ages, England was dominated by one city: London. At its demographic peak around 1290, the city's population of circa 60,000 individuals was approximately three times that of the next largest town. London's pre-eminence only increased thereafter. One in every sixty-six English people lived in London in 1300; it was one in forty by 1500. The city accounted for 2 per cent of the nation's total wealth in 1334 and nearly 9 per cent in 1515.[5] This growth was due, in some degree, to the presence of royal government in the London suburb of Westminster. Westminster's position as the realm's political capital was already assured from the twelfth century, but the Scottish wars of the late thirteenth and early fourteenth centuries had prompted institutions of royal government to move to York for extended periods of time.[6] During the reign of Edward III, however, as royal attention shifted from Scotland to France, the exchequer and courts of common pleas and king's bench became fixed in Westminster. Clerks, lawyers, litigants, judges and royal councillors (not to mention their households) fuelled London's economy as they spent money on accommodation, food, wine, luxury textiles and other consumer goods.

York was England's second largest town in 1290, with a population around 22,700; it was followed by Bristol, Lincoln and Norwich, with populations between 12,000 and 15,000. Around thirty other towns boasted 3,500 to 10,000 residents apiece (see Map 13.1).[7] These numbers declined considerably, often halving in size, in the century and a half following the plague of 1348–9. Mortality rates from late medieval epidemics were often highest in densely populated urban settings. The overall percentage of the English population resident in towns, though, remained stable into the fifteenth century: high death rates were offset by in-migration of villeins from the countryside (often women) and immigrants

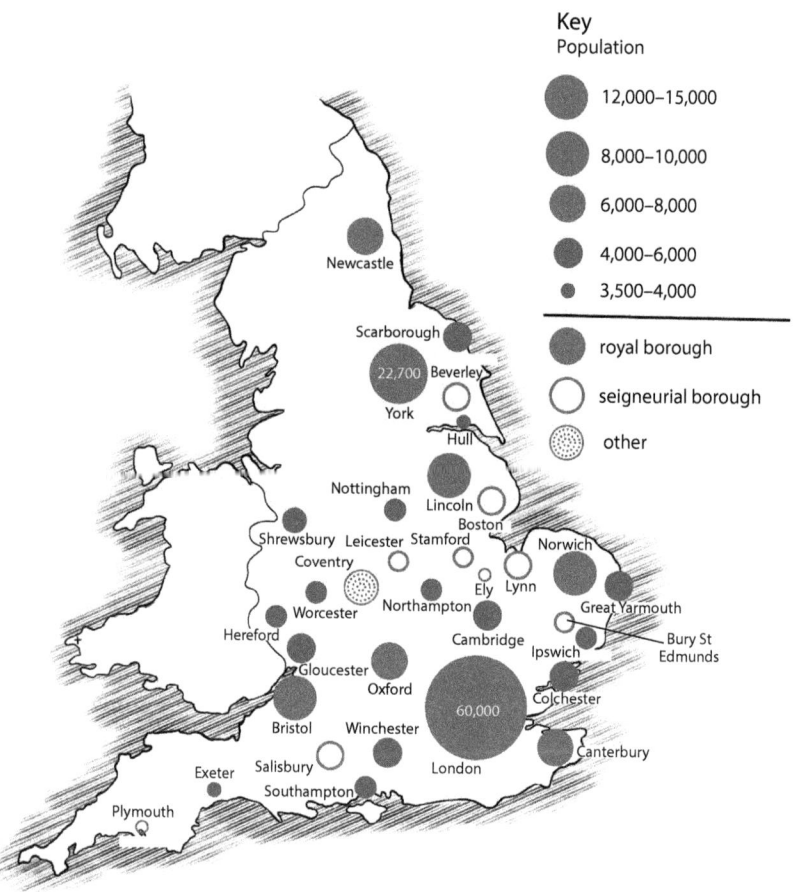

Map 13.1 Royal and seigneurial boroughs by population size, c. 1290 (source: B. M. S. Campbell, 'Benchmarking Medieval Economic Development: England, Wales, Scotland, and Ireland, c. 1290', *Economic History Review* 61 (2008), 896–945 (Table 4, pp. 908–9)

from the Low Countries, Germany, France, Scotland and Ireland. Moreover, the economic challenges faced by the likes of Beverley contrasted with the success stories of cities like Exeter, which boomed on the back of domestic coastal trade.[8] But equally important to the economy were the small market centres of 500–1,000 people which comprised the overwhelming majority of English towns throughout the Middle Ages.[9]

Citizenship, Lordship and Subjecthood

Towns 'belonged' to a lord, which could be the king (in the case of 'royal' towns) or an intermediary bishop, monastic house, noble or member of the gentry (for 'seigneurial' towns). Seigneurial overlords received the rents that burgesses paid for their plots and appointed their own officials to supervise decisions about how the town was run. It was possible for towns to have more than one lord; until becoming its own county in 1451, half of Coventry owed fealty to the earl of Chester and half to the prior of Coventry.[10] Being the 'king's town', as opposed to an abbot or bishop or earl's town, was a privilege enjoyed by a minority of English towns – typically the larger administrative centres. It enabled the burgesses to elect their own officials and implied a more direct personal relationship between town and monarch, which its residents sometimes employed to rhetorical effect. During the Wars of the Roses, the mayor of Exeter successfully avoided the earl of Devon's demands to bar his enemies from the city by citing that the citizens of Exeter 'beth [th]e Kynges tenauntes and [th]is [th]e Kynges cite' and thus could not make military decisions without royal assent.[11]

The distinction between 'king's towns' and seigneurial towns, however, can be overdrawn. Even seigneurial towns were still subject to the king, and loyalty to the monarch was expected to trump loyalty to one's overlord, especially in military matters. The city of Salisbury was under the lordship of the bishop of Salisbury but English kings made the same demands of money and troops as if it were a royal borough. Nor did Salisbury's status as an episcopal city prevent kings from conceiving their relationship in paternalist terms: Edward IV in 1465 was far from unusual in addressing his letter 'To oure trusty and welbeloued the Cite[z]eins and inhabitants of the Cite'.[12] Moreover, the vagaries of inheritance and forfeitures led some towns to shift from seigneurial to royal and back again: lordship over the seigneurial borough of Walsall in Staffordshire was assumed by the crown following the death of Richard, earl of Warwick, at the battle of Barnet in 1471 but transferred back to the earls of Warwick on several occasions during the political tumult of the 1480s and 1490s.[13] In terms of position within the economic infrastructure of the realm, conditions of lordship could matter even less. The Lincolnshire town of Boston, although belonging to the earl of Richmond, was one of England's wealthiest in the fourteenth century, and its designation as a staple in the wool trade in 1369 made it a centre for the royal supervision of imports and exports. The nearby 'king's town' of Grimsby had no such status or significance in the kingdom's commerce.[14]

In the Middle Ages, being called a 'town' did not necessarily indicate that the place in question possessed the occupational diversity, built environment or communal identity that modern sociologists and geographers designate as characteristics of 'urbanness'. Instead, specific legal criteria distinguished a town from a village. The privileges exercised by citizens/burgesses of a town were enumerated in charters, which followed standardised templates. The burgesses of Lynn, for instance, possessed the liberties already granted to the burgesses of Oxford, and the burgesses of the new towns that Edward I established in north Wales in the late thirteenth century received the same privileges as the citizens of Hereford. Charters could be issued directly by the king, or they could be granted by a seigneurial town's aristocratic or ecclesiastical overlord. While individual clauses varied, there were some liberties common to most charters. These included the right for citizens/burgesses to be tried in the town court, to trade within the town and to form a guild merchant that could establish rules for commercial transactions in the town. One of the privileges granted to citizens of royal towns was the right to trade in all towns under the king's jurisdiction (whether in England, Wales, Ireland, Scotland or France) without paying local tolls.

While seigneurial towns received their rights from an overlord, the king retained a supervisory role over the distribution of all urban privileges within his realm. It became customary for all civic governments – of royal and seigneurial towns alike – to pay for royal confirmation of their charters on the accession of a new monarch. During the thirteenth century the kings of England also established themselves as the sole authority within the realm capable of granting licences for markets or fairs to be held in any town – in contrast to elsewhere in Europe, where the monarch was one of many lords able to create a market.

Citizenship and subjecthood, far from being competing identities, were mutually reinforcing. Oaths taken by new burgesses and urban officeholders sometimes included vows of obedience to the king alongside to the town.[15] For people born outside England to non-English parents, the processes of becoming an 'English' subject of the king and becoming a citizen of a town were often closely intertwined. During the early stages of the Hundred Years War, French merchants resident in England were able to become naturalised subjects of the English king by citing their citizenship of an English town. Amiens-born Peter le Monnier, for example, gained Edward III's protection in 1346 by virtue of being a citizen of Wells, maintaining a family residence there and paying local taxes to the city. In the late fourteenth and fifteenth centuries, the situation had reversed: aliens who wished to become citizens of a town were often required to have already been recognised as English subjects.[16]

Citizens and Royal Administration: Law

People who resided in a town for a year and a day were regarded as free, and so were not obliged to use the mills and ovens of their overlords and could move or marry without their permission. Most boroughs held their own courts, with burgesses not obliged to attend manorial law courts or litigate disputes there. Practice varied, however, and the seigneurial town of Shipston-on-Stour in Warwickshire was not a complete anomaly in requiring its burgesses to use a manorial court operated by the bishop of Worcester's officials.[17] The town foundations of the thirteenth and early fourteenth centuries, nevertheless, did bring new people into a more direct relationship with English kingship: new burgesses, as freemen and freewomen, could now use the royal common law courts to settle their disputes.

It had long been common for towns to hold their own borough courts that enforced locally specific rules observed since time immemorial (known as 'customary law'), but from the reign of King John onwards many larger royal towns began to pay an annual sum (known as a fee-farm) to the exchequer which enabled municipal governments to collect fines paid to the court and gave them free rein to administer it according to their own wishes. The borough court was presided over by a mayor or bailiff: an official elected by the citizens of the town but, in royal towns, also accountable to the crown as the local delegate of royal authority. Mayors or bailiffs were often advised by councils of twelve or twenty-four men (called aldermen or jurats), again typically elected by the citizenry. Some seigneurial towns such as Leicester paid an annual fee to their lord to hold their own courts, and in such instances a very similar office-holding structure emerged, with elected mayors or bailiffs supported by councillors.[18] While officials in these types of seigneurial towns were directly accountable to their lord, they were also responsible for enforcing royal legislation. Constables in the bishop of Norwich's town of Lynn, for instance, swore an oath to 'mayntene & sustene [th]e kingis pees wi[th]ynne [th]is ffraunchise' and to keep watch according to the Statute of Winchester (1285).[19]

During the fourteenth and fifteenth centuries, some large to medium-sized towns received charters turning mayors and aldermen into justices of the peace (JPs) and royal escheators. It was thus local officials elected by the citizenry who were responsible for implementing key legislation in these towns, such as the Statute of Labourers (1351). As JPs, they investigated heretics and sat in judgement of suspected rioters, and as escheators they conducted regular surveys to ensure that no royal properties or prerogatives in the town were being usurped by other parties. In 1373, Bristol became the first town to be declared a county in its own right; the citizens of Bristol could now select their own sheriff rather than being subject to the royally appointed sheriffs of the counties of Gloucestershire and Somerset. York followed suit in 1396, and by 1485 ten more towns exercised this privilege.[20] Historians once characterised these charters as emblems of municipal 'independence' from royal administration. Christian Liddy, however, has argued more recently that the new privileges in fact transformed urban officials into agents of the crown, thereby bringing town and crown closer together.[21] Merging of civic and royal office was generally restricted to royal towns: in 1415 Henry V made the civic officers of the seigneurial town of Beverley JPs, but the town's overlord (the archbishop of York) ensured that the grant was rescinded the following year.[22]

Royal charters and parliamentary legislation concentrated a variety of legal powers in the hands of a small number of wealthy citizens: the plurality of law courts available to citizens belied the fact that many were administered by the same people. There was heated debate over whether a townsperson was allowed to appeal directly to the king and his council, chancellor or chief justices to challenge decisions made by the coterie of urban officials who dominated so many of the locally available courts. In a dispute that spanned several years in the 1450s, Henry May and other Anglo-Irish residents of Bristol claimed that the mayor and chamberlains of Bristol had stripped them of their citizenship because they had submitted a petition to the court of chancery against Bristol's discriminatory policies towards people born in Ireland seeking urban citizenship.[23]

Ultimately, mayors – though elected by the citizens of a town – could, like any other delegate of royal authority, be removed from office by the king if they were deemed to have abused that authority or been negligent in its exercise. This royal displeasure took the form of a temporary revocation of a town's chartered liberties, in which the mayor was removed in favour of a royally appointed captain or warden and the fines collected in the borough court reverted to the crown. Kings used this punishment liberally in the thirteenth century: Henry III suspended York's liberties in 1256 when the mayor and bailiffs did not obey a summons to the exchequer, and Edward I revoked York's charters no fewer than three times (in 1280–3, 1290 and 1292–7).[24] During the fourteenth and fifteenth centuries confiscation of municipal privileges tended to be reserved for occasions when urban officials had rebelled against the king (as when Canterbury lost its liberties in 1471 after its mayor, Nicholas Faunt, had taken up arms against Edward IV) or had failed in their duty to the king to preserve order within the town (as when a royal warden took control of Norwich in 1437 and 1443–7 following rioting in the city).[25] While it was usually only in royal towns that the king could suspend urban liberties, his responsibility for preserving law and order in the realm did entail intervention in the affairs of seigneurial towns. Recurring election riots in the episcopal town of Lynn, for instance, prompted Henry V's government to summon perpetrators before the royal council, change the town's constitution and even issue a royal writ in 1416 forcing the burgesses to select Thomas Hunte as mayor.[26]

Citizens and Royal Administration: Finance and War

The Angevin monarchs relied on a 'feudal' financial model: ad hoc levies on movable goods from tenants of the king's demesne lands and demands for scutage (payments from royal tenants in lieu of military service). Residents of towns contributed to many of these levies, as towns (especially royal ones) were often considered part of the king's demesne. Before their expulsion from England in 1290, Jews were liable to especially heavy taxes from the crown. Jews were regarded as property of the king and therefore had few legal or customary protections against royal demands for money. Although Jews were almost never permitted to become citizens of towns, they often lived in urban areas (with especially large communities in York, Norwich, Lincoln and Oxford) and were integral members of urban communities.

In the 1290s the English monarchy shifted to a model in which all subjects paid a percentage of the value of their goods to the crown, regardless of their 'feudal' relationship to the king. The 'borough' emerged as a separate category of taxable community, encompassing both royal and seigneurial towns. The system of fifteenths and tenths established in 1332 fixed the designations of boroughs and non-boroughs for nearly two centuries. Following assessments carried out by royal officials, each borough – whether royal or seigneurial – was to pay one-tenth of its total assessed wealth in movable goods, in contrast to the one-fifteenth owed by each rural area. The crown did not conduct new assessments after 1334, meaning that the amount paid by each urban community did not change, even as the Black Death, epidemics and the changing structure of England's international trade caused the population of each town to fluctuate wildly. From this point onwards, it was assessors selected by municipal governments and assemblies who determined how the communal tax burden was to be spread out among individuals on each occasion a tax was voted. All adult residents of towns – and not just citizens – contributed to the tenth, even though they did not generally have a voice in the assemblies or councils that determined how individuals would be assessed. All town residents felt the brunt of royal government, but citizens had the institutional power to decide who paid what and under what conditions.

When collecting taxation proved too slow to meet the needs of warfare or other emergencies, kings increasingly sought loans from their townspeople, especially following the collapse of the Peruzzi and Bardi Italian banking firms in the mid fourteenth century. These loans came both from towns as collective bodies and from individual wealthy citizens. When the town as a whole loaned money to the crown, the money was raised through a local tax on the citizenry – a process that typically required consent from an assembly of citizens. Such consent was not always forthcoming, and royal requests for loans could provoke protests against the municipal officers who administered them. In Coventry in 1351 citizens attacked the mayor in the Guildhall to prevent him from collecting the levy needed for a loan to Edward III.[27]

To sidestep the potential for public outcry, kings approached individual merchants and mercantile conglomerates to float royal initiatives. Wool exporters became especially prominent lenders to the crown, largely due to radical experiments in royal finance undertaken by Edward III. These included leasing out the management of wool customs to a group of merchants, chief among them William de la Pole of Hull.[28] A more lasting scheme was the establishment of a wool staple at Calais in 1363: anyone exporting wool to the continent from England was required to stop first at the English-held French port for their goods to be processed and taxed. The staple at Calais was managed by a group of twenty-six merchants known as the Company of the Staple. For the remainder of the Middle Ages, the merchants of the company ranked among the crown's principal lenders, as they could be repaid easily from the customs payments they collected at Calais. The crown used Stapler loans to pay the wages of soldiers stationed at Calais, and from 1466 the company funded the garrison's expenses on a permanent basis. The crown's dependence on the Company of the Staple brought risks of its own. Calais became the centre of Yorkist opposition to Henry VI's government in 1459–60, hosting the earls of Warwick, Salisbury and March after they had been declared traitors; the Staplers had greater faith that a royal government led by the duke of York would repay its debts to the company.[29]

Some merchants, such as William de la Pole of Hull and Richard Whittington of London, leveraged their financial support of the crown into prominent positions in royal government. De la Pole achieved a knighthood and his family joined the ranks of the aristocracy as earls (and later dukes) of Suffolk. Whittington – of pantomime fame – became a member of Henry IV's council in 1399–1400, with no assistance required from a cat.[30] The importance of men like Whittington, a many-times mayor of London and mayor of the Staple at Calais, to crown finance was twofold: they both contributed money from their own personal fortunes and used their roles as officeholders in municipal or mercantile organisations to influence the financial contributions made by those public bodies.

Merchants had ships as well as liquid capital at their disposal, which proved useful for a monarchy that did not have a navy of its own. Henry V's reign was one of the rare periods in which the crown built and supplied its own vessels; notably, he appointed William Soper, a citizen of Southampton, to manage his ships and shipyards.[31] Most of the time, though, the crown requisitioned merchant vessels for temporary use as warships or transport; while onerous, these demands gave port residents disproportionate influence in royal government. The confederation of the Cinque Ports – comprising the 'head ports' of New Romney, Hythe, Dover and Sandwich in Kent and Hastings, Winchelsea and Rye in Sussex, together with smaller associated 'member' towns – supplied fifty-seven vessels for the crown's use for fifteen days each year, and in turn these towns exercised political muscle far beyond their size. Citizens of the Cinque Ports held the canopy above the king at his coronation, and seven towns within the confederation regularly sent two MPs each to parliament, giving them a collective fourteen representatives compared to London's four.

Towns were an important source of troops, especially as the crown's reliance on knight service abated during the late thirteenth and fourteenth centuries. The king issued commissions of array to civic governments requesting horsemen and infantry, and municipal officials would then recruit soldiers and pay their wages through local taxes. Occasionally, as when defending Calais against Burgundian attack in 1436, urban troops took part in foreign wars, but town levies featured most often in internal warfare. Both kings and those who opposed them demanded soldiers from civic governments. Leaders of popular rebellions, too, tried to levy urban troops. In 1450, Jack Cade sent two letters to the civic government of the Kentish town of Lydd requesting military support; the jurats of the town sent their excuses but placated the rebels with the sumptuous gift of a porpoise.[32]

While urban governments were often cautious when supplying troops during periods of dynastic conflict or popular disturbance, on several occasions mayors and aldermen did throw in their lot with a particular cause. While Canterbury's participation in the rebellion of the Bastard of Fauconberg in 1471 resulted in the execution of the mayor and suspension of the city's privileges, such cautionary tales were the exception rather than the rule. More often, an urban government's overt partisanship turned the military tide in favour of the cause it supported. At the battle of Towton ten years earlier, Edward IV's success stemmed in part from his ability to attract civic troops: a Middle English poem describing the battle lauded the 'harow' of Canterbury, the 'white ship' of Bristol and the 'blak ram' of Coventry for fighting on Edward IV's behalf, undoubtedly in reference to the heraldry that festooned the civic standards under which these towns' contingents fought.[33]

The Urban Public: Parliament, Protest and Spectacle

As the concept of a 'community of the realm' developed, citizens of towns were recognised as members of the regnal community with a particular stake in its governance. London held special significance: its mayor was among the twenty-five barons sworn to enforce the terms of Magna Carta in 1215. Over the course of the thirteenth and fourteenth centuries, a wider range of towns came to be consulted about issues of 'common' interest as a matter of course.[34] In 1265, Simon de Montfort summoned towns to send representatives to parliament for the first time. Until 1310, burgess MPs were called to some parliaments but not all, and the number of burgess MPs and the towns they represented varied from assembly to assembly. From the reign of Edward II onwards, it became commonplace for each town to send two MPs to every parliament and London four. The parliament for which the fullest writs of summons survive (that of 1478) shows that representatives from towns numerically dominated the Commons: 202 out of 294 MPs were representatives from towns. Citizens of larger towns tended to elect their MPs in their own municipal councils or assemblies each time a parliament was called; the individuals chosen were typically civic officials themselves or wealthy merchants, lawyers or gentlemen with interests in the town. Members of parliament for smaller boroughs, however, were usually selected at the general meeting of the county court and were often not residents of the towns they represented.

Parliamentary business brought by boroughs varied widely, from complaints about obstructions on rivers to requests for alterations in the composition of a civic council. It is also probable that broader legislation about commerce, industry and international trade stemmed from urban MPs. The principle that merchants represented a public interest that needed to be consulted had already been established during the reigns of Edward I, Edward II and Edward III, when separate assemblies of the 'Estate of Merchants' advised on economic policy and approved grants of customs and wool subsidies. Such assemblies withered away in the late fourteenth century, but merchants in parliament continued to see themselves as champions of the 'commonweal' of the realm – a term that first appeared in parliamentary discourse in petitions about merchandise in the 1440s.[35] Petitions presented in the name of the whole parliamentary commons thus often had an urban inflection. During the Good Parliament of 1376, for instance, the impeachments of Londoners Richard Lyons and John Pecche and Great Yarmouth burgesses William Ellis and Hugh Fastolf for crimes against the king (notably, usury and the embezzlement of royal subsidies) coincided with complaints against these men for misgovernance in their home towns.[36]

Around two-thirds of burgess MPs represented royal towns.[37] As a result, parliamentary representation of urban populations was uneven: while seigneurial towns like Salisbury and Lynn did have MPs throughout the later Middle Ages, Coventry, despite being England's fourth largest town in 1377, did not regularly send MPs to parliament until after its creation as a royal county in 1451. Seigneurial boroughs that did not send MPs to parliament nevertheless engaged with the institution regularly. Beverley, a borough of the archbishop of York, was not represented in parliament between 1306 and 1563, but its burgesses used the Commons to advance their interests. In 1330, Beverley merchant John of Manby petitioned parliament for the repayment of his loan to the crown; the burgesses as a whole successfully asked parliament to petition the king for the confirmation of Beverley's charters in

1377; in 1416 the Commons petitioned that malefactors threatening violence against leading burgess John Brompton be required to take oaths to keep the peace.[38] Townspeople who were not citizens also found parliaments useful occasions to make their voices heard. The chronicler John Amundesham wrote that women from the Stocks Market in London 'came openly into parliament' at Westminster in 1427-8 to upbraid Humphrey, duke of Gloucester, for neglecting to assist his wife, Jacqueline of Hainault, in defending her inheritance in the Low Countries.[39]

The very nature of towns – where people from across the locality congregated in relatively small spaces – made them key sites for the dissemination of information. It was in urban marketplaces that many subjects heard royal proclamations, on matters ranging from legislation on weights and measures or trade treaties with foreign powers to the denunciation of rebels. Most famously, Henry V wrote letters to the mayor and aldermen of London, as well as the civic government of Norwich, detailing his military successes in France. The London letters were written in English rather than Latin or French, perhaps indicating that they were intended to be read out to the wider citizenry.[40] Rebels co-opted urban spaces to spread their own messages, often by posting bills on town gates, market crosses or important churches. Townspeople were more likely to be literate than their counterparts in the countryside, facilitated, perhaps, by the expanding number of schools located in urban settings during the fourteenth and fifteenth centuries. Bills were typically written in vernacular English with memorable rhyming slogans, to enable those townspeople able to read them to then easily spread the message by word of mouth.

Therefore, townspeople from all walks of life – citizens or not – were politically informed and their loyalties fiercely fought for. Ordinary Londoners emerged as the ultimate 'kingmakers' of the later Middle Ages. As early as 1326-7, Queen Isabella and Roger Mortimer distributed bills at the Cross in London's Cheapside and on windows across the city to rally support for the overthrow of Edward II's advisors. The commoners of the city took up arms on Isabella's behalf and influenced the city's mayor to declare himself her ally.[41] Similarly, it was the common people of London who paved the way for Edward IV's accession to the throne in 1461. Against the orders of the mayor and aldermen, they refused to allow Margaret of Anjou to enter the city following her victory at the second battle of St Albans, moved by Yorkist propaganda claiming that Margaret's army of northerners would plunder London.[42]

Outside the capital, trade networks centred on towns and municipal mechanisms for spreading news (such as the hue and cry, by which townspeople called their neighbours to witness thefts and assaults) proved essential for connecting groups of dissidents across the country and for creating the 'rumour', 'murmur' or 'clamour' that forced the crown to consider public opinion.[43] The Peasants' Revolt of 1381, while typically seen as a rural uprising, included infamous acts of violence in York, Beverley, Scarborough, Winchester, Canterbury, Bridgwater, Salisbury, St Albans, Bury St Edmunds and Great Yarmouth, among many other provincial urban locations. The man adopting the pseudonym Jack Sharpe ignited a major anti-clerical revolt in 1431 by distributing Lollard bills in Oxford, Northampton, Coventry and Salisbury as well as London, enabling his cause to reach beyond its original centre in Abingdon and drawing fullers, dyers, weavers and other textile workers to advance his mission to 'have thre prestes heedes ffor a peny'.[44]

The complex nature of urban space as a stage for political communication is exemplified by pageants that greeted kings, queens and princes when they arrived at a city for the first time following their coronation, coming of age or marriage. Entry pageants increased in number during the Wars of the Roses, as monarchs with contested claims to the throne sought to advertise their legitimacy to the widest possible audience. In 1486, less than a year after defeating Richard III at Bosworth, King Henry VII was greeted at the city of York by a field of flowers that bowed to a large Tudor rose, subsequently topped with a crown descending from a cloud.[45] While these performances had obvious propaganda value for the king, they were also a rare opportunity for residents of provincial towns to communicate with the monarch on their own turf. Individuals jointly commissioned by the crown and the civic government designed entry pageants, and their content reflected this dual patronage. The same York pageant from 1486 contained a speech from York's legendary founder, King Ebrauk, requesting that Henry VII show favour to the city's inhabitants. A public display of civic loyalty was expected to prompt a royal reward. In 1451, Henry VI made Coventry its own county as a gesture of thanks for the mayor's public homage and gift of a tun of wine and twenty fat oxen during his stay in the city.⁴⁶ Because townspeople were needed to serve as actors, suppliers and appreciative audiences for these spectacles, they also had the power to subvert these performances of majesty. Londoners twice destroyed heraldic shields set up for the royal procession to celebrate the marriage of Richard II and Anne of Bohemia in 1382 – an act perceived as bringing shame to king, queen and city.⁴⁷

Conclusion

Townspeople were an especially powerful type of subject, but they were not a homogeneous group. Residents of royal towns had a different relationship to the monarchy than did residents of seigneurial towns, and citizens interacted with kings in ways not available to non-citizen town dwellers. All townspeople bore ultimate loyalty to the king and felt the full force of royal government in military and financial matters, but in seigneurial towns the immediate source of justice and grace was their overlord and not the crown. Citizens of royal towns had special trading rights and legal privileges throughout the kingdom, elected their own MPs to parliament and could potentially exercise delegated royal authority themselves if elected as mayors, aldermen, sheriffs and councillors of their town. Citizens tended to be among the economic elite in towns, and their money, commercial expertise and ships became increasingly vital to royal financial and military initiatives from the fourteenth century onwards. Citizens thus encountered royal government through two avenues: in a public capacity as an urban community that made decisions collectively and in a private capacity as merchants with access to liquid capital.

Citizens, however, were but one component of a larger urban public. It was in urban spaces that the kings' triumphs, laws and pleas were most often broadcast. People who frequented those marketplaces and streets, whether citizens or not, were empowered as audiences who could publicly accept, ignore, protest against or negotiate with royal power. They controlled access to key sites of communication and military power in the city, such as market crosses and city gates – a fact that kings or would-be kings ignored at their peril.

Notes

1. A. Dyer, 'Appendix: Ranking Lists of Medieval English Towns', in *The Cambridge Urban History of Britain, Vol. 1: 600–1540*, ed. D. M. Palliser (Cambridge, 2000), 747–70 (at 758–64).
2. C. M. Barron, 'London and the Crown 1451–61', in *The Crown and Local Communities in England and France in the Fifteenth Century*, ed. J. R. L. Highfield and R. Jeffs (Gloucester, 1981), 88–109 (at 88); M. Kowaleski, 'The Commercial Dominance of a Medieval Provincial Oligarchy: Exeter in the Late Fourteenth Century', *Mediaeval Studies* 46 (1984), 355–84.
3. E.g. C. D. Liddy, 'The Household, the Citizen and the City: Towards a Social History of Urban Politics in the Late Middle Ages', *Social History* 49 (2024), 261–93.
4. 'The Chronology of Town Plantation in England' (319–38) and 'Gazetteer: England' (386–526), in M. Beresford, *New Towns of the Middle Ages: Town Plantation in England, Wales and Gascony* (London, 1967).
5. P. Nightingale, 'The Growth of London in the Medieval English Economy', in *Progress and Problems in Medieval England*, ed. R. Britnell and J. Hatcher (Cambridge, 1996), 89–106.
6. W. M. Ormrod, 'Competing Capitals? York and London in the Fourteenth Century', in *Courts and Regions in Medieval Europe*, ed. S. Rees Jones, R. Marks and A. J. Minnis (Woodbridge, 2000), 75–98.
7. B. M. S. Campbell, 'Benchmarking Medieval Economic Development: England, Wales, Scotland, and Ireland, c. 1290', *Economic History Review* 61 (2008), 896–945 (at 906–12).
8. J. I. Kermode, 'Merchants, Overseas Trade and Urban Decline: York, Beverley and Hull c. 1380–1500', *Northern History* 23 (1987), 51–73; E. M. Carus-Wilson, *The Expansion of Exeter at the Close of the Middle Ages* (Exeter, 1963).
9. C. Dyer, 'Small Places with Large Consequences: The Importance of Small Towns in England, 1000–1540', *HR* 75 (2002), 1–24.
10. R. Goddard, *Lordship and Medieval Urbanisation: Coventry, 1043–1355* (Woodbridge, 2004).
11. Devon Record Office, Exeter, Exeter Mayor's Court Roll 34–35 Henry VI, rot. 8d; H. Kleineke, '"[Th]e Kynges Cite": Exeter in the Wars of the Roses', in *The Fifteenth Century, Vol. 7: Conflict, Consequences and the Crown in the Late Middle Ages*, ed. L. Clark (Woodbridge, 2007), 137–56 (at 155–6).
12. Wiltshire and Swindon History Centre, Chippenham, G23/1/2, ff. 77v, 78v.
13. C. D. Liddy, 'The Making of Towns, the Making of Polities: Towns and Lords in Late Medieval Europe', *Past & Present* 264 (2024), 3–47 (at 15–20).
14. S. H. Rigby, 'Boston and Grimsby in the Middle Ages: An Administrative Contrast', *JMH* 10 (1984), 51–66.

15. E. L. Cuenca, 'Oath-taking and the Politics of Secrecy in Medieval and Early Modern British Towns', *Continuity and Change* 38 (2023), 9–29 (at 12–13).
16. B. Lambert and W. M. Ormrod, 'Friendly Foreigners: International Warfare, Resident Aliens and the Early History of Denization in England, c. 1250–c. 1400', *EHR* 130 (2015), 1–24 (at 4, 8–9, 13, 20).
17. C. Dyer, 'Courts and Urbanisation: Jurisdiction in Late Medieval Seigneurial Boroughs and Towns', in *Town Courts and Urban Society in Late Medieval England, 1250–1500*, ed. R. Goddard and T. Phipps (Woodbridge, 2019), 93–116.
18. *Records of the Borough of Leicester*, ed. M. Bateson et al., 5 vols. (London, 1899–1974), II, 149–52.
19. King's Lynn Borough Archives, King's Lynn, KL/C 9/1, f. 4v.
20. These were: Newcastle-upon-Tyne (1400), Norwich (1404), Lincoln (1409), Hull (1440), Southampton (1447), Nottingham (1449), Coventry (1451), Canterbury (1461), Gloucester (1483) and Scarborough (1485).
21. C. D. Liddy, *War, Politics and Finance in Late Medieval English Towns: Bristol, York and the Crown, 1350–1400* (Woodbridge, 2005).
22. R. E. Horrox, 'Medieval Beverley', in *A History of the County of York East Riding, Vol. 6: The Borough and Liberties of Beverley*, ed. K. J. Allison (Oxford, 1989), 2–62 (at 29).
23. E. Hartrich, 'Rebellion and the Law in Fifteenth-Century English Towns', in *The Routledge History Handbook of Medieval Revolt*, ed. J. Firnhaber-Baker and D. Schoenaers (London, 2017), 189–207.
24. D. M. Palliser, *Medieval York, 600–1540* (Oxford, 2014), 137, 139.
25. S. Sweetinburgh, 'Those Who Marched with Faunt: Reconstructing the Canterbury Rebels of 1471', *Southern History* 39 (2017), 36–57; P. C. Maddern, *Violence and Social Order: East Anglia 1422–1442* (Oxford, 1992), ch. 6.1.
26. E. Powell, *Kingship, Law, and Society: Criminal Justice in the Reign of Henry V* (Oxford, 1989), 244–6.
27. S. K. Cohn, Jr., with D. Aiton, *Popular Protest in Late Medieval English Towns* (Cambridge, 2012), 122.
28. See Chapter 5.
29. G. L. Harriss, 'The Struggle for Calais: An Aspect of the Rivalry between Lancaster and York', *EHR* 75 (1960), 30–53.
30. E. B. Fryde, *William de la Pole, Merchant and King's Banker (d. 1366)* (London, 1988); C. M. Barron, 'Richard Whittington: The Man behind the Myth', in *Studies in London History Presented to P. E. Jones*, ed. A. E. J. Hollaender and W. Kellaway (London, 1969), 197–248.
31. *The Navy of the Lancastrian Kings: Accounts and Inventories of William Soper, Keeper of the King's Ships, 1422–1427*, ed. S. Rose, Navy Records Society, 123 (London, 1982).
32. *Records of Lydd*, ed. A. Finn (Ashford, 1911), 141–2.

33. *Historical Poems of the XIVth and XVth Centuries*, ed. R. H. Robbins (New York, 1959), 217 (ll. 42–4).
34. M. McKisack, *The Parliamentary Representation of the English Boroughs during the Middle Ages* (Oxford, 1932).
35. E. Hartrich, *Politics and the Urban Sector in Fifteenth-Century England, 1413–1471* (Oxford, 2019), 96–8.
36. A. Saul, 'Local Politics and the Good Parliament', in *Property and Politics: Essays in Later Medieval English History*, ed. A. J. Pollard (Gloucester, 1984), 156–71; G. A. Holmes, *The Good Parliament* (Oxford, 1975).
37. Liddy, 'Making of Towns', 28–31.
38. *PROME*, parliament of November 1330, item 63(34); parliament of January 1377, appendix item 14; parliament of March 1416, item 45.
39. *PROME*, parliament of October 1427, appendix item 1.
40. Hartrich, *Politics and the Urban Sector*, 52–3.
41. 'The French Chronicle of London', in *Chronicles of the Mayors and Sheriffs of London, A.D. 1188 to A.D. 1274*, ed. H. T. Riley (London, 1863), 262–3.
42. Hartrich, *Politics and the Urban Sector*, 172–3.
43. A. Prescott, '"Great and Horrible Rumour": Shaping the English Revolt of 1381', in *Handbook of Medieval Revolt*, ed. Firnhaber-Baker and Schoenaers, 76–103; C. Fletcher, 'News, Noise, and the Nature of Politics in Late Medieval English Provincial Towns', *JBS* 56 (2017), 250–72.
44. *Chronicles of London*, ed. C. L. Kingsford (Oxford, 1905), 97; M. E. Aston, 'Lollardy and Sedition 1381–1431', *Past & Present* 17 (1960), 1–44 (at 25).
45. *York House Books 1461–1490*, ed. L. C. Attreed, 2 vols. (Stroud, 1991), II, 481–5.
46. *The Coventry Leet Book* ... ed. M. D. Harris, EETS, Original Series, 134, 135, 137, 146, 4 vols. in 1 (London, 1907–13), 262–6.
47. M. Meer, 'Reversed, Defaced, Replaced: Late Medieval London and the Heraldic Communication of Discontent and Protest', *JMH* 45 (2019), 618–45 (at 634–7).

Further Reading

Attreed, L., *The King's Towns: Identity and Survival in Late Medieval English Boroughs* (New York, 2001).

Barron, C. M., *London in the Later Middle Ages: Government and People, 1200–1500* (Oxford, 2004).

Cohn, S. K., Jr., with Aiton, D., *Popular Protest in Late Medieval English Towns* (Cambridge, 2012).

Fletcher, C., 'News, Noise, and the Nature of Politics in Late Medieval English Provincial Towns', *JBS* 56 (2017), 250–72.

Goddard, R. and Phipps, T., eds., *Town Courts and Urban Society in Late Medieval England, 1250–1500* (Woodbridge, 2019).

Hartrich, E., *Politics and the Urban Sector in Fifteenth-Century England, 1413–1471* (Oxford, 2019).

Holt, R. and Rosser, G., eds., *The Medieval Town: A Reader in English Urban History, 1200–1540* (London, 1990).

Liddy, C. D., *War, Politics and Finance in Late Medieval English Towns: Bristol, York and the Crown, 1350–1400* (Woodbridge, 2005).

Palliser, D. M., ed., *The Cambridge Urban History of Britain, Vol. 1: 600–1540* (Cambridge, 2000).

'Towns and the English State, 1066–1500', in *The Medieval State: Essays Presented to James Campbell*, ed. J. R. Maddicott and D. M. Palliser (London, 2000), 127–45.

Reynolds, S., *An Introduction to the History of English Medieval Towns* (Oxford, 1977).

HELEN LACEY

14
———

The 'Public'

Introduction

This chapter examines the relationship between the king and his 'ordinary' subjects and asks whether such a thing as 'public opinion' evolved over the period to play a role in politics. For medieval historians, 'the public' used to be synonymous with the nobility and gentry. They were the section of the population that had some formal role in governance and had time outside of the demands of labour to devote to political questions. In part, this argument also rested on education and literacy: would anyone lower down the social scale be able to engage with the Latin and Norman French documents of parliament, chancery and exchequer, or the writings of theorists such as Aquinas or Giles of Rome? However, recent scholarship has emphasised that most if not all people in later medieval England had *access* to texts, could hear them read aloud and discuss their contents. The texts they heard might impart ideas similar to those of jurists and theologians, even if they did not come from them directly.[1] This has led to a reappraisal of the later medieval public, towards an expansionist view that includes people below the ranks of the gentry as politically aware and engaged.[2] John Watts, Chris Fletcher and Christian Liddy have done much to shed light on emerging polities, public opinion and political communication in later medieval England. Moreover, the work of Marion Turner and Gwilym Dodd has elucidated the role of documents in public discourse and expanded our knowledge of complaint literature and parliamentary petitioning.[3] One question for this chapter, then, is to ask how far down through the social order we should extend the concept of the public? Does this meaningfully incorporate the artisans and peasants of England's small towns and villages?

One popular 'truism' often repeated about this period is that the majority of the inhabitants of England did not travel far from where they were born and lived their lives within a few miles' radius of their dwellings. Added to this, the argument goes that peasants would have felt feudal ties to the manor and the lord more keenly than a connection to a remote monarch. However, recent scholarship has emphasised the numbers of people who did travel in this period: in armies, on pilgrimage, for trade.[4] Points of contact between the crown and its people also increased: people served in armies and on juries and they heard royal proclamations in many towns and villages throughout the realm. John Maddicott estimated that a proclamation like the one issued in February 1398 to inform people of the duke of Norfolk's supposed treason was made in more than 200 small communities. Such proclamations were often made on market days when large crowds gathered and word could be spread to family members and neighbours.[5] Moreover, the number of returnable writs sent to every sheriff of England with instructions to announce new laws or taxes or news of the war suggests that people throughout England would rarely have gone a week without hearing from the crown.[6] Royal judicial courts travelled on circuits around the country, lodging in a local castle or tavern for weeks at a time while they cleared the backlog of cases against prisoners awaiting trial. On the borders of Wales and Scotland and on the coasts, people were required to maintain defences against foreign enemies. They were visited by royal purveyors who had the authority to requisition supplies for the army and issue a tally stick record of funds owed in return (sometimes never to be reimbursed). Preachers also relayed news of the war or political events. By the middle of the fourteenth century, a large and increasing number of people in England were aware of, and to varying degrees engaged in, the enterprise of royal governance and its institutions. They took part in what might be termed 'public enterprise' even if they did not have a clearly defined way of holding government to account.

Another common assumption is that feudal relations should be given primacy over the more distant power of the state. It is true that for *some* peasants, on *some* manors, lords placed heavy demands on their time and labour. But this was far from a uniform picture and it is certainly true that by the end of the fourteenth century and into the fifteenth, the feudal system was waning.[7] Language mirrored this change; as Andrea Ruddick has argued, the bond between the king and his people evolved from one expressed in feudal terms of a liege lord and his vassal to one of monarch and subject.[8] This chapter analyses the language of 'the public' and how the use of the phrase evolved in the period 1215–1485. I then examine the notion of the 'public sphere' and the extent to which 'public opinion' existed in this period. Finally, 'public action' in revolt and public belief will be examined. It is important to emphasise that political ideas were not just voiced in the socially elite spaces of courts and parliaments. Messengers and travelling-men discussed politics in fields and taverns, students gossiped in an Oxford street, rebels gathered in woods. These spaces were less regulated but still, at times, political spaces.

Res Publica

The phrase *res publica*, the idea of the 'public weal' (or 'public good'), was used by Cicero to describe the Roman Republic. In contrast to the idea of absolute power wielded by an individual or select group over the rest, this concept was grounded in the sense of a wider society of politically aware people who could hold government to account. These constitutional ideas circulated in the later Middle Ages, although they were far from agreed upon. In thirteenth-century England, the Angevin 'revolution in government' saw the establishment of governmental institutions such as parliament, the royal law courts and the administrative offices of chancery and the exchequer. Alongside these developments, intellectuals such as Robert Grosseteste and Adam Marsh sought to codify royal jurisdiction and discuss constitutional theory. Then, in the mid thirteenth century, civil war took such ideas beyond the theoretical realm.[9] By the fourteenth century, war with the French demanded well-equipped armies and therefore taxation, which in turn cemented the position of parliament as a representative body. Parliament embodied the notion of reciprocal obligation (supply and redress) even if the emphasis was always placed on the authority of the monarch. One text, the *Modus Tenendi Parliamentum* (the 'Manner of Holding a Parliament') probably written in the reign of Edward II, promoted the status of parliament as the *foremost* institution to bring about political consensus.[10] Beyond the parliamentary Commons, there was no real mechanism for 'ordinary' people to voice political opinions to those in authority. Thus, direct public action emerged in this period as a clear way for people to express their frustration with government. In 1381 the first mass revolt of the lower orders (commonly known as the Peasants' Revolt, although involving a cross-section of society) shocked the crown in its scale and intensity and made those in government warier of pushing the populace beyond the limits of their tolerance. Repeated revolts into the next century and beyond established a tradition of direct public action. By the middle of the fifteenth century, the Wars of the Roses drew yet more people into national political debate and stimulated theorists such as Fortescue to write about the role of the public in constitutional monarchy.

Throughout the later Middle Ages, then, the role and status of the public was contested. G. L. Harriss offers the phrase 'mixed monarchy' to describe the uneasy balance that existed between 'Augustinian' and 'Aristotelian' concepts of a divinely ordained powerful monarchy on the one hand and rule through the will of the people on the other.[11] The balance tipped in favour of one or other concept in England throughout the later Middle Ages, but what remained constant was the sense of a direct connection between monarch and subject. The monarch should provide military protection and dispense justice, and in return the subject would feel the reciprocal bond of loyalty and obligation (to provide military service or pay taxes, in particular).

John Watts has proposed a useful three-stage model for the changing role of the public in this period. The first stage, from 1200 to 1350, he labels 'the age of the *commune* or *communitas*', a small and socially prestigious public marked out by public discourses in French and Latin. This public expanded beyond the king and his nobles, but only so far as the gentry and urban elites who collected taxes, raised armies and enforced law and order. In return their interests were represented in parliament. For Watts in this stage 'there was not much idealisation or public consciousness of the mass of the people' (although he does mention fear of popular revolt in 1340 and a growing tradition of complaint poetry). The second stage was 'the age of the commons proper, running from the later fourteenth century to the later fifteenth', when the lower orders forced themselves into the public sphere after the revolt of 1381. The final stage, from the 1470s onwards, Watts calls 'the age of *res publica*, after its emerging catch-phrase', 'a turning away from the politics of representation towards the governance of the common wealth by educated experts'.[12] Much of the material presented in the rest of this chapter conforms to this model, although some interesting nuances can also be observed.

'Public' in Parliament

Whether those in government conceived of a wider public in this period is an interesting question. If we take parliament to represent an assembly of those who had a say in governing the realm, then the use of the word 'public' (or *publicus, publice, reipublice, publique, puplik*) as transcribed in the medieval rolls of parliament is revealing. Overall it was used relatively rarely (c. 200 times until the end of Edward IV's reign, after which its use became more frequent). In the parliaments of Edward I, II and III, 'public' either related to 'public place', 'public proclamation', 'public knowledge' or 'public talk'. In these four types of usage, the public is an audience, one who might be told things, or know things, but not part of the structure of governance. If information was made public knowledge it could be shameful or even possibly dangerous to reputation. In one case of 'public knowledge and talk' (*publica vox et fama*) from January 1316, gossip revolved around whether or not the countess of Gloucester was pregnant. This was a matter of national importance, since the inheritance of the earldom of Gloucester and the vast landholdings that went with it were at stake. If the countess, Maud de Burgh, were pregnant and had 'conceived of the aforesaid earl, her late husband', the child would inherit the earldom. If this were not the case, the earl's three sisters were set to receive a third each of the inheritance. One of the sisters, Eleanor, was married to the notorious court favourite, Hugh Despenser the Younger and he pressed for her inheritance, on the grounds that the earl of Gloucester had died at the battle of Bannockburn in June 1314, 'since which day so much time has passed that if the said countess were pregnant, according to the common course of childbirth she could not be said to have been made pregnant by the aforementioned earl'. The king's lawyers dismissed this argument, saying that the countess conceived of the earl and that 'she felt a living boy in her belly'. She had, they claimed, informed the king, the queen and the magnates of the realm 'and furthermore there was and is public knowledge and talk of this almost throughout the whole realm'.[13] This final point seemed potent: if the public knew of the supposed pregnancy, the king could not disinherit the unborn child in secret. 'Public knowledge and talk' did not give the public a recognised role in government, but it did weigh on the minds of those in power.

The first mention of *reipublice* (public weal) in the parliament rolls came in the reign of Richard II. The occasion was the opening address of the chancellor, Sir Michael de la Pole, to the parliament of November 1384. De la Pole was stoking fear of enemies surrounding the realm on all sides: 'namely the French who abound greatly in number, the Spanish who abound greatly in galleys, the Flemish who with their many great ships, and the Scots who can readily enter the kingdom of England on foot'. In the face of such danger, de la Pole emphasised that the eighteen-year-old king Richard was ready to lead an army himself. In return, his subjects should stand ready 'in body and in goods' (to fight and pay taxes). This, de la Pole argued, was necessary for the public weal:

> everyone of the same kingdom was morally bound to assume a spirit of greater fervour in freely assisting the lord king with matters necessary for the kingdom and *public weal* [reipublice], in body and in goods, since no better response could be given him.[14]

Thus in 1384, only three years after the largest mass rising seen in England, the spokesman for the crown was now using the idea of the public weal to suggest that the king's subjects were morally obliged to come together in the common enterprise of war. The same phrase was used again in January 1390, although this time the context was Richard II's support for his uncle John of Gaunt. Richard made Gaunt the duke of Aquitaine, saying that 'Amidst the illustrious cares of the *public weal* and the many solicitudes which weigh upon the royal shoulders the condign reward of merits is most sustaining to that regal power'.[15] Here the public weal was a concern that weighed heavy on the shoulders of those in power.

The Lancastrian kings continued to refer to the public in parliament. After Henry IV's usurpation of the throne, the October 1399 parliament saw several references to 'the public' as the new king attempted to ground his right to the throne in public assent.[16] Henry V, in the parliament of November 1415, spelled out a link between even-handed justice and the good of the public weal. Quoting the counsel of 'wise men', he said: 'Without justice, the public weal will not prevail' (*Sine justicia non regitur res publica*). This promotion of the interests of the public continued into the Wars of the Roses. From the 1450s onwards the parliament rolls, now in Middle English, spoke of the 'public good'. In July 1455, the duke of York's letter justifying his actions at the battle of St Albans referred to 'the good publique, restfull and politique rule and governaunce' of the realm. In October 1460 this became 'the good publique and common wele therof', assuming the form it would take from the 1470s onwards, in Watts's classic 'age of *res publica*'.[17]

Public Sphere

Outside parliament, did people conceptualise a common discursive space, a 'public sphere'? Habermas's eighteenth-century bourgeois 'public sphere' was grounded in letters, pamphlets, newspapers and coffee house discussions.[18] Since Habermas first proposed this model, other scholars developed the discussion in new directions. Nancy Fraser emphasised the performative aspect of the modern public sphere: 'a theater in modern societies in which political participation is enacted through the medium of talk'.[19] For the sociologist James C. Scott, the 'public transcript' described the way in which the powerful and the powerless interacted. Subaltern groups often adopted deferential behaviour and speech in such instances, but they would then revert to a more transgressive 'private transcript' when out of earshot among their peers.[20] Later medieval England was not, of course, the coffee house culture of the eighteenth century, nor was it the polarised, authoritarian society of Scott's fieldwork in modern Southeast Asia. But we can usefully adapt the lessons of these studies, by thinking about the discursive spaces that were part of the later medieval world, and the kinds of strategies people used when talking about, or even criticising, those in power.

John Maddicott argued for the county court as the main forum for the 'making of public opinion' from the thirteenth to the fifteenth century. In his view, these courts, often comprising upwards of 150 men, brought together county officials, magnates and their attorneys, shire officials, suitors, jurors, litigants and lawyers 'and no doubt a crowd of others who came to have their legal instruments witnessed in so public a place or merely to gossip and observe'.[21] However, Christine Carpenter cast doubt on the primacy of the county in forming any sense of community and challenged Maddicott's reading of the county court.[22] Carpenter argued that after 1300 attendance at the county court was low, with landlords only attending to fulfil historical obligations attached to particular lands. Moreover, she argued that gentry families did not often 'align' with a particular county, with land and office-holding dispersed across several different counties and marriages giving them interests not limited to one defined locale. Instead she argued that where gentry and 'lesser men' formed groupings, 'more often than not they comprised an area defined by geography and local economy, which crossed county boundaries'.[23] However, while disagreeing over location, both Maddicott and Carpenter did articulate the idea of a wider, politically informed public outside of the formal institution of parliament. There is also one piece of evidence that shows that, by at least 1429, those in power had identified the election of MPs in county courts as a focal point for wider public involvement in politics. The 'Forty-shilling freeholders' act claimed that 'folk of small means or no worth' were interfering in parliamentary elections because 'each of them claims to have a voice equivalent, in such elections, to the most valiant knights or squires'. In order to prevent this the act limited the franchise to those with a freeholding worth at least forty shillings.[24] More recently, Chris Fletcher and Christian Liddy have concentrated on the urban sphere, demonstrating the extent to which mayors and civic officeholders were engaged in political dialogue with the crown. Royal officials were 'wined and dined' by urban officers, in part to trade information about political matters, and payments were made to lawyers sent to seek out news from the royal court. Fletcher has argued convincingly that such rumours and news circulated beyond a closed oligarchy. Meetings to discuss the latest news from the royal court clearly took place in taverns where there was potential for a wider audience. In two examples cited by Fletcher, the financial accounts of the mayor of Leicester from the years 1350–1 record expenses of 1s. 4d. for wine 'consumed at the tavern of John

Cook' when a number of men returned to Leicester with news from Scotland and for 'wine consumed at the tavern of Hugh of Lille', when two men 'came from parliament' with information.[25] Thus, the circulation of news created a socially diverse, informed public. This was also a public who might be willing to inform on one another, as Liddy demonstrates, seeing this as an extension of their duties as members of tithings and heads of households who were tasked to keep a vigilant eye on those around them.

Furthermore, throughout the period we find instances of 'ordinary' people discussing royal politics in a whole host of settings, from fields and roads to mayoral courts, county courts, village centres, people's homes, churches and churchyards. The number of such instances so far identified in the records increases from only one case in the civil war of the mid thirteenth century, to a small number of cases in the 1310s–1320s, then to several more cases in Richard II's reign, finally increasing exponentially throughout the fifteenth century, in the context of the Wars of the Roses. Governments legislated against the spreading of rumours and slander on a number of occasions in the period, but enforcement varied. Willingness to prosecute people was largely determined by the relative stability of the governing regime.[26] In mid thirteenth-century Leicestershire, the villagers of Peatling Magna demonstrated their command of royal politics in an altercation in the street with royalist forces. This was at the height of the 'Barons' War' and a royalist captain was passing through their village with his retinue. The villagers were said to have accused the captain and his men of 'treason and other heinous offences because they were against the welfare of the community of the realm and against the barons'.[27] Again, when near civil war resurfaced in the 1310s between Edward II's regime and the supporters of Thomas of Lancaster, political speech was reported in the fields and in the streets.[28] In 1314, a royal messenger was reported for a conversation in the fields of Newington in Kent. The messenger, Robert of Newington, was in conversation with the sub-bailiff when he allegedly made negative comments about the recent defeat inflicted on the English army by the Scots at Bannockburn. Newington said that the king's armies had been 'confounded by the Scots' and that the king could not be expected to win battles when he was so preoccupied with 'idling and applying himself to making ditches and digging and other improper occupations' rather than hearing Mass.²⁹ In 1316, it was in the street in Oxford that a clerk called Thomas de Tynwelle supposedly spoke 'irreverently about the lord king, expressing contempt for him by means of shameful words and saying that he was not the son of lord Edward recently king of England in contempt of the lord king'.³⁰ Near to the end of Edward II's reign, in 1326, it was in public that a Yorkshireman called Nicholas de Wymbyssh of Normanton took a stand against the keeper of the king's horses, who had arrived to requisition provisions of hay. Nicholas 'created a scandal before a large number of people' by declaring that the horses did not belong to the lord king but to a certain Hugh Despenser, 'a traitor and enemy of the king and the realm'.³¹

Fewer cases can be found in the reign of Edward III, presumably because of the relative security of the regime. Jeremy Goldberg notes a case from 1356 in which a witness in the ecclesiastical court of York was accused of saying that he 'would be willing to offer a halfpenny to St Mary of Lincoln if the saint would ensure the king had ill fortune in his activities'.³² The instability of Richard II's reign led to an increase in such cases. The chronicler Thomas Walsingham noted in 1377 that public criticism of John of Gaunt was circulating in London: 'there were some who, delighting in this sort of dispute, began to write verses which slandered the duke, and to post them up in different parts of the city so that they might stir up the people's anger all the more'.³³ On 8 July 1380 Robert de Cotyngworth was imprisoned in Newgate at the suggestion of Thomas Tutbury, clerk, accused of having defamed John of Gaunt.³⁴ Other prominent men also came in for criticism: in May 1383 Thomas Depham of Norfolk was gaoled for saying that news of Bishop Despenser's 'crusade' to Flanders and other previous news from those parts was false.³⁵

Public opinion clearly took centre stage during the Wars of the Roses. John Watts, Helen Wicker and others have examined evidence of popular voices transcribed into legal records, chronicles and popular manifestos, bills, poems and songs from the mid fifteenth century onwards.³⁶ This material led Watts to argue that fifteenth-century England did not fit the 'private transcript' model proposed by James Scott (whose study focused on modern, authoritarian regimes). Rather, Watts argued that ordinary people spoke out and their voice was widely viewed as legitimate. Their complaint was 'integral in the collapse of Henry VI's authority' and played a key role in bringing Edward IV to power. Watts found popular complaint in the 1450s aligned with the criticisms made of government at elite levels: evil counsellors were intervening between the king and his true subjects, wasting taxation and oppressing the commons. For Watts, popular comments could be blunt, rude and confrontational, but this did not make them radically different from elite popular discourse. They were intended to shock and were most often presented in indictments intended to secure a conviction before the courts. As the fifteenth century wore on, there was more resigned acceptance that royal government would intrude into the lives of its subjects than there had been in the fourteenth century, but there was also a belief that people could at least debate the terms of this intrusion. By the end of the Middle Ages in England, then, there were more documented references to political speech of 'ordinary' people than ever before. What we cannot know is whether this was a change in *recording* practices or an objective increase in such speech. However, it seems telling that insecure regimes such as those of Edward II, Richard II and Henry VI recorded more instances of this type of speech than relatively more stable governments such as that of Edward III. Under the former regimes people might well have been angrier at those in power, and moved to express this discontent, which was then recorded because those in government were more anxious to prosecute their critics. A growth in royal government throughout the period gave people more opportunity to come into contact with, and sometimes get annoyed by, crown officials.[37] But recording of critical comments in the legal records relates to the relative security of the regime and their desire to prosecute dissenters.

Public Protest

The later medieval public did at times take direct, violent action. Patrick Lantschner, in his study of Italy and the southern Low Countries, argued convincingly that violence was a logical and legitimate expression of political action in many medieval cities (dependent on the particular political organisation of the urban context). In England, Sam Cohn's study has shown that violent political protest was much more frequent than previously thought and largely conformed to the model seen elsewhere in medieval Europe. However, we should of course be sensitive to the nature and purpose of the record: the sources recording this violence might well be skewed towards emphasising how extreme it was, in order to justify a harsh governmental response.[38] Large-scale public protest against royal government had emerged in England before the mass rising of 1381. Most notably, in the months before Edward II's removal from the throne, Londoners took the side of Queen Isabella and Prince Edward. They 'arrested' John Marshal on charges of spying for Hugh Despenser the Younger, and Walter Stapledon, the treasurer, beheading them both in Cheapside, along with two of Stapledon's esquires. The Londoners then went on to attack the Tower of London and liberated all prisoners connected with Piers Gaveston's execution. Elsewhere in the country there were protests against Edward II's regime: a man was imprisoned in Lynn for raising troops against the king in 1326.[39]

In 1381, however, the rising was on an unprecedented scale. Later known as the 'Peasants' Revolt', it united people from many counties of England to protest against numerous aspects of royal governance and set a benchmark for subsequent protest. New research into the judicial and manorial records of the rising shows that tens of thousands of people were involved in the revolt, coming from many areas outside the 'heartland' in the south-east and East Anglia, including Hampshire, Somerset, Derbyshire, Yorkshire and Cheshire.[40] While regional issues played a part, the failings of royal government were consistently brought up: not only the corrupt collection of the poll tax but also 'evil' councillors, manipulation of the royal judicial system and failure to defend against French attacks. The rebels referred to themselves as the 'true commons' and situated themselves as part of the 'community of the realm' that should be the concern of all those in positions of power.[41]

Seventy years later, the dynastic contests of the Wars of the Roses drew the wider populace into the political sphere. Indeed, as John Watts argues, there were times where the 'common people' drove the agenda and shaped the civil discord (such as in 1450 with Cade's Revolt, as well as in Norfolk in 1468–9, in Yorkshire in 1489 and in the Western Rising of 1497). At the very heart of these risings was a claim to speak for, and in the interests of, the wider public. There is also evidence of the claimants to the throne 'courting' public opinion. In 1452, the duke of York wrote to the 'bailiff, burgesses and commons' of Shrewsbury, exhorting them to muster as many men as they could in his support.[42] McCulloch and Jones argue that York's strategic use of proclamations, manifestos and open letters 'made the Yorkist cause the popular cause'.[43] These techniques were subsequently adopted by Warwick and Edward IV. Earlier kings had issued documents addressed to the wider populace: Edward III's justification of the war with France is a good example, but by the 1450s the dynastic rivalries drew more and more people into domestic politics and protest.[44]

New research on the spatiality of popular protest has shown that throughout this period commoners created spaces for protest.[45] These could be secluded meeting spaces where they could speak among themselves, or public symbolic spaces that they could occupy, or everyday locations where they could transgress spatial customs. In the Peasants' Revolt, plotters confessed to secret meetings in woods, taverns, inns and breweries. One group of rebels in Kent met first in a brewery in Linton and then again by night in a wood next to 'la batayle' called 'Deperfeld' and appointed deputies to command the assembled insurgents.[46] In London rebels attacked the Tower, that potent symbol of royal power. One man called Thomas atte Sole of Gravesend broke into the king's private chamber 'and with his sword split the king's bed saying that he was looking for betrayers [*seductoribus*]'.[47] Another contingent of rebels burned down John of Gaunt's Savoy Palace and ran through main thoroughfares such as Cheapside making noise and threatening violence. In Winchester insurgents 'rang the common bell and sounded the common horn of the aforesaid city' to summon support.[48] In Derbyshire rebels took the royal castle of Horston by force, raising the banner of St George to signal their takeover.[49] Popular protestors created and transformed spaces to legitimise their cause, signalling to their supporters that there was safety in numbers and shocking those in power.

These visual and aural aspects of revolt were especially important in a period when the use of written documents among those below the ranks of the gentry was not the norm. This relative lack of documentary evidence might well have distorted historians' perceptions of the participation of the 'masses' in public discourse. Occasionally, we can find evidence of political songs or poems that might well have circulated orally among the lower social orders.[50] On rare occasions we see references to written documents circulating among rebels, but very few of them survive. In 1381, a man called John Preston of Hadleigh presented a petition to the king's justices, admitting that he had drafted the petition himself (*per ipsum factam fuisse et per eum assensionem*).[51] His document expressed the concerns of rural tenants and challenged the economic and legal power of landlords. However, it survived only because it was transcribed into the records of king's bench for posterity.

Public Beliefs

Outside violent protest, the wider public often appeared in the historical record as an audience for royal pageantry, including entry processions, weddings and funerals. For Londoners in particular, these kinds of events would not have been an unusual sight. Captured foreign princes were paraded before them on their way to the Tower, coronation routes were lined with coats of arms and fountains were made to flow with wine. In the eyes of chroniclers, the 'common people' most often came into view when they were inflicted with torments. They were mentioned when illness swept through the realm or when the Scots or French attacked or when abnormal weather decimated harvests. Sometimes they comprised the armies that congregated at muster points. In September 1386, Richard II had ordered an urgent muster of troops, only to disband them a few weeks later and send them home without pay. Those soldiers, travelling long distances from the outskirts of London back to Wales, Chester and Lancaster plundered the countryside on their route home for horses and food.[52] On a few occasions, however, chroniclers mentioned the wider public doing something that gives an insight into their beliefs. In 1383, for instance, Walsingham wrote about their enthusiastic response to news of the bishop of Norwich's 'crusade' to Flanders:

> many apprentices from London, and more servants, put on white hoods, with red crosses on their right side and red sword scabbards on their left, and set off without the support of their masters and lords ... others from almost the whole of England followed their example, leaving their parents, relations, and their beloved households and departed unarmed apart from swords, bows and arrows ... Along every road and every

> track, common folk with no experience of war and simple country men were hurrying to reach the coast.[53]

Knighton, too, mentioned the public response to this 'Crusade', but he emphasised a different point, about people (women in particular) contributing more money than they could afford in order to receive papal absolution of their sins:

> And it was believed that very many gave more than they could afford, in order to secure the benefit of absolution for themselves and their devoted friends. And thus that hidden treasure of the kingdom which is in the hands of women was put at risk. That was done by both men and women, rich and poor, according to what they possessed, and beyond, that they might secure absolution for their friends who had died.[54]

Clearly, news of the crusade and the possibility of absolution had spread throughout England: this had become a public event involving apprentices, servants and others in a common enterprise.

Public expression of belief might become overtly political when, as happened in 1397, 'ordinary' people used prayer and processions to express sympathy for Richard II's political opponents. Walsingham noted that:

> prayers were said and processions held throughout all parts of the realm for these lords, and for the king, that Almighty God would make the king well-disposed towards them and turn his heart from hatred to love of these nobles.[55]

Political opinion expressed through conventional acts of religious devotion was an ingenious way for the public to intervene in the affairs of state. Political and religious beliefs also came together in the public imagination at the tombs of well-known royal opponents. The *Brut Chronicle* mentioned news of miracles at the tomb of Thomas of Lancaster, Edward II's opponent. When word spread, 'people began coming there from all parts to kneel and pray at his tomb in Pontefract priory, to ask that holy martyr for succour and help; and God heard their prayers'.[56] One peasant will, written in Suffolk in 1329, bequeathed money to fund a pilgrimage to Lancaster's shrine.[57] Again in the early fifteenth century there was a 'popular rumour' that miracles were occurring at the tomb of Archbishop Scrope, recently executed for his opposition by Henry IV. Moreover, the public might see political messages in unexplained phenomena, interpreted as 'portents' of divine will. In the spring of 1402 a comet was sighted by many in the western sky, presaging violence and bloodshed (according to at least two chroniclers).[58] The *Warkworth Chronicle* included reports of men having seen the bleeding corpse of King Henry VI, and other men witnessing a headless man crying 'Bowes, bowes, bowes' on Dunsmore Heath in Warwickshire in 1471. It has been suggested that this apparition was interpreted as a barghest, 'a fiend that is attached to a specific place'; the repetition of 'bowes' being a command 'to bow' to the will of God.[59] Belief in such portents appears to have remained a constant in a changing political landscape.

Conclusion

Over the course of this period it is clear that the English polity expanded to incorporate many people below the rank of the gentry. This is not to say that they were afforded an official role in governance, but they were informed about the political issues, they discussed them among themselves and could, if needed, make their voice heard. By the fifteenth century the language of politics had shifted from French or Latin to English, facilitating this expansion in the political community. The king's subjects throughout his realm felt the reality of royal governance whenever they paid a tax, heard a proclamation of a new law or saw armies march past (requisitioning supplies through the hated system of purveyance on their way). In 1381, the Peasants' Revolt spelled out the threat of violent destruction that could be wrought by the lower orders and the Wars of the Roses saw different factions trying to summon up and speak for the 'trewe Comyns'. By the end of the period, though, as John Watts demonstrates, ideas of *res publica* were ushering in notions of a commonwealth directed by an educated class, notably less concerned with plebeian voices.

The foregoing discussion leads us to reflect on whether 'subjecthood' is a useful concept to apply to the late medieval period. As the feudal system waned, personal fealty to a lord could shift to the more abstract notion of what it meant to be a subject of the crown. For Andrea Ruddick, late medieval subjecthood evolved alongside a more authoritarian concept of kingship, reflecting ideas from both Christian and Roman law. Obedience, rather than fealty, was required and the king dealt with his people by his grace, rather than from any sense of mutual obligation.[60] Subjecthood could also evolve alongside notions of nationhood. As the English kings lost possession of their continental territories, *subditi* no longer had to accommodate those born in the king's territories outside England. It became simpler to conflate or overlay subjecthood with English identity. The language of subjecthood, so ubiquitous by the eighteenth century, had emerged by the late medieval period as a way to conceptualise the relationship between the people and the crown.[61]

Notes

1. M. T. Clanchy, *From Memory to Written Record: England 1066–1307*, 2nd ed. (Oxford, 1993); W. Scase, *Literature and Complaint in England, 1272–1553* (Oxford, 2007).
2. J. L. Watts, 'Power, Government, and Political Life', in *The Later Middle Ages*, ed. I. Lazzarini (Oxford, 2021), 19–41 (at 21–4).
3. M. Turner, *Chaucerian Conflict: Languages of Antagonism in Late Fourteenth-Century London* (Oxford, 2007); G. Dodd, *Justice and Grace: Private Petitioning and the English Parliament in the Late Middle Ages* (Oxford, 2007).
4. J. F. Romano, *Medieval Travel and Travelers: A Reader* (Toronto, 2020).
5. J. R. Maddicott, 'The County Community and the Making of Public Opinion in Fourteenth-Century England', *TRHS* 28 (1978), 27–43 (35).
6. A. L. Brown, *The Governance of Late Medieval England, 1272–1461* (London, 1989), 43.
7. M. Bailey, *After the Black Death: Economy, Society, and the Law in Fourteenth-Century England* (Oxford, 2021).
8. A. Ruddick, *English Identity and Political Culture in the Fourteenth Century* (Cambridge, 2013).
9. Watts, 'Power, Government', 25.
10. G. Dodd, 'Parliament, Politics and Protocol: The *Modus Tenendi Parliamentum* and the Settlement of the Realm under Edward II', *JMH* 48 (2022), 631–63.
11. G. L. Harriss, *Shaping the Nation: England 1360–1461* (Oxford, 2005), 3–13.
12. J. Watts, 'The Commons in Medieval England', in *La légitimité implicite, II*, ed. J.-P. Genet (Paris, 2015), 207–22 (at 220–21).
13. *PROME*, parliament of January 1316, item 9.
14. *PROME*, parliament of November 1384, item 3.
15. *PROME*, parliament of January 1390, item 21.

16. *PROME*, parliament of October 1399, items 16 and 52.
17. *PROME*, parliament of July 1455, items 19, 36, 41; *PROME*, parliament of October 1460, item 32.
18. J. Habermas, *The Structural Transformation of the Public Sphere: An Inquiry into a Category of Bourgeois Society* (Cambridge, MA, 1991).
19. N. Fraser, 'Rethinking the Public Sphere: A Contribution to the Critique of Actually Existing Democracy', *Social Text* 25/26 (1990), 56–80.
20. J. C. Scott, *Domination and the Arts of Resistance: Hidden Transcripts* (New Haven, CT, 1990); J. C. Scott, *Weapons of the Weak: Everyday Forms of Peasant Resistance* (New Haven, CT, 1987).
21. Maddicott, 'County Community', 30.
22. C. Carpenter, 'Gentry and Community in Medieval England', *JBS* 33 (1994), 340–80.
23. Carpenter, 'Gentry and Community', 354.
24. *EHD 1327–1485*, 465.
25. C. Fletcher, 'News, Noise and the Nature of Politics in Late Medieval English Provincial Towns', *JBS* 56 (2017), 250–72 (at 258, n.35).
26. *SR*, I, 35; *CCR 1318–23*, 505–8; *CCR 1327–30*, 586–591; *SR*, II, 9; *SR*, II, 59; *SR*, I, 319–20.
27. TNA, KB 26/175, m. 28; D. Carpenter, 'English Peasants in Politics 1258–1267', *Past & Present* 136 (1992), 3–42.
28. H. Lacey, 'Defaming the King: Reporting Disloyal Speech in Fourteenth-Century England', in *Monarchy, State and Political Culture in England, 1300–1500: Essays in Honour of W. Mark Ormrod*, ed. G. Dodd and C. D. Taylor (Woodbridge, 2020), 71–93.
29. TNA, E 368/86, m. 32d; E 159/89, m. 89d.
30. TNA, E 368/86, m. 94.
31. TNA, KB 27/265 rex m. 30.
32. P. J. P. Goldberg, 'John Rykener, Richard II and the Governance of London', *Leeds Studies in English*, New Series, 45 (2014), 49–70 (65, n.95).
33. R. M. Wilson, *The Lost Literature of Medieval London* (London, 1970), 201–6; J. Taylor, *English Historical Literature in the Fourteenth Century* (Oxford, 1987), 264–7.
34. TNA, C 258/21 no. 1.
35. *Calendar of Plea and Memoranda Rolls of the City of London, Vol. 3: 1381–1412*, 36.
36. J. Watts, 'Popular Voices in England's Wars of the Roses, c. 1445–c. 1485', in *The Voices of the People in Late Medieval Europe: Communication and Popular Politics*, Studies in European Urban History 33, ed. J. Dumolyn, J. Haemers, H. R. Oliva Herrer and V. Challet (Turnhout, 2014), 107–22 (111); H. Wicker, 'The Politics of Vernacular Speech: Cases of Treasonable Language, c.1440–1453', in *Vernacularity in England and Wales c.1300–1550*, ed. E. Salter and H. Wicker (Turnhout, 2011), 171–97.

37. G. L. Harriss, 'Political Society and the Growth of Government in Late Medieval England', *Past & Present* 138 (1993), 28–57.
38. S. K. Cohn, *Popular Protest in Late Medieval English Towns* (Cambridge, 2013).
39. Ibid., 88–9.
40. 'The People of 1381' database, https://data.1381.online/ (accessed 9 June 2025).
41. E.g. TNA, JUST 1/103 m. 12; KB 9/166/1 m. 67.
42. *EHD, 1327–1485*, 269–70.
43. D. McCulloch and E. D. Jones, 'Lancastrian Politics, the French War, and the Rise of the Popular Element', *Speculum* 58 (1983), 95–138.
44. H. J. Hewitt, *The Organization of War under Edward III, 1338–62* (Manchester, 1966), 158–65; A. K. McHardy, 'Some Reflections on Edward III's Use of Propaganda', in *The Age of Edward III*, ed. J. S. Bothwell (Woodbridge, 2001), 171–92.
45. H. Serneels, 'Making Space for Resistance: The Spatiality of Popular Protest in the Late Medieval Southern Low Countries', *Urban History* 49 (2022), 709–24.
46. TNA, KB 145/3/5/1.
47. TNA, KB 9/43 m. 17; KB 9/43 m. 12.
48. TNA, KB 145/3/10/1.
49. TNA, JUST 3/56/4 m. 12.
50. V. J. Scattergood, *Politics and Poetry in the Fifteenth Century* (London, 1971); *Thomas Wright's Political Songs of England: From the Reign of John to That of Edward II*, ed. P. Coss (Cambridge, 1996).
51. TNA, KB 145/3/6/1.
52. *Knighton's Chronicle, 1337–1396*, ed. G. H. Martin (Oxford, 1995), 351.
53. *The St Albans Chronicle, Vol. 1: 1376–1394: The Chronica maiora of Thomas Walsingham*, ed. J. Taylor, W. R., Childs and L. Watkiss (Oxford, 2003), 687.
54. *Knighton's Chronicle*, 325.
55. *The St Albans Chronicle, Vol. 2: 1394–1422: The Chronica maiora of Thomas Walsingham*, ed. J. Taylor, W. R., Childs and L. Watkiss (Oxford, 2011), 75.
56. C. Given-Wilson, *Chronicles: The Writing of History in Medieval England* (London, 2004), 37.
57. *The Reign of Edward II, 1307–27*, ed. W. Childs and P. R. Schofield (Manchester, 2023), 204.
58. Given-Wilson, *Chronicles*, 31.
59. *Death and Dissent: Two Fifteenth-Century Chronicles*, ed. L. Matheson (Woodbridge, 1999), 120.
60. Ruddick, *English Identity*, 225–7.
61. H. W. Muller, 'Bonds of Belonging: Subjecthood and the British Empire', *JBS* 53 (2014), 29–58.

Further Reading

Dumolyn, J., Haemers, J., Oliva Herrer, H. R. and Challet, V., eds., *The Voices of the People in Late Medieval Europe: Communication and Popular Politics*, Studies in European Urban History 33 (Turnhout, 2014).

Firnhaber-Baker, J. and Schoenaers, D., eds., *The Routledge History Handbook of Medieval Revolt* (Abingdon, 2017).

Fletcher, C., 'News, Noise and the Nature of Politics in Late Medieval English Provincial Towns', *JBS* 56 (2017), 250–72.

Harriss, G. L., 'Political Society and the Growth of Government in Late Medieval England', *Past & Present* 138 (1993), 28–57.

Lacey, H., 'Defaming the King: Reporting Disloyal Speech in Fourteenth-Century England', in *Monarchy, State and Political Culture in England, 1300-1500: Essays in Honour of W. Mark Ormrod*, ed. G. Dodd and C. D. Taylor (Woodbridge, 2020), 71–93.

Lantschner, P., *The Logic of Political Conflict in Medieval Cities: Italy and the Southern Low Countries, 1370-1440* (Oxford, 2015).

Liddy, C. D., 'Cultures of Surveillance in Late Medieval English Towns: The Monitoring of Speech and the Fear of Revolt', in *The Routledge History Handbook of Medieval Revolt*, ed. J. Firnhaber-Baker and D. Schoenaers (London, 2017), 311–29.

Ormrod, W. M., *Political Life in Medieval England 1300-1450* (London, 1995).

Watts, J. L., 'The Pressure of the Public on Later Medieval Politics', in *The Fifteenth Century, Vol. 4: Political Culture in Late Medieval Britain*, ed. L. Clark and C. Carpenter (Woodbridge, 2004), 159–80.

'Public or Plebs: The Changing Meaning of "the Commons", 1381-1549', in *Power and Identity in the Middle Ages: Essays in Memory of Rees Davies*, ed. H. Pryce and J. Watts (Oxford, 2007), 242–60.

'Power, Government, and Political Life', in *The Later Middle Ages*, ed. I. Lazzarini (Oxford, 2021), 19–41.

PETER CROOKS

15

The King's Subjects beyond the Realm

In an era steeped in national stereotypes that bled into slanders and hatred, the English were notorious in later medieval Europe for three things: drunkenness, bearing a tail and killing their kings. But it is with the implications of another alleged propensity – for waging wars of conquest that sought to turn neighbours into subjects – that this chapter is largely concerned. These traits are combined in the hostile Latin verse of Henry of Avranches (d. 1260), where the English are depicted as not only tailed and drunken but also puffed up by violence:

> When the tailed English, who were born for drinking cups,
> Are filled up, it is with the seed of Brutus.
> Then they throw themselves into the fray, boasting they are a glorious people,
> Bringing death to all.[1]

By the later Middle Ages, the bellicose reputation of England's kings reverberated across Christendom. Jean Froissart (d. c. 1405), the chronicler of chivalry who visited the court of Edward III, noted that, because of their great conquests, the English were 'always more inclined to war than peace'.[2] In 1406, the Welsh leader Owain Glyn Dŵr (d. c. 1415) appealed to Charles VI of France (r. 1380-1422) about 'being crushed by the fury of the barbarous Saxons, who usurped to themselves the land of Wales'; while fifty years later, James II, king of Scots (r. 1439-60) complained to Charles VII (r. 1422-61) that the English were 'the principal disturbers of the peace of all Christendom'.[3]

Anglophobia was, then, one response to conquest or attempted conquest. So too, arguably, was anglophilia, among the many communities across the insular world and parts of France whose primary allegiance was to the English crown. This chapter explores the multifaceted experience of subjecthood in the Plantagenet Empire between 1200 and 1500 (see Map 15.1). The term 'subjects' here encompasses all those – the willing, the unwilling and the wilful – over whom the king claimed authority. England was a centralised and intensively governed kingdom, but its kings also had to rule *extensively* outside their realm. Just as in other imperial and colonial contexts, applying military force by sending an army on campaign proved much easier than establishing and sustaining the humdrum of royal administration. This disparity makes subjecthood a useful lens through which to examine the complex relations between the Plantagenet kings and their dominions. The chapter adopts three complementary perspectives. First, we examine how the English crown projected subjecthood as a means of embedding its claims to overlordship; second, how subjecthood was rejected by England's neighbours, who showed themselves alive to their common experience of English domination; third, how subjecthood was enacted by individuals and communities who sought to build a connection with a distant monarch and advance their interests within the composite structures of the Plantagenet Empire.

The Empire and Its Subjects

The possession of extensive territories beyond the kingdom was a defining characteristic of English monarchy in the later Middle Ages. In the era of the Norman and Angevin kings after 1066, these possessions included the continental inheritances of Normandy and Maine, as well as (from 1154) Anjou and the duchy of Aquitaine. Before the Norman Conquest, the Anglo-Saxon kings of England laid claim to an informal hegemony over the other peoples of Britain. As David Crouch has noted, the rupturing of the notion of Britain as a 'loose confederation of peoples under English presidency' was one of the key developments of the later Middle Ages.[4] Henry II pushed England's claims further by extending his dominions to Ireland. During his military expedition to Ireland in the winter of 1171/2, he took the formal submissions of the principal Irish kings. He later secured recognition of his overlordship from William the Lion, king of

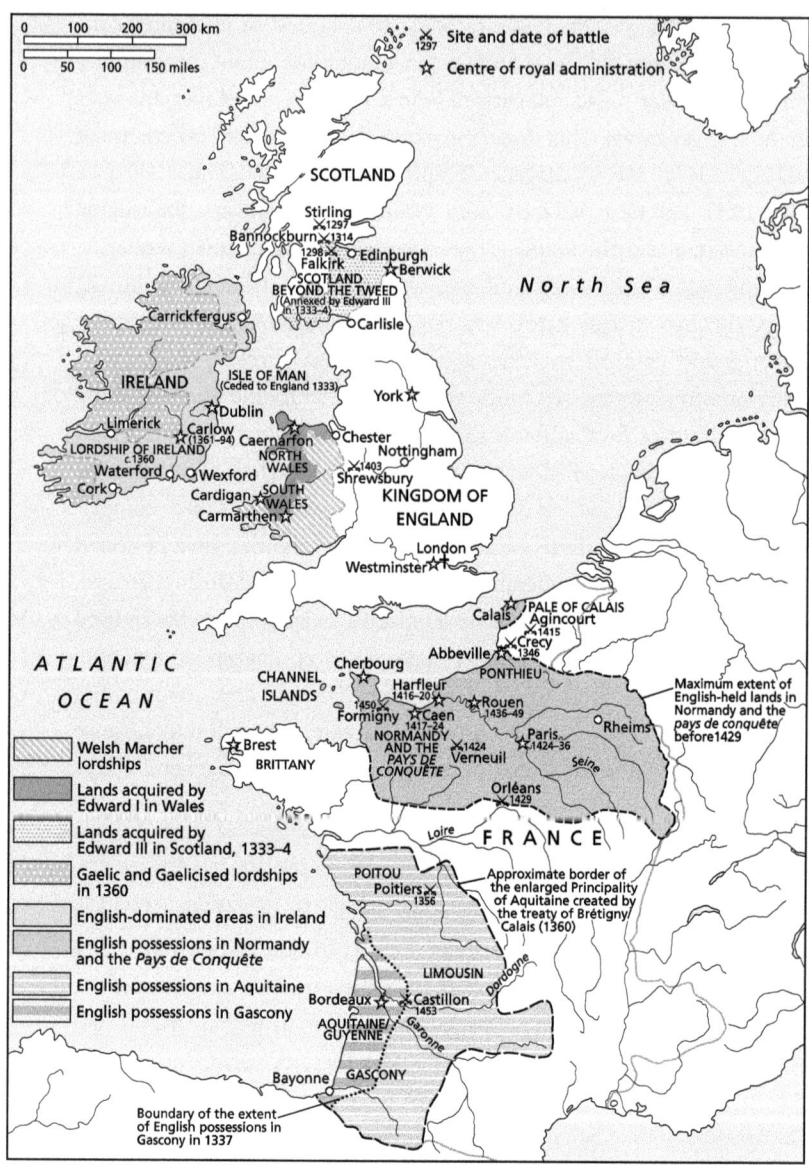

Map 15.1 England and the Plantagenet dominions in the later Middle Ages (reproduced from P. Crooks, 'Before Humpty Dumpty: The First English Empire and the Brittleness of Bureaucracy, 1259–1453', in *Empires and Bureaucracy in World History: From Late Antiquity to the Twentieth Century*, ed. P. Crooks and T. H. Parsons (Cambridge, 2016), p. 260)

Scots (r. 1165–1214), in the 'treaty' of Falaise (December 1174) while the latter was his captive, and similarly took grudging submissions in Wales from the rulers of Gwynedd in the north and Deheubarth in the south, Owain Gwynedd (d. 1170) and Rhys ap Gruffydd (d. 1197), respectively, though both maintained significant autonomy.

In 1200, it was by no means a given that Britain and Ireland would form the primary arena for the English monarchy's ambitions. King John came to the throne in 1199 and lost possession of Normandy in 1204. In 1216–17, England was invaded by the son of Philip Augustus (r. 1180–1223) – the future Louis VIII (r. 1223–6) – amid the civil war caused by John's repudiation of Magna Carta. Gerald of Wales (c. 1146–c. 1223) celebrated an alternative future in which much of Britain and France would be brought under the righteous rule of the French monarchy, a 'blessed stock of happy and natural kings' joining 'together most powerfully two or three kingdoms in one monarchy'.[5] The tempest of 'insular tyranny' was to be driven away as a 'clear day dawned in the English kingdom' under the Capetians. His optimism was premature. Prince Louis was defeated at the battle of Lincoln by the regent, William I Marshal (d. 1219), earl of Pembroke and lord of Leinster, and the succession of John's son Henry III was secured.

The centre of Plantagenet gravity shifted decidedly away from the continent in the thirteenth century. England came to lie at the core of a political system orbited by other lands in the insular world, as well as the remaining lands in France, above all the duchy of Aquitaine (Guienne/Gascony). By the later thirteenth century, these various dominions were increasingly meshed into the precocious royal administration, normally based at Westminster. The texture of power differed greatly between these territories, which ranged from significant colonial communities in Ireland and Wales to isolated garrison outposts, such as the enclaves of Berwick in Scotland (first captured by the English in 1296) and Calais in France (taken by siege in 1347), where imposed urban elites self-identified as 'English'. From 1279, the county of Ponthieu came into English possession through marriage. The king's interests also included Jersey, Guernsey, Alderney and Sark in the English Channel (fragments of Normandy), and the Isle of Man, wrested from Scotland in 1290. The inhabitants of the duchy of Aquitaine were not 'settlers', but they professed allegiance to their king-duke and cherished the duchy's enduring attachment to the English crown.

Historians have long debated whether, or to what extent, the Plantagenet dynasty ruled an 'empire' in the later Middle Ages. The title 'emperor' was not, of course, formally employed by England's kings. If we do use the term 'empire', we need to be aware of the risk of applying a modern category of analysis to a past society. The analytical move may be worth the risk if we are clear about what we mean by the term. In these pages, the concept of 'empire' refers to an 'extensive polity in which a core society exercises formal or informal power over outlying regions gained or retained by coercion'.[6] Although the king of England did not call himself an emperor, it is also important to note that 'empire' was itself a potent idea in the Middle Ages. The English monarchy drew upon imperial language, iconography and ideas when representing its overarching authority, in particular, the idea of a 'king of kings', one whose regality was enhanced by having other rulers under him.[7] An early thirteenth-century legal commentator remarked that 'by right of the excellence of the crown, [Britain] ought to be called an "empire" rather than a "kingdom"'.[8] Among the precedents that King Edward I advanced in support of his claim to sovereignty as king of England over Scotland was the example of the pre-Conquest king, Edgar. As remembered in the late thirteenth century, eight kings – the king of Scots, the king of the Cumbrians, the king of the Isles and five others – rowed King Edgar up and down the river Dee as a ritual demonstration of their submission. Seated in the prow, Edgar is said to have observed that his successors should 'rejoice in being kings of England, for they enjoyed so great a prerogative of honour in having subject to them such powerful kings'.[9]

Subjecthood Projected, 1200–1300

Ireland was neither England's first colony nor its oldest possession, but the twelfth-century conquest of the island nonetheless provides an early example of a phenomenon that would become important in later centuries: the projection overseas of English identity, liberties, law and governing institutions. The conquest of Ireland, beginning in 1169, brought in its train not only a new French-speaking aristocracy but also the transplantation of English-style administration and common law. In February 1217, a version of Magna Carta was notified to

Ireland for observance, and by the later thirteenth century a separate parliament provided a focus for the collective political activities of the English settler community.[10] The expectation was that law in Ireland, and administrative structures at central and local level, would be subordinate to, and modelled upon, English practice. These developments came at the expense of native power structures. Access to English law became a key marker of identity, and the Irish who wished to access the royal courts found it necessary to purchase a charter of English law and liberty.[11]

Subjecthood in Ireland was, then, a privilege that divided the colonists (the king's faithful English lieges of Ireland) from the colonised (the king's Irish enemies). In Wales, subjecthood became a predicament for the native dynasties, binding them to the English crown to a degree that was, in the end, intolerable. Following the death of King John in 1216, Llywelyn ap Iorwerth (d. 1240) of Gwynedd had consolidated his position as ruler over much of Wales, while also acknowledging Henry III as his overlord. His grandson, Llywelyn ap Gruffydd, achieved even greater recognition as 'prince of Wales', a title conferred upon him by Henry III in the treaty of Montgomery (1267). This treaty was in one sense a concession to Llywelyn, whose power was acknowledged to extend not only over Gwynedd but across native Wales. The language of the treaty is expansive: Henry III, 'wishing to magnify the person of Llywelyn and honour his successors', granted that he and his successors should be called 'princes of Wales' and should have the fealty of 'all the Welsh barons of Wales' (*baronum Wallie Wallensium*). The very form of the document served, however, to consolidate Henry III's status as the superior lord, by whose 'liberality and grace' the title 'prince' might be created.[12] That grace might equally be withdrawn. Across the next fifteen years, Llywelyn's power was steadily eroded. The treaty of Aberconwy (1277) shrank his effective authority. Welsh rebellion provoked a full-throated conquest in 1282–3 that extinguished the ruling house of Gwynedd. The Statute of Rhuddlan (1284) annexed Wales to the English crown. In place of the native principality, the principalities of north and south Wales were created, to be administered directly by English royal officials from castles at Carmarthen in the south and Caernarfon in the north, whose striped masonry and octagonal towers evoked the grandeur of Constantinople.[13] What emerged from the Edwardian conquest was a Wales in which communities and allegiances were cleaved. While the principality was tightly controlled, the Welsh Marches – a fragmented and semi-independent collection of lordships along the Welsh side of the border with England – retained a marked autonomy.[14]

In Scotland, too, subjecthood became a site of contestation – marked first by cautious acquiescence and negotiation, then progressively struggle, rebellion, attempted conquest and, finally, a fierce reassertion of the independence of the Scottish monarchy. The reigns of Alexander II (1214–49) and Alexander III (1249–86) were generally peaceful ones in Anglo-Scottish relations, marked by extensive cross-border landholding by the aristocratic elite. The kings of Scots were willing to perform homage for the estates they held in England. This period of relative harmony was both reflected in and reinforced by dynastic marriages between the two royal houses: Alexander II married Joan (d. 1238), the sister of Henry III, while Alexander III later married Henry's daughter, Margaret (d. 1275). Anglo-Scottish cordiality forms the background to a proposed union of crowns. When Alexander III died unexpectedly in 1286, he left as heir his four-year-old granddaughter Margaret, the 'Maid of Norway', daughter of Erik II. The Guardians who governed Scotland during the hiatus looked south to England to ensure the continuity of the Scottish line. Margaret was to marry Edward of Caernarfon (the future Edward II). Under the agreement of July 1290, Edward was to rule in Scotland solely as 'king of Scots', not in his future, separate, capacity as 'king of England', thereby protecting the independence of the Scottish monarchy. The principle was clearly enunciated that 'Scotland shall remain separated and divided and free in itself *without subjection to the realm of England*'.[15] In the event, the negotiations were for nothing. The Maid of Norway died in September 1290 in Orkney while travelling to Scotland. Her death caused a vacancy and a new crisis for the Scots. Edward I was invited to arbitrate the succession to the kingship. He used the opportunity to bind the 'competitors' for the Scottish throne into recognition of his superior lordship over Scotland. John Balliol (d. 1314), the chosen vassal king, tried to resist Edward I's summons before the English parliament and defied a request to serve with the English against the French. Instead, Balliol negotiated a treaty with Philip IV of France in 1295. This provoked war with England.

An illustrated royal genealogy created at St Mary's Abbey in York presents a compelling visual case for the legitimacy of English claims over Scotland through dynastic and historical continuity. Across a length of four metres of parchment, the roll unfurls the history of the kings of Britain from the mythical Brutus of Troy. The final section entwines the Plantagenet family tree with that of the kings of Scots. Dating the document to 1301, R. R. Davies interpreted it as a sign of English imperialist pretensions to Scotland: 'The English needed the solace of history – a history of England *ab origine* – as the ideological arm of their subjugation of the island.'[16] More recently, the manuscript has been attributed to the period after 1296, when the victorious Edward I not only stripped Balliol of his kingship but symbolically denuded the Scottish monarchy by transporting the Stone of Scone to Westminster.

In this context, the web of connections shown in the genealogy between the royal families – culminating with the Scottish line apparently converging with the English – visually asserted the supposed legitimacy of Edward I's claim to lordship over Scotland.[17] Between May and August 1296, Edward I received submissions from more than 1,500 Scots. These acts were later copied in triplicate by a public notary in manuscript enrolments known as the 'Ragman Rolls'. When Pope Boniface VIII (r. 1294–1303) challenged English rights in Scotland in 1299 and asserted that Scotland was a papal fief, the 'Ragman Rolls' provided evidence for the collective and individual recognition by Scottish landholders of Edward I's overlordship – giving Edward I wholesale proof with which to rebut the pope's claim.

Subjecthood Rejected

From the perspective of England's kings, war might be justified to vindicate rights and to punish defiant subjects in rebellion; but the unleashing of armies against fellow Christians provoked criticism, and – in what was to become a recurring theme – the validity of England's territorial claims was rejected by the victims of the aggression. The stakes became higher in the late thirteenth century, as expectations of obedience grew.[18] A 'subject' who departed from their allegiance could now be punished as a traitor. Such was the grisly fate of Dafydd ap Gruffydd (d. 1283) in

Wales and William Wallace (d. 1305) in Scotland. After being hanged and eviscerated, Wallace's dismembered body was sent to Newcastle-upon-Tyne, Berwick, Stirling and Perth – four significant locations in the Anglo-Scottish wars. The next year, 1306, Robert Bruce murdered his rival claimant to the kingdom of the Scots, John Comyn, and took the throne for himself, in spite of his previous homage to Edward I. It was a turning point. In 1314, Bruce won a major victory over the army of Edward II at Bannockburn. In 1328, under the treaty of Edinburgh–Northampton, the regime of Queen Isabella and Roger Mortimer renounced the English claim to Scotland, recognising its independence under Robert Bruce. After Mortimer's overthrow in 1330, the young Edward III sought to overturn this 'shameful peace' and install Edward Balliol (d. 1356) as his vassal king. His campaigns in the 1330s – most notably his victories over Scottish forces at Dupplin Moor (1332) and Halidon Hill (1333), as well as the siege and capture of Berwick (1333) – demonstrated that an English army, under capable leadership, remained formidable. However, sustaining a conquest regime proved beyond England's capacity.[19] Although Edward III conquered much of lowland Scotland and appointed sheriffs to the Scottish shrievalties, the Bruce monarchy endured and regained the lost ground, even during David II's long captivity following his defeat at Neville's Cross in 1346.[20]

In Ireland, the English advance across the island was often predicated on splintering Gaelic dynasties on the principle of divide and rule. Despite their political fragmentation, the Irish kings rallied in collective resistance, and their horizons extended beyond the island to natural allies in western Scotland. In the winter of 1314/15 Domnall O'Neill (d. 1325), king of Tír Eoghain, transferred his claim to the kingship of Ireland to Robert Bruce's brother, Edward. For three years (1315–18), Scottish armies in Ireland challenged the English lordship, until the death of Edward Bruce at the battle of Faughart, county Louth, on 14 October 1318. The grievances of the Irish and the Scots were expressed eloquently in letters addressed to the papacy: the 'Remonstrance of the Irish Princes' (1317) and the 'Declaration of Arbroath' (1320). These two documents were closely related in inspiration, language and ideas. Rejecting outright the claims of England's kings, they cast English rule in terms of 'tyranny and deceit' and asserted their need to wage a deadly war in order 'to shake off the harsh and insupportable yoke of servitude'.

The Remonstrance still served a didactic purpose a century later. Abbot Walter Bower (d. 1449), author of the monumental *Scotichronicon*, inserted the full text of the Irish Remonstrance into his narrative 'so that the Scots may learn never to be willing to be subject to the tyranny or the insufferable rule of the English'.[21]

The harsh lessons of English subjecthood were taught too in Gaelic vernacular history and poetry. The mid fourteenth century was a period of Gaelic resurgence, cultural and political. A prose history known as *Caithréim Thoirdhealbhaigh* ('The Triumphs of Turlough') was written in the 1350s, narrating the resistance of the O'Briens of Thomond to the attempted English conquest of north Munster by the Clare lords of Thomond in the second half of the thirteenth century up to the eventual defeat of Richard Clare (d. 1318). A vivid episode from 1318 describes Clare and his retinue encountering a supernatural figure at a river-crossing on the eve of the battle of Dysert O'Dea, where he would meet his demise. A hideous crone stands in the water, vigorously dipping armour and wringing the blood-soaked garments so that the river runs red. These are the strippings of a foreign host dressed in finery: satin, gold thread, and other 'handsome oversea-fashioned wares'. When asked whose armour she is washing, the woman explains that they belong to Clare, his barons and knights, 'his oversea-men' and his Gaelic allies:

> Blood and gore of their hurts and wounds and bodies are these crimson rills ... carried away with this rushing stream. Haughty as ye go on this your errand, your immolation all together ... is very near to you.

It was a vision of Clare's own impending destruction in the battle of Dysert O'Dea, and with it the fracturing of English colonial settlement in north Munster. The premonition was not just a warning; it was a comment on the futility of foreign conquest and the resilience of the old order. The *Caithréim* was a celebration of military victory; but, composed several decades after the events it describes, it also reflected broader anxieties about domination, identity and resistance in a conquest culture, casting the English in the sharpest terms as the 'abominable perverse English gang, cruel and insatiable, overbearing, surly, sullen, full of spite, malevolence, and ill-design'.[22]

In the 1360s, Robert I's son, David II, king of Scots – who had been captured at the battle of Neville's Cross on 17 October 1346 and only ransomed in October 1357 by Edward III after eleven years in captivity – proposed a dynastic union with one of the sons of Edward III, probably Lionel of Antwerp (d. 1368). After two generations of warfare with England, the proposal was roundly rejected by the Scottish parliament. The episode provoked a scholarly treatise on the 'proposals of the king of England'. A later gloss refers to the union as being 'very damaging and dangerous to the kingdom of Scotland which would altogether betray, weaken and destroy the whole freedom of the kingdom, and would wipe out not only the freedom of the kingdom, but also, in the course of time, all the magnates and people'. The recent experiences of Ireland and Wales were cited as reasons not to acquiesce: 'they themselves [the English] treat the Welsh altogether, and the Irish so far as they can, so inhumanely and so like slaves that now the name and nobility of the Welsh has altogether vanished ... and it is to be presumed that they would treat us more inhumanely and cruelly, whom they perceive as hitherto opposing them more seriously'.[23]

For over a century after the Edwardian conquest of the 1280s and 1290s, Wales lay relatively quiescent. After the Lancastrian revolution of 1399, Henry IV invested his eldest son, the future Henry V, with the title 'prince of Wales' in his first parliament. In September 1400, the same title was revived by Owain Glyn Dŵr, a lord from the *uchelwyr* ('squirearchy') class, whose descent from the royal houses of Wales was celebrated in Welsh poetry.[24] The acclamation of Glyn Dŵr as prince of Wales was a riposte to the future Henry V. Part of the interest of Owain Glyn Dŵr's career lies in how closely integrated he was into the English mainstream prior to his revolt: he studied law at the Inns of Court and fought in Scotland in Richard II's 1385 expedition. His revolt in 1400 represented the most significant challenge to English rule in Wales since Edward I's conquest. It tapped into deep-rooted Welsh discontent and aspirations for self-rule in a world caused by English arrogance (W. *Llyma fyd rhag sythfryd Sais!*), as the poet Iolo Goch conjured it in an ode written to Owain. The Westminster parliament passed punitive legislation that forbade social interactions between Welsh and English.[25] Two months after the battle of Shrewsbury 1403, the Welsh found themselves expelled from the city of Chester by order of Henry, prince of Wales, and forbidden to gather in groups of more than three.[26]

The anti-Welsh laws were the most severe interethnic inhibition of the period, comparable in chauvinist intention and impracticability to legislation then current in Ireland. The Statute of Kilkenny (1366) had been passed at a parliament presided over by Lionel, duke of Clarence, when lieutenant of Ireland in the 1360s.[27] It was a wide-ranging statute regulating many aspects of warfare in the frontier conditions of the lordship of Ireland, but it included a number of clauses that were intended as a bulwark against the cultural degeneracy of the English of Ireland. The Irish language was forbidden, as was the patronage of Irish entertainers, and the custom of fosterage. Marriage between the English of Ireland and their neighbours, the Irish – even though they were fellow Christians – was prohibited. In reality, the statute did not prevent such social practices, but the law was enforced and some women were prosecuted for marrying Irishmen.[28] Cross-cultural exchange remained one of the most pervasive features of life in late medieval Ireland, and from the perspective of the crown, one of the most intractable precisely because it blurred the visual and cultural markers between the king's natural English subjects and his mortal enemies among the Irish.[29]

Subjecthood Enacted

We have so far examined how subjecthood could be projected by the king onto territories and communities outside the bounds of the kingdom, and conversely how those claims might be rejected by various would-be subjects in Ireland, Wales and Scotland. Subjecthood was not, however, merely transmitted outwards; it was rather a form of interaction between the king and his subjects. Often the impetus came not from the king himself but rather from dominions fearful that the king's enemies were intent on gobbling them up and absorbing them into their own emerging polities. The king was normally physically distant, but his far-flung subjects were adept at using arts of political persuasion to bring him closer, ensuring he remained attentive to their interests and – so they fervently hoped – ready to send armies in their defence. Subjecthood, in this sense, had to be enacted, theatricalised and performed to become real.

The point is made vividly in the song of a Gascon troubadour composed in the years following the war of Saint Sardos (1324–5), a brief conflict that compelled Edward II to cede key territories in Gascony to Charles IV of France. The text was at once critical and loyalist. The song enjoins the 'king-duke' to come to Gascony to wage war, promising that his presence would increase the love the Gascons felt for him and enable them, together, to recover the duchy. The alternative, so the song says, would be that the flower (of France) would force the king-duke to abandon the duchy altogether, just as his ancestors had been forced to quit the duchy of Normandy – a reference to the retaking of Normandy by Philip Augustus in 1204.[30]

Ireland and Aquitaine shared certain characteristics in the era of the Hundred Years War (1337–1453): internally fractious, the king's subjects in the two lands were protective of their liberties and coordinated their political activities through assemblies, such as the Irish Parliament and Gascon Estates. In 1390, Richard II granted the duchy of Aquitaine to his uncle, John of Gaunt, to hold for his life. Across the next five years, the Gascons – through the Estates – organised themselves in the form of a loyalist opposition to this perpetual grant to John of Gaunt, especially as it was made by Richard II styling himself as 'king of France'. Their allegiance was to the king of England, whose representative in Gascony was normally a seneschal. In 1394–5, in an escalation, the Estates met in Bordeaux: the assembly included the archbishop of Bordeaux, nobles, the mayor of Bordeaux and representatives of other towns. Together they formed a 'Union', and now rejected Gaunt's regime on the basis that 'the duchy is, and should be, annexed to the Crown of England'.[31]

The language of annexation was also current in fifteenth-century Ireland. An Irish great council in 1441 petitioned the king and council in England that 'the said land of Ireland is your lordship of old time annexed to your crown'.[32] With a quick switch, the petitioners then asserted the separate status of the lordship of Ireland, with its distinct institutional apparatus, right to appoint officers and the primacy of the great seal of Ireland. Representatives of the English community in Ireland – whether through parliament, local assemblies or towns – often clamoured for royal attention. Collective grievances were typically couched in this language of loyalty to the monarch, while criticising royal ministers and exhorting the king to attend to the island for fear that it would be overrun by his Irish enemies. It was the English of

Ireland who assembled the arguments for the reconquest of the island and proposed schemes for the colonisation of the land. In reality, English kings were limited both in what they could feasibly achieve and were willing to undertake. Large parts of Ireland remained unconquered or outside direct royal control. As Gaelic Ireland was increasingly autonomous, a typical fifteenth-century pattern was for an English chief governor to achieve temporary subjection through a destructive raid, and to celebrate this as a 'conquest'. Little wonder that these butcher-and-bolt agreements were brittle. We cannot, however, entirely discount the idea that individual Gaelic lords found advantage in becoming the liegemen of the English crown, as a means of wriggling out of other provincial hierarchies.

The largest set of submissions in Ireland were those taken by Richard II on his first expedition of 1394–5. The Gaelic lords who submitted to the king did so in a mode that emphasised their long obedience: 'I, together with my predecessors, have been obedient and devoted to your Magnificence', said Tadhg O'Carroll: 'now, God be witness, I declare that I have stood forth firmly and signally as your special subject'. O'Carroll handed over his sons as hostages for his good behaviour and surrendered himself to the king as his 'immediate servant and special subject absolutely exempt from the lordship of other Irishmen'. O'Carroll claimed to be the direct liege of the crown, independent of any other Gaelic lord in Leinster. The same pattern is evident in the correspondence between the O'Neill lords of Tír Eoghain (in the northern part of Ireland), who sought recognition as 'princeps' directly from the king, rather than through the earl of Ulster, who claimed lordship over the northern part of Ireland.[33] Richard II's settlement started to unravel perhaps even before he had himself departed for England in May 1395. But the pattern of submission continued into the fifteenth century, creating a form of diplomacy in which Gaelic lords interacted with English royal government while remaining mostly outside the framework of political and governmental institutions in English Ireland.

England's fluctuating claims of lordship over Scotland, though increasingly tenuous in the fifteenth century, found occasional moments of revival, even in the absence of military intervention. Since Henry IV's Scottish expedition of 1400, England had largely refrained from launching major invasions northwards. Although Henry V briefly considered a Scottish campaign in 1416, his ambitions lay overwhelmingly in France. The early Stuart monarchy, particularly under James I (r. 1406–37), solidified its authority within Scotland, while English kings, absorbed in their dynastic struggles and continental wars, lacked both the inclination and the capacity to press claims to overlordship. Yet such claims were not abandoned and continued to be articulated in legal, diplomatic and propagandistic forms. One striking example is the work of the Northumbrian chronicler and spy John Hardyng (d. c. 1464), whose forgeries sought to provide a documentary basis for English suzerainty over Scotland. Hardyng forged a career over decades in which he purveyed spurious evidence supporting England's claims to overlordship, using the *inspeximus* formula (by which the king inspected and confirmed instruments of much earlier date) to cover his palaeographical tracks.[34] His fabrications included records of the submissions in 1291 of the Scottish competitors for the throne at Norham, alongside later letters supposedly from David II and Robert II. Yet Hardyng's forgeries extended far beyond recent history. Most audaciously, he produced a purported submission of Malcolm III to Edward the Confessor, dated 5 June 1065, at a 'parliament' in York attended by Malcolm's queen, Margaret, Edgar Ætheling and other English magnates. The document described Edward the Confessor as *dominus superior regni Scotie et insularum adjacentium* – an assertion of English overlordship over Scotland and the surrounding islands.[35] This was, of course, entirely spurious – parliament, as an institution, did not exist in the eleventh century – but the forged tradition Hardyng constructed speaks to the political anxieties of the fifteenth century. The claim that Margaret of Scotland, an Anglo-Saxon princess, had advised her husband to submit to English overlordship was a direct negation of Scottish chronicles that instead asserted an independent Scottish right to rule Britain. While Hardyng's claims found no real purchase in English foreign policy – by the mid fifteenth century, the Stuart monarchy was firmly established and English attention was overwhelmingly fixed on France – his work exemplifies how, even in periods of relative Anglo-Scottish peace, the ideological underpinnings of English claims to lordship persisted.

In Wales, in the decades following the revolt of Owain Glyn Dŵr, the king's Welsh subjects also found ways to accommodate themselves and assimilate to English society. The end of the revolt was marked by a series of collective submissions, and the imposition of punishing financial penalties. Six hundred men knelt in submission on 10 March 1414 before the king's ministers and admitted they deserved to be punished with death for their rebellion. Instead, they were pardoned and admitted to the king's peace for a collective fine of £100.[36] Gruffydd Don, a member of the notable Don family of Kidwelly, who had supported Glyn Dŵr's revolt, was nimble enough to answer Henry V's summons for troops to fight in France in 1415. In 1421 he was granted exemption from laws barring Welsh-born individuals from buying land in England. His service to the English crown extended to familial ties, as he married into the Scudamore family, linking his Welsh lineage with a prominent English family. This integration exemplifies how a former rebel family adapted to and prospered under English rule.[37]

Henry V's ambitions in France after 1415 transformed the course of the Hundred Years War. Normandy was invaded and conquered between 1417 and 1420. The reduction of Normandy was consolidated with a wave of land grants to English proprietors, creating, albeit only for a generation, a new settler colonial community across the English Channel – a Norman conquest in reverse. The political situation was complicated by the treaty of Troyes (1420), by which Charles VI acknowledged Henry V as his heir to the kingdom of France. The dual monarchy became a reality in 1422, when Henry VI acceded as an infant to the kingdoms of England and France.[38]

From this moment until the continental empire came tumbling down between 1449 and 1453, the Lancastrian dynasty faced the challenge of presenting Henry VI as a legitimate king to his French subjects. Such was the purpose of the elaborate propaganda of the dual monarchy, which placed emphasis on Henry VI's descent not only from St Edward the Confessor and St Louis but also from Arthur and Charlemagne. Even in Paris during the years of Anglo-Burgundian rule, the citizens (according to the anonymous 'bourgeois' whose chronicle is an indispensable source for this period) complained that the regent of France, John, duke of Bedford, had been absent from France for too long, to their detriment. A French poem translated as 'On the English title to France' emphasises 'unity, peace and accord' soothing the previous state of mortal war between the kings of England and France:

> That this Henry, standing in the line,
> Through God's hand and providence divine,
> Is justly born to void all variance,
> For to be king of England and of France.[39]

The years of English rule in Paris (1420–36) were especially rich in ceremonial entrances, processions and other forms of public display. These moments provided opportunities not only for the dual monarchy to transmit its propaganda but for Parisian subjects to communicate the city's significance, its illustrious history and municipal interests. At the grand entrance of the boy king Henry VI into Paris for his French coronation in 1431, a spectacle costing 1,837 *livres parisis* was put on by the citizens. The pageant included a scene with nine worthies, both male and female, adorned with the arms of Paris.[40]

Between 1449 and 1453, England's once-formidable holdings in France crumbled under the advance of Charles VII's forces. First Normandy, then Gascony fell. Four centuries of English cross-channel kingship ended. Besides the Channel Islands, only the town and Pale of Calais remained in English possession, until it too was lost to the French in 1558. The collapse was sudden, and it took another two or three generations for English kings to come to terms with the humiliation. Both Edward IV and Henry VIII planned French expeditions intended to rekindle the glories of Edward III and Henry V. William Worcester's *Boke of Noblesse*, addressed to Edward IV, offered an extended argument for the justification for a 'new conquest, to be had for your very right and true title in the inheritance of the said realm of France and duchy of Normandy'.[41]

Conclusion

'Realms without justice are but tyrannies and robberies, more consonant to beastly appetites, than to the laudable life of reasonable people': such was the admonition of Henry VIII to Thomas Howard, earl of Surrey (d. 1554), when praising his diligence as lieutenant of Ireland (1520–2) upon the 'reduction of that our dominion and the disobedient subjects of the same, to peaceable governance, due order, subjection, and obedience'.[42] The king advised Surrey to use moderation in extending royal authority over Gaelic lords. The letter presents conciliation and conquest as alternative means towards a common end. The king's preference was for 'sober ways, politique drifts, and amiable persuasions, founded in law and reason'; this he contrasted with 'rigorous dealing ... or any other enforcement by strength or violence'. After a year in Ireland, Surrey provided a contrary perspective. Without the king's personal determination to reduce the island with a sustained campaign, he said, the island 'will never be brought to good order and subjection other than by conquest'.[43] Clinching the point, Surrey cast back to the precedent of Edward I, whose conquest of Wales more than two centuries earlier took some ten years and was accomplished at vast expense. Ireland was, he reminded Henry VIII, five times larger than Wales. Moreover, Edward I had campaigned in person, and no sea separated England and Wales. The tragic history of the next century in Ireland was to show that even as seasoned a campaigner as Surrey underestimated the scale and contradictions inherent in a conquest that aimed at total assimilation.[44]

Here the different faces of subjecthood that we have been examining are brought together in a single frame. Despite their reputation as warmongers, England's kings often sought to extend their authority as cheaply as possible through what Henry VIII called, euphemistically, 'amiable persuasions'. Persuasion faltered when it required conquest to be persuasive. This was precisely the dilemma: military conquest was not only prohibitively expensive; it was also a form of war that could be rejected as illegitimate and fiercely resisted. Even so hawkish a career soldier as Sir John Fastolf (d. 1459) acknowledged the conundrum during the negotiations with the French and Burgundians at the Congress of Arras (1435). The proposed peace would have seen the king of England relinquish his claim to the crown of France: should this be accepted, he warned, 'it might be said, noised, and deemed in all Christian lands where it should be spoken of, that neither the king nor his noble progenitors had, nor have, any right in the crown of France, and that all their wars and conquests have been but usurpation and tyranny'.[45] Subjecthood in the Plantagenet Empire was, to coin a phrase, subjective. For those who felt themselves in thrall to a hostile power, it meant subjugation and fuelled cycles of rebellion and reprisal. In other contexts, subjecthood was a prized status that conferred liberties and opened pathways to advantage and preferment.

Subjecthood was not merely the outcome of conquest; it was, rather, a primary means by which English kings extended and consolidated their power. Moreover, when embraced and enacted – for instance, within the settler communities of Ireland and Wales, and the king's possessions in Gascony and Normandy – subjecthood provided one of the principal binding agents within the Plantagenet Empire.

Notes

1. C. Weeda, *Ethnicity in Medieval Europe, 950–1250: Medicine, Power and Religion* (York, 2021), 182.
2. M. Keen, 'Chivalry and English Kingship in the Later Middle Ages', in *War, Government and Aristocracy in the British Isles, c.1150–1500: Essays in Honour of Michael Prestwich*, ed. C. Given-Wilson, A. J. Kettle and L. Scales (Woodbridge, 2008), 250–66.
3. *Owain Glyn Dŵr: A Casebook*, ed. M. Livingston and J. K. Bollard (Liverpool, 2013), 124–5; *Letters and Papers Illustrative of the Wars of the English in France during the Reign of Henry the Sixth*, ed. J. Stevenson, 2 vols. in 3, RS (1861–4), I, 325.
4. D. Crouch, *Medieval Britain, c.1000–1500* (Cambridge, 2017), ix, 299, 362 (quotation).
5. *Gerald of Wales*: De principis instructione: *Instruction for a Ruler*, ed. R. Bartlett (Oxford, 2020), 732–3.
6. P. Crooks, 'State of the Union: Perspectives on English Imperialism in the Late Middle Ages', *Past & Present* 212 (2011), 3–42 (at 4).
7. P. Crooks, D. Green and W. M. Ormrod, 'The Plantagenets and Empire in the Later Middle Ages', in *The Plantagenet Empire, 1259–1453*, ed. P. Crooks, D. Green and W. M. Ormrod (Donington, 2016), 1–34 (esp. 24).
8. *Munimenta Gildhallae Londoniensis: Liber Albus Liber Custumarum et Liber Horn*, ed. H. T. Riley, RS, 4 vols. (London, 1860–2), II, 645.
9. *Anglo-Scottish Relations, 1174–1328*, ed. E. L. G. Stones (Oxford, 1965), 200–1 (no. 30); *Edward I and the Throne of Scotland, 1290–1296: An Edition of the Record Sources for the Great Cause*, ed. E. L. G. Stones and G. G. Simpson, 2 vols. (Oxford, 1978), II, 302.
10. *Law and the Idea of Liberty in Ireland: From Magna Carta to the Present*, ed. P. Crooks and T. Mohr (Dublin, 2023), chs. 1–4.
11. R. Frame, 'Ireland after 1169: Barriers to Acculturation on an "English" Edge', in Frame, *Plantagenet Ireland* (Dublin, 2022), 62–84.
12. *The Acts of Welsh Rulers, 1120–1283*, ed. H. Pryce, (Cardiff, 2005), 32, 536–42 (no. 363).

13. R. A. Griffiths, *The Principality of Wales in the Later Middle Ages: The Structure and Personnel of Government* (Cardiff, 1972).
14. R. R. Davies, *Lordship and Society in the March of Wales, 1282–1400* (Oxford, 1978).
15. W. B. Stevenson, 'The Treaty of Northampton (1290): A Scottish Charter of Liberties?', *Scottish Historical Review* 86 (2007), 1–15.
16. R. R. Davies, *The First English Empire: Power and Identities in the British Isles, 1093–1343* (Oxford, 2002), 42–3.
17. J. A. Holloway, *Genealogy and the Politics of Representation in the High and Late Middle Ages* (Cambridge, 2019), 113, 124–5.
18. A. Ruddick, *English Identity and Political Culture in the Fourteenth Century* (Cambridge, 2013), esp. ch. 5.
19. P. Crooks, 'Before Humpty Dumpty: The First English Empire and the Brittleness of Bureaucracy, 1259–1453', in *Empires and Bureaucracy in World History: From Late Antiquity to the Twentieth Century*, ed. P. Crooks and T. H. Parsons (Cambridge, 2016), 250–87.
20. I. A. MacInnes, *Scotland's Second War of Independence, 1332–1357* (Woodbridge, 2016).
21. *Scotichronicon by Walter Bower in Latin and English, vol. 6: Books XI–XII*, ed. N. F. Shead, W. B. Stevenson and D. E. R. Watt *et al.* (Aberdeen, 1987–98), 384–5; S. Duffy, 'The Irish Remonstrance: Prototype for the Declaration of Arbroath', *Scottish Historical Review* 101 (2002), 395–428.
22. *Caithréim Thoirdhealbhaigh: The Triumphs of Turlough*, ed. S. H. O'Grady, Irish Texts Society, 2 vols. (1929), II, 124–5.
23. 'A Question about the Succession, 1364', ed. A. A. M. Duncan, *Miscellany of the Scottish History Society*, 12 (Edinburgh, 1994), 1–57 (quotations at 29, 39).
24. H. Fulton, 'Owain Glyn Dŵr and the Uses of Prophecy', *Studia Celtica* 39 (2005), 105–21.
25. *Owain Glyndŵr*, ed. Livingston and Bollard, 70–1.
26. P. Morgan, 'Cheshire and Wales', in *Power and Identity in the Middle Ages: Essays in Memory of Rees Davies*, ed. H. Pryce and J. Watts (Oxford, 2007), 208.
27. D. Green, 'The Statute of Kilkenny (1366): Legislation and the State', *Journal of Historical Sociology* 27 (2014), 236–62.
28. Add. MS 3104, Cambridge University Library.
29. S. Booker, *Cultural Exchange and Identity in Late Medieval Ireland: The English and Irish of the Four Obedient Shires* (Cambridge, 2018).
30. G. Pépin, 'Le sirventés *"El dugat ... "*: une chanson méconnue de Pey de Ladils sur l'Aquitaine anglo-gasconne', *Les Cahiers du Bazadais* 152 (2006), 5–27.

31. J. J. N. Palmer, *England, France, and Christendom, 1377–99* (Chapel Hill, NC, 1972), ch. 9.
32. TNA, E 101/246/16, m. 1; P. Crooks and L. Kilgallon, '"Of Old Time Annexed to Your Crown": Documents on the Irish Parliament and the Crisis of 1441–2', *Analecta Hibernica* 53 (2023), 97–123.
33. TNA E 159/171/Recorda/T/25, rot. 25 dorse; *Richard II in Ireland, 1394–5, and the Submission of the Irish Chiefs*, ed. E. Curtis (Oxford, 1927), no. XX, 182–3.
34. A. Hiatt, *The Making of Medieval Forgeries: False Documents in Fifteenth-Century England* (London, 2004), ch. 5.
35. TNA, E 39/87, published in *Documents and Records Illustrating the History of Scotland, and the Transactions between the Crowns of Scotland and England*, ed. F. Palgrave (London, 1837), 367; *Edward I and the Throne of Scotland*, ed. Stones and Simpson, II, 385.
36. R. R. Davies, *The Revolt of Owain Glyn Dŵr* (Oxford, 1995), 2.
37. R. A. Griffiths, 'After Glyn Dŵr: An Age of Reconciliation?', *Proceedings of the British Academy* 117 (2002), 139–64, esp. 159–60. For the theme of integration at an earlier point in the history of the march of Wales, see M. F. Stevens, *Urban Assimilation in Post-Conquest Wales: Ethnicity, Gender and Economy in Ruthin, 1282–1348* (Cardiff, 2010).
38. A. Curry, 'Two Kingdoms, One King: The Treaty of Troyes (1420) and the Creation of a Double Monarchy of England and France', in *The Contending Kingdoms: France and England 1420–1700*, ed. G. Richardson (Aldershot, 2008), 23–42.
39. 'To King Henry VI on His Coronation', in *Political Poems and Songs Relating to English History*, ed. T. Wright, 2 vols. (London, 1861), II, 141.
40. G. L. Thompson, *Paris and Its People under English Rule: The Anglo-Burgundian Regime* (Oxford, 1991), 199, 203–5.
41. *The Boke of Noblesse: Addressed to King Edward the Fourth on His Invasion of France in 1475*, ed. J. G. Nichols (London, 1860), 3 (spelling normalised).
42. *State Papers Henry VIII, II, iii: 1515–1538* (1834), no. 12 (51–3), no. 20 (73).
43. S. G. Ellis, 'Prelude to the Tudor Conquest: Henry VIII and the Irish Expedition of Thomas Howard, Earl of Surrey, 1520–22', *Irish Historical Studies* 47 (2023), 19–37.
44. *Age of Atrocity: Violence and Political Conflict in Early Modern Ireland*, ed. D. Edwards, P. Lenihan and C. Tait (Dublin, 2007).
45. *Letters and Papers Illustrative of the Wars of the English in France during the Reign of Henry the Sixth, King of England*, ed. J. Stevenson, 2 vols. (London, 1864), II, pt. ii, 576 (spelling modernised). For this theme, see A. Curry and R. Ambühl, *A Soldiers' Chronicle of the Hundred Years War: College of Arms Manuscript M 9* (Woodbridge, 2022), ch. 3.

Further Reading

Allmand, C. T., *Lancastrian Normandy, 1415-1450: The History of a Medieval Occupation* (Oxford, 1983).
Aurell, M., *The Plantagenet Empire, 1154-1224*, trans. D. Crouch (Harlow, 2007).
Booker, S., *Cultural Exchange and Identity in Late Medieval Ireland: The English and Irish of the Four Obedient Shires* (Cambridge, 2018).
Brown, M., *Disunited Kingdoms: Peoples and Politics in the British Isles, 1280-1460* (Harlow, 2013).
Crooks, P., Green, D. and Ormrod, W. M., eds., *The Plantagenet Empire, 1259-1453: Proceedings of the 2014 Harlaxton Symposium* (Donington, 2016).
Davies, R. R., *Domination and Conquest: The Experience of Ireland, Scotland and Wales, 1100-1300* (Cambridge, 1990).
The Age of Conquest: Wales, 1063-1415 (Oxford, 1991).
The Revolt of Owain Glyn Dŵr (Oxford, 1995).
Frame, R., *The Political Development of the British Isles, 1100-1400* (Oxford, 1990).
Colonial Ireland, 1169-1369 (Dublin, 2012).
Simms, K., *From Kings to Warlords: The Changing Political Structure of Gaelic Ireland in the Later Middle Ages* (Woodbridge, 1987).
Thompson, G. L., *Paris and Its People under English Rule: The Anglo-Burgundian Regime 1420-1436* (Oxford, 1991).
Vale, M. G. A., *English Gascony, 1399-1453: A Study of War, Government and Politics during the Later Stages of the Hundred Years' War* (Oxford, 1970).
The Ancient Enemy: England, France and Europe from the Angevins to the Tudors (London, 2007).
Watson, F., *Under the Hammer: Edward I and Scotland, 1286-1307* (Edinburgh, 1998).

Part IV

Representations

LAURA SLATER

16

Art and Architecture

Late medieval kings varied in their level of personal interest in the visual arts and architecture. Henry III sent his workmen detailed and impatient personal directives for the commissioning of vestments, liturgical furnishings and the decoration of palaces and chapels. For the adornment of the church of St Peter in the Tower of London in 1240, he ordered cherubim with a 'joyous and cheerful countenance' to be placed on either side of its great cross.[1] The lectern for Westminster Abbey's chapter house was to be like that at St Albans, but 'if possible even more handsome and beautiful'.[2] In 1447–8, Henry VI ordered his new college of Eton to be built in the fashionable Perpendicular architectural style: 'in large fourme, clene and substancial, wel replenysshed with goodely wyndowes and vautes leyng', without any 'besy moldyng'.[3] The surviving records for other kings are sparser. Yet for all late medieval kings, images, buildings and material objects played an important role in projecting, representing and inviting wider reflection on their power and authority.

The stereotyped depictions of royal majesty encountered in coins, seal imagery and public sculpture were often the closest encounter many subjects ever had with their rulers. Monumental statues of English kings (sometimes including queens) were installed on the interior choir screens of numerous English cathedrals and great churches. They can still be seen at York Minster (Figure 16.1) and Canterbury Cathedral, guarding the entrance to the sacred area of the choir and acting as witnesses to liturgical processions and prayers made in the nave. Lines of kings were also placed on exterior façades, visible

Figure 16.1 Choir screen at York Minster, c. 1452–61. (Photo by Angelo Hornak/Corbis via Getty Images.)

today on the west fronts of Exeter and Lincoln cathedrals. Sometimes representing the kings of Judah rather than the kings of England, they again ensured a powerful royal presence on the threshold of sacred space.

The magnificence of the late medieval king's household and courtly ceremony, the splendour of his palaces and castles and the piety expressed by his religious foundations shaped both the reputations of individual kings and wider conceptions of royal power. Collars, liveries and badges could significantly personalise royal authority, stressing one particular ruler or dynasty over another. Whether giving a general impression of royal majesty or a more specific message of individual political legitimacy, art and architecture powerfully shaped common expectations and understandings of kingship in late medieval England.

Westminster Palace

Two sites were central to the practice, representation and ritual performance of late medieval English kingship: Westminster Palace and Windsor Castle. A royal residence since the eleventh century, by the late Middle Ages, Westminster had become the traditional centre of English royal government. The exchequer had been based permanently at Westminster since the twelfth century and Magna Carta decreed the establishment of the court of common pleas in the Norman 'great hall' built by William Rufus, known today as Westminster Hall. By the fourteenth century, the courts of the chancery and the king's bench also sat permanently in Westminster Hall. Their working hours were sounded out by the four-ton bell of a clocktower built in 1365–7. This medieval equivalent of Big Ben was known as 'Edward of Westminster'. The meeting place of the king's council was rebuilt on the east side of Westminster Hall from 1349. Known from 1366 as the Star Chamber, its name was probably derived from the decoration of the chamber, most likely its ceiling, with gilded stars. The river Thames ran along the east side of the palace precinct and Westminster Abbey adjoined the palace to the west (Figure 16.2).

From at least the early fourteenth century, there was a distinction between the official, legal and administrative areas of Westminster great palace centred around Westminster Hall to the north and the privy palace to the south, primarily for the personal use of the royal family. The privy palace contained a 'lesser hall', apartments reserved for the king, queen and their courtiers and a Jewel Tower (Figure 16.3) to house the king's personal plate and jewellery, built at its south-western corner after 1343. Yet the privy palace was never as secluded as its name suggests. Royal audiences, alms-giving ceremonies, the opening of parliament and parliamentary assemblies were regularly held in rooms in the privy palace.[4] One of the most famous of these rooms, used for all of these activities, was the Painted Chamber.

Figure 16.2 View of Westminster, with Parliament House (the former St Stephen's Chapel), Westminster Hall and Westminster Abbey, 1647. Original artwork: illustrated by Wenceslaus Hollar (1607–77), the Bohemian print maker and draughtsman. (Photo by Henry Guttmann Collection/Hulton Archive/Getty Images.)

Figure 16.3 Jewel Tower, Westminster Palace, c. 1365. (Photo by English Heritage/Heritage Images/Getty Images.)

An originally twelfth-century room renewed by Henry III from 1236 and again after a fire in 1263, its focal point was a large state bed where the king formally received visitors. Henry III ordered an image of the coronation of St Edward the Confessor, the holy Anglo-Saxon king and ancestor of the Plantagenet dynasty, to be painted at its head. St Edward enjoyed special importance at Westminster. His shrine was next door at the abbey and 'his' coronation regalia was stored there. His legendary ancient laws were believed to have guaranteed the peace and liberties of England.

The bed in the Painted Chamber was flanked by depictions of the guardians of Solomon's bed (Canticles 3:7). Two further scenes from the life of the Confessor (Figure 16.4) were painted on the window splays opposite. The splays of the other Gothic windows in the chamber depicted crowned female personifications of the Virtues trampling the Vices underfoot, holding shields emblazoned with the arms of England, the Holy Roman Empire, St Edward and St Edmund of Bury. The imperial arms referred to Henry III's younger brother, Richard of Cornwall, elected king of Germany in 1257. As Henry III named his two eldest sons Edward and Edmund, the decoration of this section of the Chamber showcased Plantagenet family wisdom and virtue. The king in bed was reminded to follow the saintly example of the Confessor and practise virtues such as *largesce* (generosity) and *debonereté* (tranquillity).

Between 1292 and 1297, Edward I added a large frieze of Old Testament narratives across all but the west wall of the Painted Chamber. Rather than celebrating royal wisdom, virtue and holy kingship, the master painter Walter of Durham depicted battle scenes from the biblical books of I and II Maccabees, II and IV Kings and Judges. Alongside military heroics, the frieze focused on the grim deaths of wicked, tyrannical rulers such as Abimelech and Sennacherib. This type of imagery warned and cautioned its audiences about the divine punishment that followed any misuse of royal power.[5]

The year 1292 also saw Edward I's foundation of St Stephen's Chapel, Westminster, eventually completed by his grandson, Edward III (Figure 16.5). The construction and decoration of the chapel took place in 1292–7, 1320–5, 1331–4 and 1340–63, halted in between by financial crisis, political instability and wars with Scotland and France. On 6 August 1348, Edward III founded a college of canons dedicated to God, St Stephen the Protomartyr and the Virgin Mary to staff the chapel.

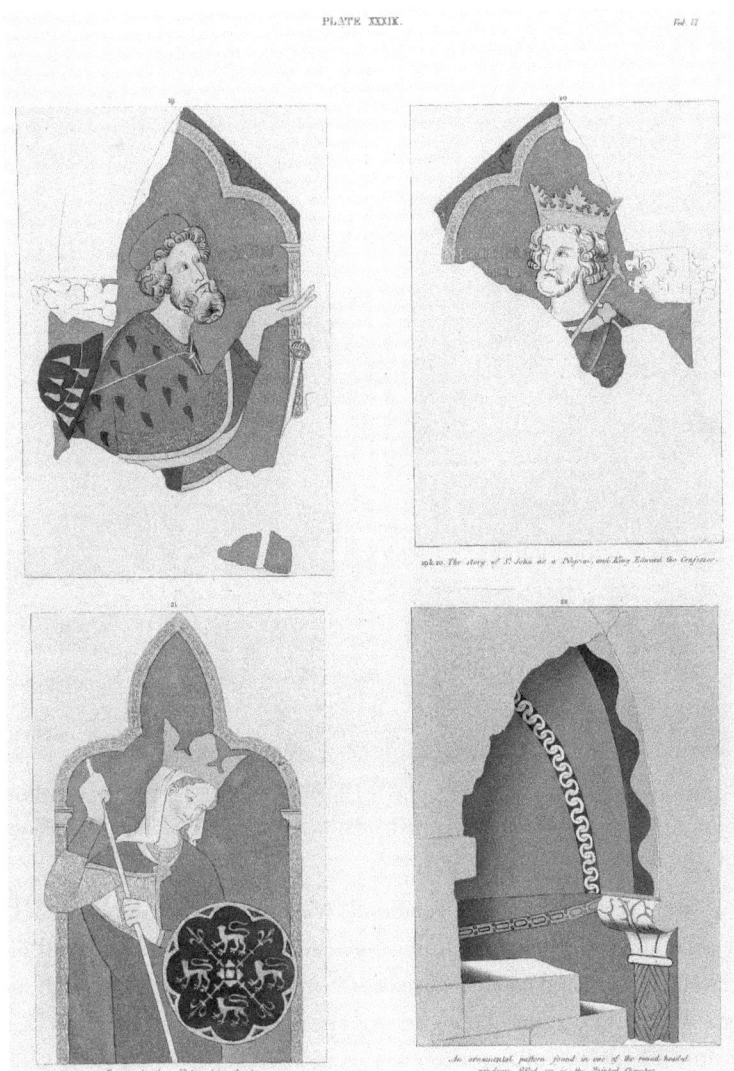

Figure 16.4 Antiquarian copies of decoration in the Painted Chamber, Westminster Palace. Fragments of scenes from the life of St Edward the Confessor and a triumphant Virtue, c. 1819–20. Original artwork: illustrated by Charles Alfred Stothard FSA (1786–1821), antiquarian draughtsman. Society of Antiquaries of London. (Photo by Sepia Times/Universal Images Group via Getty Images.)

Figure 16.5 Depiction of St Stephen's Chapel, Westminster Palace in 1830, prior to its destruction in 1834. Artist unknown. Original artwork, 1881 (Photo by The Print Collector/Getty Images.)

Like everything at late medieval Westminster, St Stephen's was a rebuilding and renovation. A single-storey chapel already stood on the site in 1292 and had been used as the main palace chapel throughout the thirteenth century. Edward I was strongly influenced by Louis IX's Sainte-Chapelle, built between 1241 and 1248 at the Palais de la Cité, Paris. Echoing the Sainte-Chapelle, the new building designed by Michael of Canterbury had two storeys. The upper chapel dedicated to St Stephen was reserved for the royal family. The lower chapel below, known as St Mary Undercroft, was accessible to the wider court. On the south side of the chapel in between its easternmost buttresses was the small chapel of St Mary le Pew, which housed a miraculous image of the Virgin. The east end of the chapel faced directly onto the Thames and became a notable London landmark.[6]

From 1351 to 1360, a team of painters led by Master Hugh of St Albans are recorded in royal accounts to have given the interior of St Stephen's brightly coloured, textured and gilded decoration. Biblical scenes and images of saints were arranged in tiers below the chapel windows. Fragmentary painted panels depicting scenes from the histories of Job and Tobit are now preserved in the British Museum, London. Their architectonic elements and handling of space and perspective suggest the influence of contemporary Italian artistic innovations. The programme culminated on the arcaded east wall with a depiction of the royal family, destroyed, like most of St Stephen's, by a devastating 1834 fire. To the north of the high altar was depicted the Adoration of the Magi and, beneath, St George leading Edward III and five of his sons to prayer. On the south side were representations of Queen Philippa and female members of the royal family, below a cycle concerned with the Infancy of Christ. Antiquarian drawings show the royal figures kneeling in devotion, framed within microarchitectural niches below miniature gabled canopies.

The unprecedented family portrait at St Stephen's was part of a growing image-consciousness on the part of late medieval western rulers. From the later fourteenth century onwards, European rulers were commissioning more individualised (if not necessarily naturalistic) representations of themselves. English kings were just as attentive to the political possibilities of portraiture as their continental counterparts. For the childless Richard II, the first stage of his rebuilding of Westminster Hall was another form of dynastic display. In 1385, he commissioned thirteen painted and gilded stone kings to stand in the great hall, depicting the kings of England from the Confessor to Richard himself. Like the royal statues in English great churches, Richard's kings would form a grand display of lineage and dynastic continuity. Another likely influence was the statues of French kings installed in the Grand Salle of the Palais de la Cité by Philip IV of France (d. 1314).

Richard renovated Westminster Hall from 1394. The walls were heightened and refaced and the old Norman posts or columns supporting its existing roof were removed. The royal master mason, Henry Yevele, added buttresses to take the thrust of an extraordinary hammer-beam oak roof spanning the full width of the hall, overseen by the master carpenter Hugh Herland (Figure 16.6). Carved wooden angels

Figure 16.6 Interior of Westminster Hall, Westminster Palace, c. 1395. (Photo by Pawel Libera/Getty Images.)

holding shields with the royal arms project from each hammerbeam terminal. The wooden vaults that support the braces spring from stone corbels, decorated with the heraldic arms of Richard and the Confessor. New traceried windows in the Perpendicular style replaced the original Romanesque ones with their connecting wall passages. A string course runs below the windows, stamped at intervals with Richard's personal badge of the chained white hart, adopted in 1390.[7]

Richard's thirteen sculpted kings may have been intended to stand in front of these personal devices, directly below the carved angels. Only six kings were eventually set up in the hall by the 1390s. The principal north doorway of Westminster Hall was remodelled with flanking towers to create a grand ceremonial entranceway, echoing the west façades of great churches. Richard commissioned two additional, even larger statues of kings to be placed above the north doorway. They probably represented himself and the Confessor.

The new hall bore Richard's symbols and arms and suggested his permanent royal presence throughout. The highly personalised decoration conflated his kingship with the ordinary offices of the English state, such as the law courts working there daily. Much of medieval government was a matter of routinely delegated authority. Yet the way that these activities and officials were visually reframed in the new Westminster Hall combined 'corporate' with 'personal' kingship, emphasising to all who entered that the English judiciary and state bureaucracy functioned only at the continued pleasure and will of the king.

When formally enthroned at Westminster before his subjects, Richard's presence was amplified by the repetition of his personal heraldry and devices. Statues of past rulers presented the king as culmination of the exemplary English kingship embodied by his ancestors, especially the Confessor. Richard's renovation of Westminster Hall created a powerful stage for both the ordinary practice and the ritual performance of kingship. Yet ironically, the first ceremony that took place in the new hall was his own deposition in 1399.

Westminster Abbey

Late medieval kings ruled in state at Westminster and spent increasing periods in residence there, but the sacred ritual of coronation took place next door at Westminster Abbey. A fifteenth-century history of the abbey attributed its foundation to Lucius, the first Christian king of Britain. Like his later medieval successors, he supposedly used the abbey as coronation church, burial place and regalia store.[8] The church was rebuilt in the Romanesque style under Edward the Confessor and likely completed by William I in the 1070s. It remained largely unchanged until 1245, when Henry III embarked on a rebuilding that cost the exchequer more than £40,000 (Figure 16.7).

Henry's spectacular generosity was partially motivated by his special devotion to St Edward and intimately tied to his own personal vision of kingship. St Edward's strong associations with Westminster made him a natural symbol of wider state, or national, as well as dynastic and personal (royal) virtue, power and authority. Like King Arthur, Edward was key to medieval English mythologies of the past and his figure could help frame and formulate contemporary notions of kingship and statehood.[9]

Although he did not visit Paris until 1254, Henry was keenly aware of the latest advances in Gothic architecture. He closely followed the construction of the Sainte-Chapelle by his brother-in-law, Louis IX.

Figure 16.7 Interior of crossing and east end of Westminster Abbey, c. 1245–53. (Photo by John Harper/Getty Images.)

He knew about the rebuilding of the French coronation church of Reims (1210–41) and the abbey of St Denis, the royal regalia store and necropolis (1231–64). Their splendour glorified the French crown. Westminster could not risk appearing outdated or unworthy in comparison.

It has been debated if the master mason first appointed by Henry III for Westminster, Henry of Reyns, was of French or English origin. Whatever his nationality, Henry certainly knew the Gothic churches of the Île-de-France well, especially Reims, Amiens and the Sainte-Chapelle. Numerous French influences were incorporated into his work on Westminster between 1245 and 1253, including an east end and elevation modelled on Reims. Henry of Reyns oversaw construction of the abbey's eastern arm and its remarkable octagonal chapter house. He was followed by masters John of Gloucester (worked 1253–60) and Robert of Beverley (worked 1260–72), who completed the work as far as the eastern bays of the nave.

Westminster did not solely imitate French Gothic architecture. Its deep projecting transepts, long nave, lavish use of Purbeck marble, rich sculptural decoration and elaborate mouldings conformed to customary English building practices. Throughout the interior, stylised leaves, flowers and rosette or 'diaper' work cover doorways, wall arcades and spandrels. Originally painted and gilded, sculptures of angels can be seen in the abbey transepts, aisles and radiating chapels, alongside depictions of kings, biblical figures and saints. A grand north transept portal (now lost) was built to provide a ceremonial entrance for the king to arrive directly from Westminster Palace. The galleries, transepts and crossing were designed to accommodate crowds of spectators and provide clear sightlines for royal ceremonial.

Work on the abbey was disrupted by the Barons' War of 1258–66 but does not seem to have stopped. On the north and south choir aisles of the abbey, rows of carved and painted shields depict the arms of the English peerage. They include the heraldry of Simon de Montfort, earl of Leicester. An unlikely royal choice after Simon's 1263 rebellion, it is also possible that the shields marked continued baronial support for the rebuilding of Westminster.

The most distinctive embellishments of the new abbey were added in the 1260s and 1270s by a father-and-son team of craftsmen from Rome.

The sanctuary around the high altar, and the chapel and shrine area of St Edward the Confessor behind it, contain several Cosmati mosaic works (Figure 16.8). Cosmati is a distinctive *opus sectile* ('cut work') technique in which large, specially cut rare stones are framed by smaller, precious stone and glass tesserae to form complex patterns and roundels. In Westminster, the mosaics contain porphyry marble, the quarries for which had been lost since late antiquity. The only porphyry available in medieval Europe was recycled from ancient monuments and usually sourced from Rome. All ancient ruins were the property of the papacy, giving porphyry strong associations of place and sacred power. The purple porphyry used at Westminster had further significance, due to the ancient Roman and then Byzantine practice of reserving rare purple dyes for the clothes of the imperial elite. After 750, imperial children were born 'in the purple' (*porphyrogennetos*), in a special room lined with porphyry and purple silk in the Great Palace in Constantinople. The use of purple porphyry linked Henry III, St Edward and Westminster to ancient, imperial and papal Rome.

The Cosmati works consist of a large sanctuary pavement before the high altar, a base for the shrine of the Confessor, a smaller pavement

Figure 16.8 Sanctuary pavement before the high altar, Westminster Abbey, 1268. (Photo by Dan Kitwood/Pool/AFP via Getty Images.)

laid down in the Confessor's chapel below the new shrine base and the tomb of Henry III. The sanctuary pavement contains numerous inscriptions, dating the pavement to 1268 and making obscure cosmological speculations. It may have been modelled on the pavement of the chapel of St Maurice in Old St Peter's in Rome, the dedicated place of unction for imperial coronation ceremonies.[10] The Cosmati work at Westminster was likely steered by the papal legate sent to England after the Barons' War, Ottobuono Fieschi, the future Pope Adrian V, and the abbot of Westminster, Richard Ware (d. 1283). He is recorded travelling to the papal court multiple times (1259, 1260, 1261 and 1266) and returning with Roman craftsmen and materials.

Even if visitors did not pick up the precise associations of the mosaics and their materials, the unique Cosmati work affirmed the sanctity of the Confessor, the magnificence of the abbey and Henry's Christian kingship. The shared use of Cosmati and purple porphyry for the shrine of the Confessor and the tomb of Henry III gave visible form to the spiritual connection between the king and St Edward. Subsequent royal burials in the Confessor's chapel transformed the abbey into a royal mausoleum. Just as Westminster was the unchallenged political capital of late medieval England, its abbey became the spiritual and cultural centre of the English crown.

Although he lacked interest in finishing Westminster Abbey, Edward I commissioned the Coronation Chair (Figure 16.9) in 1296–7 to house the Stone of Scone, one of the most important trophies of his military campaigns in Wales and Scotland. After his 1283 conquest of Gwynedd, Edward I presented the Crown of Arthur and the Cross of Neith, a supposed fragment of the True Cross kept at Aberconwy, to the Confessor's shrine in 1285. In 1296, the king removed the Stone of Scone, the traditional coronation seat of the kings of Scotland, from the abbey of Scone. He presented it to Westminster alongside the Scottish coronation regalia. The Stone was later identified by the English as that on which the biblical patriarch Jacob rested his head at Bethel (Genesis 28:18). The Scots believed the Stone was brought from Egypt by the mythical foundress of Scotland, Scota, daughter of Pharaoh and witness to the preaching of Moses.[11]

Edward intended the Coronation Chair to be made of bronze, set up at the shrine of St Edward and used at coronation services. Like Richard

Figure 16.9 Coronation Chair, Westminster Abbey, c. 1300–1. (Photo by Werner Forman/Universal Images Group/Getty Images.)

II's statues at Westminster Hall, the Chair would act as a permanent signifier of royal presence in the abbey. Financial crisis led to the chair's construction not in bronze but in painted and gilded wood. Open quatrefoil tracery beneath the seat displayed the Stone to viewers. Glass and pastework suggested the reliquary-like appearance of precious metalwork. Edward also ordered 'two small leopards made, painted and gilt' for each arm of the chair.[12] Flanking leopards or lions echo biblical descriptions of the throne of Solomon (III Kings

10:18–20 and II Chronicles 9:17–19). Solomon was held up to late medieval kings as an exemplar of wise rulership.[13]

Windsor Castle

Windsor Castle was founded by William I around 1070 as a motte-and-bailey castle, that is, it had a large central raised mound (the motte) where the main keep was located, a walled courtyard below (the castle ward or bailey) and further defensive structures such as walls, ditches and palisades. At Windsor, there were two baileys, referred to as the upper and lower wards. The site occupied by the State Apartments in the upper ward today has been a royal residence from the early twelfth century. Henry III was the first late medieval king to spend significant sums on Windsor. After his marriage in 1236, he made the castle one of his main residences and significantly remodelled the queen's apartments. Between 1240 and 1248, the king built a chapel dedicated to St Edward the Confessor in the lower ward. The thirteenth-century chapel survives in fragments such as the Gilebertus door, its former main entrance. In 1263, the *Flores historiarum* celebrated the castle as unrivalled in Europe for its splendour.[14]

Windsor fell out of favour under Henry's successors and Edward III spent very little time there during the first half of his reign. Yet at a tournament at Windsor in early 1344, he announced his intention to establish an Order of the Round Table for 300 knights on the model of King Arthur. Construction began on a jousting arena in the upper ward, abruptly cancelled in November 1344. Following his victories at Calais and Crécy, Edward returned in triumph to England in October 1347 and resided for extended periods at Windsor for the first time. In June 1348, he instituted the Order of the Garter. On 6 August 1348, Henry III's chapel of St Edward was refounded as a college of secular canons dedicated to the Confessor, the Virgin and St George.

The foundation of the Order of the Garter and St George's provided the impetus for major building work at Windsor from 1350 until the end of the king's reign. The former chapel of St Edward's was refurbished. The institutional buildings required for a college of canons were constructed on three sides of a rebuilt cloister in the lower ward, now the Dean's Cloister. At its north-west corner stands the lierne-vaulted

Aerary Porch of 1353–4, originally leading into the Galilee Porch of the fourteenth-century St George's Chapel. The adjacent Canon's Cloister, built in 1352–5, provided timber-framed domestic accommodation for the canons and priest-vicars of St George's.

A mechanical striking clock was set up by 1354 in the keep. The royal lodgings in the upper ward were renovated in 1350–75, creating an eighteen-bay hall and chapel above an undercroft. Edward's birthplace became a grand centre of court spectacle and a public statement of his chivalric and Arthurian kingship. Windsor had no legendary connection to Arthur, but Edward's reconstruction of the castle as a new Camelot was on a spectacular enough scale for at least two later fourteenth-century chroniclers to assume an ancient Arthurian history for the site.[15]

In 1475, Edward IV started rebuilding the chapel of St George (Figure 16.10) on a new site to the west of the original chapel. Edward III's chapel of St George (the former St Edward's Chapel built by Henry III) was completely replaced by Henry VII and is now the Albert Memorial Chapel. Edward IV's chapel of St George was still unfinished at his death. It was constructed by the master mason Henry Janyns in the Perpendicular style, with a prominent transept located halfway down its seven-bay nave. Edward IV intended to be buried at St George's on the north side of the choir. The elaborate iron gates to his personal chantry chapel, the work of royal smith John Tresilian, can still be seen. From 1478 to 1481 the 'Horseshoe Cloister' was built to house the vicars choral of St George's.

Other Royal Works

Edward III's Arthurian posturing was not new. In 1289–90, Edward I added a round table evoking Arthur's assembly of knights to the great hall in Winchester Castle. Winchester had long been identified with the Arthurian Camelot. Its great hall was rebuilt by Henry III in 1222 with Gothic pointed arches and clustered Purbeck marble columns. Edward's round table now hangs on its west wall (Figure 16.11). Edward also sought to connect Arthurian sites and legends to the royal family when he rebuilt Caernarfon Castle from 1283.

As part of his conquest of north Wales, the king constructed a formidable series of castles with townships below. The rebuilding of

Art and Architecture 341

Figure 16.10 Interior of St George's Chapel, Windsor Castle, c. 1475–1528, restored 1863–73. (Photo by Tim Graham Photo Library via Getty Images.)

Caernarfon (Figure 16.12) was loaded with Arthurian and imperial symbolism. Caernarfon was the ancient centre of the Welsh kingdom of Gwynedd and site of the Roman city of Segontium. The supposed body of Magnus Maximus, father of Constantine, the first Christian

Figure 16.11   Interior of Great Hall, Winchester Castle, 1222–35. (Photo by Franz Marc Frei/Getty Images.)

Figure 16.12   Caernarfon Castle, Gwynedd, Wales, 1283–1330. (Photo by Gallo Images/Getty Images.)

emperor, was discovered at Caernarfon in 1283 and reburied in a nearby church on Edward I's orders. Caernarfon has polygonal rather than round towers and walls striped with bands of coloured stone.

These features echo the Theodosian walls of the Byzantine imperial capital of Constantinople. Its 'Eagle Tower', intended as the official residence of the constable of Caernarfon, was crowned by three turrets bearing an imperial eagle. The town's west gatehouse, built at the same time, was called the *Porth yr Awr*, or Golden Gate, recalling both Constantinople and Jerusalem.

By making Caernarfon the birthplace of the future Edward II in 1284, Edward I may have been trying to associate the new prince of Wales with the prophecies of Merlin and other legends connected with the castle. The romance of Macsen Wledig records the emperor Maximus's dream of a great fort with towers of many colours, for example. Although never finished, Edward I spent more than £20,000 on the castle and clearly intended it to be a lasting memorial to his conquests.

The foundation and benefaction of religious houses, chantries and colleges was a routine way for the late medieval king to seek divine favour and support and to publicise his piety to his subjects. Royal religious patronage is discussed in Chapter 10 and little, if anything, survives in material relation to foundations such as Vale Royal Abbey in Cheshire, the Dominican house of King's Langley in Hertfordshire and Henry V's Thameside foundations of Sheen and Syon (both Greater London). Henry VI's foundations of King's College, Cambridge and Eton College, Berkshire still preserve elements of their original art and architecture.

The status, scale and ambition of these colleges changed multiple times before the fundamental threat to their existence posed by the king's 1461 deposition. Henry laid the foundation stone for a royal college dedicated to St Nicholas near the Old Schools site in central Cambridge on Easter Sunday 1441. He dramatically expanded his foundation (commonly known as King's) in 1443, when the college was rededicated to the Virgin and St Nicholas and explicitly connected to Eton. In 1445, King's College was enlarged again to support seventy scholars. At this point, the king acquired the land that now comprises the main college site.

The first stone of King's College Chapel (Figure 16.13) was laid on 25 July 1446. In his 'will' of 1448, the king planned an aisleless chapel of great height and length. It would form the north side of an enormous

Figure 16.13 King's College Chapel, Cambridge, 1446–1536. (Photo by Ian Cumming/Design Pics Editorial/Universal Images Group via Getty Images.)

court, with three-storied living accommodation on its east and south sides and a gate tower. A grand Provost's Lodge would straddle the south and west corners of the court, while the rest of the west range contained the college hall, buttery, pantry and library. A second, smaller court would house the kitchen and domestic offices. Between the college and the river would be a detached cloister with a cemetery and belltower. Construction work proceeded apace until 1455, after which financial support from the duchy of Lancaster dried up. In 1461, only the eastern range of the great court had been started and the chapel was a roofless shell.

Royal support for the college was renewed in 1480 by Edward IV and continued by Richard III. By 1485, five eastern bays of the chapel were virtually complete and two side chapels had been glazed and vaulted. The chapel remained in this partially finished but usable state until Tudor adoption of the foundation by Henry VII in 1506. The chapel was finally completed in the 1530s under Henry VIII. Its magnificent fan vaulting, carpentry and stained glass all date from that period.

Founded in 1440 in honour of the Virgin, Eton College had an even more disrupted building history. Henry VI's acquisition of a site close to his birthplace at Windsor Castle included the parish church of Eton, already dedicated to the Assumption of the Virgin. Henry appropriated the church to be used for college services until a dedicated college chapel had been built. Construction of the college began in summer 1441. The original cloister buildings formed a quadrant with the new chapel on the south side. Still extant on the north side of what is now School Yard is the circa 1441–4 red-brick range of Lower School buildings. A stone hall was built on the south side of the cloisters between 1443 and 1450.

By 1448, the chapel was almost finished. Extant accounts record the construction of its roof and stalls. Yet, between 1446 and 1448, Henry drastically revised his plans for Eton. An expanded college required a larger chapel, which he redesigned three times. His clerk of works took measurements from Salisbury and Winchester cathedrals in 1449. The third and final design for the college chapel, if carried out, would have given the chapel a vast nave comparable in length to the nave of Lincoln Cathedral. Despite seven years of work, the original chapel was demolished. Building work restarted in 1449 and a new east end was nearing completion by 1458–9.

After Henry's deposition in 1461, Edward IV transferred much of the college's land and revenues to his refoundation of St George's, Windsor. All work stopped and the college never fully recovered its lost income. Building work resumed at the expense of William Wainfleet, bishop of Winchester (and former provost of Eton), in 1469. The choir of the chapel was completed in 1469–75 (Figure 16.14). No nave was ever built, but a modest transverse antechapel was added between 1479 and 1483. What was intended solely to be the east end of the church today consists of eight bays divided by clustered wall-shafts and tall transomed windows. Its large, nine-light east window may have been reused from the original chapel demolished in 1448–9. The chapel's length, spaciousness and large windows all conform to the vision of its royal founder. Yet some of the most significant artistic work at Eton is not the product of late medieval kingship. The circa 1477–87 grisaille paintings on the north and south sides of the chapel, strongly influenced by southern Netherlandish art, were commissioned by Wainfleet.

Figure 16.14 Eton College Chapel, Berkshire, 1441–83. (Photo by DeAgostini/Getty Images.)

Royal Portraiture and Tombs

Representations of late medieval kings were rarely 'portraits' as we understand the term today, in the sense of a mimetic artistic representation that convincingly depicts the actual physical appearance of the sitter. Instead, kings were shown in highly stereotyped and formalised ways. Decorated charters, collections of royal statutes and compilations of historical and legal documents usually showed the king enthroned before his subjects. More important than the king's person was his heraldry, a key visual identifier and sign of royal presence. Change was rare, making Edward III's quartering of the arms of England and France in January 1340 a major shift in monarchical representation. The royal arms were widely reproduced in late medieval England as a sign of loyalty. They were added to church architecture and furnishings, devotional manuscripts, memorial brasses, tombs and stained glass to combine patriotic celebration with prayer and commemoration. The circa 1350s east window of Gloucester Cathedral places the armorials of Edward III and the Black Prince at the centre of a tier of heraldry. All the arms refer to veterans of royal military campaigns, particularly the 1346 battle of Crécy. The window honours the military bond between the king and his nobility and places royal victories in a wider spiritual context.[16]

Medieval coinage followed a consistent visual template. Surrounded on both sides by written 'legends', Henry III's gold penny showed a frontal-face depiction of a bearded, crowned king on its obverse and a cross on the reverse. It set the pattern for English coinage until Edward III's 1344 introduction of a new coin, the gold noble. On the obverse, the crowned king was depicted within a ship, holding an upright sword and a shield with the royal arms. The image evoked the familiar medieval allegory of the 'ship of state' steered by the king and celebrated Edward's 1340 naval victory at Sluys. The noble's reverse showed an ornate cross and further heraldic motifs.

Heraldry frequently featured on medieval seals, the visual equivalent of an official signature to documents. Royal seals usually showed the monarch as an armed and mounted warrior on one side, crowned and holding some of the regalia bestowed at his coronation on the other (Figure 16.15). Aside from the crown of St Edward, this could include a sceptre topped with a cross or fleur-de-lis, symbolising the monarch's

EDWARD I. ON THE GREAT SEAL.

Figure 16.15 Obverse of the Great Seal of Edward I, 1272–1307. (Photo by Bettmann/Getty Images.)

temporal power. The dove-topped 'rod of virtue and equity' was associated with the sovereign's moral virtue and spiritual role. The dove symbolised the holy spirit. The king held an orb or a sword of state, signifying royal authority and justice.

The enthroned king might be represented trampling a lion and dragon beneath his feet (as in Psalm 90:13) or flanked by lions echoing the throne of Solomon. From 1340, the seated monarch was depicted in an increasingly elaborate niched and canopied throne of state, rather like an altar reredos, filled with royal heraldry and/or patron saints such as St George or the Virgin. Seal and coin iconography were remarkably consistent throughout the late medieval period, irrespective of the current age or appearance of the ruling monarch. Seals and coins were among the most important ways that royal government was made visible and tangible to the king's subjects. Conformity to established visual traditions was essential for the currency and documents that royal seals confirmed to be recognised and accepted as valid.

Tomb effigies did not play the same authenticating social role, but firmly established visual conventions again held sway. The effigy sculpted in stone or metal above the tomb chest was intended to replicate the temporary wooden effigy placed over the royal coffin during the king's funeral procession. The king was shown as a peaceful, recumbent crowned figure, dressed in some form of coronation robes. He usually held an orb and sceptre. The crown and regalia might be carved as part of the effigy or included as separate gilt and jewelled additions. Expensive textiles were sometimes used to 'dress' the effigy further. The king's feet rested on lions or other beasts. His head might be supported by saints or angels or framed within a microarchitectural canopy.

While emphasising the sacrality of the king's body, there was still scope for widespread variation in form, design, materials and location. A painted tester or canopy might be installed above the tomb. An elaborate grille kept onlookers at a distance. Henry III, Edward III and Richard II (who commissioned a double tomb effigy showing him holding hands with his first wife, Anne of Bohemia) were all depicted in gilt-bronze effigies. The alabaster form of Edward II's effigy echoed the contemporary French royal use of white marble and was likely the choice of Edward's wife, Isabella of France.

No effigy was ever set over the plain, polished Purbeck marble tomb chest of Edward I. Such simplicity was likely the king's personal choice, although a potentially elaborate canopy originally stood above it. Edward III's Purbeck marble tomb chest alternates the royal arms with the arms of St George along its base. Small bronze statues of his children (six of the original twelve survive) are set within microarchitectural niches above. Often referred to as 'weeper figures', they are not in fact depicted in attitudes of grief and mourning and so make Edward's tomb a 'tomb of kinship', emphasising his family and dynasty.

Like his predecessor Richard II, Henry IV was commemorated by a double tomb, this time of alabaster (Figure 16.16). It was probably commissioned by his wife, Joan of Navarre, made by a specialist workshop in Derbyshire and completed in the early 1420s. In his 1415 will, Henry

Figure 16.16 Detail of the double tomb of Henry IV and Joan of Navarre in Canterbury Cathedral, 1420s. (Photo by RDImages/Epics/Getty Images.)

V founded a chantry chapel in Westminster Abbey for his tomb. Only the oak core remains of an originally dazzling silver and silver-plated effigy.

Queens' tombs are outside the scope of this chapter but for one major act of commemorative patronage. After the death of Eleanor of Castile in

1290, Edward I ordered a series of stone crosses to mark the twelve places at which her funerary cortege rested overnight on its journey from Harby in Nottinghamshire to Westminster. Only three crosses survive today, at Geddington and Hardingstone in Northamptonshire (Figure 16.17) and

Figure 16.17 Eleanor Cross at Hardingstone, Northamptonshire, 1291–3. (Photo by Dave Porter/Getty Images.)

Waltham Cross in Hertfordshire. Likely inspired by the sculpted *montjoies* marking Louis IX's funerary procession, the three-storied hexagonal or triangular crosses enclose multiple idealised statues of Eleanor under arched and gabled canopies, with heraldry and ornament below.

Richard II commissioned several painted portraits of himself. A lost 1382–94 altarpiece for the English College in Rome is recorded to have shown the king and his first wife flanked by saints including St George and St John the Baptist.[17] Around 1395, Richard commissioned the wooden panel painting now known as the Westminster Abbey portrait (Figure 16.18). The earliest known extant portrait of an English monarch, Richard is shown in ceremonial dress and regalia as if at his coronation. The full-frontal view recalls contemporary images of the face of Christ. Richard may have wanted to project a similar image of timeless majesty.

More personal than the Westminster Abbey portrait is the circa 1395 Wilton Diptych, a small altarpiece likely made for Richard or a member of his family. Made from Baltic oak and painted with egg tempera on a gold ground, the diptych is made in the luxury International Gothic or Beautiful style (*Schöne Stil*) prized by courts across later medieval Europe. Yet its content is distinctively English and Ricardian. The outside of the diptych displays personal emblems of Richard II; his first wife, Anne of Bohemia; his second wife, Isabella of Valois; and a shield impaling the royal heraldry with the fictive arms of the Confessor. On the interior left wing of the diptych (Figure 16.19), St Edmund, St Edward and St John the Baptist stand in a desert, holding their identifying attributes of an arrow, a ring and a lamb. A dark forest can be glimpsed behind them. Richard kneels in adoration before the Virgin and Child. Among the many personal emblems on his clothes, the king wears a gold and pearl collar, its links formed by gold broom pods. In 1396, gifts to Richard from his new father-in-law, Charles VI of France, included a gold broom pod collar, part of the French king's livery.

Livery collars and badges became increasingly important to the visual culture of late medieval English kingship. The Lancastrian SS collar and the Yorkist collar of alternate or inset suns and roses (*roses-en-soleil*) came to symbolise royal authority, dignity and, above all, loyal service. Earlier in his reign, Richard publicly wore the livery collar of John of Gaunt, the likely originator of the Lancastrian SS collar, to signal his love for, and trust in, his uncle. By wearing the broom pod in the Wilton

Art and Architecture 353

Figure 16.18 Westminster Abbey portrait of Richard II, c. 1395. (Photo by Fine Art Images/Heritage Images/Getty Images.)

Figure 16.19 Interior left wing of the Wilton Diptych, c. 1395 (London, National Gallery NG44451). (Photo by Imagno/Getty Images.)

Diptych, Richard suggests similar personal loyalty to Charles VI. Henry IV legislated to make the distribution of livery collars and badges exclusive to royalty. By the second half of the fifteenth century, livery collars were bestowed on royal servants, local officers and loyal followers. Recipients of collars sometimes wore them on their tomb effigies as a proud sign of honour and royal service. These associations are already present in the liveries and personal badges in the Wilton Diptych.

On the interior right wing of the diptych (Figure 16.20), the Virgin and Child are surrounded by angels wearing the king's livery collar

Figure 16.20 Interior right wing of the Wilton Diptych, c. 1395 (London, National Gallery NG4451). (Photo by Fine Art Images/Heritage Images/Getty Images.)

and badge of the white hart. One angel carries a white standard with a red cross. It is through works such as the Wilton Diptych that the cross of St George came to symbolise England. At the top of the standard is a tiny orb depicting an island, set within a sea of tarnished silver leaf. Its white tower suggests the Tower of London. From 1400 if not earlier, England was widely assumed to be the dowry of the Virgin (the *Dos Mariae*) and placed under her special protection. The miniature island, English flag and Marian host in the Wilton Diptych may refer to that legend.

The Christ Child leans forward towards Richard, making a blessing gesture. The interlocking gazes, gestures and interactions between Richard, king of England; Christ, the king of kings; and the Virgin Mary, queen of heaven, are at the heart of the Wilton Diptych. Richard's kingdom and Christian rulership are given heavenly validation and placed under saintly protection.

Conclusion

The Wilton Diptych's exaltation of Richard's kingship encapsulates what late medieval English kings sought in art and architecture. Late medieval rulers made grand public statements through official portraiture or their (re)building of secular and sacred spaces. Their artistic commissions might have deep personal meaning. Whether intended as memorials to conquest or as devout offerings to God, glorification of king and kingship was a constant. Art and architecture expressed political power and could act as instruments of political power in late medieval England. Yet they constituted more than propaganda to an audience with limited literacy. Beyond the personal or political interests of the monarch and official state iconographies, a wider visual culture of late medieval government emerged. The king's subjects chose to display the royal arms and wear livery collars, created schemes of royal imagery in great churches independently of the crown, supported royal religious foundations and reproduced royal portraiture in their own manuscripts and documents. They engaged with the state on a personal as well as institutional level. Through their artistic choices, we start to understand how kingship and royal government were understood and experienced in late medieval England.

Notes

1. D. Carpenter, *Henry III: The Rise to Power and Personal Rule 1207–1258* (London, 2020), 345.
2. Carpenter, *Henry III*, 334.
3. H. M. Colvin, *The History of the King's Works*, 4 vols. (London, 1963–82), I, 288.
4. Colvin, *King's Works*, I, 534–46; E. Biggs, *St Stephen's College Westminster: A Royal Chapel and English Kingship, 1348–1548* (Woodbridge, 2020), 4–8.
5. P. Binski, 'The Painted Chamber at Westminster, the Fall of Tyrants and the English Literary Model of Governance', *Journal of the Warburg and Courtauld Institutes* 74 (2011), 121–54 (at 140–1).
6. Colvin, *King's Works*, I, 510–22; Biggs, *St Stephen's*, 1–8, 16–17.
7. Colvin, *King's Works*, I, 528–33; E. Scheifele, 'Richard II and the Visual Arts', in *Richard II: The Art of Kingship*, ed. A. Goodman and J. Gillespie (Oxford, 1999), 255–72 (at 260–1).
8. J. Flete, *The History of Westminster Abbey* ed. J. A. Robinson (Cambridge, 1909), 76.
9. P. Binski, *Westminster Abbey and the Plantagenets: Kingship and the Representation of Power 1200–1400* (New Haven, CT, 1990), 3–7, 134.
10. P. Binski and C. Bolgia, 'The Cosmati Mosaics: Art, Politics, and Exchanges with Rome in the Age of Gothic', *Römisches Jahrbuch der Bibliotheca Hertziana* 45 (2021–2), 7–76 (at 15–18, 22–5).
11. P. Binski, 'A "Sign of Victory": The Coronation Chair, Its Manufacture, Setting and Symbolism', in *The Stone of Destiny: Artefact and Icon*, ed. D. J. Breeze, T. O. Clancy and R. D. E. Welander (Edinburgh, 2003), 207–24.
12. Binski, *Westminster Abbey*, 136.
13. F. Wormald, 'The Throne of Solomon and St Edward's Chair', in *De Artibus Opuscula XL: Essays in honor of Erwin Panofsky I*, ed. M. Meiss (New York, 1961), 532–9.
14. *Flores Historiarum*, ed. H. R. Luard, 3 vols. (London, 1890), II, 481.
15. Colvin, *King's Works*, I, 864–88; W. M. Ormrod, 'For Arthur and St George: Edward III, Windsor Castle and the Order of the Garter', in *St George's Chapel, Windsor, in the Fourteenth Century*, ed. N. Saul (Woodbridge, 2005), 13–34.
16. N. Clavner, 'The Great East Window of Gloucester Cathedral and Its Heraldic Glass', *Journal of the British Archaeological Association* 171 (2018), 100–30.
17. Scheifele, 'Richard II', 257; D. Gordon, 'A New Discovery in the Wilton Diptych', *The Burlington Magazine* 134 (1992), 662–7 (at 665–6).

Further Reading

Alexander, J. J. G. and Binski, P., eds., *Age of Chivalry: Art in Plantagenet England 1200-1400* (London, 1987).

Binski, P., *The Painted Chamber at Westminster* (London, 1986).

Westminster Abbey and the Plantagenets: Kingship and the Representation of Power 1200-1400 (New Haven, CT, 1990).

Borenius, T., 'The Cycle of Images in the Palaces and Castles of Henry III', *Journal of the Warburg and Courtauld Institutes* 6 (1943), 40-50.

Colvin, H. M., *The History of the King's Works*, 4 vols. (London, 1963-82).

Gordon, D., Monnas, L., and Elam, C., eds., *The Regal Image of Richard II and the Wilton Diptych* (London, 1997).

Howe, E., 'Divine Kingship and Dynastic Display: The Altar Wall Murals of St Stephen's Chapel, Westminster', *The Antiquaries Journal* 81 (2001), 259-303.

Marks, R. and Williamson, P., eds., *Gothic: Art for England 1400-1547* (London, 2003).

Slater, L., 'Visual Reflections on History and Kingship in the Medieval English Great Church', *Journal of the British Archaeological Association* 167 (2014), 83-108.

Art and Political Thought in Medieval England, c. 1150-1350 (Woodbridge, 2018).

Ward, M., *The Livery Collar in Late Medieval England: Politics, Identity and Affinity* (Woodbridge, 2016).

SARAH L. PEVERLEY

17

Kingship and Historical Writing

Chronicles and other forms of medieval historical writing have persistently shaped how English kings and their legacies are represented and remembered. Ever since insular monks like Gildas and Bede began recording royal deeds in the fifth to eighth centuries, medieval historiography has been an invaluable repository of information, anecdotes and observations, illuminating the triumphs and tribulations of individual reigns. From glowing endorsements to virulent attacks on sovereign power, how historiographers captured or elided the most impactful events of a reign affected how a king's legacy was transmitted and preserved. In some cases, kings directly influenced what was written about their reign; in others, their reputation was determined by other men of authority, including their successors. Taking a long view, this chapter examines the most prolific types of historical writing from the thirteenth to the fifteenth century, the contexts and authors that produced them, and the ways in which historiography was shaped and used by kings and their supporters at times of political crisis.

Historical Writing: Types, Contexts and Development

In 1447, Walter Bower, abbot of Inchcolm Abbey, concluded his *Scotichronicon* 'as a comfort' for Scotland and its young king, James II. Musing on why he had ended his nation's history in 1437 with the death of James I, rather than continuing to cover the first decade of James II's reign, he explained that he wished to avoid accusations of flattery. Chroniclers, he said, should not praise a man in his own lifetime, but rather wait until he had 'met his end'. With this in mind, Bower went on to paint an idealised picture of how the English avoided nepotism when producing their chronicles:

> [I]t has been suitably laid down in very many countries (including England, I have heard) that each monastery founded by kings should have its scribe or writer appointed from among the community, who should make a dated record of all noteworthy things during a king's reign which affect the kingdom and neighbourhood at any rate as seems to be the truth of the matter; and at the first [parliament or] general council after a king's death all the annalists should meet and produce openly their sworn statements or writings. The council should choose wise men who are skilled and expert in such matters to examine the writings, make a careful collation of them, extract a summary of what has been brought together, and compile a chronicle. And they should store away the writings of the copyists [of this work] in monastic archives as authenticated chronicles which can be trusted, lest by the passing of time memories of happenings in the kingdom perish ... I pray to Christ by the gift of his mercy to bring the king up as the kind of man who will give us something worthy of eternal memory (just as we have from the outstanding kings his ancestors), which we may transmit to posterity with the help of writings about him.[1]

While this passage forms part of a longer, anxious reflection about how Bower's own chronicle would be received and how his nation's history was being preserved, it also gets to the heart of the uneven ways in which historical writing was produced across the Middle Ages, particularly in England. The fanciful image of government and church working in harmony to produce a balanced record of a king's achievements was not how the English (or the Scots) produced their histories. Monastic authors had the freedom to record whatever interested them, but many focused on matters that affected their religious house and when they wrote about kings they tended to evaluate them according to how well they defended or encroached on ecclesiastical liberties. Rarely did they understand or acknowledge the precarious balancing act that sovereigns had to perform to keep both religious and secular lords satisfied and the mechanisms of government working. Moreover, though Bower is correct about England's historical writing being examined by governments as a trustworthy source of information, there was never a single, authorised account of a monarch's reign produced in the manner he describes. Instead, historical writing was subject to individual bias, reframing by later authors and interference from kings themselves.

Where information about the authors of historical writing in England is known, or can be gleaned from their texts, they were educated men, who wrote largely at the request of a secular or ecclesiastical patron, or for their own delectation. Historiographers' visions of the past were therefore attuned to the world view of their benefactor, their regime or their religious order. Although powerful women patronised historical writing alongside, and independently from, men, there is, to date, no evidence of women writing historiography in England, as their (rare) European counterparts did.[2] Historical writing in England was therefore inherently biased towards the affairs and interests of educated men in the orbit of power and influence (secular, civic and ecclesiastical), and its infrequent depiction of lower ranks or female entanglements with such power structures was always mediated through a privileged male voice.

The late medieval period covered by this book ushered in significant changes to the way that historical writing was sourced and written in England. Before the late fourteenth century, historiography was almost exclusively the preserve of monks like Ralph of Coggeshall (fl. 1207–26) and secular clerks (i.e. priests and clerics outside monastic orders with responsibility for ecclesiastical administration and pastoral care) like Geoffrey le Baker (fl. 1350). Their most common outputs were monastic annals and chronicles, which served as aides-memoires for the future and had limited circulation among a readership of educated religious and politically active men. Monastic annals provided brief chronological notes about key events deemed worthy of remembrance by the annalist(s), and did not usually evaluate or comment further on what was recorded. Chronicles provided lengthier accounts of local, national or international affairs and offered commentary from the chronicler, who would often look for patterns of cause and effect in the narrative.[3] Both types of historical texts were heavily reliant on earlier works and oral accounts from eyewitnesses that the authors deemed to be trustworthy. However, these methods of gathering source materials did not prevent authors from being selective in what they included or from fabricating sources and details to suit their own agenda.[4]

The types of evidence available to writers increased significantly from the thirteenth century onwards. As Chris Given-Wilson has noted, a prolific body of bureaucratic materials in the form of 'copies of writs, charters, memoranda, and various other documents' began to circulate 'to monasteries, county courts, parish churches, foreign courts, and so forth'.[5] Such a proliferation of information provided fertile material for chroniclers to enrich their works in tandem with the more traditional methods of gathering information. While some authors threaded the information contained in these official and semi-official documents through their narratives in subtle and inspired ways, others elected to include verbatim copies of the materials or direct their readers to where they could be viewed for verification. Henry Knighton, for example, preferred integrating parliamentary reports, private letters, proclamations, writs and other official materials directly into the account of the reigns of Edward III and Richard II that he produced at Leicester Abbey in the fourteenth century. The anonymous royal chaplain who authored the *Gesta Henrici Quinti* in 1416 and 1417 preferred to direct his readers to independent reference works, such as the register of Archbishop Arundel and an independent book of 'royal evidences and records'.[6] Meanwhile, Matthew Paris (c. 1200–59) combined both working practices in the chronicles he produced at St Albans. When writing his *Chronica Majora*, one of the most important sources for the reign of Henry III, Paris began by copying the documents that informed his history into the main body of the text but, as the work progressed, he switched to presenting them in a separate book called the *Liber Additamentorum* (*Book of Additions*) and urged his readers to consult that.[7]

Where possible, chroniclers researched and adjudicated between conflicting sources for their readers, but, in some cases, they merely repeated and bolstered official accounts without intervention. Context and caution are therefore required when reading them, as they are not without inherited or authorial bias. This is especially true of texts produced during and in the wake of a political rupture, when historical writing became one of the most important mechanisms for transmitting and preserving how one king fell and another took his place (see 'Historical Writing and the Succession' later in the chapter).

The chronicle's ability to capture more information and evaluate events made it the pre-eminent form of late medieval historical writing.

Chronicles were time-consuming to write and expensive to produce, but they also had great flexibility of form. They could be confined to the deeds of a specific monarch or period, like the *Vita Edward Secundi* (discussed later in the chapter), or they could adopt a more expansive approach like two of the most widely read and influential histories of the fourteenth century: the *Prose Brut* and Ranulf Higden's *Polychronicon*. Following the pattern established by Geoffrey of Monmouth's twelfth-century *De Gestis Britonum* (*On the Deeds of the Britons*), the anonymous Anglo-Norman *Prose Brut* (c. 1272–c. 1300) placed British and English kings at the centre of its narrative, depicting them as an illustrious line of legitimate successors that stretched all the way back to Britain's mythical founder Brutus via legendary figures like King Arthur.[8] This model proved to be so popular with readers and writers of history that the *Prose Brut* was continued, revised and translated into English and Latin throughout the fourteenth and fifteenth centuries. It was owned by religious houses and secular readers ranging from merchants to royalty, and in all its linguistic forms, but especially in its English translation which is extant in more than 200 manuscripts, it helped shape English identity and memorialise the deeds of the late medieval kings.[9] As the most prolific secular work to survive in Middle English, its influence on other genres of literature, such as romance, can be seen in works invoking the 'Matter of Britain', or stories about King Arthur, like *Sir Gawain and the Green Knight*.[10]

Taking a different approach, Ranulf Higden's universal chronicle put the inheritance and deeds of England's kings in conversation with broader world history (as defined by the medieval Christian mind). Written in three versions between 1327 and 1352, the encyclopaedic *Polychronicon* began with the Creation, tracing exemplary leadership through biblical patriarchs and classical figures to Higden's own times. Though his coverage of world leaders provided good and bad models of kingship for his readers, he nonetheless questioned whether figures like King Arthur were real and acknowledged the complex co-mingling of peoples, languages and cultures that took place through centuries of invasion in Britain's past. For Higden, the affairs of the English kings and their forebears formed an integral part of his work, but they were situated alongside other details of equal import, such as geographical information, religious history, archaeological curiosities and folklore. Higden's extensive coverage of the ancient and classical world, the papacy and the histories of other European countries inevitably offered readers a God's-eye view of the past in which the kingdoms of men rose and fell in mere moments against the vastness of eternity. Like the *Prose Brut*, the *Polychronicon* inspired numerous continuations and translations all the way through to William Caxton's famous printing and expansion of the text in 1482.

While these two types of chronicles provided models for many subsequent historical works, including shorter digests of history used by scholars to memorise English history, they also helped to inspire new demographics of writers to take up their pens. As the fourteenth and fifteenth centuries progressed, historiography written by noblemen, civic officials, heralds and soldiers emerged with greater frequency, bringing about a marked shift from Latin to vernacular chronicles. With the broadening of authorship came a bigger assortment of historiographical forms and audiences. The chivalric chronicles written by Sir Thomas Gray (d. 1369) and John Hardyng (1378–c. 1465) captured history from the perspectives of seasoned military men who experienced, first-hand, England's ongoing wars with Scotland and France. Writing as only northerners who had lived on the habitually contested border with Scotland could, both chroniclers measured and interpreted the affairs of kings according to the ideals of knightly conduct and sovereign dominion. Through the lens of England's foreign conflicts, they advanced models of good kingship centred on justice, martial prowess and the protection of England's territorial rights (as they perceived them). Gray, for example, used Edward II's truce with the Scots in 1322 to depart from his largely favourable account of the king and explain the emergence of unchivalrous behaviour that led to the loss of his crown:

> From this time on, the king made a truce with the Scots for thirteen years, keeping himself wholly quiet, in peace, concerning himself with nothing of honour or prowess, but only with getting rich ... he gave himself completely to that which completely debarred him from chivalry, delighting himself in avarice and in the delights of the flesh, disinheriting his men who had rebelled against him, and at the same time getting rich from their great landholdings.

A few passages later, Edward abandons his domestic duties and household 'to leave with Hugh le Despenser by sea for a foreign land', a betrayal that prompts his followers to desert him and which, in turn, facilitates his deposition.[11] Robust kingship in this text is clearly equated with honourable conduct, strength and uncompromising martial action conducive to England's interests.

Gray, who has the distinction of being the first English knight to write a history, and Hardyng, a former soldier and gentleman in the service of the Percy and Umfraville families, were writing with noble and gentry audiences in mind. They therefore began their chronicles with the descent of the first British king from Adam, the first man, and utilised a variety of source materials, including Trojan and Arthurian narratives, to appeal to courtly tastes. Such legendary material, paired with unique insights into the social and political realities of their own times, enabled both men to produce valuable histories that spoke to the importance of noblemen in helping their monarchs to protect and govern the kingdom across time. These were not just chronicles about kings but about the men who helped them expand and retain their realms through heroic deeds and loyalty.

Other historiographical forms that flourished under an expanded range of authors included campaign narratives focused on the martial excellence of individual princes, like the *Gesta Henrici Quinti*, and town chronicles like the *London Chronicles*. The *Gesta Henrici Quinti* (1416–17) provides an important example of how historical writing helped to secure the positive reputation of Henry V and advance his royal policy of war against France. Authored by an anonymous religious clerk who was eyewitness to the events of 1413 to 1416, the text was written for consumption at home and perhaps abroad against the diplomatic backdrop of the Council of Constance (1414–18). Shamelessly propagandist in tone, the methods used by the author to cast Henry as the perfect Christian prince align with the traditional criteria for establishing good kingship in contemporary mirrors for princes. Piety, prudence, martial resilience, the maintenance of wise councillors and a desire to protect the commonweal of his realm are all praiseworthy qualities manifest in Henry, but the narrative really turns on the motif of a divine test to show the king's 'worth' and uses his piety to underpin the narrative of his successful French campaign. It is Henry's 'sacred meditations' on how to promote God's honour that lead to the creator burdening him with a 'furnace of tribulation'.[12] By nullifying domestic uprisings, like Sir John Oldcastle's insurrection and the Southampton Plot of 1415, Henry proves his worth in foreign trials and successfully returns home to honour his political ally, the Emperor Sigismund, with the Order of the Garter. The author's closing prayer for a final victory in France looks forward to a peace between the two kingdoms that will allow Henry to pursue 'the heathen' and recoup the Holy Land, exposing the text's political slant.[13] In this piece, England and its sovereign are located at the heart of European affairs and Christendom's hopes for the recovery of its lost territory.

While the *Gesta* and other campaign narratives looked beyond England's borders, offering insights into how the English kings sought and justified territorial expansion, civic chronicles, like the *London Chronicles*, always kept an eye on the mechanisms of government at home and on the men who exercised power in the name of the king. The authors' inclusion of material was determined by their civic identity and the city's historic relations with the centre of power (good or bad). Though such chronicles often discuss foreign affairs, there is usually an insularity of focus centred on how external and economic matters, such as trade and war, affect the city, or an emphasis on the spatial dynamics of the metropolis as a site for displays of royal authority. A fine example of the city's ceremonial role in royal and foreign affairs is the *London Chronicles*' preservation of John Lydgate's poetic account of 'Henry VI's Triumphal Entry into London on 21 February 1432'. The poem was commissioned by John Welles, mayor of London, to commemorate the fine pageantry that the city staged for the king's return to England following his coronation in France. By its nature the pageantry was an ephemeral affair, but the poem provided an official textual record of the king's engagement with the urban landscape and its people. Surviving in several *London Chronicles*, the closing stanzas of the poem allude to London's foundational role as the first locus of power in Britain by calling it 'Newe Troye', the name given to it by Brutus, the first king in the *Brut* chronicles. Comparisons with Rome and Carthage similarly align it with the great capitals that conquerors of the classical world returned to after their foreign conquests, placing it in a historic line of special cities.[14] In the same way that the chivalric chronicles of Gray and Hardyng sought to provide histories that captured the importance of the nobility in protecting and governing the kingdom, the *London*

Chronicles helped to foster civic identity and pride in the city's superior and long-lived history.

The final historiographical form that rose to importance as consumption of historical texts increased among lay readers in the fourteenth and fifteenth centuries was the genealogical chronicle, which became an increasingly popular (and cheaper) means of visualising the ancestry of royal or noble families than the weightier texts discussed hitherto. Frequently taking the form of a roll with the pictorial descent of a sovereign marked by familial lines and decorative roundels depicting his ancestors, the pedigree was supplemented with a brief textual narrative in Latin, Anglo-Norman or English, which captured important historical details about a monarch and traced their succession back from the English kings to Adam via legendary British and biblical figures, such as King Arthur, Brutus and Noah. Noble genealogies likewise began with a legendary ancestor, such as the two rolls produced by John Rous (discussed and illustrated in the next section). Of all the forms of historical writing available to authors, genealogies were the easiest to manipulate and modify, which may explain their ubiquity in the fifteenth century when the question of the succession was most hotly contested.

Historical Writing and the Succession

Historical writing in late medieval England had to speak to the chaotic power shifts brought about by the unseating of six kings: Edward II, Richard II, Henry VI, Edward IV, Edward V (who was never crowned) and Richard III. In some instances, contemporaneous chronicles survive from before the monarchs lost their crowns, offering incomparable insights into the final years of their reign before the end was known and their successors' version of events had time to influence accounts of their demise. A rare example for the reign of Edward II is the *Vita Edwardi Secundi*, which was written in journalistic stints from around 1310–12 to 1326. It responds to the problems generated by Edward II's favouritism of Piers Gaveston, maintaining 'a relatively tolerant and balanced view of most political individuals', and while critical of Edward's court it is 'not sympathetic to baronial lawlessness and rebellion'.[15] The chronicler's reflection on the downfall and execution of Thomas, earl of Lancaster (d. 1322), an arch critic of the king in the 1310s, provides a good illustration of his stance:

> Oh, what a sight! To see the earl of Lancaster, who was recently the terror of the whole country, receiving judgment in his own castle and home ... Oh! Earl of Lancaster! Where is your power, where are your riches, with which you hoped to subdue all, and that no one could resist you? If you had been steadfast in your early faith, you would never have come to be forsaken ... The earl of Lancaster once cut off Piers Gaveston's head, and now by the king's command the earl of Lancaster has lost his head. Thus, perhaps not unjustly, the earl received like for like, as it is written in Holy Scripture: 'for with the same measure that you shall mete withal it shall be measured to you again'.[16]

Founded on the author's own knowledge, the testimonies of others and occasional information from letters, documents and newsletters, the *Vita* is a precious and unusual survival because almost all of the chronicles covering the end of Edward II's rule were written or altered after his deposition and were weighted in favour of his son's accession under the regency of Isabella of France.

Generally speaking, chroniclers invoked divine providence, prophecy and a healthy dose of hindsight to explain why kings were usurped or murdered, but memories of their reigns were also indelibly shaped by the regime in ascendance. A case in point is Richard II, whose reign chroniclers wrote and rewrote about to chime with the shifting political landscape of the fifteenth century. Like the reign of Edward II, few wholly contemporary chronicles charting the close of Richard's rule survive from before his deposition in 1399. The exceptional examples that do survive tend to offer a sympathetic or neutral view of the king, rather than depicting him as a failed ruler on the brink of losing his crown, whereas those written during or immediately after Henry IV's accession are coloured by the new Lancastrian dynasty's version of events.[17] The *Short Kirkstall Chronicle* and the *Dieulacres Chronicle* capture this transition perfectly. The *Dieulacres Chronicle* was composed in two parts. The first, covering the period 1337–1400, was written around 1403 by a single monk who remained sympathetic to Richard and unmoved by the rhetoric that justified Henry Bolingbroke's election as Henry IV. The second part, written by another individual in the initial years of Henry IV's reign, extended the text from 1400 to 1403 and censured the previous author's attitude to Richard, lamenting that 'this commentator in many places condemns what should be praised and praises what should be condemned'.[18] The first section of the *Short Kirkstall Chronicle*, written in 1398 to 1399, follows the same pattern and is positive towards Richard II, but its concluding section, written after Henry IV's accession in 1399, has a marked tonal shift in the new king's favour. The striking difference here is that, unlike the *Dieulacres Chronicle*, both parts were written by the same anonymous Cistercian author, who changed his mind about Richard either of his own volition or through necessity. Historiographers appear to have had the freedom to write critically about incumbent monarchs, but many exercised a degree of caution, especially when recording dynastic transitions. Tempering his writing to account for the change in monarch, the Kirkstall chronicler closed his work with a description of the years 1399 to 1400 that repeated the speeches made by Richard II and Henry IV in a pro-Henrician account of Richard's deposition known as 'The Record and Process of the Renunciation and Deposition of Richard II'.[19]

First enrolled in the rolls of parliament for October 1399, 'The Record and Process' was circulated at the start of Henry IV's reign alongside other documents as a formal record of the injustices of Richard II's regime and justification for Henry's accession. Straddling fact and fiction, it described the assembly that gathered on 30 September 1399 to accept Richard's resignation and listed the many ways in which Richard allegedly broke his coronation oath and ruled tyrannously. Copies were distributed to religious houses like the abbeys at Kirkstall, Evesham and St Albans, and Grey Friars Convent, Canterbury, where they made their way into the chronicles produced there, shaping how historical writing from 1400 onwards remembered the transfer of power. The *Short Kirkstall Chronicle*, the *Historia Vitae et Regni Ricardi Secundi*, Thomas Walsingham's *Chronica Maiora*, Richard Fox's *Chronicle* and the *Continuatio Eulogii* all attest to the propaganda's reach and influence.[20]

Beyond generating official documents to influence Richard II's presentation in the historical imagination of the early fifteenth century, Henry IV is known to have based his claim to the throne on a false genealogy that promoted his descent from Henry III. From as early as the 1390s, Henry IV's father, John of Gaunt, duke of Lancaster, attempted to circulate a fake chronicle claiming that Edward I was the youngest of Henry III's sons and that he inherited the crown instead of his brother Edmund, earl of Lancaster, on account of Edmund being 'crouchbacked' or disabled.[21] Both Adam of Usk's *Chronicle* and the *Continuatio Eulogii* report that Gaunt's chronicle was proven to be false when compared with other histories in English monasteries, but this did not stop Henry IV alluding to the 'Crouchback' story again in 1399 when he produced a genealogy outlining his claim to the throne as a descendant of Henry III.[22] On this occasion, the *Annales Ricardi Secundi et Henrici Quarti* reports that the leaders of all major religious houses in possession of chronicles relating to England's governance from the time of William the Conqueror to the present were required to send their books to London with representatives who could speak to their contents.[23] Chris Given-Wilson has suggested that as well as looking for evidence to support the Crouchback legend, Henry IV was interested in how previous depositions were handled and intended to 'ensure that the major religious houses of the realm were issued with copies of his version of events ... for both the St Albans and Evesham chronicles are dependent in varying degrees on the handouts concocted by Henry and his supporters for their accounts of the deposition and usurpation'.[24] It is possible that Henry also went so far as destroying a chronicle that contained material casting doubt on the legitimacy of his claim. Walter Bower, the Scottish chronicler with whom this chapter began, reported that the king destroyed the chronicle belonging to Glastonbury Abbey because it indicated that the daughters of Roger Mortimer 'ought to succeed'.[25]

Henry IV's active manipulation of England's historical outputs is nonetheless only a small part of the bigger picture. Other kings (and those in their orbit) also used the tactics employed by Henry to shape popular opinion and further their own political ends. Henry III famously visited St Albans to request that Matthew Paris attend the ceremonial installation of the Holy Blood Relic he had obtained for Westminster to record the event in his chronicles for posterity.[26] Similarly, in March 1291, when Scotland entered into a succession crisis following the death of Margaret, the Maid of Norway, Edward

I instructed heads of England's religious houses to consult their chronicles and report whatever they found relating to England's role in the historic governance of Scotland. Two months later, the fruits of those enquiries were brought to Norham by representatives of the houses, where it was established that the Scottish kings had paid homage to their English overlords on numerous occasions. When the claimants to the Scottish throne acknowledged Edward's right to decide the next successor, the king ensured that the principal religious houses recorded this fact for posterity.[27] When Edward decided to claim the Scottish throne for himself, the epistolary exchange he had with Pope Boniface VIII was likewise copied into several English chronicles to ensure it remained available to his successors and was not forgotten.

One of the best examples of an historiographical intervention stemming from the heart of government is *The History of the Arrival of Edward IV*. Based on newsletters written to explain Edward IV's recovery of the English throne to his allies abroad, the text covers the period from 2 March to 26 May 1471 and was written by 'a servaunt off þe kyngs that presently saw in effect a great parte of his exploytes, and the resydwe knew by trwe relation of them that were present at every tyme'.[28] It persistently positions Edward IV as a superlative Christian king dispossessed of his crown by the 'traytor & rebell' Richard Neville, earl of Warwick, who aided 'the vsourpowre' Henry VI.[29] Although the author takes great care to record Edward IV's movements and tactics, a significant amount of space is devoted to outlining the king's devotion to God and to reflecting on moments of divine intercession, which include assistance from St George in battle and a miracle performed by Saint Anne at Daventry on Palm Sunday. Crucially, Edward's decisive recovery of the kingdom and martial acumen is steered by the grace of God, and his opponents' defeat reveals divine judgement in action.

This clever narrative demonstrates the importance of historical writing in disseminating the story of Edward's recovery of the crown, but it was not the first time the Yorkists had exploited the past. As the dynasty that overthrew Henry IV's grandson, Henry VI, the Yorkists and their supporters had encouraged and deployed other forms of historiography to reframe accounts of Richard II's deposition as an ambitious Lancastrian grasp for the throne. In the 1460s and 1470s, a prolific cluster of genealogical rolls were produced by a small group of craftsmen who saw an opportunity to monetise the hereditary right to the English throne that Richard, duke of York, had presented when he became heir apparent to Henry VI under the Act of Accord of October 1460, and which was subsequently invoked when Edward IV took the throne in 1461. Seeing a market for historiography that made 'what had been achieved by military force and good fortune ... acceptable in conscience to both nobles and commons', a single metropolitan scribe and his artist associates began producing genealogical rolls that repeated and enshrined the Yorkist descent in material form for those wishing to educate themselves about the claim or demonstrate their allegiance to the new dynasty.[30]

It was also in this period that John Hardyng, the aforementioned author of a chivalric chronicle, began writing his second history. His first text had been completed in 1457 for Henry VI, but its Lancastrian tone no longer suited the new political circumstances that emerged through the Act of Accord of 1460.[31] Prefacing his new history with a prologue that outlined York's superior claim to the throne as a descendant of Edward III's second son, Lionel, duke of Clarence, Hardyng utilised the ancestral information that the duke had presented to parliament and which had been circulating as a genealogical roll in the environs of London from the 1460s onwards. By 1464, when the Yorkist ascendancy was secure under Edward IV, Hardyng, who was still working on his second history, also elected to include copies of letters relating to Richard II's deposition and Archbishop Scrope's rebellion of 1405. Issued by the rebels, the letters emphasised Richard's death by starvation and Henry IV's perjury of an oath taken at Doncaster in which he swore to claim only the duchy of Lancaster.[32] With this historiographical intervention, Richard II was recast as a martyr. The downfall of the Lancastrian dynasty under Henry VI became the inevitable consequence of Henry IV's unlawful seizure of the throne and Edward IV's accession was framed as the legitimate restoration of the royal line. Most of the surviving manuscripts of Hardyng's second *Chronicle* bear evidence of being produced in London and/or owned by late medieval residents of that city, suggesting a degree of popularity in the capital at the same time that the genealogies that Hardyng drew on were also in demand.

Such flagrant refashioning of historical events was endemic in times of crises and civil war and serves as an example of how difficult the task of writing history could be for medieval writers when kingship was contested or in flux. Whether Hardyng acted of his own free will or was encouraged to update his work by a pro-Yorkist patron, his engagement with the legality of the succession sits alongside the efforts of other late fifteenth-century historiographers, like John Rous (1420–92), who famously changed his portrayal of Richard III in one of the two genealogical rolls he prepared between 1477 and 1485 (see Figure 17.1). Designed to show the history of his patrons, the earls of Warwick, both rolls traced their decent from Guthelinus, legendary founder of Warwick, to Prince Edward, son of Anne, daughter of Richard Neville, earl of Warwick, and Richard III, in whose reign the rolls were completed. After Richard III's

Figure 17.1 A depiction of Richard III with his wife, Anne Neville, and son, Edward in the armorial roll-chronicle by John Rous, The Rous Roll, c. 1483–5 (London, British Library Additional MS 48976). Short passages beneath the figures praise the family, who stand on a muzzled and chained bear representing the house of Warwick (Anne) and boars representing Richard II's badge (Richard and Edward). Between them are representations of the kingdoms Richard holds with a reference to Saint Edward too (labelled clockwise from the top right: England, Ireland, Walys, Gascyon and Gyan, Francia, and Seynt Edward). (Photo by: Universal History Archive/Universal Images Group via Getty Images.)

demise, the first roll written in English was unavailable for Rous to edit the images and passages of praise he had included about Richard and his son, but he updated the second Latin roll by erasing the images it contained of the Yorkist monarchs Edward IV and Richard III and replacing them with the figures of Edward III and Henry VI's son, Prince Edward. The text praising Richard was also erased. Another of Rous's historical outputs, the *Historia Regum Angliae*, was started in the reign of Edward IV at the request of John Seymour, canon of Windsor, and finished in the reign of Henry VII in 1486. In this, references to Richard's great building works at Westminster, Nottingham, Warwick, York, Middleham and London were overshadowed by Rous attuning his narrative to Tudor efforts to vilify the king. In a much-cited passage, Rous presented Richard as a monstrous hunchback, who had an unnaturally long gestation in his mother's womb and emerged with a full set of teeth and shoulder-length hair.[33] The text also condemns Richard for the murder of Henry VI, his wife, Anne, and his nephews, Edward V and Richard of Shrewsbury, duke of York.

Conclusion

It will be evident by now that the production of historical writing in late medieval England fell far from Walter Bower's idealised image of how a king's reign should be memorialised. All medieval historiography was in some way prejudiced by those who authored it, the patronage or political events that prompted it and the sources, ephemera and hindsight that informed it. The sheer variety of authors and historiographical forms that have pushed and pulled in different directions across the centuries cannot provide a complete picture of kings long dead, only a tangle of insights that are not easily unpicked from the contexts that produced them. This is not to say that the rich body of historical writing that has come down to us is useless. On the contrary, amid the threads of truth, fiction and uncertainty inherent in the historiography there is an inexhaustible supply of insights and details that can deepen knowledge about individual monarchs. But what late medieval historical writing offers is far more valuable than a series of royal portraits. It provides a window into the world of the medieval kings and their subjects. It speaks to the messiness, confusion, concerns and aspirations of those, like Bower across the border, who were attempting to preserve something of their times for posterity. It reveals what was important to the writers, whether religious, civic or noble, in the moment they took up their parchment and ink, and how they responded to royal power. The snapshots historiography affords of England's kings belong to the complex and changeable times that generated them and the worldview of the people who compiled them. Kings were the custodians of the kingdom, but historiographers were the custodians of communal memory. What they left behind might not reveal the whole picture, but the glimpses they supply illuminate the world that kings had to navigate on their journey to immortality at the mercy of others' pens.

Notes

1. *Scotichronicon by Walter Bower*, ed. D. E. R. Watt, 8 vols. (Aberdeen, 1987), VIII, 338–9.
2. The *Encyclopedia of the Medieval Chronicle* records only 15 female chroniclers among its 2,500 entries, the majority of whom are from Germany: G. Dunphy, 'Women Chroniclers and Chronicles for Women', in *Encyclopedia of The Medieval Chronicle*, ed. G. Dunphy, 2 vols. (Leiden, 2010), II, 1521–4 (at 1521).
3. For the problems inherent in defining 'Annals' and 'Chronicles', see Dunphy, *Encyclopedia of the Medieval Chronicle*, I, 45–52, 274–82.
4. On forgery in medieval chronicles, see R. F. Berkhofer III, *Forgeries and Historical Writing in England, France and Flanders, 900–1200* (Woodbridge, 2022); A. Hiatt, *The Making of Medieval Forgeries: False Documents in Fifteenth-Century England* (London, 2004); and A. Hiatt, 'Forgery as Historiography', in *Medieval Historical Writing: Britain and Ireland, 500–1500*, ed. J. Jahner, E. Steiner and E. M. Tyler (Cambridge, 2019), 404–19.
5. C. Given-Wilson, 'Official and Semi-Official History in the Later Middle Ages: The English Evidence in Context', *The Medieval Chronicle* 5 (2008), 1–16 (at 3).
6. *Gesta Henrici Quinti: The Deeds of Henry the Fifth*, ed. F. Taylor and J. S. Roskell (Oxford, 1975), 8–9, 14–15, 18–19, 56–7, 94–5.
7. *Matthæi Parisiensis, Monachi Sancti Albani, Chronica Majora*, ed. H. Richards Luard, 7 vols. (London, 1872–3), II, 606.
8. *The Oldest Anglo-Norman Prose Brut Chronicle*, ed. J. Marvin (Woodbridge, 2006).
9. L. M. Matheson's *The Prose Brut: The Development of a Middle English Chronicle* (Tempe, AZ, 1998) provides the best overview of the various versions and continuations. For the text of *The Middle English Prose Brut*,

see *The Brut of the Chronicles of England*, ed. F. W. D. Brie, EETS, Old Series, 131 and 136 (London, 1906–8).

10. For the 'Matter of Britain' in romance, see W. R. J. Barron, *English Medieval Romance* (London, 1987), ch. 7.
11. *Sir Thomas Gray, Scalacronica 1272–1363*, ed. and trans. A. King (Woodbridge, 2005), 89, 91, 93.
12. *Gesta Henrici Quinti: The Deeds of Henry V*, ed. F. Taylor and J. S. Roskell (Oxford, 1975), 3.
13. Ibid., 133, 181.
14. *A Chronicle of London, from 1089 to 1483*, ed. N. H. Nicolas (London, 1827), 235–50 (at 250) and *Chronicles of London*, ed. C. L. Kingsford (Oxford, 1905), 97–116 (at 115–16).
15. *Vita Edwardi Secundi*, ed. W. R. Childs (Oxford, 2005), xxxii.
16. Ibid., 215.
17. Sources for Richard's reign are covered by L. Duls, *Richard II in the Early Chronicles* (The Hague, 1975) and C. Given-Wilson, *Chronicles of the Revolution, 1397–1400* (Manchester, 1993), but see also P. Strohm, *England's Empty Throne: Usurpation and the Language of Legitimation 1399–1422* (New Haven, CT, 1998); J. Nuttall, *The Creation of Lancastrian Kingship* (Cambridge, 2007), 17–18; and S. Walker, 'Remembering Richard: History and Memory in Lancastrian England', in *The Fifteenth Century, Vol. 4: Political Culture in Late Medieval Britain*, ed. L. Clark and C. Carpenter (Woodbridge, 2004), 21–31. Other chronicles written before the deposition include *The Westminster Chronicle* (which ends in 1394) and Henry Knighton's *Chronicle* (which ends in 1396); see: *The Westminster Chronicle, 1381–1394*, ed. L. C. Hector and B. F. Harvey (Oxford, 1982) and *Knighton's Chronicle, 1337–1396*, ed. G. H. Martin (Oxford, 1995).
18. *Iste commentator in locis quampluribus vituperat commendanda et commendat vituperanda*: M. V. Clarke and V. H. Galbraith, 'The Deposition of Richard II', *BJRL* 14 (1930), 125–81 (at 174–5). The editors suggest that the author was a clerk of Henry IV who joined Dieulacres after Richard's deposition (133).
19. *The Kirkstall Abbey Chronicles*, ed. J. Taylor (Leeds, 1952), 80–81, 123–5.
20. *Historia Vitae et Regni Ricardi Secundi*, ed. G. B. Stow (Pennsylvania, 1977), 157–60; *The Chronica Maiora of Thomas Walsingham (1376–1422)*, ed. and trans. D. Preest and J. G. Clark (Woodbridge, 2005), 309–11; *Continuatio Eulogii*, ed. and trans. C. Given-Wilson (Oxford, 2019), 92–5. Richard Fox's copy of 'The Record and Process' survives (unedited) in Woburn Abbey MS 181, ff. 205r–226v. For 'The Record and Process', see *Chronicles of the Revolution*, ed. Given-Wilson, 168–89.
21. For the crouchback legend, see T. P. J. Edlin, 'The Crouchback Legend Revisited', *The Ricardian* 14 (2004), 95–105; G. T. Lapsley, 'The Parliamentary Title of Henry IV', *EHR* 49 (1934), 577–606, and A. R. Allan, 'Political Propaganda Employed by the House of York in England in the

Mid-Fifteenth Century, 1450-71', unpublished Ph.D. thesis (University of Wales at Swansea, 1981), 193, 196-8, 269, who notes a connection between the crouchback myth and the account in the *Continuatio Eulolgii*, which details Richard II naming Mortimer as his heir.

22. *Continuatio Eulogii*, ed. and trans. Given-Wilson, 70-1, and *The Chronicle of Adam of Usk, 1377-1421*, ed. and trans. C. Given-Wilson (Oxford, 1997), xix, 64-7. The episode is also reported by John Hardyng : *Chronicle of Iohn Hardyng*, ed. H. Ellis (London, 1812), 353-4.
23. 'Annales Ricardi Secundi et Henrici Quarti', in *Johannis de Trokelow et Henrici de Blaneforde Monachorum S. Albani*, ed. H. T. Riley, RS (London, 1866), 155-420 (at 252).
24. C. Given-Wilson, *Chronicles: The Writing of History in Medieval England* (London, 2004), 72.
25. *Scotichronicon*, ed. D. E. R. Watt, VIII, 20-1. Some degree of caution is nonetheless required here due to Bower's anti-English stance.
26. *Chronica Majora*, ed. H. Richards Luard, IV, 640-4, and VI, 138-44. For the cultural and political contexts of the relic, see N. Vincent, *The Holy Blood: King Henry III and the Westminster Blood Relic* (Cambridge, 2006).
27. On this, see E. L. G. Stones, *Anglo-Scottish Relations 1174-1328: Some Selected Documents* (Oxford, 1970); R. Griffiths, 'Edward I, Scotland and the Chronicles of English Religious Houses', *Journal of the Society of Archivists* 6 (1979), 191-9; and A. Duncan, 'Revisiting Norham, May-June 1291', in *War, Government and Aristocracy in the British Isles, c.1150-1500: Essays in Honour of Michael Prestwich*, ed. C. Given-Wilson, A. Kettle, and L. Scales (Woodbridge, 2008), 69-83.
28. *The Contemporary English Chronicles of the Wars of the Roses*, ed. D. Embree and M. T. Tavormina (Woodbridge, 2019), 157.
29. Ibid.
30. These genealogies were also responding to, and correcting, Lancastrian genealogies circulating in the 1430s and 1440s that omitted the line of Lionel, duke of Clarence. See R. Griffiths, 'The Sense of Dynasty in the Reign of Henry VI', in *Patronage, Pedigree and Power in Later Medieval England*, ed. C. Ross (Gloucester, 1979), 13-36; A. Allan, 'Yorkist Propaganda: Pedigree, Prophecy and the "British History" in the Reign of Edward IV', in *Patronage, Pedigree and Power in Later Medieval England*, ed. C. Ross (Gloucester, 1979), 171-92; and Allan, 'Political Propaganda'.
31. *John Hardyng, Chronicle*, ed. J. Simpson and S. Peverley (Kalamazoo, MI, 2015).
32. *The Chronicle of Iohn Hardyng*, ed. Ellis, 351-4. These claims certainly chime with those in earlier chronicles, such as the *Dieulacres Chronicle*, which mentions Richard's death by starvation and Henry's perjury of the oath (although the location is given as Bridlington): Clarke and Galbraith, 'The Deposition of Richard II', 179. Starvation is also mentioned in: the

Historia Vita et Regni Ricardi Secundi, ed. Stow, 166; the *Prose Brut*, ed. Brie, II, 360; Capgrave's *Abbreuiacion of Cronicles* (*John Capgrave's Abbreuiacion of Cronicles*, ed. P. J. Lucas, EETS, Old Series, 285 (1983), 217); and John Rous's *Historia Regum Angliae* (*Joannis Rossi Antiquarii Warwicensis, Historia Regu, Angliae*, ed. T. Hearne (Oxford, 1745), 206). The *Continuatio Eulolgii* and the *Chronicque de la Traïson et Mort de Richart Deux Roy Dengleterre* are likewise of interest, as they mention a series of letters circulated by Henry 'calling himself duke of Lancaster and steward of the realm, saying he wanted to restore the kingdom to its accustomed form of government and ancient liberty' (*Continuatio Eulogii*, ed. and trans. Given-Wilson, 88–9, and *Chronicque de la Traïson et Mort de Richart Deux Roy Dengleterre*, ed. B. Williams (London, 1846), 180–3. See also J. Sherborne, 'Perjury and the Lancastrian Revolution of 1399', *The Welsh History Review* 14 (1988), 217–41.

33. *biennio matris utero tentus, exiens cum dentibus et capillis ad humeros*: Rous, *Historia Regum Angliae*, ed. Hearne, 215.

Further Reading

Allan, A. R., 'Political Propaganda Employed by the House of York in England in the Mid-Fifteenth Century, 1450–71', unpublished Ph.D. thesis (University of Wales at Swansea, 1981).

Dunphy, G., ed., *Encyclopedia of the Medieval Chronicle*, 2 vols. (Leiden, 2010).

Given-Wilson, C., *Chronicles of the Revolution, 1397–1400* (Manchester, 1993).

Chronicles: The Writing of History in Medieval England (London, 2004).

'Official and Semi-Official History in the Later Middle Ages: The English Evidence in Context', *The Medieval Chronicle* 5 (2008), 1–16.

Gransden, A., *Historical Writing in England II: c. 1307 to the Early Sixteenth Century* (London, 1997).

Jahner, J., Steiner, E. and Tyler, E. M., eds., *Medieval Historical Writing: Britain and Ireland, 500–1500* (Cambridge, 2019).

Kennedy, E. D., *A Manual of the Writings in Middle English, 1050–1500, Vol. 8: Chronicles and Other Historical Writings* (New Haven, CT, 1989).

McLaren, M, *The London Chronicles of the Fifteenth Century* (Woodbridge, 2002).

Nuttall, J., *The Creation of Lancastrian Kingship* (Cambridge, 2007).

Radulescu, R. and Kennedy, E. D., eds., *Broken Lines: Genealogical Literature in Late-Medieval Britain and France*, Medieval Texts and Cultures of Northern Europe 16 (Turnhout, 2008).

Rajsic, J., Kooper, E. and Hoche, D., *The Prose Brut and Other Late Medieval Chronicles* (Woodbridge, 2016).

CHRISTOPHER FLETCHER

18

Conceptualisations of Kingship

Introduction

The brief for this chapter is to consider kingship in the abstract, that is both how late medieval people theorised kingship but also their assumptions, prejudices and expectations about what a king could and should do. The difficulty with this task is that, although these two domains overlap, they are distinct. The hard, theoretical categories of professional thinkers are different from the unspoken assumptions that a time-travelling anthropologist might uncover. In the case of late medieval England, indeed, the two can sometimes seem quite remote from one another. If, taking the conceptualisation of kingship in strict philosophical terms, we define conceptualisation as the formation of a concept, and a concept as a mental model of a class of objects which unites all their aspects, then it is difficult to find a pure example of concept-building based solely on the systemisation of contemporary beliefs about late medieval English kingship.

Instead, the English took their political theory from different ages and places, occasionally adapting it to fit local conditions. This might seem surprising, since the period was rocked by momentous developments in the powers of kings and what their subjects expected them to do. It certainly irritated nineteenth- and early twentieth-century historians, keen to find a rugged English theorist of the late medieval English constitution. A less self-confident age might admit that, in uncertain times and with an unknown arrival point, existing concepts might be adapted to provide good models for new situations but also that established ideas can prove surprisingly resilient despite their inapplicability to changed circumstances.

No late medieval Thomas Hobbes went back to fundamentals to produce a model that captured the essence of political relations in that time and place. The closest approximation came in the early 1470s when Sir John Fortescue declared, boldly but simply, that there were two kinds of kingdoms, one, like that in France, in which the king could make laws and raise taxes 'such as he wol hym self' and the other, like England, in which the king could not make laws or raise taxes without the assent of the people.[1] Instead, the most widely circulated and intellectually complete models of kingship in late medieval England came from different times and places. Two of these came from the capacious genre identified by historians as 'mirrors for princes': works that use direct address to a ruler to confer advice concerning the business of government and consequently transmit lessons about the ideal nature of rule. The first of these was the *Secretum Secretorum*, a twelfth-century Latin translation of the Arabic pseudo-Aristotelian work *Kitāb Sirr al-asrār*, presented as a series of letters from Aristotle (the most revered ancient philosopher in the later Middle Ages) to the equally famous war leader, Alexander the Great.[2] The second was the *De Regimine Principum*, composed between 1277 and 1281 for the future king of France by the Italian Augustinian friar, student of Thomas Aquinas and major Parisian professor, Giles of Rome.[3]

Both of these works aimed to adapt the riches of the Aristotelian canon to the day-to-day practice of kingship. Unfortunately for present purposes, they did so in places other than late medieval England, and they circulated over a period when rulership across Europe increasingly diverged from the model cases they had in mind. Nevertheless, it is clear that English readers and writers found much that they wanted in these monumental works. The *De Regimine Principum* survives in some 350 copies, 60 of which are of English medieval origin.[4] Into the fifteenth century, changing practices of copying, manuscript arrangement, annotation and indexing make it possible to show how the use of Giles's work changed over time, foregrounding the multifarious possibilities of its voluminous contents.

The advice on bodily and ethical self-government provided by the *Secretum Secretorum* was more independent of time and place, but its tips on good diet and lifestyle, on the king's role as justice-giver, even its introduction to physiognomy, evidently seemed as useful in late medieval England as in tenth-century Syria. When in the late fourteenth and early fifteenth century writers such as John Gower and Thomas Hoccleve compiled the first English-language guides to kingly rule, they still drew on the *Secretum Secretorum* and the *De Regimine Principum*.

And yet, throughout our period, English writers composed works, often anonymous, in Latin, Anglo-Norman and, from the fourteenth century, Middle English, which have been characterised as complaint, satire or political poetry. These often survive in a single manuscript, or perhaps two or three. They take on the faults of the time in a fashion which sometimes aligns them with the 'mirrors' and sometimes foregrounds different aspects of kingship. The poems known to historians as *The Simonie* (c. 1321), *Against the King's Taxes* and *The Song of the Husbandman* (before 1340) treat royal counsellors and officials as estates within society which failed to fulfil their allotted role.[5] They can be usefully analysed alongside prose works of moral counsel for kings which stuck close to the *Secretum Secretorum*, like Walter of Milemete's *On the Nobility, Wisdom, and Prudence of Kings* (1326–7), or struck out from the familiar lessons of 'mirrors for princes' to present a more bracing message, as in William of Pagula's *Mirror of King Edward III* (1331–2).[6] From mid-century, alliterative poetry in English took on kingship more directly, in *Winner and Waster* (1350s or early 1360s), the B-text of *Piers Plowman* (c. 1379) and its imitators, *Richard the Redeless* (1399), *Mum and the Sothsegger* (1406) and the *Crowned King* (c. 1415).[7] In this latter tradition, the genre of the dream vision allowed the author to expose contradictions in the way that accepted conceptions of kingship related to practice in late medieval England. To this, we might add texts like Chaucer's *Knight's Tale* and his *Tale of Melibee*, which raise parallel questions about kingship.

This chapter considers how a knowledge of 'mirrors for princes' composed outside late medieval England, but widely circulated within it, can help us to identify what was mainstream and what was divergent in the ideas of kingship which are suggested by complaint poetry, dream vision, narrative fiction and prose treatises. First, one important way that both groups of texts conceptualised both kingship and society was through the opposition between the common profit and individual, self-serving interests. This opposition was central to Aristotle's vision of politics, where it identified good as opposed to tyrannical regimes. The 'mirrors' and English-authored works adapted this logic to the circumstances of late medieval kingship, in which the king was a lord, a household head and a military leader but also the head of a judiciary, a legislator and a recipient of tax grants. They also adopted but slightly tempered the consequences of providing a readily applicable means of identifying a tyrannical regime, that is, one that served the particular interests of the ruler and not the common good. A tyrant would most probably be deposed and killed, probably by the rebellion of his people, although writers preferred to obscure the question of how this might come about.

Second, we will focus on one area where the 'mirrors' and English conditions might be thought to differ, notably in the relationship between the king and the law and in their conceptions of justice, severity and mercy. In conclusion, we will briefly evoke the linked questions of counsel and expertise, flattery and liberality. In each of these cases, English kingship might have been conceived of as different from kingship in general, as for Fortescue, but more commonly it was not.

These themes and discourses were not restricted to either 'mirrors for princes' or the English works discussed here. The conceptualisations of kingship dealt with here were not just transmitted to each generation by the mastery of one or two well-circulated texts. Nonetheless, it is useful to pay particular attention to Giles of Rome's *De Regimine Principum* since it presented with clarity Aristotelian knowledge which circulated elsewhere but which Giles was the first to adapt to late medieval kingship. This makes it particularly helpful as a lens through which to view not only late medieval English texts but also the practice of late medieval English kingship.

Lordship and Kingship, the King's Profit and the Common Profit

In the later Middle Ages, the king of England was still a lord. That is to say, he was a nobleman and a war leader, deriving his title from hereditary right. He had extensive estates, lands and residences and a complex accretion of jurisdictional and fiscal rights, which it was his officials' duty to administer for his profit. He also, most of the time, had a wife and, ideally, children. He most certainly had a household, his *mesne*, that group of men and women organised to provide for his material and spiritual needs, to serve his interests and to do his bidding in peace and in war. On the other hand, he was also the head of a fearsomely complex judicial apparatus, quite different from the jurisdiction over courts which a lesser lord might have but which could never be entirely left to function on its own.

To preserve peace, the king had to be seen as a fair arbiter. He was not just a lord like any other; he had to rise above division where an earl or baron might choose his faction. He was an anointed monarch, with a special mission to defend Holy Church and the thaumaturgical power to heal certain illnesses by his touch. Moreover, from the mid thirteenth century, and with increased intensity from the 1290s, the English king was able to raise taxation reckoned as a proportion of the movable goods of his people, granted in response to a specific necessity, increasingly by the representatives of the Commons in parliament. No English earl or baron could do that. In parliament, too, in response to the petitions of the Commons, he promulgated new legislation. So the English king was not just a lord, but a lord he was. He had his own knot of interests, resources and dependants, and his success in preserving them lay with his personal qualities as a man.

In the twelfth-century cathedral schools, as the Aristotelian canon was gradually rediscovered in western Europe, 'practical philosophy' was divided between 'ethics', 'economics' and 'politics', that is to say: the science of governing oneself, a household and a community. It was Giles of Rome's innovation to show how this schema could be made to fit the practice of late medieval kingship. The *De Regimine Principum* was divided into ethics, economics and politics not only because philosophical orthodoxy said that it should be but also because kingship was a kind of lordship that was exercised personally (as a reflexive process to decide how one should act), over a household (meaning wife, children, servants and material resources directly managed) and over public affairs in peace and war. The twist that Giles gave this was to use this progression to direct kingship to the common good.

De Regimine Principum begins with an introduction seeking to demonstrate that the purpose of a king's rule must be the common good of his people, rather than riches, honour and glory, power and might or the pleasures of the body. Giles is here clearer and more robust than the *Secretum Secretorum*, which does however aim to show that the king's well-being was served by pursuing virtue, conceived in terms of moderation and the mastery of bodily desires, and that his interests were promoted by pursuing the prosperity of his people. Giles enumerated the virtues which enable the king to deliver the goal of the common good and the passions to be mastered to put virtuous intention into practice.

In book II, Giles then considered the household, dealing with marriage, the rule of wives, of children and of servants and how the king should meet his material needs. Each man should acquire riches and maintain his household according to his estate, and a king should take appropriate rents and acquire goods as his ancestors had done, not taking the goods of others without reason (II.iii.12). Giles thus takes an ethical but also pragmatic view of kingship, centred on the king as a man and moving outwards to establish how his good will can be put into practice. As a result, his account of the king's virtues and the good arrangement of his household would suit almost any prosperous household head. In particular, in increasing contrast with practice both in France and in England, he imagines the king living on his ancestral resources, without raising additional taxation, by consent or otherwise.

This conception of kingship as a form of lordship committed to the common profit can also be perceived in fourteenth-century English complaint poetry, although in less explicitly Aristotelian terms. These poems complain that the people are brought low by the king's fiscal demands, and yet they do so not by contesting taxation in itself but through an ethical and pragmatic model of good management, focused on the misdeeds of officials. The early fourteenth-century *Song of the Husbandman*, for example, begins in the voice of men of the land complaining that they must work ceaselessly to live since 'every fourth penny must go to the king' (8). This at first seems an unambiguous reference to the direct taxation of the late thirteenth and fourteenth centuries, raised as a proportion of the movable goods of the kingdom, before it is realised that a tax had not been raised at such a high level since 1194. In fact, this is a more general, hyperbolic complaint against royal taxation. Indeed, the next stanza moves away from royal demands to manorial officials: the hayward and woodward, the bailiff and, later, the beadle. It is they who 'rob the poor man who is of little account' (19). This part of the poem recalls treatises on estate management aimed at lords and their senior officers, such as the late thirteenth-century *Senechaucy*, which list the different types of manorial officials, explaining how to supervise them and how to avoid being cheated.[8] The *Song of the Husbandman* then returns to the king's taxes, but from the poet's point of view, and that of real peasants, their suffering was just as bad whether the self-serving officers who afflicted them worked for the lord or the king.

A similar conception of the faults of royal government as a result of the misdeeds of officials is seen in *Against the King's Taxes* and *The Simonie*. In the former, a specific expedition of the king 'over the sea' (8) is condemned since it was undertaken without the consent of 'the commons (*la commune*) of his land' (13–14) and 'without counsel' (20). This leads to a tax of a fifteenth, passed on from year to year, inflicting 'common harm' (24) and forcing the 'common folk' (*commune gent*) to sell cows, tools and clothing (27–8). Not only were these taxes granted as a result of evil counsel but the king does not even benefit from them, as a result of the misdeeds of his agents. The king does not receive half of what is raised (33–4), yet he could easily find enough among the rich (61–70), in particular those who granted the tax (87–90). The poor suffer and the rich are spared, people grow proud on the goods of others, which is just like robbery (81–104). If this continues, and the poor find a leader, they might rise in rebellion (121–30).

The Simonie situates similar complaints about how the king's profit is compromised by the corruption of his agents within a more general account of how all ranks of society pursue personal gain at the expense of their allotted role. After passing from the faults of venial clergy to those of knights, this poem arrives at the errors of the justices, sheriffs, mayors and bailiffs who 'could make dark night out of the fair day' ('kunnen of the faire day make the derke nihti') (289–90). When troops are raised for the king's wars, the strongest men in each vill pay to stay at home, sending forth 'a wretch that could not help himself | if he needed to | so the king is deceived and poor men injured by bribery' ('a wrecche that may noht helpe himselve | At nede | Thus is the king deceyved and pore men shent for mede') (298–300). Again, half the money raised in tax goes missing before it reaches the king (313–17). If the king was well advised, he would have no need to pillage the poor, since he could easily find the money among his own officials (319–24). Such men 'play with the king's silver' ('pleien wid the kinges silver') and the king is left with little, 'When every man has had his part, the king has the least | Every man is out to fill his own purse' ('Whan everi man hath his parte, the king hath the leste, | Everi man is aboute to fille his owen purse') (332–3).

These poems do not deny the legitimacy of raising extraordinary, direct taxation in itself but attack specific levies since the money does not profit the king but is diverted to his self-interested agents. These works thus represent an extension of the conceptualisation of kingship as an amalgam of lordship and the common profit found in *De Regimine Principum*. Royal lordship should be directed towards the common good of the people, and if this is so then the common profit can be served simply by ensuring efficient administration. If all was well, and the king well advised and supported by trustworthy officers, then the king's profit and the common profit would be identical. Even *Against the King's Taxes*, which ascribes the royal expedition to bad counsel, does not argue that the king should wage war out of his own resources.

One of the first poems of the alliterative revival, *Winner and Waster*, which dates from the 1350s or 1360s, goes even further in this direction. Whereas the poem was once seen as a critique of excessive fiscal demands, it has recently been convincingly argued that it is better to interpret it as a staged debate between the drive to accumulation (Winner) and the drive to expenditure (Waster) implicit in any lordly household, including the king's.[9] Winner's money-raising activities are not linked to the impoverishment of the poor by taxation but on the contrary to the improved management of the king's lands (288–93). Waster's critique of Winner focuses on the absence of charity implied by accumulating riches for riches' sake, not on the suffering that was caused by extracting them in the first place (253–62). The poet does not mention exceptional taxation, nor does he worry about the legitimate raising of profit from the king's lands.

Even the most radical of our texts chose different targets than negotiated direct taxation. William of Pagula wrote his *Mirror of King Edward III* (1331–2) to condemn 'purveyance', that is, the compulsory purchase of goods, initially supposed to supply the royal household but which was increasingly used to victual the king's armies. William not only compared this activity to theft, and alluded darkly to the likely rebellion it would cause, but even went so far as to threaten the young Edward III with the recent fate of his deposed father. Yet it is telling that it was purveyance, not taxes on movables, that William chose to criticise, even though he was writing after the four decades of unprecedented direct taxation that had begun in the 1290s, and as negotiations were once more ongoing for a further grant to fund war in Scotland. More typical was the convenient advice of Walter of Milemete who noted, in the tradition of the *Secretum Secretorum*, that it was 'useful for the king and productive for the republic that the king has rich subjects, inasmuch as the greater the amount of the riches subjects possess, the better they are able to serve the king in all royal business'.[10] It was lords who oppressed their tenants whom the king ought to be careful to correct, so that his projects might prosper.

It took the sharp wit of William Langland to dare to observe that the 'the Kynges profit' could threaten both the 'confort of the commune' and the 'Kynges soule' (*Piers Plowman*, B-text, IV.150–1). He would later have Conscience upbraid a king who, speaking after a lord who sees no problem having his officers take all they can from his peasants, asserts that he can take his subject's goods simply because he is their head and they are mere members (XIX.463–80). Yet Conscience's correction is milder than William of Pagula's, imposing only the condition that the king defend his kingdom 'in reson, right wel and in truthe | That thow have thyn askyng as the lawe asketh' (481–3). The king's profit and the common profit were usually held to be identical, an identity guaranteed by the king's conscience, his concern for his reputation and his fate in the afterlife, and especially by the diligent monitoring of officials.

The King and the Law, Justice and Mercy

Another way the king was different from other lords was in his relationship to justice and law. Justice is discussed as an essential characteristic of the king in the *Secretum Secretorum*, book III, in the exercise of which he came to resemble God through his use of reason. Yet already in Giles of Rome's *De Regimine Principum* it was clear that there is more to it than that.

In the second part of book III, which considers government in times of peace, Giles argues that hereditary kingship is the best form of government, explicitly contradicting Aristotle. This argument is constructed in terms of the likelihood of promoting the common good, notably in ensuring peace (III.ii.3–5). Later, Giles argues, again against Aristotle, that a good king is better than a good law, since the law determines things in general and cannot account for the conditions specific to each particular case (III.ii.29). A good ruler could consider particular circumstances, sometimes behaving more mildly than the law prescribed, sometimes more harshly.

This argument used to be cited in isolation as evidence for Giles's 'absolutist' views, contrasted with those imagined to be characteristic of English kingship.[11] Yet Giles was as keen to demonstrate that the king should know and follow the law as he was to argue for its flexibility in the name of mercy or severity. Giles insists that the law, whether established by the prince or the people, must be both rightful and directed to the common profit:

> For If the common profit is not desired in the law, then it is not rightful (*recta et regularis*), but perverse and tyrannical. For as the king differs from a tyrant, because a king (*rex*) is so called who acts rightly (*recte agit*) and desires the common good, whereas the tyrant rules perversely and desires his own private profit, a law is rightful and royal in that it intends the common good, and differs from perverse and tyrannical [law] which intends private good. (III.ii.26)

Ruling by laws, indeed, is the essence of 'politics', since just as medicine serves to regulate and balance the humours of the human body using medicines, so 'political science is [the science] of the rule of the kingdom and the city, by laws and by other things which are taught in it to balance and regulate human actions, so that the citizens live justly, and behave as they should' (III.ii.28). Even if it is the king who legislates, and even if he exercises mercy or severity on occasion, Giles's account of the evil fate of tyrants makes it clear that to make laws or bypass the laws for personal gain invited a bad end (III.ii.14).

How did this view of the relationship between the king and the law compare to the conceptualisation of the same in England? Did, for example, the English believe that the laws of the kingdom were established, perhaps by authority of the king, but only with the assent of the people? Was the English king, perhaps, more tightly bound to observe the letter of established law than was the king of France? What immediately springs to mind here is the English king's coronation oath as it existed after the addition of a fourth clause, probably at the coronation of Edward II in 1308. The king first swore to confirm the laws and customs granted by his predecessors, and especially those granted to the clergy and the people by Edward the Confessor; he swore to keep peace in God, for God, Holy Church, the clergy and the people; he swore to do, in all his judgements, equal and right justice, in mercy and truth. In 1308, however, the English king also swore to keep the laws and rightful customs which the community of his realm *would* choose, to defend and to enforce them. It was thus implied that the community of the kingdom would legislate in the future and that the king was bound by oath to defend and enforce the resulting laws and customs.

As we have seen in earlier chapters, this was not an abstract problem. Civil wars had been fought in an attempt to impose Magna Carta and the reforms laid out by the Provisions of Oxford in 1258, at first accepted by the king and then repudiated. Since the political crisis of 1297, it had proved impossible to make Edward I abide by the concessions he made in parliament. In the reign of Edward II, this problem returned, as the political community repeatedly attempted to enforce the extensive reform programme known as the Ordinances. Finally, in 1327, Edward II was deposed and replaced by his fifteen-year-old son. What did all this do to English conceptions of the relationship between the king and the law?

In fact, neither the dream vision works of the alliterative revival nor later English 'mirrors for princes' give us reason to believe that English writers fundamentally reworked their conception of kingship to fit local practice. Instead, as in the case of taxation, they supplemented and adapted thirteenth-century scholastic orthodoxy. Once again, William Langland is the most radical. On his arrival in the Prologue of *Piers Plowman* in the B-text (c. 1379), the King is led by knighthood, but '[m]ight of the communes made hym to regne' (112–13). The strength of the 'commons' is thus the basis of his reign, but does that mean that it is on their authority that he rules? The next lines cast doubt on this. The embodiment of natural law, 'Kynde Wit' arrives and makes 'clerkes' who are charged '[f]or to counseillen the Kyng and the Commune save' (114–15). The King, Knighthood and Clergy then decree that 'the Commune sholde hem communes fynde' (116–17): the Commons provide 'commons', that is, food. Led by Kynde Wit, the 'Commune' then contrive crafts and ordain ploughmen 'for profit of al the peple' to till and work 'as trewe lif asketh' (118–20). It thus seems that the commons make the king reign in the sense that they provide the material basis for the existence of king, knights and clergy, much as is described in book II, part ii of *De Regimine Principum*.

But not quite: we are then told that '[t]he Kynge and the Commune and Kynde Wit the thridde' together shape 'lawe and leaute', or lawfulness (121–2). This at first sounds like a shared legislative power between king, commons and natural law, but it is then glossed as 'each should know his own' (122), invoking the idea that justice consisted in each fulfilling the role apportioned to his estate, found also in complaint poetry. Three speakers then intervene, foregrounding different aspects of the relationship between the king and the law. The 'lunatik' first provides the carrot, commending the King and his kingdom to Christ's keeping. He wishes that the King shall 'lede thi lond so leaute thee lovye' ('lead thy land so lawfulness loves you'), and that he shall be rewarded in heaven for his 'rightful rulyng' (125–7). An angel then proffers the stick, declaring that though he is now king and ruler, he will perhaps be neither one day, a remark with which William of Pagula had threatened Edward III.[12] That said, the laws to be enforced are the laws of Christ the King, and the angel's message is that the King should rule according to divine law, by which human laws should be corrected (128–38). Finally a 'goliardeis' answers the angel: 'Since "king" (*rex*) is said to take his name from "ruling" (*regere*) | You will have the name without the thing unless you take care to keep the laws' (141–2). These criss-crossing declarations are followed by a final pronouncement, addressed by 'the commune' to 'the Kynges counseil', acknowledging that 'The king's precepts are to us the chains of law!' (145). This in turn serves to announce Langland's famous depiction of a parliament of rats and mice, with its proposal to bell the cat 'for oure commune profit' (169), an idea which a wise mouse rejects since 'hadde ye rattes youre wille, ye kouthe noght rule yourselve' (201).

Langland thus puts forward multiple aspects of a problem without seeking to reconcile them. What emerges is that, in England, law is shaped by the king, the commons and natural law, rather than just the first and the last of this Trinity. The king is encouraged to rule lawfully by the prospect of a reward in heaven, warned to temper human laws by divine law, but also urged that unless he has the laws observed he will have the name of king without the substance. The commons confirm that the king's orders are binding upon them, and even mice victimised by a bothersome cat accept that a flawed authority is better than no authority at all, lest the rats do even worse. The result is a multifaceted picture which modified scholastic theory only slightly to produce a conceptualisation of kingship which fitted English practice rather well.

The English-language 'mirrors for princes' in book VII of John Gower's *Confessio Amantis* (1386–90) and the second half of Thomas Hoccleve's *The Regiment of Princes* (1410–11) are if anything more affirmative than *Piers Plowman* that the king must obey the law.[13] That said, they are considerably less 'left wing' in their account of where these laws derive from. John Gower begins his account of 'Practique' or practical philosophy with its traditional threefold division into the 'thre thinges | Toward the governance of kings' (1649–50), that is, 'Etique', 'Iconomique' and 'Policie'. The first two are outlined swiftly before turning to the five points of 'Policie', which Gower identifies as Truth, Liberality, Justice, Pity and Chastity, in a manner closer to the *Secretum Secretorum* than Giles of Rome. Gower's discussion of 'politics' actually incorporates 'ethics' and (under 'liberality') 'economics' too.

Gower packs the desiderata of law and justice, which occupy book III, part ii of Giles' *De Regimine Principum*, into the section on Justice in *Confessio Amantis*. It is first asked, rhetorically: 'What is a king in his ligance, | Wher that ther is no lawe in londe? What is to take lawe on honde, | Bot if the jugges weren trewe?' (2698–701). Much as in the *Secretum*, this is less about the Thomist distinction between divine, natural and positive law which animates Giles's discussion than about the king's obligation to rule rightly, following conscience and reason. We are told that the power of a king is great, but that a worthy king should avoid wrong where he can (2725–7). The marginal Latin gloss aligns this to the observance of laws, but as an aid to the king, not a bridle: 'It is fitting for imperial majesty to be armed not only with weapons but also with laws.' The king must first ensure his own deeds are virtuous before delivering justice to poor and rich without exception (2743–5). Gower then observes, like Giles, that since the king cannot do justice everywhere at once, he must appoint judges to govern his people, and that they should be 'lerned', 'trewe' and 'wise' (2751–3). The people are glad and 'stant upriht' when 'lawe stonde with the riht' (2759–60). The 'comun poeple' can be readily ruled where the 'lawe is resonable' but 'if the lawe torne amis, | The poeple also mistorned is' (2760–4). A bad law thus leads to an unquiet people, but this law does not derive from the collective will.

Gower explains where the law should come from through the story of Ligurgius, king of Athens. Ligurgius, we are told, held the laws and ruled so well that there was peace without discord, and '[r]ichesse upon the comun good | And noght upon the singuler | Ordeigned was' (2928–34). One day, Ligurgius calls a parliament. He tells his subjects that the god Mercury taught him the laws he established and now wants Ligurgius to meet him on an island. He has his people swear to observe his laws in his absence, but then never returns. Consequently, they are bound to observe his laws in perpetuity. Thus, in Athens, no good law was ever annulled that was 'for comun profit set' (3004–7). So it is in the present day: 'lawe is come among ous alle' and 'every king' is held to it, because 'thing which is of kinges set, | With kinges oghte it noght be let' (3071–2). There can be no right where there is no law in the land, and a king 'which is to lawe swore' must understand that if the law is not executed '[i]t makth a lond torne up so doun | Which is unto the king a sclandre' (3075–83). The king must enforce the law, and if he does not the kingdom will fall into disorder, but this law derives from earlier kings, inspired by God. There is no sense here that the king needs the assent of the people to make law, or indeed that fresh legislation ever occurs. All this in a kingdom where, as Gower well knew, the king regularly called parliaments which promulgated a considerable volume of new laws, certainly by the king's authority, but undeniably in response to the petitions adopted by the Commons on the grounds they served the common good.

In Thomas Hoccleve's *Regiment of Princes*, the king is unambiguously bound to keep the law, notably by his coronation oath, but the content of law and justice is treated as self-evident and eternal: a matter of doing to each according to their estate, following the law of God, suppressing crime and protecting peace and property. The question of how and by whom law might be determined is simply not raised. Hoccleve begins his 'mirror' by insisting on the king's duty to 'truth', that is, keeping faith and especially his oaths (2158–465), before moving on, like Gower, to 'justice'. Again, this means 'gevynge unto every wight | That longeth to his propre dignitee' (2466–7). He who wishes to keep lawful justice must learn to follow the law of Christ (2501–3). Justice restrains shedding of blood and punishes guilt; it defends possessions and keeps people from oppression (2511–14). It is, indeed, the purpose of kingship: 'A kyng is maad to keepen and mayteene | Justice, for shee makith obeissant | The misdoers that prowde been and keene' (2515–17). It is also the purpose of the coronation oath: 'A kyng is by covenant | Of ooth maad in his coronacioun | Bownde to justice sauvacion' (2519–21).

Yet this leads not to a discussion of how the king might align his own behaviour to the law but rather to how he should ensure that his officials do justice. Hoccleve tells the future Henry V to keep 'your lawes', observe them and not offend against them (2774–8). Law is both the lock and the key of 'seuretee' and 'whyl lawe is kept in londe, | A prince in hist estat may sikir stonde [i.e. stand sure]' (2778–80). The point is that the king must have the law enforced, preventing evildoers from violently taking the goods of others. This, too, is the thrust both of the invitation to think on death and to consider the importance of the voice of the people. A king should 'governe and gye' his kingdom since 'whoso lyveth wel, wel shal he dye' (2870–1). If he does so, he shall win the people's voice, which is a potent intercessor with God. That is how Hoccleve construes the expression *Vox populi, vox Dei*: 'wynneth your peples vois, | For peples vois is Goodes vois, men seyn' (2885–6).

The purpose of the king therefore is to maintain law and justice, the purpose of law and justice is to maintain peace, and the king who does so will be rewarded with worldly felicity and eternal salvation. Exemplary rigour is only half the story, however, and Gower and Hoccleve go on to consider the importance of pity. Yet neither of these works are interested in how legislation occurred in their own day, and to what extent the king might be bound by that. What concerns them is the balance between due severity and appropriate mercy. Langland, too, in the complaint of Peace against Wrong in Passus IV of *Piers Plowman* insists on the consequences of over-hasty and ill-motivated forgiveness. The King refuses to acquit Wrong for his physical assault against Peace, simply because the latter has been bought off by Mede, the embodiment of material reward. As the King notes, if Wrong gets off so lightly, he will soon reoffend (106–7). Mercy should only come when the guilty party has shown humility and should only be exercised when 'the Kynges counseil be the commune profit' (123).

These were problems which interested Chaucer, too.[14] His *Tale of Melibee* stages a similar assault against a man's household, and the dialogue between Melibee and Dame Prudence serves to steer him away from the desire for extra-legal vengeance towards the observation of due process. The portrayal of Theseus in the *Knight's Tale*, meanwhile, shows a king whose first impulse is for rigorous application of the letter of the law but who is steered by female intervention and the passage of time into a more amenable, merciful stance. When he comes across the protagonists Palamon and Arcite, openly declaring their offences against him, Theseus's first judgement is to have them both summarily executed. But this sentence is tempered by the intervention of his queen and his sister, Emilia, the object of their competing affections, and replaced with a judicial battle, with the winner taking Emilia's hand. This is once more downgraded on the day itself to a judicial tournament with non-fatal weapons. Theseus thus moves step by step from rigour to mercy, combining a respect for the law with a willingness to temper it. The people react by intervening for Theseus with God: 'The voys of peple touchede the hevene | So loude cride they with murie stevene | "God save swich a lord, that is so good, | He wilneth no destruccion of blood!"' (2561–4).

Conclusion: Counsel and Expertise, Flattery and Liberality

Late medieval kingship, in England as elsewhere, was conceptualised as an extended form of lordship. The most decisive contribution to reconceptualising kingship in the later Middle Ages was a twofold adaptation from scholastic Aristotelianism: the progression from 'ethics', to 'economics', to 'politics'; and the primacy of the common good over individual interests. So well were these imports welded onto the kind of kingship-lordship prevalent in France and England in the later thirteenth century that although it proved possible to adapt it to incorporate some developments – direct taxation justified by necessity and negotiated by forms of political representation – it took considerably longer to incorporate others – the role of the community in legislation, for example. The king could be called upon to combat the offences of his self-interested officials against the profit of both himself and the kingdom, and English writers never tired of walking the line between exemplary justice and mercy, but the involvement of the people in legislation proved much more difficult to incorporate.

Arguably, this was a result of the kind of men who wrote these treatises: men of education, royal officials and university graduates, sometimes clerics and sometimes laymen, but never the great nobles or powerful ecclesiastics who had the right and even the duty to offer the king their counsel. Such lesser men risked being considered impertinent in offering their advice to kings, and even treasonous if that advice shaded into the kind of criticism that might label a king as a tyrant, and thus likely to suffer deposition and death. Like Giles of Rome or the *Secretum Secretorum*, what they offered was counsel, which is to say expertise, and the acceptance of their advice relied on the perceived value of that expertise. Yet Giles was the first Augustinian regent master of theology at the university of Paris, and the *Secretum Secretorum* author was supposed to be Aristotle himself. Our English writers had no such claims to authority. This is one reason why, if they accuse a king of tyranny, that is, ruling for his own interests not the common good, it is only once he has been safely deposed.

It also helps explain why these writers constantly hark on the importance of counsel and decry the evils of flattery, going considerably beyond the practical advice on choosing good counsellors offered by their sources. These men had to be good counsellors and not flatterers, otherwise they were nothing, yet they were engaged in an activity which looked a lot like flattery: talking up the merits of their advice in the hope of favour.[15] Thus although the author of the *Crowned King* recommends the advice of 'suche a man that loueth not to lye, | A faithfull philosophre that flatre woll never' (109–10), he has already literally lied himself by asserting that he will talk in plain prose, not verse (46–7). Establishing the desirability of speaking out is the major purpose of *Mum and the Sothsegger*, and Thomas Hoccleve and the poet of *Richard the Redeless* spend much of their work bemoaning the excessive influence of overdressed youths, contrasted with their own earthy, aged directness.[16] In the *Confessio Amantis*, too, the flatterer is the perfect Aristotelian bad advisor: proffering advice which serves his own interests, not the common good, by telling the king what he wants to hear (VII.2165–694).

The ambiguous status of these writers also partly explains why they are so interested in liberality as a mean between prodigality and avarice, already a prominent theme in the *Secretum Secretorum* (book I). The king must be liberal enough to preserve his estate without exceeding measure, that is, without impoverishing himself (e.g. VII.2152–8). Yet, although this was a good model for a late medieval lord, and even for an early thirteenth-century English king, it was an inadequate account of the economics of kingship by the end of that century, now that the king's finances had been transformed by grants of taxation negotiated in parliament. 'Economics' was no longer reducible to estate and household management. It was itself a political problem.

In financial matters as elsewhere the opposition between the common good and private interest showed its effectiveness as a rhetoric and as a way of organising thought, but also its limitations as a practical guide to political action. *Richard the Redeless* decries the foolishness of the deposed King Richard II in putting his faith in the badges which attached men to his cause but spread division in society. Did he not realise that at his coronation he had been made lord of all, not simply of a faction (II.47–52)? Certainly, political success could lie in creating belief in a common profit which included the interests of all, and if a king flagrantly behaved like a lord pursuing the sectional interests of himself and his followers, everyone would know he was a tyrant. Yet kingship and the common good could not always be reconciled by standing above the mêlée, as philosophers and poets imagined, since the king often found himself with no option but to act against those who had other ideas about how he should rule. The king was in politics, not above it. The king's profit should have been the common profit, but often it was not.

Notes

1. Sir John Fortescue, *The Governance of England*, ed. C. Plummer (London, 1885), 109.
2. Latin text in *Opera hactenus inedita Rogeri Baconi: Fasc. V*, ed. R. Steele (Oxford, 1920). For English translations, adaptations and expansions: *Secretum Secretorum: Nine English Versions*, ed. M. A. Manzaloui (Oxford, 1977).
3. For a close Middle English translation: *The Governance of Kings and Princes: John Trevisa's Middle English Translation of the De Regimine Principum of Aegedius Romanus*, ed. D. C. Fowler, C. F. Briggs and P. G. Remley (New York, 1997).
4. C. F. Briggs, *Giles of Rome's De Regimine Principum: Reading and Writing Politics at Court and University, c. 1275–c. 1525* (Cambridge, 1999), 3, 5.
5. *The Simonie*, ed. J. Dean (Kalamazoo, MI, 1996); *The Complete Harley 2253 Manuscript*, ed. S. G. Fein, D. Raybin and J. Ziolkowski (Kalamazoo, MI, 2015), items 114, 31.
6. *Political Thought in Early Fourteenth-Century England: Treatises by Walter of Milemete, William of Pagula and William of Ockham*, ed. and trans. C. J. Nederman (Tempe, AZ, 2002).
7. *Wynnere and Waster and The Parlement of the Thre Ages*, ed. W. Ginsberg (Kalamazoo, MI, 1992); William Langland, *The Vision of Piers Plowman: B-Text*, ed. A. V. C. Schmidt (London, 1978); *The Piers Plowman Tradition*, ed. H. Barr (London, 1993).
8. *Walter of Henley and Other Treatises on Estate Management and Accounting*, ed. D. Oschinsky (Oxford, 1971).
9. W. M. Ormrod, *Winner and Waster and Its Contexts: Chivalry, Law and Economics in Fourteenth-Century England* (Cambridge, 2021).
10. *Political Thought*, ed. Nederman, 50–1.
11. Briggs, *Giles of Rome's DRP*, 60–2.
12. *Political Thought*, ed. Nederman, 105.
13. John Gower, *Confessio Amantis*, in *The English Works*, ed. G. C. Macaulay (London, 1900); Thomas Hoccleve, *The Regiment of Princes*, ed. Charles R. Blyth (Kalamazoo, MI, 1999).
14. For the texts, see *The Riverside Chaucer*, 3rd ed., ed. L. D. Benson (Oxford, 1988).
15. J. Ferster, *Fictions of Advice: The Literature and Politics of Council in Late Medieval England* (Philadelphia, 1996), 137–59.
16. H. Barr, *Signes and Sothe: Language in the Piers Plowman Tradition* (Cambridge, 1994), 51–94.

Further Reading

Baldwin, A. P., *The Theme of Government in Piers Plowman* (Cambridge, 1987).
Briggs, C. F. and Eardley, P. S., eds., *A Companion to Giles of Rome* (Leiden, 2016).
Ferster, J., *Fictions of Advice: The Literature and Politics of Counsel in Late Medieval England* (Philadelphia, 1996).
Giancarlo, M., *Parliament and Literature in Late Medieval England* (Cambridge, 2007).
Kempshall, M., *The Common Good in Late Medieval Political Thought* (Oxford, 1999).
Kendall, E., *Lordship and Literature: John Gower and the Politics of the Great Household* (Oxford, 2008).
Matthews, D., *Writing to the King: Nation, Kingship and Literature in England, 1250–1340* (Cambridge, 2010).
Nuttall, J., *The Creation of Lancastrian Kingship: Literature, Language and Politics in Late Medieval England* (Cambridge, 2007).
Perkins, N., *Hoccleve's Regiment of Princes: Counsel and Constraint* (Cambridge, 2001).
Perret, N.-L. and Péquignot, S., eds., *A Critical Companion to the 'Mirrors for Princes' Literature* (Leiden, 2023).
Rigby, S. H., *Wisdom and Chivalry: Chaucer's Knight's Tale and Medieval Political Theory* (Leiden, 2009).
Williams, S. J., *The Secret of Secrets: The Scholarly Career of a Pseudo-Aristotelian Text in the Later Middle Ages* (Ann Arbor, MI, 2003).

Part V

Reflection

JOHN WATTS

19

English Kingship in a European Context

Introduction

If Edward I had died in the course of his conquest of Wales in the early 1280s, his successor would not have been the notorious Edward II, but King Alfonso I, born at Bayonne in 1273, and named after his godfather, the queen's brother and king of Castile. In fact, Alfonso was to die a child in 1284, just as Edward's first two sons had done, but the details of his life are a reminder that English kingship was not just – or even, at times, very – English.[1] The kings of England, descended from Normans and Angevins in the male line, wished to be leading figures on the European stage, and they jealously defended lands, rights and connections across the continent, as well as in these islands. Historians have often been impatient with Richard II's scheme to seek election as Holy Roman Emperor, the grandest secular estate in Latin Europe, but – as Michael Bennett has recently pointed out – Richard had nobbled two of the seven Electors, and the son of one of these obtained the Empire just a year after his deposition.[2] Twelfth- and thirteenth-century kings had maintained a close interest in the Empire, and Henry III's brother, Richard of Cornwall, was actually elected Emperor in 1257, and managed to exercise power in large parts of the huge territory. A few centuries later, Henry VIII's interest in the role was at least as serious as that of the king of France, even if both of them were out-classed by the Habsburg heir, Charles of Ghent. Henry III had also been angling for the quasi-imperial position of papal lieutenant, which was offered to his brother in the early 1250s, in preference to Charles of Anjou, and was then bestowed on his younger son, Edmund Crouchback, complete with the crown of Sicily.[3]

These plans failed, just as Edmund of Langley's and John of Gaunt's attempts to secure Castile failed (though both Castile and Portugal acquired English queens in the wake of the conflict); so too did Humphrey of Gloucester's plan to rule a large part of the Low Countries, with similar territories later offered by the French king to Edward IV, and then to Warwick the Kingmaker; but – as is well known – English kings and their families succeeded in ruling other lands outside England.[4] They conquered and held great swathes of France between the 1340s and the 1370s and again between the 1410s and the 1450s; Edward III, in 1359, and Edward IV, in 1475, made attempts on the French crown only to withdraw, but Henry V accepted the succession to that honour in 1420, and his son was crowned king of France in 1431. The English kings of this period also made multiple attempts to assert their claim to the throne of Scotland, and Richard of Gloucester was set up with a palatine principality of Cumberland in the early 1480s to encourage him in that enterprise. Later in the fourteenth century, and again from the 1490s, and more determinedly from the 1530s, there were quite serious efforts to extend and flesh out royal rule in Ireland, which was elevated from the status of lordship to kingdom by Henry VIII in 1541.

So English kings repeatedly sought to rule over a much larger space than their small kingdom in southern Britain, and this must have implications for how we think about 'English kingship': it is not clear that the rule of England can be isolated from the wider concerns of the ruler. At the same time, however, the crown of England was the centrally important asset possessed by this family of Franco-Hispano-British adventurers. The Plantagenets were kings at all because they were kings of England, and that ancient kingdom supplied the bulk of their financial, military and political resources. England was also a political community with its own institutional and constitutional definition, its own laws and customs and its own church, already recognised as *ecclesia anglicana*. This community was closely bound up with the king who ruled it, and he in turn swore to protect its laws, church, territory and people, demanding the *iura regni* – the rights of the kingdom, in fact the service of his subjects and a share in their property – in return. From this perspective, then, the king of England was a public officer, with a series of rights and duties in relation to English subjects, whatever else he might claim and seek to realise outside the kingdom: as Sir John Fortescue put it, in the mid fifteenth century, 'though his estate be the highest estate temporall in the erthe, yet it is an office in wich he mynestrith to his reaume defence and justice'.[5]

From this perspective, then, it is not wrong to think of an English government, and to assume that it entailed a prominent role for the king. And it is also not wrong to compare the English political system, or polity, to others in Europe (and elsewhere). In fact, synchronic comparisons of this kind are still quite unusual. There are some British Isles examples, and some Anglo-French and Anglo-German comparative work; there are also some pan-European treatments, some by historians and some also by political scientists, both in the 'grand historical sociology' tradition of the 1970s and 1980s and, more recently, in the wake of the 'historical turn' in political science. But the main comparative tradition in the study of English kingship has been diachronic, rather than synchronic – it has looked at English kingship over time, typically in relation to the rise of liberal institutions: the common law; parliament; and government by cabinet or prime minister. In the classic – 'whig' – narratives of English constitutional history in the nineteenth century, the best kings accepted legal and representative restraints and gradually surrendered their prerogatives, while the worst ones fought to retain or even to extend them, provoking a series of confrontations, culminating in the seventeenth-century civil war, the execution of Charles I and the short-lived republic that followed. This well-established and long-standing developmental account – only partially discarded today – has a number of interpretative consequences. It minimises the connections of the kings with the rest of Europe, drawing a sharp distinction between internal politics (which it prioritises) and foreign affairs, which are regarded as interruptions to the national story. It makes English kingship seem unique, simply through its insular focus, although, as we shall see, England's kings and their regime shared many characteristics with other European rulers. Inasmuch as there were unusual features of English kingship – and every other regime and polity had these too, of course – they arose as much from geography, economy and contingency as from a special path of constitutional development.

In placing English kingship in a European context, then, we have to do two things. We can make comparisons and ask what was distinctive about the English political system and the part the king played in it; but we must also acknowledge the connections that linked these kings to the many other players on the European scene, both their common European inheritance and their determined maintenance of interests and relationships throughout our period. Historians of the 'global middle ages', who have faced this same tension between comparison and the study of connection, have argued for a 'combinative' approach, and that is what will be attempted here.[6] The same rulers who spent the bulk of their time at Westminster, Windsor and other Thames-side palaces, wished to exercise power and influence all over Europe and not only in the tight little English kingdom. At the same time, the dynamics of that kingdom influenced their capacity to exert themselves outside it.

Comparison: Underlying Structures

The king of England, like every other king, moved in a world shaped by structures which were common to much of Europe: in particular, the Latin church, headed by the papacy, and its sizeable body of law, theology and philosophy, its Vulgate Bible and common liturgies; the Roman Law which underpinned church (canon) law and was read in every university and chancery; Latin rhetorical tradition, or *dictamen*, which influenced all governmental writing; epics, romances and fables, shared across European languages; the cultures of warfare, chivalry and courtliness; and the customary hierarchies and service ties of aristocrats and peasants associated with what we used to call 'feudalism'. Its kings were crowned according to rites which would have been recognisable to other Europeans; they inherited and married according to customs shared with other parts of the continent; they benefited from similar processes of legal and bureaucratic development to the rulers of other territories. But, of course, like the rulers of everywhere else, they also had some distinctive characteristics, born from local conditions. In the shaping of English monarchy, great emphasis has always been laid on the Norman Conquest of 1066, which established a line of kings who claimed to own all the rights of the crown and all the land of England, so that everyone else held land of them, according to the laws and customs that they agreed to enforce.[7] This major event, and the destruction or suppression of the Old English aristocracy which followed, laid the foundations for an unusually complete royal authority over English subjects, but it was afforced by two other major factors. One of these was the well-established administrative tradition of pre-Conquest England, with its shires and their courts and officers, its universal taxes and its traditions of governmental writing and inquiry. The other was the accident of geography which established a single kingdom in the lowlands, centred on London and Kent, Wessex and Mercia, protected by the sea, and extended into the north, east and west by an ongoing process of conquest which ultimately engulfed Wales and hammered out a boundary with Scotland.

These basic features of English kingship underpinned three distinctive phenomena in our period: first, a common law, which was the custom of the king's court and was imposed practically everywhere by a net of officers and institutions; second, a tradition of intense government by royal officers – judges, sheriffs, tax collectors and commissioners of various kinds – albeit that many of these were unpaid amateurs, aristocrats in the shires and oligarchs in the towns; and third, a bicameral parliament, developing between about the 1230s and the early fourteenth century, in which all freeborn English people were understood to be represented. All three phenomena developed over the period of this book. The common law grew in volume and authority, encompassing statutes from Magna Carta onwards, as well as new forms of writ-based action. It reached down into manors, as villeins gained their freedom in the second half of the fourteenth century; and royal jurisdiction was imposed more forcefully and consistently on counties and towns, on privately held liberties and franchises, and even on the church, whose officers were held in check by the 1340s Statutes of Provisors and Praemunire, before being subjected to explicit royal authority in the 1530s (canon law – the law of the church – was permitted to continue, but only under royal supervision). The intensity of royal government persisted and increased, and the social elites whose property was protected by the law – lords, knights and esquires, wealthy merchants – were managed and monitored by the crown as far as was practicable: their private networks were circumscribed and infiltrated by a mixture of formal regulation and informal supervision. Importantly, there was no privileged caste – nobles were rich and powerful and esteemed, but they were formally subject to the same laws as everyone else, and they and their tenants paid the same taxes; social hierarchy was a fact of life, but – especially after the decline of serfdom – it was only defined informally. Meanwhile, parliament became a well-established institution, meeting virtually every year or two between the 1310s and the 1460s, and levying taxes, receiving petitions, making laws and providing a venue for important public business. The English kingdom had an unusually comprehensive and authoritative representative institution for its size.

These arrangements made the king awesomely powerful. He authorised all government action – judicial and regulatory, military, fiscal – and he led a great deal of it in person; he could intervene in justice, exempt people from the operation of law, direct the spending of incomes, including the large sums levied from his subjects; he insisted on the right to appoint his own officers and counsellors; he had his own household establishment for service and entertaining; and he could use his rights as feudal overlord to shape the holdings of the greatest landowners. These rights and powers were the practical basis of royal authority and could be used to promote order and harmony and the successful defence of the realm (or the conquest of neighbouring peoples). But they were also in tension with the more standardised or public aspects of royal authority – the expectation, enshrined in Magna Carta, that the king was subject to the law and would administer it properly; that he would use his and the realm's resources for the common good, and not waste them or hand them over to private interests; that he would take good advice, from leading figures – lords, bishops, judges – rather than paying too much attention to flimsier types with better access to him. Kings who frustrated these expectations faced conflicts with their subjects, especially when taxation was high or the realm was in peril. Many of these conflicts featured the temporary withdrawal from the king of the power to govern, as supposedly representative councils or regencies were set up in his place; several of them resulted in the deposition, and then the murder, of the king and/or in the usurpation of the throne by one of his near relatives. So there were some contradictory trends in the way the English monarchy had developed: the political system was highly combustible, and the powerful king could be – and often was – brought low by his subjects.

In its underlying structures, England was certainly distinctive when set against other European kingdoms. No other ruler, apart from the pre-1282 kings of Sicily who ruled over territory of a similar size, combined such complete tenurial claims with such complete jurisdiction (see Map 19.1).[8] While the Emperor, the king of France and some other rulers exercised significant authority over great fiefs and apanages, and could regrant them in default of male heirs, their kingdoms contained numerous allods – territories held autonomously – and their control of jurisdiction was much weaker. The French king offered subjects the opportunity to appeal to his high court, the *parlement*, and claimed authority over a widening number of *cas royaux* – cases that only the king could judge – but a great deal of 'middle' and 'low' justice remained in the hands of lords and towns, and the situation in the Empire was worse, with most princes, lords and towns having 'high' justice in their own territories and the Emperor's courts having merely arbitrative authority. Similarly, while kings across the continent created ordinances and royal law codes, these were by no means systematically enforced – indeed royal codes were directly resisted in thirteenth-century Castile and fourteenth-century Bohemia, while the king of Hungary's attempt to bring property cases into his own courts provoked rebellion in 1351. Rulers typically had high courts, for the judgement of their greatest subjects, but sometimes these were under the control of lords (as in Bohemia and Aragon) or towns (as in Catalonia), and a great deal of justice was administered locally and independently of the king in most European kingdoms. Only selectively could most kings intervene judicially, so the political arts of favour or disfavour and a general trend towards appeasement of all but the most unpopular offenders were more prominent features of their administration of justice than the systematic authority of the English king and his judges.

Equally, the relative clarity of lines of authority in England was unusual on the continent. Most kingdoms contained large areas that were only tenuously obedient to the ruler or were claimed by a neighbouring king or lord. In contrast to the English situation, towns, churches and lords had often developed their jurisdictions at the same time as the king, or even ahead of him, and were consequently able to operate with more independence. European rulers had other means of power – taxes from the fourteenth century, networks of vassals and allies, incomes from their extensive domains, and from silver mines and

Map 19.1 Western Europe, c. 1300 (reproduced from J. Watts, *The Making of Polities: Europe, 1300–1500* (Cambridge, 2009), p. 160)

other perks – and they enjoyed all the advantages of ancient prestige or sacrality and personal wealth, but it would not be wrong to argue that their authority was typically superimposed on territories which were full of smaller polities, partly independent and often able to league together or to find other ways of protecting their rights. Although the rulers of continental Europe were centrally important figures in their realms, with exceptional powers, they mostly lacked the penetrative capacity of the English king and were reliant on semi-independent princes, lords or towns to rule the regions under them. Some, like the French kings, had enclaves in the territories of the great princes – based on churches under royal protection.[9] More of them had close relations with towns, which they could use to gather resources and project their power in distant areas, though large towns were complex places, with multiple contending networks and a strong interest in their own independence.

Most continental kings and princes also had their own networks of supporters, including men in the entourages of their greatest subjects, and these too were an important political resource.[10] Equally, many European kingdoms had high-level representative institutions, often with the power to consent to taxes, to petition, or to make laws with the king's agreement. But almost none of these institutions had the power to bind subjects in the manner of the English Parliament: the real negotiations over taxes and laws were carried on outside them, and sometimes not at all; they could be important in signifying a collective voice, whether for or against the ruler's policy, but they were not the main gateways to extraction, and kings frequently made laws without them.[11] In all, then, the rule of continental kings might be characterised as presidential and political, whereas the rule of the English king was almost overwhelming – administratively intense, judicially rooted, but also, like everywhere else, backed by the more flexible political resources entailed in the power to appoint and endow.

Finally, English kings did not typically share authority with their wives or children. Whereas queens were prominent figures in the Iberian kingdoms, often with a constitutional role as their husbands' or sons' lieutenants or regents, their counterparts in England were generally excluded from formal authority: Eleanor of Provence and Philippa of Hainault acted as keepers of England during royal campaigns abroad, but this was unusual, and the general preference was to appoint a male and a council of lords to govern when the king was away. Queens were powerful figures, and many of them acted alongside their husbands, but if they took the lead, like Isabella of France in the mid and late 1320s, or Margaret of Anjou in the later 1450s, this was highly controversial, and even the informal influence of the queen over her husband could be denounced.[12] Royal children were endowed with estates, and often given lieutenancies in Ireland, Gascony, Wales or on the northern border, but when Henry V offered leadership at the centre during his father's illness between 1409 and 1413, this caused tensions.[13] Nothing like the cooperative rule of Emperor Frederick III and his son, Maximilian, king of the Romans, occurred in England (though it is not hard to find evidence of kings' sons leading opposition movements on the continent, just as the relatives of Edward II or Richard II led the critics of these kings). In general, the English system was intensely personal, and no one was allowed to interrupt the key political and constitutional relationship between the king and those counsellors and agents who represented the concerns of his subjects to him.

At the same time, however, it would not do to draw too sharp a contrast between English and continental kings, especially as we are generalising over a very large space and a long time and trying to deduce patterns from bitty evidence which is often highly circumstantial. Something of the judicial penetration of the English king was matched by the fiscal machineries of continental rulers – the networks of Jews and *conversos* (Christian converts) that managed the Castilian king's incomes from his lucrative sales tax, the *alcabala*, for instance: these dominated the governments of the cities, which were the main nodes of provincial authority in Castile.[14] Likewise, the *élus* and lenders who managed the *gabelle* and the *taille* in France, and the royal habit of sharing the massive incomes from taxes with urban governments and tax-exempt princes and lords, whether via pensions or less centralised arrangements, created ties between the ruler and the subjects of every part of his realm.[15] But that reference to sharing is important: these powers and resources were not under the king's exclusive control and could do more to sustain local powers – provinces, cities, lords – than the centre. To some extent that was true of the English king too. He did have direct management of his own tax incomes, and he freely appointed judges and other officers to exercise his jurisdiction, but he had to share elements of the administration of justice with lords and gentlemen, and they looked after a great deal of judicial business, including the task of enforcement, on his behalf. For the maintenance of order, and also for defence, the king was dependent for most of the period on good relations with great lords whose influence rested on legal property and the networks they had built up themselves. In these ways, then, he was not so different from other kings.

That was even more the case in his rule of territories beyond England itself. In England, the king normally had the upper hand in relations with the nobles: he could prevent the outright perversion of justice through checks, balances and close supervision; he could manage the men who raised and commanded his armies by a mixture of laws and funding and his own commitment to military leadership and courtly culture. Outside England, though, his rule was much more like that of a continental king, and often less effective – he had centres of government in Dublin, Bordeaux and for a time Paris and Rouen; he had vassals, allies and supporters in Wales and many parts of France and Ireland, even in some parts of Scotland; but his authority in these areas was essentially political – dependent on his ability to make it effective – and, in practice, it was frequently contested or absorbed by local potentates.

Comparison: Dynamics

The main political and constitutional trajectory across Europe in the centuries covered by this book was a process of governmental expansion and political consolidation, which has often been captured by terms like 'state growth' or 'state formation'. Between the thirteenth century and the sixteenth, European regimes developed a widening range of governmental functions and elaborated these so that they pushed more deeply and consistently into society. These regimes were of all shapes and sizes: even if kings and popes usually led the way, lords, towns, provinces and lesser churches were not far behind. Equally, governments provoked reaction from those they ruled – a mixture of compliance and upward colonisation on the one hand, as subjugated elites sought to exploit the new dispensations, and resistance on the other, as populations sought to amend or shape the terms of their subjection. Both factors meant that the governmental growth of the period was accompanied by copious amounts of conflict. Over the long term, the trend was towards political consolidation – the growth of larger, more complex and more effective polities, typically kingdom-sized and kingdom-like ('regnal', to echo Susan Reynolds), with lesser units, such as towns, lords and churches, accepting subordinate positions – and there were parallel developments in political consciousness: the growth of cultures, histories, literatures, acknowledged customs, associated with each polity; and the rise of comparisons, and interstate relations, between them.[16] As the previous section has already suggested, England followed these paths alongside everywhere else. The question in this section is: did it follow them in the same way? How did it – and its king, specifically – weather the conflicts and challenges of this overall pattern of development?

While all the regnal polities ultimately got better at managing the tasks of government and political inclusion, there is one major difference between England and most others. At the start of our period, England had been a comparatively rich and militarily aggressive kingdom, and its resources grew in the era of taxation, to reach a peak around the middle of the fourteenth century; by the end of the period, its tax incomes had significantly reduced, and its military capacity was distinctly limited. Most European kingdoms went the other way, building up their tax incomes in the fifteenth century, developing large standing armies and investing extensively in artillery, navies and fortifications. Once they had escaped from the Wars of the Roses, English kings tried to do some of the same things, especially under Henry VIII, but they were forced to operate within a much smaller fiscal envelope and to accept the continuation of older mechanisms for raising armies, dependent on the aristocracy and temporary levies.[17] Shut out of France from the 1450s and effectively unable or unwilling to intervene in Scotland between the mid 1480s and the 1540s (the great victory at Flodden in 1513 was the fruit of a Scottish invasion), the English government focused more exclusively on domestic matters – its reformation of the church, its regulation of society and its promotion of commerce – and focused military investment mainly on defence, including in Ireland and on the seas.

Why this was is hard to determine. Part of the answer lies in the civil wars of the second half of the fifteenth century, though similar (if shorter) conflicts also occurred in France and Spain, without halting the expansion of military-fiscal machinery in these countries. Part of the answer lies in the parliamentary basis of taxation, which allowed the classes represented there to limit extraction to what was absolutely necessary for the defence of England, as opposed to the servicing of royal and noble adventurism. Part of the answer probably lies in the thickness of the legal and administrative tradition, which steered the government towards the preservation of the common good of the subjects, who were considered equally as citizens, even if they were highly differentiated in wealth and power. Geography was surely also a factor: unlike almost everywhere else in Europe, as foreign observers noted, England was relatively untouched by war – it had not been invaded since 1216, and its people were used to a higher standard of peaceful government than others.[18] As coastal defences improved, on both sides of the English Channel, English aggression became unthinkably expensive, and the kingdom's protection from foreign invasion was all the stronger; an inward turn and a sharper distinction between 'internal' and 'external' made sense.

Alongside this overall trajectory, and apart from its relative immunity from warfare, the English kingdom experienced a similar gamut of political events to other European kingdoms – popular revolts, succession disputes and inadequate kingship, noble uprisings, civil wars. How did its comparatively centralised and interfering government affect the working out of these challenges? Perhaps the first thing to say is that English political crises were just as highly centralised as the political system, and in two senses: they were, for the most part, national and collective, particularly in their presentation, but also to a large extent in their causation; and they quickly affected the king in person. Let us take these points in turn.

English political crises arose mainly on two grounds – failure of government (wastage of resources, disorder, failure to defend the realm, the king not listening to the complaints of his people) or excessive pressure (unbearable taxation, administrative or judicial high-handedness, tyranny). The people who confronted the king, whether in parliament, or in publicly circulated petitions and manifestos, or in face-to-face confrontations, such as those of Bigod and Bohun with Edward I in 1297, or of Cade's rebels with Henry VI in 1450, almost always acted in peer groups and claimed to act for the common weal of the realm.[19] Of course, there was also usually a personal dimension in the grievances of magnates who challenged the king, and there were regional grievances or influences in popular uprisings – those of Kent and Essex in 1381, or of Kent and Sussex in 1450, or of the south-west in 1497 – but there was certainly something public and national or communitarian in all these risings. So it was that, for instance, Richard Marshal and his allies, rising against Henry III in 1233–4, denounced the infringements of Magna Carta perpetrated by the regime of des Roches and des Rivaux; the Percies, rising against Henry IV, portrayed themselves as defenders of the *res publica*; the Yorkshire rebels of 1489 planned to march on London and claimed to defend the king and the 'Comowns of Engelond, for suche unlawfull poyntes as Seynt Thomas of Cauntyrbery dyed for'.[20] Many confrontations occurred in parliaments, in which the 'community of the realm' was believed to be represented, and the massive popular uprisings of 1381 and 1450, both occurring in the south-east, and both converging on London, saw themselves as completing the reforming work of earlier assemblies: the 'Good Parliament' of 1376 and the parliament that impeached the duke of Suffolk and imposed resumption on Henry VI in 1449–50. Of course, there were many who did not rise in each of these confrontations, and some who defended the government, but the latter were often identified as 'traitors' or 'evil counsellors', and settlements tended to vindicate the protests of the opposition, even if they also insisted on the king's right to be obeyed.

So uprisings claimed to be collective and were – at least to some extent – caused by collective factors: fiscal, judicial, administrative or military failings or oppressions. They were also targeted on the king in person, even though critics and opponents started out by claiming that they were trying to defend him from enemies around him. The English were notorious in France for killing their kings, and five of the eleven kings of our period were indeed murdered.[21] Two of them were formally deposed by their subjects, one declared a bastard, one attainted following his replacement by the true heir to the throne and the other killed in battle. Even the kings who survived confrontations – Henry III in 1258 and 1264, Edward I in his final years, Edward III in 1340–1 – were obliged to accept humiliating restrictions on their freedom to govern, even if these were subsequently overridden or withdrawn; and Edward II, Richard II, Henry IV and Henry VI were subjected to the rule of councils for long periods of time. Paradoxically, these moves were the flip side of the king's overwhelming power: to oppose him was dangerous, and those who started down that path found they had to finish the job. The typical English political crisis consequently involved ever more direct assaults on the king's immediate environment – his council, his household, his friends. The king could best regain the authority to govern by showing that he was listening to his people's complaints, typically by reducing taxation, taking counsel from magnates and prelates, and improving justice and defence. If he dug his heels in, the crisis would deepen, and – however much damage he might do to his opponents (and his friends) – he was likely to face deposition proceedings or a dynastic coup.

Continental confrontations were by no means completely unlike these. It was not uncommon for groups of subjects, typically headed by magnates, to protest against royal rule and demand reforms: that is what happened in France in the 'affair of the leagues' in 1314–15 and in the 'war of the public weal' in 1465, or in Castile between the 1270s and the 1320s and again in the 1460s, when *hermandades*, or brotherhoods, representing the towns and the royal estates (*realengo*), rose up on behalf of the political community against a series of overbearing or inadequate kings.[22] Similar episodes happened almost everywhere, and sometimes they were connected to representative assemblies, as in Aragon in the 1340s, France in the 1350s or Bohemia in the 1390s, but they almost never led to the deposition or death of the king.[23] Castilian rebels deposed their king in effigy in 1465, and had Henry IV or Louis XI of France been captured in the confrontations of that year, they may well have suffered a similar fate to Edward II, Richard II or Henry VI, but continental crises were often less about how a particular person governed and more about clashes of rights and interests between the crown and other powers. In part, this reflected the less unified jurisdiction of continental polities. In part, it was a matter of size – in the large and populous kingdoms of France, the Empire and Castile, the king was physically remote from many of his subjects, whereas England was small in both scale and population, and even its remoter parts were in touch with its overbearing centre. On the continent, conflicts often bore a regional character, where the matters in question were the liberties of a distant or disputed province and its rulers or officers. Tensions over the rule of the north and west in France, or between 'Little' and 'Great' Poland, or between opposing parties in the Holy Roman Empire, or between the rulers of the Kalmar Union and their three kingdoms in fifteenth-century Scandinavia, could persist for decades without leading to the deposition of the kings of these places, and still less to their deaths (Wenceslas IV *was* deposed from the Empire, but there was no question of imprisoning or murdering him).[24] England did not really have these kinds of conflict (though its subject territories did rebel – Gascony in the 1390s, Wales in the 1400s and Ireland was only loosely and partly subordinate).[25]

On the other hand, factional struggles or disputes over the succession could happen anywhere, and these were often both personal and bloody, as in the war of the Armagnacs and Burgundians, or the conflict between Peter I of Castile and his illegitimate competitor Henry of Trastámara (and that explains why Peter was killed, as were several Scottish kings in what were effectively feuds with leading magnates).[26] So there were similarities and differences between English and European political dynamics, but we can say that English crises over kingship were particularly intense, coming to a crescendo quickly, and often resulting in royal bloodshed; if they were not typically regional, they were both constitutional and personal, cutting to the heart of the royal office and the king's own management of his government.

English crises of kingship were also very prolonged. There was a foretaste of this in the twelfth century, when the deadlock of Stephen's reign lasted more than fifteen years, but – as the integration of government and society proceeded – periods of political unease became ever longer. The difficult last years of Edward I set the stage for utter disaster under Edward II, and it took Edward III about a decade to rebuild. Later crises were more enduring still: Edward III's dotage in the 1370s fed into the war-torn reign of Richard II, but trouble persisted under the usurper, Henry IV; only in the 1410s was order fully restored. And the collapse of Henry VI's authority in 1450 led to five more decades of civil war and political uncertainty, which was only laid to rest by the uncontested succession of Henry VIII. These long crises gave the later Middle Ages their bad reputation in English history. We should not exaggerate them – despite the uncertainty at the top, and the greater frequency of parliamentary confrontations, risings, battles, murders and executions, justice was administered, taxation collected and the realm defended during all but the worst few years of each of these periods. To some extent, their identification as times of trouble by both contemporaries and historians reflects the high expectations of political order in the English realm. While continental political crises were typically shorter – the wars of the Burgundians and Armagnacs in France between the 1400s and the 1430s (or later) and the troubles in Naples between the 1340s and the 1440s are exceptions – they often involved more serious and extensive violence, and the differences between external war, internal war and normal politics were less stark.[27]

Connection and Combination

Notwithstanding the famous English victories at Crécy, Poitiers and Agincourt, and the associated conquests of Calais, Normandy and the Île-de-France, we often think of the early Plantagenet period as the high tide of English assertion on the continent – Henry II's empire, stretching from Scotland and Ireland to Bayonne; the ambitions of Henry III's brother and sons in the Empire, Gascony, Sicily and the Holy Land – but the activities and aims of later Plantagenets like Edward III and Henry V were just as far-reaching. Edward bestrode France for a time, and sought to place his sons in Scotland, Ireland, the Low Countries and Castile. Henry V missed becoming king of France by a matter of weeks; his networks reached deeply into the kingdom and also into the Burgundian lands to its north and east; he had the king of Scots in his possession; the Emperor was his ally; and his agents played a central role in the ending of the papal schism and the restoration of papal authority in 1417. We have noted earlier that English kings gradually detached themselves from these horizons over the century from 1450 and shifted to a more consistently determined posture in Britain and Ireland, along (in time) with an Atlantic orientation; but while a continental frame of reference still dominated the thinking of English rulers, as it did for almost all the period of this book, how did it affect the politics of English kingship?

The effects of war on English constitutional development are well known. War had been the engine of English fiscal development and played a central role in the evolution of parliament. As a result, the pursuit of the king's overseas claims always had to be justified in terms of defence and other domestic priorities. So it was that Richard II's government pointed out that war against the French in France was greatly preferable to war against them in England; Edward III and Henry V both had to guarantee that their English subjects would not be made subject to their kingdom of France; and Edward IV tried to claim that his intervention in France would bring unity and order back to England.[28] But war was not the only by-product of the king's overseas interests: he also had to maintain defences and networks of support and manage the conduct of international relations. These were continual concerns for the lords and ministers around him, and this kind of business was a major stimulus to the activity and development of the king's council.

There has been a tendency to note that the most successful kings of the period – Edward I, Edward III and Henry V – were also its most successful warriors, and this is hard to contest, but the causal dynamic may lie in either direction. It seems likely that the same range of skills that underlay military victory also underlay domestic rule – the cardinal virtues of prudence, justice, temperance and fortitude were essential to the management of political relationships, good decision-making and the balancing of aims and resources. Certainly, victory alone did not create political harmony: Edward III endured some of his most difficult parliaments following his victories at Sluys in 1340 and Calais in 1347; by the 1350s, MPs were finding it hard to understand why war taxation was continuing when the king's initiatives had been so successful. Equally, defeats could have a galvanising effect, as Baugé in 1421 produced extensive lending and a will to return to fighting after the pause of 1419–20 and Orléans in 1429 induced Henry VI's parliaments to resume grants of taxation. Both Edward III and Henry V gave as much attention to the management of justice, administration and public finance as they did to the wars in France: McFarlane noted that Edward III only spent short periods of time in parliament, but he only spent a similar length of time at war outside his kingdom.[29]

In all, it may be better to see the king's European aspirations and his governance of England as deeply intertwined. These enterprises not only involved the same political dispositions and techniques; they also meant interaction with more or less the same political classes – pre-eminently nobles but also prelates, clerks and knights – combining administrative skill, personal connections, wealth and a sense of how to behave in a courtly world. One of the signal developments in the recent historiography of later medieval England is a recognition that the political world was multiple and sprawling – it was not all about the management of landed power, just as it was not all about the rise of parliamentary limited monarchy. This rich political scene included people and places outside England as well as those within.

Conclusion

It is clear, then, that while English kingship and the English political system had much in common with their continental counterparts, they also had some distinctive features. Tensions between the person of the king and the other bodies in which his realm was represented – whether official ones like parliament or unofficial ones like popular and aristocratic uprisings – were posed particularly sharply and were difficult to resolve. There was also perhaps a stronger distinction between the internal and the external, notwithstanding the investment of the king, his government and many of his subjects in both these worlds. English political life was deeply shaped by its distinctive history and geography and the relatively clear boundaries, overwhelming royal jurisdiction, and high expectations of centrally protected peace that these conferred. Outside England, the rule of the English king was much more typical of European models: he could sometimes mobilise the resources of the English polity in foreign adventures, and this enabled him to punch above his weight, but it is not altogether surprising that England's imperial ventures on the continent, and even in the British-Irish archipelago, faced so many reverses.

Notes

1. M. Prestwich, *Edward I* (London, 1988), 126–7.
2. M. Bennett, 'Richard II in the Mirror of Christendom', in *Ruling Fourteenth-Century England: Essays in Honour of Chris Given-Wilson*, ed. R. Ambühl, J. Bothwell and L. Tompkins (Woodbridge, 2019), 263–88 (at 282–4, 287).

3. B. Weiler, 'Image and Reality in Richard of Cornwall's German Career', *EHR* 113 (1998), 1111–42; 'Henry III and the Sicilian Business: a Reinterpretation', *HR* 74 (2001), 127–50.
4. P. E. Russell, *The English Intervention in Spain and Portugal in the Time of Edward III and Richard II* (Oxford, 1955); R. Vaughan, *Philip the Good* (London, 1970), 34–50; C. L. Scofield, *The Life and Reign of Edward the Fourth*, 2 vols. (London, 1923), I, 412, 556–7.
5. Sir John Fortescue, *The Governance of England* . . ., ed. C. Plummer (Oxford, 1885), 127.
6. C. Holmes and N. Standen, 'Introduction: Towards a Global Middle Ages', in *The Global Middle Ages*, ed. C. Holmes and N. Standen (Oxford, 2018) 1–44 (at 23–4).
7. G. Garnett, *Conquered England: Kingship, Succession and Tenure, 1066–1166* (Oxford, 2007).
8. J. Watts, *The Making of Polities: Europe, 1300–1500* (Cambridge, 2009), 79, 88–9, 126 and, for other details in this paragraph, 207–19, 393–6.
9. J. Richard, 'Royal "Enclaves" and Provincial Boundaries: The Burgundian Elections', in *The Recovery of France in the Fifteenth Century*, ed. P. S. Lewis (London, 1971), 216–41.
10. P. S. Lewis, 'Reflections on the Role of Royal Clientèles in the Construction of the French Monarchy (mid-XIVth/end-XVth centuries)', in *L'Etat ou le Roi?*, ed. N. Bulst (Paris, 1996), 51–67; P. Moraw, 'The Court of the German King and of the Emperor at the End of the Middle Ages, 1440–1519', in *Princes, Patronage and the Nobility: The Court at the Beginning of the Modern Age, c. 1450–1650*, ed. R. G. Asch and A. M. Birke (London, 1991), 103–38.
11. D. Boucoyannis, *Kings as Judges: Power, Justice, and the Origins of Parliaments* (Cambridge, 2021); M. Hébert, *Parlementer* (Paris, 2014), introduction and conclusion.
12. *Later Plantagenet and Wars of the Roses Consorts: Power, Influence and Dynasty*, ed. A. Norrie, C. Harris, J. Laynesmith, D. R. Messer and E. Woodacre (Cham, 2023), 27–47, 195–213; T. Earenfight, *Queenship in Medieval Europe* (Basingstoke, 2013), especially 176–9 and 238–42.
13. C. Given-Wilson, *Henry IV* (London, 2016), pt. 5.
14. M. A. Ladero Quesada, 'Corona y Ciudades en la Castilla del Siglo XV', in *En La España Medieval V* . . ., ed. M. A. Ladero Quesada, 2 vols. (Madrid, 1986), I, 551–74.
15. D. Grummitt and J.-F. Lassalmonie, 'Royal Public Finance (c.1290–1523)', in *Government and Political Life in England and France, c.1300–c.1500*, ed. C. Fletcher, J.-P. Genet and J. Watts (Cambridge, 2015), 116–49 (at 127, 130, 141–3).
16. S. Reynolds, *Kingdoms and Communities in Western Europe, 900–1300*, 2nd ed. (Oxford, 1997), 250–331.

17. S. Gunn, D. Grummitt and H. Cools, *War, State and Society in England and the Netherlands, 1477-1559* (Oxford, 2007), 20-38.
18. Philippe de Commynes, *Memoirs*, ed. M. C. E. Jones (Harmondsworth, 1972), 345.
19. J. Watts, 'Public or Plebs? The Changing Meaning of "the Commons", 1381-1549', in *Power and Identity in the Middle Ages*, ed. H. Pryce and J. Watts (Oxford, 2007), 242-60 (at 248-52).
20. Quotation from *The Paston Letters*, ed. J. Gairdner, 6 vols. (London, 1904), VI, 131.
21. P. S. Lewis, 'Two Pieces of Fifteenth-Century Political Iconography', in Lewis, *Essays in Later Medieval French History* (London, 1985), 189-92 (at 191-2).
22. Watts, *Making of Polities*, 3-7, 101-4, 168, 172-3, 346-7, 350.
23. Ibid., 103, 181, 185, 199.
24. G. Small, *Late Medieval France* (Basingstoke, 2009), 43-52 and 95-131; T. Scott, 'Germany and the Empire', in *The New Cambridge Medieval History, Vol. 7: c.1415-c.1500*, ed. C. Allmand (Cambridge, 1998), 335-66; Watts, *Making of Polities*, 310-17.
25. C. S. L. Davies, 'The Wars of the Roses in European Context', in *The Wars of the Roses*, ed. A. J. Pollard (Basingstoke, 1995), 162-85 (at 181-2).
26. Watts, *Making of Polities*, 317-20; C. B. Estow, *Pedro the Cruel of Castile, 1350-1369* (Leiden, 1995); K. Stevenson, *Power and Propaganda: Scotland, 1306-1488* (Edinburgh, 2014), 52-87.
27. F. Senatore, 'The Kingdom of Naples', in *The Italian Renaissance State*, ed. A. Gamberini and I. Lazzarini (Cambridge, 2012), 30-49.
28. *PROME*, parliament of March 1340, item 9 (Edward III); parliament of 1385, item 5 (Richard II); parliament of 1420, item 25 (xiv) (Henry V). *Literae Cantuarienses*, ed. J. B. Sheppard, 3 vols. (London, 1887-9), III, 274-85 (Edward IV).
29. K. B. McFarlane, *The Nobility of Later Medieval England* (Oxford, 1973), 120.

Further Reading

Abulafia, D., ed., *The New Cambridge Medieval History, Vol. 5: c.1198-c.1300* (Cambridge, 1999).

Allmand, C., ed., *The New Cambridge Medieval History, Vol. 7: c.1415-c.1500* (Cambridge, 1998).

Boucouyannis, D., *Kings as Judges: Power, Justice, and the Origins of Parliaments* (Cambridge, 2021).

Carpenter, C., *The Wars of the Roses: Politics and the Constitution in England, 1437-1509* (Cambridge, 1997).

Crooks, P., Green, D. and Ormrod, W. M., eds., *The Plantagenet Empire, 1259–1453* (Donington, 2016).

Fletcher, C., Genet, J.-P. and Watts, J., eds., *Government and Political Life in England and France, c.1300–c.1500* (Cambridge, 2015).

Frame, R., *The Political Development of the British Isles, 1100–1400* (Oxford, 1990).

Harriss, G. L., *Shaping the Nation: England, 1360–1461* (Cambridge, 2005).

Holmes, C., Van Steenbergen, J. and Weiler, B., eds., *Political Culture in the Latin West, Byzantium and the Islamic World, c.700–c.1500* (Cambridge, 2021).

Jones, M., ed., *The New Cambridge Medieval History, Vol. 6: c.1300–c.1415* (Cambridge, 1999).

Lazzarini, I., ed., *The Later Middle Ages*, Shorter Oxford History of Europe (Oxford, 2021).

Reynolds, S., *Kingdoms and Communities in Western Europe, 900–1300*, 2nd ed. (Oxford, 1997).

Watts, J., *The Making of Polities: Europe, 1300–1500* (Cambridge, 2009).

Index

Aberconwy, 337
  treaty of (1277), 303
Abingdon, 272
Acre, 12, 14
admiralty, court of, 118, 123
Ætheling, Edgar, 312
Æthelwulf of Wessex, 174
Agenais, 10, 13
Agincourt, battle of, 47, 49, 100, 134, 135, 141, 145, 146, 200, 243, 417
Alderney, 301
Alexander II, king of Scots, 3, 8, 304
Alexander III, king of Scots, 8, 14, 304
Alfonso I, 401
Alnwick Castle, 227
Amiens, 13, 263, 335
  mise of, 11
Amundesham, John, 271
Angoulême, Isabella of, 7, 187
Anjou, Charles of, 401
Anjou, Margaret of, queen of England, 49, 50, 51, 53, 96, 175, 177, 178, 180, 185, 187, 202, 271, 410
Appellants, the, 35, 36, 37, 84, 137, 229
Aquinas, 278, 380
Aquitaine, 10, 32, 33, 138, 140, 147, 283, 299, 301, 310
Aquitaine, Eleanor of, 29

Aragon, 407, 415
Arbroath, Declaration of, 306
Aristotle, 380, 382, 383, 384, 388, 395, 396
Arras, Congress of (1435), 48, 315
Arthur, legendary king of Britain, 131, 143, 144, 161, 173, 313, 334, 337, 339, 340, 363, 367
Artois, Robert of, 29
Arundel, Thomas, archbishop of Canterbury, 45, 46, 202, 206
Audley, Hugh, the Younger, baron, 226
Avignon, 25, 96, 200, 202, 205
Avranches, Henry of, 298

Baker, Geoffrey le, 361
Balliol, Edward, 306
Balliol, John, 15, 138, 304, 305
Bannockburn, battle of, 26, 29, 38, 132, 133, 137, 282, 286, 306
Banstead, 157
Bardi, of Florence, 99, 267
Bardolf, Thomas, Lord, 120
Barnet, battle of, 53, 54, 121, 134, 135, 262
Barons' War, 14, 19, 137, 286, 337
Basset, Gilbert, 5, 9
Battle Abbey, 207

Baugé, battle of, 47, 418
Bayonne, 401, 417
Beauchamp, Guy, earl of Warwick, 230
Beauchamp, John, of Holt, 223
Beauchamp, Richard, earl of Warwick, 218, 227
Beauchamp, Thomas, earl of Warwick, 35
Beaufort, Edmund, duke of Somerset, 50, 51, 84, 167, 230
Beaufort, Henry, bishop of Winchester, 48, 49, 100, 187, 201, 202
Beaufort, Margaret, 56
Beaufort, Thomas, duke of Exeter, 223
Beaumont, Robert de, 220
Becket, Thomas, 197, 204, 210, 211
Bede, 359
Bedford, 5
  riots in, 250
Bedford, John, duke of, 47, 48, 313
Beler, Roger, 127
Bellegarde, 15
Benhall, 222
Berkeley Castle, 28
Berwick, 133, 134, 142, 301, 306
Beverley, 261, 264, 270, 272
  Robert of, 335
Big Ben, 325
Bigod, Roger, earl of Norfolk, 9, 10, 15, 413
Black Book, 152
Black Death, the, 30, 31, 34, 98, 198, 245, 259, 260, 266
Blackheath, 175
Bluet, John, 241
Bohemia, 407, 415
Bohemia, Anne of, queen of England, 36, 37, 38, 41, 128, 181, 182, 183, 184, 188, 273, 349, 352
Bohun, Humphrey, earl of Hereford, 15, 413

Boniface VIII, pope, 25, 305, 371
Boniface IX, pope, 202
Boniface, archbishop of Canterbury, 7
Booth, Laurence, 180
Bordeaux, 30, 33, 46, 50, 160, 310, 411
Boroughbridge, battle of, 27, 135, 223
Boston, 262
Bosworth, battle of, 57, 134, 272
Boteler, Ralph, 167
Bower, Walter, 307, 359, 360, 370, 374
Bracton, 7, 124
Bramham Moor, battle of, 45
Breauté, Falkes de, 5
Brétigny, treaty of (1360), 32, 140, 146
Brian, Guy, baron, 225
Bridgwater, 272
Bristol, 259, 264, 265, 269
British Museum, 331
Brittany, 5, 56, 173
Brompton, John, 271
Brotherton, Margaret of, duchess of Norfolk, 220
Bruce, David (David II, king of Scots), 27, 29, 30, 143, 155, 306, 307, 312
Bruce, Edward, 306
Bruce, Robert (Robert I, king of Scots), 16, 26, 28, 133, 140, 306
Brut Chronicle, 135, 292, 363, 364, 366
Brutus, 298, 305, 363, 366, 367
Burgh, Hubert de, 4, 5
Burgh, Maud de, countess of Gloucester, 282
Burgh-on-Sands, 16
Burgundy, Charles, duke of, 54, 97
Burgundy, John, duke of, 47
Burgundy, Philip, duke of, 47, 48, 49, 52
Burley, Simon, 120
Burnell, Robert, bishop of Bath and Wells, 201
Burstwick, lordship of, 155
Bury St Edmunds, 50, 272
  Abbey, 211

Cade's Rebellion, 50, 128, 138, 167, 268, 289, 413
Caerlaverock Castle, 136
Caernarfon, 14, 303, 340, 341, 342, 343
Cahors, 10
Calais, 32, 45, 46, 47, 48, 49, 51, 53, 54, 97, 105, 134, 137, 142, 172, 183, 267, 268, 301, 314, 339, 417, 418
Cambridge, 343
  University of, 123
Cambridge, Richard, earl of, 46
Camelot, 144, 227, 340
canon law, 117, 123, 197, 405
Canterbury, 173, 265, 269, 272
  Cathedral, 57, 173, 323
  Grey Friars Convent, 369
  St Augustine's Abbey, 207, 211
Carlisle, 126
  diocese of, 196, 205
Carmarthen, 303
Castile, 29, 188, 401, 402, 407, 410, 415, 417
Castile, Peter of, 31, 155, 416
Castillon, 137
Catalonia, 407
Caxton, William, 131, 132, 135, 143, 145, 146, 162, 364
chancery, 67, 68, 69, 70, 96, 153, 183, 209, 212, 278, 280, 404
  court of chancery, 122, 123, 124, 265, 325
  the chancellor, 36, 50, 68, 71, 104, 112, 122, 137, 142, 183, 209, 212, 223, 265, 283
Charlemagne, 313
Charles I, 403
Charles IV, king of France, 310
Charles VI, king of France, 47, 95, 97, 145, 146, 298, 313, 352, 354
Charles VII, king of France, 48, 49, 50, 298, 314
Charny, Geoffroi de, 135
Chaucer, Geoffrey, 162, 381, 394

Chaucer, Thomas, 244
Cheapside, 271, 289, 290
Cherbourg, 50
Chertsey Abbey, 58
Cheshire, 37, 198, 248, 289, 343
Chester, 291, 308
Chester, Ranulf, earl of, 4
Chichester, diocese of, 207
Chirk, 222
chivalry, court of, 118, 119, 120, 121, 123
Cicero, 280
Cinque Ports, 268
Clanvowe, John, 162, 163
Clare, Gilbert de, earl of Gloucester, 11, 12
Clare, Margaret de, 26
Clare, Richard (d. 1318), 307
Clare, Richard de, earl of Gloucester, 9, 11
Clarence, George, duke of, 53, 54
Clarence, Lionel, duke of, 32, 219, 308, 309, 372
Clarence, Thomas, duke of, 46, 47
Clifford, Thomas, Lord, 226
Clipstone, 157
Cobham, Reginald, 221
Coggeshall, Ralph of, 361
Colchester, 257, 258
Columbers, Matthew de, 160
common pleas, court of, 113, 114, 123, 259, 325
Company of the Staple, 267
Comyn, John, 16, 306
Confessor, St Edward the, 198, 312, 313, 328, 331, 333, 334, 336, 337, 339, 347, 352, 389
Constance, Council of (1414–18), 200, 365
Constantinople, 303, 336, 343
convocation, 92, 93, 203, 204, 205, 206
Coppini, Francesco, 187
Corfe Castle, 3

Cornwall, 136
Cornwall, Richard of, 5, 11, 328, 401
Coterels, criminal gang, 127, 252
Courtenay, Hugh, earl of Devon, 225
Courtenay, Richard, bishop of
    Norwich, 58
Courtenay, William, archbishop of
    Canterbury, 206
Coventry, 53, 261, 267, 269, 270,
    272, 273
Cravant, 48
Crécy, battle of, 30, 31, 34, 134, 135,
    140, 141, 144, 339, 347, 417
Cumberland, 55, 402

Darcy, John, baron, 229
Dartford, 50
Daventry, 371
Dedham, 222
Dee, river, 302
Deheubarth, 301
Denbigh, honour of, 229
Derbyshire, 136, 227, 289, 290, 349
Despenser, Henry, bishop of
    Norwich, 287, 291
Despensers, the, 27, 28, 120, 166, 183,
    229, 230, 231, 282, 287, 289, 364
Devon, 53, 136, 225, 250
Dominicans, the, 181, 198, 199, 343
Don, Gruffydd, 313
Doncaster, 372
Dover, 4, 173, 268
Dublin, 411
Dumfries, 16
Dunsmore Heath, 293
Dupplin Moor, battle of, 29, 306
Durham, 134
    diocese of, 196, 205, 207
Dysert O'Dea, battle of, 307

East Anglia, 250, 251, 289
Eddington, William, 73
Edgar, king of England, 302

Edgecote, battle of, 53
Edward I, 3, 13, 14, 15, 16, 17, 18, 20,
    24, 71, 77, 82, 90, 92, 93, 96, 97,
    99, 111, 112, 125, 132, 133, 135,
    136, 138, 140, 141, 142, 143,
    144, 157, 160, 161, 162, 163,
    164, 173, 174, 177, 179, 181,
    182, 185, 188, 197, 198, 199,
    201, 202, 204, 208, 210, 219,
    220, 231, 239, 240, 246, 259,
    262, 265, 270, 282, 302, 304,
    305, 306, 308, 315, 328, 330,
    337, 340, 342, 343, 349, 351,
    370, 371, 389, 401, 413, 414,
    416, 418
Lord Edward, 10, 11
Edward II, 14, 24, 26, 28, 36, 38, 40,
    41, 75, 76, 79, 83, 84, 85, 90, 95,
    96, 125, 127, 132, 133, 135, 137,
    140, 141, 142, 161, 162, 166, 177,
    180, 182, 185, 186, 188, 189, 198,
    221, 223, 226, 229, 230, 231, 269,
    270, 271, 280, 282, 286, 287, 289,
    292, 304, 306, 310, 343, 349, 364,
    367, 368, 389, 401, 410, 415, 416
Edward III, 24, 27, 28, 29, 30, 31, 32,
    33, 34, 36, 39, 41, 44, 70, 73, 75,
    80, 82, 93, 94, 95, 96, 97, 98, 99,
    102, 111, 127, 133, 135, 138, 139,
    140, 141, 142, 143, 144, 146, 154,
    155, 157, 160, 161, 162, 163, 164,
    166, 173, 176, 177, 181, 182, 184,
    186, 197, 198, 199, 200, 201, 219,
    220, 221, 222, 223, 225, 229, 230,
    232, 245, 248, 259, 263, 267, 270,
    282, 287, 288, 290, 298, 306, 308,
    314, 328, 331, 339, 340, 347, 349,
    362, 372, 374, 381, 387, 390, 402,
    414, 416, 417, 418
Edward IV, 51, 53, 56, 58, 61, 80, 90,
    95, 97, 101, 121, 127, 132, 134,
    135, 136, 145, 152, 158, 160, 162,
    172, 173, 176, 182, 183, 184, 187,

199, 211, 230, 261, 265, 269, 271,
    282, 288, 290, 314, 340, 344, 345,
    367, 371, 372, 374, 402, 418
Edward V, 54, 55, 56, 59, 62, 186,
    367, 374
Eglesfield, Robert de, 180
Eleanor Crosses, 351
Eleanor of Castile, queen of England,
    177, 181, 182, 184, 186, 188, 350
Eleanor of Provence, queen of
    England, 7, 155, 171, 173, 174,
    176, 178, 179, 180, 181, 182, 184,
    185, 186, 187, 189, 409
Ellis, William, 270
Eltham, 157, 158
Ely, diocese of, 197
Erik II, king of Denmark, 304
Erik of Pomerania, 96
Eton College, 49, 58, 199, 323,
    343, 345
Evesham
    Abbey, 369
    battle of, 12, 19
exchequer, the, 15, 17, 67, 68, 69, 70,
    89, 90, 95, 98, 102, 103, 104, 105,
    113, 176, 228, 248, 259, 264, 265,
    278, 280, 325, 334
    treasurer, 68, 69, 71, 73, 104,
    209, 289
Exeter, 258, 261
    Cathedral, 324
    diocese of, 207

Falaise, treaty of (1174), 301
Falkirk, battle of, 16, 133, 135,
    142, 143
Fastolf, Hugh, 270
Fastolf, Sir John, 251, 315
Faughart, battle of, 306
Faunt, Nicholas, 265
Ferre, Guy, 186
Fiennes, James, 167
Fiennes, Roger, 167

Fieschi, Manuele, 28
Finstock, 75
Fitz Geoffrey, John, 9
Fitzalan, Richard, earl of Arundel, 35,
    37, 100, 222
Flanders, 15, 29, 32, 133, 139, 142,
    287, 291
    Matilda of, 181
Flodden, battle of, 412
Folvilles, criminal gang, 127, 252
Formigny, battle of, 50
Fortescue, John, 80, 124, 225, 380,
    382, 403
Fotheringhay, 199
Fourth Lateran Council (1215), 199
Fox, Richard, 369
Frederick II, Holy Roman Emperor,
    7, 97
Frederick III, Holy Roman
    Emperor, 410
Frescobaldi, of Florence, 99
Froissart, Jean, 298

garderoba, 103
Gascony, 7, 10, 13, 14, 15, 16, 25, 27,
    29, 31, 32, 34, 41, 45, 46, 49, 50,
    92, 93, 96, 136, 137, 142, 184,
    301, 310, 314, 316, 410, 416, 417
Gaunt, John of, duke of Lancaster, 32,
    33, 35, 37, 56, 202, 219, 223, 228,
    248, 249, 250, 283, 287, 290, 310,
    352, 370, 402
Gaveston, Piers, 26, 39, 40, 166, 228,
    230, 289, 367, 368
Geddington, 157, 351
Ghent, 139
    Charles of, 401
Gildas, 359
Giles of Rome, 172, 278, 380, 382, 383,
    384, 388, 391, 392, 395
Glastonbury Abbey, 370
Gloucester, 28
    Abbey, 3, 38

Gloucester (cont.)
  Cathedral, 347
  John of, 335
Gloucester, Humphrey, duke of, 47,
  48, 49, 271, 402
Gloucestershire, 264
Glyn Dŵr, Owain, 45, 134, 206, 298,
  308, 312, 313
Goch, Iolo, poet, 308
Gower, John, 57, 162, 381, 391, 392,
  393, 394
Gower, lordship of, 231
Grandisson, Catherine, countess of
  Salisbury, 166
gravamina, 93, 203
Gray, Sir Thomas, 364, 365
Great Cause, the, 15
Great Schism, the, 200
Great Seal, the, 68, 119, 125, 132
Great Yarmouth, 270, 272
Greenwich, 177
Grey, Thomas, marquess of
  Dorset, 54
Greyfriars, 180
Grimsby, 262
Grosmont, Henry of, duke of
  Lancaster, 220, 221, 227
Grosseteste, Robert, bishop of
  Lincoln, 199, 280
Gruffudd, Dafydd ap, 14, 18, 305
Gruffydd, Llywelyn ap, 8, 11, 12, 13,
  14, 137, 303
Gruffydd, Rhys ap, 301
Guernsey, 301
Gwynedd, 3, 8, 301, 303,
  337, 341
Gwynedd, Owain, 301

Hainault, Jacqueline of, 271
Hainault, Philippa, queen of England,
  27, 41, 128, 155, 173, 177, 179,
  180, 181, 182, 183, 184, 188,
  331, 409

Halidon Hill, battle of, 29, 133, 135,
  141, 142, 306
Hall, Edward, 44
Hampshire, 289
Harby (Notts.), 351
Harclay, Andrew, 120, 223
Hardingstone, 351
Hardyng, John, 312, 364, 365, 366,
  372, 373
Harfleur, 46, 47
Harlech, 52
Hastings, 268
Hastings, William Lord, 55
Haxey, Thomas, 165
Hedgeley Moor, 52
Henry I, 232
Henry II, 29, 110, 151, 197, 204, 210,
  211, 232, 299, 417
Henry III, xvii, 3, 5, 7, 9, 16, 18, 19, 33,
  44, 76, 85, 90, 96, 97, 133, 137,
  138, 141, 155, 157, 162, 166, 171,
  173, 182, 184, 186, 187, 188, 198,
  199, 202, 204, 208, 229, 265, 301,
  303, 304, 323, 327, 328, 334, 335,
  336, 337, 339, 340, 347, 349, 362,
  370, 401, 414, 417
Henry IV, 35, 36, 37, 44, 52, 57, 60, 71,
  75, 79, 83, 96, 120, 134, 135, 136,
  142, 157, 165, 173, 174, 175, 180,
  199, 200, 205, 206, 218, 232, 248,
  268, 283, 293, 308, 311, 349, 354,
  368, 369, 370, 371, 372, 414,
  415, 416
Henry V, 38, 45, 46, 57, 60, 75, 80, 90,
  96, 98, 100, 126, 132, 134, 135,
  136, 139, 141, 145, 146, 147, 157,
  159, 163, 177, 199, 200, 201, 202,
  205, 207, 209, 219, 223, 243, 264,
  265, 268, 271, 284, 308, 312, 313,
  314, 343, 350, 365, 393, 402, 410,
  417, 418
Henry VI, xvii, 47, 49, 50, 51, 52, 53,
  58, 61, 75, 76, 83, 85, 96, 101, 112,

120, 127, 134, 137, 141, 145, 147, 157, 159, 161, 167, 175, 185, 186, 187, 199, 202, 226, 230, 231, 232, 267, 272, 288, 293, 313, 314, 323, 343, 345, 366, 367, 371, 372, 374, 413, 414, 415, 416, 418
Henry VII (Henry Tudor), 56, 60, 111, 183, 232, 272, 340, 344, 374
Henry VIII, 44, 145, 147, 183, 197, 204, 314, 315, 344, 401, 402, 412, 416
Hereford, 262
Herefordshire, 224
Herland, Hugh, 331
Hertfordshire, 352
Hexham, 52
Higden, Ranulf, 39, 363
Hobbes, Thomas, 380
Hoccleve, Thomas, 381, 391, 393, 394, 396
Holderness, 53
Holinshed, Raphael, 41
Holland, 53
Holy Land, 12, 186, 366, 417
Horston Castle, 290
Howard, Thomas, earl of Surrey, 314
Hull, 99, 230, 259, 267
Hunte, Thomas, 265
Hythe, 268

Île-de-France, 48, 335
Inchcolm Abbey, 359
Inns of Chancery, 123
Inns of Court, 112, 123, 124, 308
Iorwerth, Llywelyn ap, 3, 8, 303
Ireland, 32, 33, 35, 36, 37, 41, 51, 93, 96, 134, 136, 137, 142, 144, 261, 262, 265, 299, 301, 302, 303, 306, 308, 309, 310, 311, 315, 316, 402, 410, 411, 412, 416, 417
Isabella of France, queen of England, 27, 28, 139, 173, 177, 179, 180, 181, 182, 183, 189, 223, 232, 271, 289, 306, 349, 368, 410

Isabella of Valois, queen of England, 37, 41, 97, 176, 352
Isle of Man, 37, 301
Ismanie, Lady Scales, 180

James I, king of Scots, 45, 147, 312, 359
James II, king of Scots, 298, 359
Janyns, Henry, 340
Jersey, 301
Joan 'the Fair Maid' of Kent, 33, 187
John II, king of France, 31, 32, 135, 143, 155
John, king of England, xvii, 3, 90, 91, 218, 263, 301, 303
Joinville, Jean de, 18

Katherine of Valois, queen of England, 47, 145, 163, 187
Kenilworth
 Castle, 227
 Dictum of, 12
Kent, 290, 405
Kidwelly, 313
Kilwardby, Robert, archbishop of Canterbury, 201
King Ebrauk, 272
king's bench, court of, 114, 115, 125, 126, 127, 259, 291, 325
King's College, Cambridge, 58, 199, 343
King's Langley, 38
 friary of, 198, 343
Kingston, treaty of (1217), 4
Kirkstall Abbey, 369
Knighton, Henry, 292, 362

Lacy, Edmund de, earl of Lincoln, 218
Lacy, Walter, baron, 224
Lancashire, 136, 250
Lancaster, 291
Lancaster, duchy of, 32, 37, 90, 251, 344, 372

Lancaster, Edmund ('Crouchback'), earl of, 370, 402
Lancaster, Edward of, 50, 52, 53, 186, 374
Lancaster, Philippa of, 96
Lancaster, Thomas of, son of Henry IV, duke of Clarence, 45, 46
Lancaster, Thomas, earl of, 26, 27, 84, 120, 137, 226, 286, 292, 368
Langham, Simon, archbishop of Canterbury, 201
Langland, William, 387, 389, 391, 394
Langley, Edmund of, earl of Cambridge, 32, 33, 219, 402
Latimer, William, 166
Leicester, 57, 62, 264, 285, 286
    Abbey, 362
Leicestershire, 286
Leinster, 311
Leulinghem, truce of, 144, 147
Lewes, 11
    battle of, 19, 133
    priory of, 207
Ligurgius, king of Athens, 392
Limoges, 10
Lincoln, 4, 126, 259, 266, 287
    battle of, 301
    Cathedral, 188, 324, 345
    diocese of, 197, 201, 207
Lincolnshire, 53, 262
Littleton, Thomas, 124
Livery and Maintenance, Ordinance of (1390), 249
Llull, Ramon, 131
Lollards, the, 60, 213, 272
London, 3, 11, 12, 34, 35, 51, 52, 53, 55, 95, 100, 101, 123, 126, 143, 145, 157, 175, 178, 180, 182, 183, 185, 198, 258, 259, 267, 268, 269, 271, 272, 287, 290, 291, 330, 331, 343, 366, 370, 372, 374, 405, 414
Louis IX, king of France, 5, 10, 11, 12, 18, 182, 198, 313, 330, 334, 352

Louis VIII, king of France, 301
Louis XI, king of France, 52, 53, 54, 95, 415
Louis, Prince of France, 3, 4, 5, 301
Low Countries, 14, 15, 93, 97, 155, 261, 271, 288, 402, 417
Lusignan, Aymer de, bishop of Winchester, 9
Lusignan, Hugh de, 7, 155
Lydd, 268
Lydgate, John, 132, 366
Lynn, 262, 264, 265, 270, 289
Lyons, Richard, 100, 270

Magna Carta, 4, 5, 6, 8, 9, 16, 25, 81, 83, 90, 111, 112, 113, 128, 231, 269, 301, 302, 325, 389, 405, 406, 414
Maine, 48, 49, 50, 299
Malcolm III, king of Scots, 312
Manby, John of, 270
Map, Walter, 151
Margaret of France, queen of England, 16, 173, 174, 177, 179, 181, 183
Margaret of Norway, 15, 304, 370
Marlowe, Christopher, 40
Marsh, Adam, 280
Marshal, John, 289
Marshal, Richard, earl of Pembroke, 5, 133, 414
Marshal, William, earl of Pembroke, 4, 301
Marston Maisey, 229
Martel, William, 241
Mauny, Walter, 155
McFarlane, K. B., 20, 60, 61, 246, 418
Meaux, 40, 47
Merchants Estates, assemblies of, 270
Mercia, 405
Messager, Robert le, 137
Middleham, 374
    Edward of, 56, 373
Milemete, Walter of, 381, 387

Modus Tenendi Parliamentum, 221, 280
Moleyns, Adams, 167
Monmouth, Geoffrey of, 139, 363
Montagu, John, 162
Montagu, John, earl of Salisbury, 227
Montagu, Thomas, earl of Salisbury, 48
Montagu, William, earl of Salisbury, 221
Montfort, Simon de, earl of Leicester, 9, 10, 11, 12, 20, 84, 133, 185, 219, 233, 269, 335
Montgomery, treaty of (1267), 12, 13, 303
Mortimer, Edmund, 44, 45, 46, 50
Mortimer, Roger, 28, 133, 222, 223, 231, 232, 271, 306, 370
Mortimer's Cross, battle of, 51, 134
Mowbray, John, baron, 225
Mowbray, Thomas, earl of Nottingham, 35, 120, 279

Naples, 417
Navarre, Joan of, queen of England, 57, 173, 174, 175, 177, 178, 180, 349
Neath, 27
Nefyn, 143
Neville, Anne, queen of England, 53, 54, 185, 373, 374
Neville, Isabel, 53, 54
Neville, John, Lord Montagu, 52
Neville, John, of Raby, 166
Neville, Richard, earl of Salisbury, 50
Neville, Richard, earl of Warwick, 51, 52, 53, 184, 262, 267, 290, 371, 373, 402
Neville's Cross, battle of, 30, 306, 307
New College, Oxford, 209
New Romney, 268
Newark, 3
Newcastle-upon-Tyne, 306

Newington, 137, 286
  Robert of, 286
Newton (Dorset), 259
Norfolk, 251, 289
Norham, 312, 371
Norman Conquest, 227, 238, 299, 404
Normandy, 30, 46, 47, 48, 49, 50, 91, 137, 146, 147, 299, 301, 310, 313, 314, 316, 417
Normanton, 287
North Sea, 53
Northampton, 11, 272
  battle of, 51, 134
Northampton/Edinburgh, treaty of (1328), 28, 140, 306
Northamptonshire, 172, 351
Northumberland, 52, 137
Norwich, 126, 259, 264, 265, 266, 271
Nottingham, 126, 374
  Castle, 28, 127
Nottinghamshire, 250

O'Carroll, Tadhg, 311
Oldcastle, John, 213, 366
O'Neill, Domnall, king of Tír Eoghain, 306
Ordainers, 26, 27
Order of the Garter, 120, 144, 161, 198, 339, 366
Ordinances, the New, 26, 83, 106, 231, 389
Orkney, 304
Orleans, 48, 418
Orleton, Adam, 40
Otterburn, battle of, 137
Oxford, 262, 266, 272, 280, 287
  University of, 123, 213
Oxfordshire, 75

Pagula, William of, 381, 387, 390
Paper Constitution, the, 7

Paris, 10, 32, 47, 48, 134, 182, 313, 314, 330, 334, 395, 411
Paris *parlement*, 14, 407
Paris, Matthew, 17, 18, 174, 185, 362, 370
Paris, treaty of (1259), 10, 13, 14, 138
parliament (general), 4, 6, 7, 13, 16, 25, 28, 30, 31, 47, 51, 74, 77, 79, 80, 92, 93, 94, 98, 104, 105, 106, 112, 113, 119, 121, 126, 128, 141, 154, 165, 200, 204, 205, 221, 223, 280, 282, 283, 285, 286, 325, 372, 383, 396, 405, 406, 409, 413, 418, 419
  the Commons, 33, 45, 60, 79, 80, 92, 93, 94, 98, 104, 105, 106, 110, 111, 112, 132, 141, 142, 146, 165, 202, 225, 240, 244, 245, 249, 250, 269, 270, 271, 281, 383, 390, 393
  the Lords, 79, 94, 110, 119, 120, 202, 218, 219, 220, 221, 222, 225
parliament (sessions of)
  1258, 8, 10
  1264, June, 11
  1265, January–March, 11
  1327, 244
  1337, March, 223
  1341, 230
  1362, 102
  1376 (the Good Parliament), 33, 142, 166, 225, 245, 270, 414
  1377, October, 249
  1378, 142
  1381, 165
  1384, April, 249
  1384, November, 283
  1385, 225
  1386 (the Wonderful Parliament), 36, 84, 137
  1388 (the Merciless Parliament), 36, 84, 120, 166, 167
  1390, January, 283
  1397, January, 106
  1398, 120
  1399, 37, 283, 308, 369
  1401, 45, 308
  1404, 45
  1406, 45, 106, 120
  1414, 139
  1415, 284
  1416, March, 271
  1416, October, 223
  1427–8, 271
  1449–50, 414
  1472, 136
  1478, January, 54, 142
  1484, 56, 172
Paston Letters, the, 251
Peasants' Revolt, 34, 118, 138, 205, 245, 272, 281, 282, 289, 290, 293, 414
Peatling Magna, 286
Pecche, John, 270
Pecham, John, archbishop of Canterbury, 197, 200, 201
Percy, Henry (Hotspur), 45
Percy, Henry, baron, 225
Percy, Henry, earl of Northumberland, 120, 134
Périgueux, 10
Perrers, Alice, 166, 182, 183
Peruzzi, of Florence, 99, 267
Peter I of Castile, 31, 155, 416
Philip II (Augustus), king of France, 301, 310
Philip III, king of France, 13
Philip IV, king of France, 14, 16, 139, 304, 331
Philip VI, king of France, 29, 135
Picquigny, treaty of (1475), 54
Pisan, Christine de, 184
Plantagenet, Arthur, 183
Poitiers, battle of, 31, 32, 34, 140, 417
Poitou, 5, 7, 133, 155
Poland, 416

Pole, Michael de la, earl of Suffolk, 36, 137, 222, 230, 283
Pole, William de la, duke of Suffolk, 49, 50, 82, 84, 99, 137, 167, 414
Pole, William de la, merchant, 154, 155, 267
Policraticus, 238
Pontefract, 292
    Castle, 37
    honour of, 218
Ponthieu, 301
Portugal, 402
Powicke, Maurice, 19, 20
privy seal office, 67, 68, 69, 71, 153, 209, 223
Provisions of Oxford, 11, 25, 83, 389
Provisions of Westminster, 10, 25

Queen's College, Oxford, 180

Radcot Bridge, battle of, 36
Ralegh, William, 7
Reading Abbey, 173, 211
Reims, 32, 335
requests, court of, 122, 126
Reyns, Henry of, 335
Ricciardi, company of, 99
Richard Coeur de Lion, 131
Richard II, xvii, 24, 33, 35, 36, 38, 39, 40, 42, 44, 46, 60, 70, 76, 83, 84, 85, 90, 95, 97, 100, 101, 106, 111, 118, 134, 136, 137, 140, 144, 159, 160, 161, 162, 165, 166, 176, 182, 183, 187, 198, 200, 201, 205, 206, 220, 222, 223, 225, 229, 230, 232, 247, 248, 273, 283, 286, 287, 288, 291, 292, 308, 310, 311, 331, 349, 352, 362, 367, 368, 369, 371, 372, 396, 401, 410, 415, 416, 418
Richard III, xvii, 56, 57, 58, 62, 63, 111, 127, 131, 133, 134, 145, 172, 182, 185, 232, 272, 344, 367, 373, 374
    as duke of Gloucester, 54, 55, 56, 172, 402
Roches, Peter des, bishop of Winchester, 4, 5, 6
Rochester, diocese of, 197, 207
Roman law, 40, 42, 77, 123, 125, 141, 294, 404
Rouen, 47, 48, 49, 50, 411
round table, 143, 144, 161, 339, 340
Rous, John, 131, 132, 367, 373, 374
Roxburgh, 142
Rye, 268

Saint Sardos, war of, 27, 177, 309
Saintonge, 13
Salisbury, 56, 261, 270, 272
    Cathedral, 345
Salisbury, John of, 238
Sandwich, 268
Sark, 301
Savoy, Peter of, 7, 9
Savoy, William of, 7
Scandinavia, 416
Scarborough, 272
    Castle, 26
Scone, Stone of, 305, 337
Scotichronicon, 307, 359
Scotland, 8, 14, 15, 16, 20, 24, 25, 26, 28, 29, 30, 41, 44, 45, 51, 54, 55, 97, 133, 134, 136, 137, 138, 139, 140, 141, 142, 145, 147, 155, 157, 183, 202, 240, 259, 261, 262, 279, 286, 301, 302, 304, 305, 306, 308, 309, 311, 312, 328, 337, 359, 364, 370, 387, 402, 405, 411, 412, 417
Scotland, Margaret of, 312
Scrope, Richard, archbishop of York, 45, 60, 197, 200, 292, 372
Scrope, Richard, baron, 70
Sens, 145
Seymour, John, 374
Shakespeare, 40, 41, 60, 61, 62
Sharpe, Jack, 272

Shaw, Ralph, 56
Sheen, 157, 158, 182, 199, 343
Shipston-on-Stour, 263
Shore, Elizabeth, 182
Shrewsbury, 126, 290
  battle of, 45, 58, 134, 135, 308
Shrewsbury, Richard of, duke of York, 55, 374
Sicily, 7, 204, 402, 407, 417
Sigismund, Emperor, 366
signet seal office, 68
Sluys, battle of, 29, 133, 135, 140, 142, 347, 418
Smithfield, 143, 144
Snowdonia, 14
Somerset, 264, 289
Song of Lewes, 18, 19
Soper, William, 268
Southampton, 46, 104, 268
Southeray, John de, 182
St Albans, 51, 272, 362
  Abbey, 17, 211, 323, 369, 370
  battle of, 272, 284
  Master Hugh of, 331
St Denis Abbey, 335
St Edmund, 198, 328, 352
St Edward the Confessor, 162, 313, 328, 334, 336, 337, 348
St George, 59, 157, 290, 331, 339, 348, 349, 352, 356, 371
St John the Baptist, 352
St Paul's cathedral, 51
St Pol, Marie de, countess of Pembroke, 220
Stafford, Henry, duke of Buckingham, 55, 56
Staffordshire, 250, 262
Stamford, 127
Stapledon, Walter, 289
Star Chamber, 325
Statutes
  Statute of Merton (1235), 7
  Statute of Mortmain (1279), 210

Statute of Rhuddlan (1284), 14, 303
Statute of Winchester (1285), 111, 264
Statute of York (1322), 3
Statute of Labourers (1351), 30, 264
Statutes of Provisors (1351 & 1390), 200, 405
Statute of Treasons (1352), 119
Statutes of Praemunire (1353, 1360, 1390 & 1393), 200, 405
Statute of Pleading (1362), 31
Statute of Purveyors (1362), 102, 164
Sumptuary Laws (1363), 242
Statute of Kilkenny (1366), 309
Statute of Additions (1413), 242
Staunton, John de, 152
Stirling Bridge, battle of, 16, 141
Stocks Market, London, 271
Stratford, John, archbishop of Canterbury, 70, 197
Stubbs, William, 19, 60
Sturmy, Richard, 166
Sudbury, Simon, archbishop of Canterbury, 35
Suffolk, 292
Swynford, Katherine, 202
Syon, 199, 343

Tattershall Castle, 227
Tewkesbury Abbey, 53
Tewkesbury, battle of, 53, 121, 134
Thatcher, Margaret, 35
The Rydalle Book, 158
Tír Eoghain, 311
Topples Wood, 75
Tours, truce of, 49
Tout, Frederick, 20
Tower of London, 17, 50, 52, 53, 54, 55, 56, 62, 95, 98, 100, 175, 289, 290, 291, 323, 356
Towton, battle of, 51, 134, 135, 269
Trastámara, Henry of, 416

Tresilian, John, 340
Trevet, Nicholas, 18, 132
Troyes, treaty of (1420), 47, 146, 313
Tuddenham, Thomas, 167
Tudor, Owen, 187
Tunis, 12
Tyler, Wat, 35
Tynwelle, Thomas de, 287

Ufford, William, earl of Suffolk, 222
Upavon, manor of, 5
Urban VI, pope, 202
Usk, Adam of, 370

Vale Royal Abbey, 198, 343
Vere, John de, earl of Oxford, 54
Vere, Robert de, earl of Oxford, 36, 220, 229
Versailles, 96, 158
Vincennes, 47
Violante Visconti of Milan, 33

Wainfleet, William, bishop of Winchester, 345
Wakefield, battle of, 51
Wales, 8, 12, 13, 14, 16, 20, 26, 27, 41, 45, 47, 52, 53, 93, 96, 133, 136, 141, 143, 177, 197, 205, 206, 229, 231, 259, 262, 279, 291, 298, 301, 303, 304, 306, 308, 309, 312, 315, 316, 337, 340, 401, 405, 410, 411, 416
Wales, Gerald of, 301
Wallace, William, 16, 306
Walsall, 262
Walsingham (Norf.), 181
Walsingham, Thomas, 287, 291, 292, 369
Waltham Cross, 352
Ware, Richard, abbot of Westminster, 337
Warenne, John de, earl of Surrey, 15, 16, 230

Warkworth Chronicle, 293
Wars of the Roses, 120, 137, 172, 228, 252, 261, 272, 281, 284, 286, 287, 289, 293, 412
Warwick, 374
Warwickshire, 250, 263, 293
Weardale, 133, 139
Welles, John, 366
Wells, 257, 263
Wenceslas IV, Holy Roman Emperor, 416
Wessex, 405
Westminster Abbey, 17, 38, 39, 46, 52, 55, 58, 96, 100, 158, 162, 175, 188, 189, 198, 323, 325, 326, 333, 334, 335, 336, 337, 338, 350, 351, 352
 Coronation Chair, 337, 338
 Cosmati Pavement, 336, 337
Westminster Portrait, 40, 352, 353
Westminster, Palace, 67, 68, 69, 71, 103, 114, 119, 121, 123, 126, 128, 157, 158, 174, 175, 178, 224, 259, 271, 301, 305, 325, 374, 404
 great hall, 9, 114, 118, 325, 326, 331, 332, 333, 338
 Painted Chamber, 119, 325, 328, 329
 St Stephen's Chapel, 198, 326, 328, 330, 331
Weymouth, 53
Whittington, Richard ('Dick'), 100, 267, 268
William I ('the Conqueror'), king of England, 132, 334, 339, 370
William Rufus, 232, 325
William the Lion, king of Scots, 299
Willoughby, Richard, 127
Wilton Diptych, 40, 198, 352, 354, 355, 356
Winchelsea, 134, 259, 268
Winchelsey, Robert, archbishop of Canterbury, 197, 201, 204

Winchester, 143, 161, 173, 272, 290, 340
  Cathedral, 345
  College, 209
  diocese of, 197, 201, 207
Windsor, 96, 126, 144, 157, 158, 187, 198, 325, 339, 340, 345, 404
  St George's Chapel, 55, 58, 59, 198, 339, 340, 345
Wingfield Manor, 227
Woodstock, Edward of (the Black Prince), 31, 32, 33, 144, 186, 205, 219, 220, 248, 347
Woodstock, Thomas of, duke of Gloucester, 35, 36, 37
Woodville, Anthony, Earl Rivers, 55, 56
Woodville, Elizabeth, queen of England, 52, 55, 56, 172, 177, 182, 183
Woodville, Richard, Earl Rivers, 52, 53, 227
Woolmer, 157
Worcester, William, 314
Wycliffe, John, 213
Wykeham, William, bishop of Winchester, 104, 209
Wymbyssh, Nicholas de, 287
Wynnere and Wastoure, 39

Yevele, Henry, 331
York, 126, 156, 259, 264, 265, 266, 272, 287, 374
  diocese of, 205
  St Mary's Abbey, 305
York Minster, 56, 173, 207, 323
York, Cecily, duchess, 187
York, Edward, duke of York (d. 1415), 227
York, Margaret of, 53, 97
York, Richard, duke of, 48, 49, 50, 51, 84, 232, 233, 267, 284, 290, 372
Yorkshire, 51, 53, 56, 103, 259, 289, 414

For EU product safety concerns, contact us at Calle de José Abascal, 56–1°,
28003 Madrid, Spain or eugpsr@cambridge.org.

www.ingramcontent.com/pod-product-compliance
Ingram Content Group UK Ltd.
Pitfield, Milton Keynes, MK11 3LW, UK
UKHW021119111125
464942UK00022B/1198